THE
TRUMP
TAPES

— THE HISTORICAL RECORD —

Bob Woodward's Twenty Interviews
with President Donald Trump

BOB WOODWARD

Simon & Schuster Paperbacks
New York   London   Toronto   Sydney   New Delhi

Simon & Schuster Paperbacks
An Imprint of Simon & Schuster, Inc.
1230 Avenue of the Americas
New York, NY 10020

Copyright © 2022 by Bob Woodward
This title was previously published in 2022 in audio format
by Simon & Schuster Audio

First Simon & Schuster trade paperback edition January 2023

SIMON & SCHUSTER PAPERBACKS and colophon are
registered trademarks of Simon & Schuster, Inc.

For information about special discounts for bulk purchases,
please contact Simon & Schuster Special Sales at 1-866-506-1949
or business@simonandschuster.com.

The Simon & Schuster Speakers Bureau can bring authors to your live
event. For more information or to book an event, contact the Simon &
Schuster Speakers Bureau at 1-866-248-3049 or visit our website
at www.simonspeakers.com.

Manufactured in the United States of America

1 3 5 7 9 10 8 6 4 2

ISBN 978-1-6680-2814-8

TABLE OF CONTENTS

AUTHOR'S PERSONAL NOTE

Claire McMullen, 28, a lawyer and writer from Australia, was my full collaborator on this project. She poured over the Trump tapes for countless hours this past year, pushing me to reflect and explain my reporting methods and Trump's presidency for listeners and readers. Her brilliant insights on American politics, the presidency and Trump were invaluable to me. This historical record—the transcript of more than eight hours of interviews with President Trump and my 227 new commentaries—is a testament to her hard work. I will always cherish her friendship and commitment.

Karen Pearlman, producer and director of *The Trump Tapes*, was also an extraordinary behind-the-scenes force on this project. This is the first time in 50 years of reporting that I have released full audio and transcripts of my work. Karen's attention to detail and to the sound production quality was instrumental to the audiobook. Her energy and candor in the studio for days as I read the new commentary into the microphone made an unnatural process for me feel comfortable.

Thank you to the great Jonathan Karp, CEO of Simon & Schuster, for his counsel and unflagging support. My profound gratitude to Chris Lynch, president and publisher of Simon & Schuster Audio, for his advice at every step of the audiobook process. Chris understood immediately the value of these interviews. His full engagement in this project was a steady guide through new, uncharted territory for me. Many thanks to Elisa Shokoff, vice-president and executive producer, for her management; Robert B. Barnett, my lawyer and confidant, for being at my side for too many years to count; and Aileen Boyle, my publicist, for helping this project reach listeners and readers around the world.

Finally, my eternal thanks to my wife, Elsa Walsh, who has worked on 19 of my 21 books in the 41 years we have been together. She played an extraordinarily pronounced role in my book *Rage* that was based on these interviews. As you see in the transcripts, Elsa lived these interviews with me. Trump would call our home at any time, and I had the rare opportunity to be able to call him. Elsa jokes there were three people in our marriage. She is a brilliant and clear-eyed editor, always identifying the intrigue and the essential follow-up questions. I will never be able to thank her enough for her contributions to my work and our life together.

presidential election. And many criminal and civil investigations into Trump's conduct are ongoing, including the FBI search in August of his Mar-a-Lago estate to recover documents Trump took from the White House.

Some of the documents at the center of Trump's disputes with the National Archives and the Justice Department were first revealed during these interviews and quoted in my book *Rage*. The extraordinary letters between Trump and North Korean leader Kim Jong Un are, for example, discussed extensively in these tapes.

But after Trump's four years as president, there is no turning back for American politics. Trump was and perhaps still is a huge force and indelible presence.

"On history's clock it was sunset," the brilliant author Barbara Tuchman wrote of 1914 before World War I in her book *The Guns of August*. Just over a century later, the year 2016 and the election of Trump as president turned out to be another sunset. The old political order was dying and is now dead.

INTERVIEW 1:
The Lone Ranger

Old Post Office Pavilion Trump Hotel

March 31, 2016

TRUMP: I am a person that's going to bring this country
together; I'm a person that is going to unify the
country.

COMMENTARY: This was March 31, 2016. Trump had the Republican nomination almost in his grasp. My colleague at *The Washington Post*, Robert Costa, a remarkable political reporter known for his objectivity and knowledge of Republicans, had suggested we go interview Trump together.

He did not think Trump was being taken seriously enough as a candidate. We sent Trump a two-and-a-half-page list of questions. I saw the interview as an opportunity to ask Trump questions about the presidency—many I had asked prior presidents.

This interview was held at a make-shift conference room at the Trump International Hotel in the Old Post Office Pavilion on Pennsylvania Avenue just blocks from the White House. It was still under construction. You will hear construction noise and hotel clamor in the background of this interview.

BW: Where do you start the movie of your
decision—
TRUMP: Yeah, I saw that.
BW: —to run for president? Because that is a big deal.
A lot of internal/external stuff, and we'd love to
hear your monologue on—

TRUMP: Okay. I thought it was very interesting. I saw that.

BW: —how you did it.

TRUMP: Where do you start the movie? I think the start was standing on top of the escalator at Trump Tower, on June 16th . . . I mean, it looked like the Academy Awards. I talk about it. There were so many cameras. So many—it was packed. The atrium of Trump Tower, which is a very big place, was packed. It literally looked like the Academy Awards. And . . .

BW: But we want to go before that moment.

TRUMP: Before that? Okay, because that was really—

BW: Because, other words, there's an internal—

TRUMP: Yeah.

BW: —Donald with Donald.

RC: Maybe late 2014 or—before you started hiring people?

TRUMP: Well, but that was—okay, but I will tell you, until the very end . . . You know, I have a good life. I built a great company. It's been amazingly—I'm sure you looked at the numbers. I have very little debt, tremendous assets. And great cash flows. I have a wonderful family. Ivanka just had a baby. And, you know, doing this is not the easiest thing in the world to do. You know, people have—many of my friends, very successful people, have said, why would you do this?

COMMENTARY: Let's pause here to address Trump's assertions about his finances. They have always been suspect and frequently exaggerated, at times wildly so. It's never been clear what the exact numbers were, what he'd made and what he'd spent his money on. In the six years working on Trump, it is one of the continuing mysteries.

BW: So is there a linchpin moment, Mr. Trump, where it went from maybe to yes, I'm going to do this? And when was that?

TRUMP: Yeah. I would really say it was at the beginning

of last year, like in January of last year. And there were a couple of times. One was, I was doing a lot of deals. I was looking at it very seriously one time, not—you know, they say, oh, he looked at it for many—I really, no. I made a speech at the end of the '80s in New Hampshire, but it was really a speech—it was not a political speech, anyway, and I forgot about it.

BW: And that was the real possibility? Or the first . . .

TRUMP: Well no, the real possibility was the Romney time. This last one four years ago. I looked at that, really. I never looked at it seriously then. I was building my business. I was doing well. And I went up to New Hampshire, made a speech. And because it was in New Hampshire, it was sort of like, Trump is going to run. And since then people have said, Trump is going to run. I never was interested. And I thought that Romney was a weak candidate. I thought Obama was very beatable. Very, very beatable. You know, you had a president who was not doing well, to put it nicely. And I looked at that very seriously. I had some difficulty because I was doing some big jobs that were finishing up, which I wanted to do. My children were younger. And four years makes a big difference. And I also had a signed contract to do *The Apprentice* with NBC. Which in all fairness, you know, it sounds like—when you're talking about "president" it doesn't sound much, but when you have a two-hour show, primetime, every once a week on a major network . . .

BW: So when did it go to yes?

TRUMP: So—okay.

BW: Because that's—having made, you know, we all make minor decisions in our lives.

TRUMP: Okay.

BW: This is the big one.

TRUMP:	Big decision. Yeah, this is a big decision. And I say, sometimes I'll say it in the speeches. It takes guts to run for president, especially if you're not a politician, you've never . . .
BW:	When did it become yes?
TRUMP:	What happened is, during that time that I was just talking about, I started saying I'd like to do it, but I wasn't really in a position to do it. I was doing a lot of things, and I had a signed contract with NBC. But I started thinking about it. And the press started putting me in polls, and I was winning in the polls. And I was essentially leading right at the top, without doing any work. Not one speech, not one anything. But every time I was in a poll, I did very well in the poll.

COMMENTARY: I intentionally asked Trump: when does the movie begin because I knew that Trump thought in terms of movies, visuals, big spectacular events. He wants to talk about his success, not his decision to run for the presidency.

The question for Costa and myself is why does he want to be president? Perhaps because it's the biggest movie or the biggest stage?

RC:	What happened between 2011 and 2014?
TRUMP:	During this period of time, I said, you know, this is something I really would like to do. I think I'd do it really well. Obviously the public seems to like me, because without any . . .
BW:	Who are you saying that to? Your wife?
TRUMP:	To myself.
BW:	To your family?
TRUMP:	To my family, but to myself.
BW:	To yourself.
TRUMP:	Yeah, to myself, and . . .
BW:	This is interior dialogue.
TRUMP:	This is thought process.
BW:	Can you isolate a moment when it kicked to yes?
TRUMP:	I just felt there were so many things going wrong with the country. In particular, because I'm a

very natural person when it comes to business, I assume—I mean, I've done really well, and I do have an instinct for that.

BW: So when did you tell somebody in your family or your circle, I've decided to run. Other words, I've pulled the switch.

TRUMP: Well, I would tell my family about it all the time. Don is one of my sons, and doing a really good job. He's involved very much in this job. He's here today, so I said come and meet—

BW: Thank you.

DONALD TRUMP, JR.: Of course.

TRUMP: —the great genius and the current great genius. Right? The great genius of all time. But Don and my family, I would talk about it a lot. I would say, I can't believe they're doing it.

BW: Did anyone recommend no? Did your wife, or did your son?

TRUMP: Oh. Yeah.

BW: Did anyone say, Dad, Donald, don't do it?

TRUMP: I think my wife would much have preferred that I didn't do it. She's a very private person. She was a very, very successful—very, very successful model. She made a tremendous amount of money and had great success and dealt at the . . .

BW: What'd she say?

TRUMP: She was, she said, we have such a great life. Why do you want to do this? She was . . .

BW: And what'd you say?

TRUMP: I said, I sort of have to do it, I think. I really have to do it. Because it's something I'd be—I could do such a great job. I really wanted to give something back. I don't want to act overly generous, but I really wanted to give something back.

COMMENTARY: This was standard presidential and political jargon about giving back. Something I had heard many times over 50 years of reporting.

BW: That's the important moment, when you say, I have to do it.

TRUMP: Yeah, I had to.

BW: That's the product of the endless internal dialogue.

TRUMP: Well, she's a very private person, and very smart person. I'm sure you've seen a couple of interviews that she's done. She's very smart. And there's no games. You know, it's boom, it's all business. But a very smart person. And considered one of the great beauties.

BW: Did she give you the green light?

TRUMP: And she said, why are we doing the . . . Oh, absolutely. She said, if you want to do it, then you should do it, but . . . And she actually said something that was very interesting. She's very observant. And she would go around with me. And look, I've been around for a long time at a high level. She said, you know if you run, you'll win. I said, I don't know if I'm going to win. She said, if you run, you'll win. But if you say you're going to run, people are not going to believe it. Because people were let down the first time, I will tell you. They really wanted me to run, and I would've beaten Romney. So for the most part the polls didn't include me. And then one poll included me, and I didn't do that well. I was down at like three percent. I said to my wife, I don't think I can run. I'm down at three percent. Boy, that's a long way to go up.

TRUMP: And she goes, no, no, no, you're only at three percent because they don't believe you're running. If they thought you were going to run . . . I said, no, no, the poll said I'm going to run. She said, no, no, they still don't believe it. It doesn't matter what the poll says. The poll can say, you are going to run, Donald Trump is going to absolutely run. It was very interesting. Sort of like—I called her my pollster. She said, no, no, they won't believe that. I don't care if they put it at the top of your building, I'm going to run. They're not going to believe it unless you go out and announce that you're going to run. And she said, I hope you don't do it, but if you run, you'll win.

RC: So it was an evolution. Let's turn to . . .

TRUMP: So it was an evolution.

BW: Yeah.

RC: Let's turn to the presidency. You're nearing the nomination . . .

TRUMP: And then the big thing, by the way, the big thing was standing at the top of that escalator, looking down into that room, which was a sea of reporters. That was as big as anything we've had. And getting up and saying, all right. And I remember. I took a deep breath. I said, let's go, to my wife. And we came down. You know, pretty famous scene, the escalator scene. Boom. And we started, and we talked illegal immigration, and it became a very big subject, and that's where we started.

COMMENTARY: His speech announcing his run for the presidency included these well-known words:

TRUMP: *When Mexico sends its people, they're not sending their best. They're not sending you, they're not sending you. They're sending people that have lots of problems. And they're bringing those problems with us. They're bringing drugs, they're bringing crime, they're rapists, and some I assume are good people. But I speak to border guards, and they tell us what we're getting . . . (fade out)*

RC: Let's say you're the president, though. How do you see the office of the presidency?

BW: Other words, what's the definition of the job?

TRUMP: Well, I think more than anything else, it's the security of our nation. I mean, that's number one, two, and three. The military, being strong, not letting bad things happen to our country from the outside. And I certainly think that that's always going to be my number one part of that definition.

BW: You are running for the nomination in the Republican Party.

TRUMP: Right.

BW: Which is the party of Lincoln and the party of Nixon.

TRUMP: Right. Right.

BW: And if you look at Lincoln, he succeeded. Why? And if you look at Nixon—sorry—he failed. Why?

TRUMP: Because of you. [*laughter*]

BW: No. No. No, no. [*laughs*] That's not the—I mean there's . . .

TRUMP: Hey, you helped. [*laughter*]

[DONALD TRUMP, JR.]: I think there's more truth in that statement than most would want.

BW: No, no, he did it to himself.

TRUMP: Yeah. Well—yeah.

BW: And it was the Republican Party in the end, in the person of Barry Goldwater, who turned on him. And so we have this party that you are running to be the nominee in, and it's got two heritages. Lincoln and Nixon.

TRUMP: That's true. That's true.

BW: And why did Lincoln succeed? Thought about that at all?

TRUMP: Well, I think Lincoln succeeded for numerous reasons. He was a man who was of great intelligence, which most presidents would be. But he was also a man that did something that was a very vital thing to do at that time. Ten years before or 20 years before, what he was doing would never have even been thought possible. So he did something that was a very important thing to do, and especially at that time. And Nixon failed, I think to a certain extent, because of his personality. You know? It was just that personality. Very severe, very exclusive. You know, in other words, people couldn't come in. And people didn't like him. I mean, people didn't like him.

BW: And he broke the law.

TRUMP: And he broke the law, yeah. Yeah. He broke the law. Whether that's insecurity . . .

BW: I mean, you listen to those tapes, and he's a criminal.

TRUMP: Yeah. Whether that's—right. And he broke the law.

BW: And time and time again, break in, get the FBI on this, get the IRS on it.

TRUMP: Sure. Sure.

BW: I mean, it is an appalling legacy of criminality.

TRUMP: Right.

BW: And at the end, the day he resigned, an amazing day, he gives that speech which is kind of free association about mom and dad.

TRUMP: Right.

BW: He's sweating. And then he said, "Always remember: others may hate you, but those who hate you don't win unless you hate them, and then you destroy yourself." The piston was hate.

TRUMP: Well, and he was actually talking very much about himself, because ultimately, ultimately, that is what destroyed him. Hate is what destroyed him. And such an interesting figure. I mean, you would know that better than anybody. But such an interesting figure. And such a man of great talent. I mean, Nixon had great potential, great talent. Unfortunately, it was a very sad legacy. Such an interesting figure to study.

BW: Do you take any lessons from that? Because

what he did is he converted the presidency to an instrument of personal revenge.

TRUMP: Yeah.

BW: You're my enemy, I'm going to get you. I'm going to get so-and-so on you. And . . .

TRUMP: Yeah. No, I don't. I don't see that. What I am amazed at is, I'm somebody that gets along with people. And sometimes I'll notice, I'll be, I have the biggest crowds. Actually we've purposefully kept the crowds down this last week. You know, we've gone into small venues and we're turning away thousands and thousands of people, which I hate, but we didn't want to have the protest. You know, when you have a room of 2,000 people, you can pretty much keep it without the protesters. When you have 21 or 25,000 people coming in, people can start standing up and screaming. What has been amazing to me—I'm a very inclusive person. We have some amazing endorsements, some amazing people, but I'm amazed at the level of animosity toward me by some people. I'm amazed.

RC: But you're going to have to overcome that, Mr. Trump, if you're going to be the nominee and the president. So this . . .

TRUMP: I think you may be right. I think you may be right.

RC: I think this is such a pivot moment for you.

TRUMP: Okay.

RC: You're nearing the nomination. The presidency is possible. How do you expand your reach, your appeal, right now?

TRUMP: Well, let me tell you the biggest problem that I have. I get a very unfair press. And a lot of times I'll be making a speech, as an example, in front of a—in Orlando, where you have 20, 25,000 people show up. And I will be saying things, and Bob, it won't be reported what I say. It will be reported so differently.

RC: So how do you—so regardless of your view of the
               press, how do you navigate the . . .

TRUMP: Well, the problem with my view of the . . .

RC: The candidate has to get beyond all these different
               obstacles.

TRUMP: No, you're right, but if the press would report
               what I say, I think I would go a long way to
               doing that. Now, there is a natural bias against
               me because I'm a businessperson, I'm not in the
               club. Okay? You understand that. I'm not in the
               club. I'm not a senator. I'm not a politician. I'm
               not somebody that's been in Congress for 25
               years, and I know everybody, I'm somebody—I'm
               very much an outsider. I am also somebody that's
               self-funding my campaign, other than small
               contributions.

BW: But the press likes outsiders. I mean . . .

TRUMP: But the press doesn't like me. For the most part.

BW: And would you blame the problem on the press,
               on the media coverage?

TRUMP: No, I—but I think . . . I do say this: my media
               coverage is not honest. It really isn't. And I'm not
               saying that as a person with some kind of a, you
               know, complex. I, I just—I'm just saying, I will be
               saying words that are written totally differently
               from what I've said. In all fairness, the editorial
               board of *The Washington Post*. I was killed on
               that.

COMMENTARY: Trump was interviewed by *The Washington Post*
editorial board on March 21st, 2016.

TRUMP: I left the room, I thought it was fine.

RC: But what are some concrete steps you could take
               right now to project a bigger presence, a more
               unifying presence? Regardless of your view of the
               press, which is noted. How do you take steps now
               to really become a nominee?

TRUMP: Well, I think—it's a great question, and it's a question I've thought about a lot. I think the first thing I have to do is win. Winning solves a lot of problems. And I have two people left. We started off with 17 people. I have two people left.

COMMENTARY: The two remaining primary challengers, though not for long, were Senator Ted Cruz of Texas and Governor John Kasich of Ohio.

TRUMP: And one of the problems I have is that when I hit people, I hit them harder maybe than is necessary. And it's almost impossible to reel them back. Jack Nicklaus is a friend of mine. Jack Nicklaus is a killer. He is so tough, you have no idea. Are you a golfer? Do you play golf?

BW: Some.

TRUMP: By the way, Jack is tough. Jack was a killer, mentally. He's a brilliant guy. You have to have something special when you can sink the 30-foot putt and nobody else can. You know, the under— with 200 million people watching, okay? So Jack would just kill people. So he calls me up about a month ago, right after I beat Rubio. And I beat him by 20 points. You know that was a big beating. Don't forget, he was the face of the Republican Party. He was the future of the Republican Party. So Jack called me up. And he said, hey Donald, could you do us all a favor? We love you. Don't kill everybody. Because you may need them on the way back.

BW: What Bob Costa and I were talking about as—and we appreciate this moment to really get into these things. Having done this, reporting, so many years—too many decades—

TRUMP: Right. Right.

BW: What's politics? All successful politics, is about coalition building.

TRUMP: It's true.

BW:	Do you agree?
TRUMP:	I do. I agree. I agree.
BW:	And if you look . . .
TRUMP:	But I think you have to break the egg initially. In other words, I agree with you, but when you're coming from where I'm coming from—I came from the outside. By the way, I was establishment. I was an establishment guy until I said I'm running. And then when I said I don't want anyone's money, that drove everyone cra—I mean, outside of the small contributions.
BW:	But you said it: sometimes you have to break an egg.
TRUMP:	Sometimes you have to break an egg.
BW:	And haven't you broken enough eggs?
TRUMP:	Well, if that's the question, I think I have two more left.
BW:	And . . . Okay, but at this point of—as you, you know, Bob Costa, from his perspective of knowing the Republican Party as well as anybody in journalism, and the question is, how do you coalition-build, how do you unbreak those eggs?
TRUMP:	So that's the question.
RC:	It seems like you're not working as much as I would've thought to bring the party together.
TRUMP:	I'm looking to win first. My life has been about victories. I've won a lot. I win a lot. When I do something, I win. And even in sports, I always won. I was always a good athlete. In golf, I've won many club championships. Many, many club championships. And I have people that can play golf great, but they can't win under pressure.
RC:	And at some point the nomination battle ends.
TRUMP:	Yeah. And at some point the nomination . . .
RC:	Maybe I'm mishearing you, but I feel like you're almost comfortable being the Lone Ranger.
TRUMP:	I am. Because I understand life. And I understand how life works. I'm the Lone Ranger.
BW:	But can you be president and be Lone Ranger?

TRUMP:	Um . . .
BW:	I mean, as we were talking about Lincoln— if we may.
TRUMP:	Yeah.
BW:	Lincoln's second inaugural, he's won the war, he has broken more eggs than any president ever.
TRUMP:	He broke a lot of eggs.
BW:	And he comes out and in his second inaugural he said, "Malice toward none, charity for all, bind up the nation's wounds."
TRUMP:	Right.
BW:	Other words, he's saying, let's go back and coalition-build between the North and the South. Isn't that a moment you're going to have to face?
TRUMP:	Totally, totally.
BW:	Or is that not right now, this moment?
TRUMP:	I don't think it's now.
BW:	You don't?
TRUMP:	No, because I think I have to win before I can do that. Look, I've had . . .
BW:	Might that not assist in the winning?
TRUMP:	No, because you have two people that want to win also, and they're not going to be changing their ways.
RC:	What does it look like, though, when you pivot to the general election? Let's say you win the nomination. How does that coalition-building, that unity message—what does that look like? How is Trump the unifier different than Trump the primary battler?
TRUMP:	Okay. As you know, certain polls have me beating Hillary Clinton, but I haven't focused on Hillary Clinton yet. Okay? And I say that all the time. I have not focused on her. I've only focused on the people that are ahead of me, and right now I have two people. I don't have to think about whether it's going to be Hillary or somebody else. I'd love

your view on what's going to happen with Hillary from the other standpoint, okay? Because that's really going to be a very interesting question.
And it seems to be heating up, which is almost a little surprising, because it looked to me like she's being protected. But my family said to me—and Don has said this, and Ivanka, and my wife has said this—be more presidential. Because I can be very presidential. I jokingly say, I can be more presidential than any president that this country has ever had except for Abraham Lincoln, because he was sort of—right? You can't out-top Abraham Lincoln.

BW: Isn't that what people want to see now?

TRUMP: Yeah. Yeah, but but they said . . . Yes.

BW: Isn't that—I mean in the Republican Party, I mean, Bob Costa is an expert on this, there is a lot of angst and rage and distress.

TRUMP: A lot. Record-setting.

BW: Record-setting.

TRUMP: I bring . . .

BW: And you have to tame that rage, don't you?

TRUMP: Yes, yes, but I bring that out in people. I do. I'm not saying that's an asset or a liability, but I do bring that out.

BW: You bring what out?

TRUMP: I bring rage out. I do bring rage out. I always have. You know, I think it was . . . I don't know if that's an asset or a liability, but whatever it is, I do. I also bring great unity out, ultimately. I've had many occasions like this, where people have hated me more than any human being they've ever met. And after it's all over, they end up being my friends. And I see that happening here. But when my wife and Ivanka and the rest of my family, they said, be presidential, Dad, be presidential. Last debate. I said, wait a minute. If I get hit, I'm gonna hit back. That's not going

to look very presidential, because you know I
hit back and you hit back. I said, I'm going to
give it a shot. And I was actually—you know,
the last debate was actually a much different
debate . . .

RC: Right.

TRUMP: . . . in terms of my tone. And I actually got my
highest ratings on that debate.

RC: But I'm just struck by—we're asking the questions
about "being presidential." So many other people
have asked, can Trump pivot, can he shift to a
different kind of tone? And correct me if I'm
wrong, but my view, listening to you, is that you
actually don't really have that much interest in
changing too much.

TRUMP: Not yet. Not yet.

RC: But it seems your natural inclination is to
fight . . .

TRUMP: Yes, always to fight. My natural inclination is to
win. And after I win, I will be so presidential that
you won't even recognize me.

BW: When—when Ted Cruz—

TRUMP: You'll be falling asleep, you'll be so bored.

RC: I don't think a lot of people know that much
about how much you value discretion, loyalty
within your business.

TRUMP: Great loyalty, yes. Great discretion, great loyalty.

RC: But it's different when you're running the federal
government.

TRUMP: Well, it's . . .

RC: And one thing I always wondered, are you going
to make employees of the federal government sign
nondisclosure agreements?

TRUMP: I think they should. You know, when people are
chosen by a man to go into government at high
levels and then they leave government and they
write a book about a man and say a lot of things
that were really guarded and personal, I don't like

that. I mean, I'll be honest. And people would say,
oh, that's terrible, that's, you know, you're taking
away his right to free speech. Well, I do have
nondisclosure deals. That's why you don't read
that . . .

BW: With everyone? Corey has one, Hicks has one.

TRUMP: Corey has one, Hope has one. Did you sign one?

HOPE HICKS: Of course.

LEWANDOWSKI: Steven has one.

TRUMP: Steven has one.

LEWANDOWSKI: Donny has one.

DONALD TRUMP, JR.: I don't got one. I'm in the middle of the book, baby. [*laughter*]

LEWANDOWSKI: Donny has two. [*laughter*]

TRUMP: I know, I forgot, he's the one I'm most worried about.

DONALD TRUMP, JR.: I'm not getting next week's paycheck until I sign one.

BW: Do you think these are airtight agreements?

TRUMP: Yeah, totally. I think they're very airtight. They're very . . .

BW: And that no one could write a book or . . .

TRUMP: I think they're extremely airtight. And anybody that violated it—let's put it this way: it's so airtight that I've never had . . . You know, I've never had a problem with this sort of thing. I don't like people that take your money and then say bad things about you. Okay? You know, they take your . . .

RC: But it's so different when you're in the federal government.

TRUMP: It's different, I agree. It's different.

RC: But you are recommending nondisclosure . . .

TRUMP: And I tell you this, I will have to think about it. I will have to think about it. That's a different thing, that I'm running a private company and I'm paying people lots of money, and then they go out and . . .

BW: The taxpayers are paying the other people in the federal government.

TRUMP: Sure. Sure. They don't do a great job, and then you fire them, and they end up writing a book about you. So it's different. But I will say that in the federal government it's a different thing. So it's something I would think about. But you know, I do right now—I have thousands and thousands of employees, many thousands, and every one of them has an agreement, has a . . . I call it a confidentiality agreement . . .

BW: Say you're elected president. Would one four-year term be enough?

TRUMP: I would say that every time I see somebody make that statement and then they're feeling good and doing a great job, and they run, they lose because of that statement. So I would never want to limit myself to four years. I think I can do a tremendous job in four years. One of your questions, I noticed, is what would be your first 90 days in terms—and we'll talk about that next.

BW: Good.

TRUMP: But, so I think I can do a terrific job. And I think this: if I'm doing a terrific job, and if I'm feeling well, I would say I would continue to go for the extra four years. Because again, I don't wanna, I don't wanna put that burden on myself. If I'm doing a good job, I should be allowed. And I only say it because, you know, Bob, I've seen so many people say it. Even for local positions. And if they decide to then go, they always lose because they make that statement. So I don't want to say that. But I think I will be able to do a fantastic job in four years.

BW: Real quickly, at the *Post* editorial board interview, you referred to the $19 trillion in debt, and then you said the U.S. is "probably sitting on a bubble."

TRUMP: Yeah, a bubble.

BW:	What bubble?
TRUMP:	Well, I think we're sitting on an economic bubble. A financial bubble. I think that if you look at the stock market . . .
BW:	In the stock market you mean?
TRUMP:	Yeah.
BW:	It's not a housing bubble.
TRUMP:	No, no, I'm talking about . . .
BW:	Or a real estate building bubble?
TRUMP:	I'm talking about a bubble where you go into a very massive recession. Hopefully not worse than that, but a very massive recession. Look, we have money that's so cheap right now. And if I want to borrow money, I can borrow all the money I want. But I'm rich. And I don't need the money. I don't have to borrow. I don't even call banks anymore. I use my own money to do things. If I want to borrow money or if another rich person wants to borrow money, you can borrow money at, like, LIBOR plus nothing. And you're paying one and a half percent interest, it's crazy, and they'll give you all you want. If somebody is a great, wonderful person, going to employ lots of people, a really talented businessperson, wants to borrow money but they're not rich? They have no chance.

COMMENTARY: LIBOR is the average interest rate global banks charge each other for loans in London's lending market. It's a standard international measure.

A few years later various government investigations have now established that Trump's finances were a bit of a shell game. For example, records showed that Trump was able to lease the Old Post Office Pavilion from the federal government and convert it to a hotel with a $170 million loan from Germany's Deutsche Bank that Trump guaranteed personally. The loan terms, which Trump did not disclose, permitted him to delay principal payments for years.

But perhaps more important was that Trump failed to include over $1.1 billion in outstanding loan balances in properties in New York,

Chicago, Las Vegas, and San Francisco in the most recent balance sheets provided to the government. So this self-confidant declaration of vast wealth was certainly suspect.

BW:	Bubbles are scary to economists.
TRUMP:	Oh, bubbles are scary.
BW:	Alan Greenspan, the former chairman of the Fed, used to say, there may be a bubble out there, but you don't know it's a bubble until it bursts.
TRUMP:	Yeah.
BW:	Is that true?
TRUMP:	That's true. I think that's true. I think you had a lot of signs, because you had all those exploding mortgages.
BW:	And you say there are signs now.
TRUMP:	I told people . . .
BW:	We're "sitting on a bubble."
TRUMP:	Okay, so I made many speeches for different groups on success, where people would pay me a lot of money, I gave it to charity. People would pay me money for speeches on success. So I would do that, before this. And I would tell people, don't invest that, don't go—I was pretty good at prognostication, at telling people what to do in terms of . . . Now, I'd talk about success, but I'd say, this is a bad time to invest. I also said, this is a good time to invest.
BW:	What is it now? Is it a good time to invest now?
TRUMP:	Oh, I think it's a terrible time right now.
BW:	You really do?
TRUMP:	Yeah. I think it's precarious times. Part of the reason it's precarious is because we are being ripped so badly by other countries. We are being ripped so badly by China. It just never ends. Nobody's ever going to stop it. And the reason they're not going to stop it is one of two. They're either living in a world of the make-believe, or they're totally controlled by their lobbyists

and their special interests. Meaning people that
want it to continue. Because what China, what
Mexico, what Japan, what—I don't want to
name too many countries, because I actually do
business in a lot of these countries—but what
these countries are doing to us is unbelievable.
They are draining our jobs. They are draining our
money.

BW: So you are really pessimistic, to say the least?

TRUMP: I'm pessimistic. Unless . . . unless changes are
              made. Changes could be made.

BW: Could you fix it? Next year, if you became
              president?

TRUMP: Yes, I can fix it. I can fix it pretty quickly.

BW: Okay. Tell us that.

TRUMP: When I was at your editorial board meeting, I
              talked about NATO. And I'm not a world expert
              on NATO. But I have a natural instinct for certain
              things, okay? Like I said, keep the oil. Well, now
              ISIS has the oil.

RC: So what's your instinct, your plan, for let's say
              first 100 days, how do you turn this all around?

TRUMP: Okay, well, I say this. Look—Okay. I would do
              a number of things. Number one, I would start
              negotiating great trade deals using—I know the
              best people. You know . . .

BW: You think that can turn around in 100 days?

TRUMP: No, no, it can't, no, but I would start the
              negotiation. No, these are complicated
              transactions. What I would do—and before I talk
              about legislation, because I think frankly this is
              more important. Number one, it's going to be a
              very big tax cut. You have to do a tax cut. But I
              would immediately start renegotiating our trade
              deals with Mexico, China, Japan and all of these
              countries that are just absolutely destroying us.
              And they have been for years. It's an incredible
              tribute to our country that we can lose hundreds

of billions of dollars consistently, year in and year out and still even survive. We have rebuilt China single-handedly. Now, they've done okay with Europe, too.

RC: On trade deals, dealing with a company, it's dealing with people and corporations.

TRUMP: And I'm negotiating over 100 deals. We're negotiating 114 deals.

RC: But aren't deals with countries and foreign leaders different than the kind of transactions you do at the corporate level? And how do you make that transition?

TRUMP: No.

RC: Because you can't say to a country, I'm going to sue you.

TRUMP: No. Well, you know, it depends on what your definition of "sue" is. We will be able to make great trade deals. It'll be good for the countries. It will be good for us.

BW: How long will it take? A year? Two years?

TRUMP: It will go . . . Yeah, I would say within the first year a lot of it will be done.

BW: Sir, in listening to this . . .

TRUMP: But you have to be able to walk. You have to be able to . . .

BW: . . . in covering lots of presidents, if I may go back to that experience.

TRUMP: Go ahead.

BW: Trying to understand them. Reagan was Morning in America. And it's almost like you're saying, at least for a while, morning in the ditch. That we are just not going to be able to get out because of these trade deals, because of your pessimism about the economy.

TRUMP: Look, we are losing $500 billion a year on trade deficits with China. Okay? We've been for a long time, from 200 to 500. We are losing hundreds and hundreds of billions of dollars a year on trade.

COMMENTARY: Trump's claim that the U.S. is losing about $500 billion because of the trade deficit with China is a significant misunderstanding. The trade deficit means Americans are buying approximately $500 billion more in goods from China than China is buying from the U.S. The money is not lost. Americans get the goods they purchased. China often winds up with more money in the form of U.S. treasury bonds.

TRUMP: You look at Japan. They send their cars in here by the hundreds of thousands. You go to Los Angeles, you look at those docks, and these cars get driven off those boats at 40 miles an hour. You've never seen anything like it. They just come pouring into our country. And yet when—you talk about an imbalance, when it comes to us selling to Japan? They take very little.

BW: Where's the optimism to get out of this?

TRUMP: Oh, I have great optimism.

BW: You do?

TRUMP: Oh. Oh, okay. With all of that, I'm an optimistic person. You know, "Make America great again." That's actually a very optimistic—you know, that's not—Some people say, oh, that's so pess—because they hate the word "again." I said, no, no, you don't understand. We're going to make America great again. People view that as very positive.

LEWANDOWSKI: We have [to be on the other side of town] in 15 minutes.

COMMENTARY: Trump's campaign manager Corey Lewandowski wanted to move Trump along to his next meeting.

TRUMP: You know what, we can delay that meeting for 20 minutes. I love this.

LEWANDOWSKI: I know, but it's a very important—and it's respectful. I just—we set it up, and . . .

TRUMP: Could you call them up and say could we delay half an hour?

LEWANDOWSKI:	I can, but we promised these guys—an hour, an hour and 15?
TRUMP:	Do me a favor. Call them back, tell them we'll be 45 minutes late, if it's okay? Only if it's okay. If he can't do it . . .
LEWANDOWSKI:	I don't know. Let me find out.
TRUMP:	Okay. Because I'd like to finish with these guys.
BW:	Thank you. We appreciate it.
TRUMP:	This is like a great—having you in the room is a honor. Is "an" honor.
BW:	No, this is important. This is at the center of— and you have . . .
TRUMP:	So just so you understand, mine is a message of great optimism.
RC:	Bob was in New Haven, Connecticut, the other day, and he met a maid in a hotel who identified herself as Mexican. And one of the things she said was, "He does not like me."
BW:	Meaning you. I asked her about you. What do you think of Trump?
TRUMP:	Was she here . . .
RC:	Wait. And she said, "All I want is my dignity."
TRUMP:	Yeah. I'll give her great dignity. Let me hear the question—you may not know the answer.
RC:	What do you have to say to her?
TRUMP:	Was she here legally or illegally?
BW:	I asked her, and she would not say.
TRUMP:	That means she was here illegally. Okay. So here . . .
BW:	Possibly. And she says . . . "He doesn't like me." She took it personally. And then she said, "I just want my dignity."
TRUMP:	I understand that.
BW:	What would you say to her?
TRUMP:	I'll tell you what I'd say to her. Number one, she was probably here illegally. The polls are all showing people—Hispanics—that are here legally like me very much. In Nevada,

you saw the poll, I was . . . I'm leading with the Hispanics. People that vote, people that therefore are here. I'm leading with Hispanics. They don't want their jobs taken. And they know I'll bring jobs back from China. I'll bring jobs back from Japan and from Mexico and from all these countries. You look at what Mexico's doing, Bob. Mexico is the new China, smaller level. Mexico, what they're doing to us on trade and at the border is unbelievable. Okay? And I was right. When I got up and made that initial speech at Trump Tower on June 16th, and I talked about illegal immigration and the problems, that hit a nerve. You know? Because . . .

RC:
It's not all economic. Because some of these people we encounter on the campaign trail, whether it's an undocumented Mexican maid or it's a Muslim, one consequence of your campaign has been they feel isolated in America. And you may disagree with the reason they feel that, but that is how they feel as a consequence of your message. And just how do you speak to those people who think you don't want them in this country? Including legal Muslims.

TRUMP:
I am a person that's going to bring this country together. I'm a person that's going to unify the country. President Obama is a divider. He is not a unifier. When he first got elected, I didn't have great feelings for the fact that he was going to do well. But the one thing I thought, he would be able to unify the country. African American, white, I thought that he would be a unifying factor. He has not been. He's been a great . . .

BW:
But Bob Costa's right, Mr. Trump, that you talk to people and they feel you're not a unifier.

TRUMP:
I know. They feel that now.

BW:
And you say you are. The question becomes . . .

I mean, this is one maid, but I think there are a countless number of people out there who want their dignity, and the question is, how are they going to get it from you if you're president?

TRUMP: Well again, so I asked you the very important question, was she here legally or illegally?

BW: I don't know.

TRUMP: Because if she was here legally, I think you would find that she would like me very much. In Nevada, where you have a huge Hispanic population, when they did the exit polls, I won with the people that are Hispanic in the state of Nevada. But—not by a little bit, by a lot. I think that's a—it's an important question to ask. I will give people back their dignity because I'm going to bring jobs back. Our jobs are being taken away from us like candy from a baby. Our jobs are being ripped out of our country.

RC: People understand the economic argument. But people—I think what she was looking for, and others—is do you have empathy for the immigrant experience? You think back to your grandfather coming over in 1885.

TRUMP: That's right. Totally. I do. I mean, totally. I mean, ultimately we're all immigrants, okay? I mean, I have total empathy. At the same time, we need borders, otherwise we don't have a country and you have to come into the country legally. And that's been a big theme of my campaign, and for the most part, I think it's a hit.

BW: But this maid doesn't have a lawyer, I suspect. And she came to the country, we don't know. And she didn't do anything that put her in the position she may be in, you're right. And what she's saying is—and I was floored by what she said, quite frankly. "I just want my dignity."

TRUMP: Yeah. Well.

BW: And a giant question, pulsing out there, is how do

people get their dignity that you seem to be quite critical of? Illegal immigrants . . .

TRUMP: No. I'm . . .

BW: Well, you are critical.

TRUMP: Well, illegal immigrants, yeah. Just so you understand, I want people to come into this country. I want to make it much easier to come into the country. But they have to come in through a legal process. Were you able to do that, Corey? Huh?

COMMENTARY: Campaign Manager Lewandowski tries again to get Trump to go to the next meeting.

[*Lewandowski speaks inaudibly.*]

TRUMP: I'd love to keep it going. I actually enjoy this. I'll probably end up ruing the day. I'll say, how could they have said that stuff about me? But I do really enjoy this.

BW: What would . . .

TRUMP: I think I'll do really great. With the African Americans. And a lot of people think that. And you know that a lot of people think that. But I think I'm going to do great with the African Americans. I think I'm going to do great with Hispanics. I'm going to bring jobs back to our country, Bob. And that's going to . . .

BW: Understand. Let me ask, this is a really . . .

TRUMP: Jobs is a very big answer, because that's going to give . . .

BW: Of course. Although this maid has a job.

TRUMP: That's right. But dignity. And maybe she'll have a better job. She'll have more options.

BW: Okay. What would be the most challenging situation that the next president might face? And this is a serious issue.

TRUMP: I—go ahead.

BW:	I asked President Obama this a number of years ago. And he said, what I worry about most— sitting in the Oval Office, and I think he really meant this—I worry the most about a nuclear weapon going off in an American city.
TRUMP:	Okay.
BW:	That is the game-changer.
TRUMP:	It's funny, it's very interesting. I'm surprised he said that, because I heard him recently say that the biggest problem we have is global warming, which I totally disagree with. Okay?
BW:	But he told me . . .
TRUMP:	Okay.
BW:	Sat there. And I thought, you can read between— do you agree with that?
TRUMP:	It's very interesting. I have . . . I absolutely agree. I think the single greatest problem that this world has is a nuclear—the power of nuclear. The tremendous power. You look at Hiroshima and multiply it times a thousand.
BW:	And he's, President Obama's having this summit now, right here in Washington, down the street. And he is a strong advocate for eliminating nuclear weapons entirely.
TRUMP:	Okay.
BW:	Would you agree with that?
TRUMP:	Well, if it's done in an equal basis, absolutely.
BW:	You would.
TRUMP:	But the problem you have now is you have Pakistan. You have India. You have so many countries now with nuclear already. You have some very bad people trying very hard to get nuclear. So I think that's something that in an ideal world is wonderful, but I think it's not going to happen very easily.
BW:	Would you pick up the baton on that effort on his part?
TRUMP:	I would love to see a nuclear-free world. Will

that happen? Chances are extremely small that will happen. Look, Russia right now is spending a tremendous amount of money on re-doing their entire nuclear arsenal.

RC: Did you read Jeffrey Goldberg's article about Obama's foreign policy? Regardless, in *The Atlantic*, Obama gave . . .

TRUMP: Oh, *The Atlantic*, okay.

RC: So one of the quotes Obama said in there is, "The notion that Russia is somehow in a stronger position now in Syria and Ukraine than they were before they invaded Ukraine or before he had to deploy military forces in Syria is to fundamentally misunderstand the nature of power in foreign affairs. Real power means you can get what you want without having to exert violence." That's Obama on global power. Do you agree?

TRUMP: Well, I think there's a certain truth to that. Real power is through respect. Real power is, I don't even want to use the word, fear. But we have to strengthen our military. Now, one of the things that *The Washington Post* treated me very badly on, when I talked about NATO. We're spending too much money, and we're not getting treated with respect from the 28 countries that we're dealing with.

RC: This comes back to the Lone Ranger point. I think even globally, you're comfortable being the United States president . . .

TRUMP: No.

RC: Not being . . .

TRUMP: I didn't say I'd get out of NATO. I say it's got to be . . . First of all, it's obsolete. Our big threat today is terrorism. Okay? And NATO's not really set up for terrorism. NATO was set up for the Soviet Union more than anything else. And now you don't have the Soviet Union.

RC: Well, you don't have a great belief in these international institutions.

TRUMP:	No, because we seem to get ripped off by everybody. We seem to always be the one that pays the bill and gets the least. And we're going to stop doing that.
BW:	But you're talking about reform of NATO, aren't you, rather than making . . .
TRUMP:	Yes, I'm talking about reform.
BW:	You're not just saying, let's move out.
TRUMP:	I'm talking totally about reform. But you have to be—in order to get reform, you have to be prepared to walk.
BW:	One really important question.
TRUMP:	Go ahead.
BW:	A couple of years ago, I had a breakfast with one of the leaders, heads of state, of our best allies. And I asked him about Obama. And he was talking off the record, and he said, "I like him. He is smart. But no one in the world is afraid of him." Do you agree with that? And in a Trump administration—are you formulating a new doctrine of "you better be afraid of me"?
TRUMP:	Yeah, I don't want people to be afraid. I want them to respect our country. Right now, they don't respect our country.
BW:	But do they respect you if you kind of . . .
TRUMP:	People have respected me. My life has been a life where I've been respected. I want them to respect our country. I want them to respect our leader. But I want them to respect our country. Now, you could use . . .
BW:	How do you achieve that, sir?
TRUMP:	Through the aura of personality. Through having the goods. You know, so Muhammad Ali is a friend of mine. He's a good guy. I've watched many people over the years. Muhammad Ali would get in the ring, and he'd talk and talk and scream and talk about the ugly bear, and this, that, you know. And then he'd win. And respect

is about winning. We don't win anymore. I see
it in my—we don't win anymore. And he'd win.
I've seen many fighters that were better than
Muhammad Ali, in terms of talking. I've seen guys
that were so beautiful, so flamboyant, they'd get
into the ring—and then they'd get knocked out.
And guess what? It's all gone. Let me just say: we
don't win anymore.

BW: So do you want Putin to be afraid of you?

TRUMP: I want Putin to respect our country, okay?

BW: And what would he respect?

TRUMP: Well, first of all, it's sort of interesting. He said
very good things about me.

BW: Understand.

TRUMP: You saw that. He said, Trump is brilliant, and
Trump is going to be the new leader and all
that. And some of these clowns said, you should
repudiate Putin. I said, why would I repudiate
him? He's not going to get anything. Because I've
been through this stuff before. But he said very
positive things about me. And I say to myself—
and I say to people—wouldn't it be nice if we
actually could get along with Russia? And if we
could get along with these people? China takes
advantage of us. Look at what they're doing
in the South China Sea. They're not supposed
to be playing that game. Okay? Look at what
they're doing. That is a lack of respect. When
they're building a massive, like nobody's ever
seen before—they're building islands in the
middle of the South China Sea for a massive
military complex. Beyond runways. I mean, this
is a complex. So what I'm saying is there's a
tremendous lack of respect for our country. And I
think for our leader.

BW: But what does Putin respect? The former KGB
lieutenant colonel? Force. Power.

TRUMP: I think he respects strength. Okay? I think Putin

respects strength. And I've said it before, I think
I will get along well with Putin. Now you never
know. I don't say that—only a fool would say,
"I will," but I feel that I will get along well with
Putin. I feel that if we can get along with more
countries, that's a positive thing. That's not a bad
thing. Some people—for instance, when Putin
came out and he wanted to bomb the hell out
of ISIS, we had people standing on the stage,
we don't want that, we want . . . Let me tell you
something. If we have somebody else dropping
bombs that cost a half a million dollars a piece
on the top—if we have somebody helping us,
that's not so bad. We have a situation in Libya
where a friend of mine is just saying, so, we had
Qaddafi, he killed the terrorists, he ran his place.
Not a good man. Same thing you could say with
Iraq, with Saddam Hussein. Saddam Hussein was
a plus-10 at killing terrorists, that's one thing. If
our presidents would have gone away and gone to
the beach, the Middle East would be a far better
place than it is right now. I don't say it would be
run by nice people, but you know, it would be a
far better place. The mistakes we've made in the
Middle East are so astronomical. Now here's the
thing: ISIS is controlling the oil now in Libya.
How did we let that happen?

RC: So just turning back to . . .

TRUMP: And by the way, that oil? That is a great oil, and
           it's a lot of oil.

RC: We were looking over your 1990 book,
           Surviving at the Top.

TRUMP: Right.

RC: And thinking about, what would happen if
           Trump's president of the United States? And
           you—this is a line from your book, then: "The
           same assets that excite me in the chase often, once
           they are acquired, leave me bored. For me, you

see, the important thing is the getting, not the having." If you get the presidency, you are going to have it.

TRUMP: Yeah, but see, that's not the getting. The getting, for me, is to make our country great again. The getting—that's just a part of it. The getting the position is not the real getting. For me, the getting is—and that's when I'll say, congratulations everyone, my job is finished. We will make our country financially strong again. I had a woman come up to me. She said, Mr. Trump, I love you. You're so incredible. I'm voting for you 100 percent, but could you stop saying you're going to make our country rich again? I said, I understand what you're saying—it doesn't sound nice. But without being rich again, we can't be great again. You look at our military budget, it's massive compared to any other country. But what are we doing? We're taking care of the military needs of all these countries. And these countries are much richer than us. We're not a rich country. We're a debtor nation. I talked about bubble. We've got to get rid of the $19 trillion in debt.

BW: How long would that take?

TRUMP: I think I could do it fairly quickly, because of the fact the numbers . . .

BW: What's fairly quickly?

TRUMP: Well, I would say over a period of eight years. And I'll tell you why.

BW: Would you ever be open to tax increases as part of that, to solve the problem?

TRUMP: I don't think I'll need to. The power is trade. Our deals are so bad.

BW: That would be $2 trillion a year.

TRUMP: No, but I'm renegotiating all of our deals, Bob.

BW: When does the coalition building begin?

TRUMP: The coalition building begins—I believe—when it's decided who wins. Hopefully I'm going to win. The coalition building for me will be when I win. Vince Lombardi, I saw this. He was not a big man. And I was sitting in a place with some very, very tough football players. Big, strong football players. These are tough cookies. He came in, screaming, into this place. And screaming at one of these guys who was three times bigger than him, literally. And very physical, grabbing him by the shirt. Now, this guy could've whisked him away and thrown him out the window in two seconds. This guy was—the player—was shaking. A friend of mine. There were four players, and Vince Lombardi walked in. He was angry. And he grabbed—I was a young guy—he grabbed him by the shirt, screaming at him . . . And I said, wow. And I realized the only way Vince Lombardi got away with that was because he won.

BW: But to do that—a colleague of ours . . .

TRUMP: No, to do that you have to win.

BW: Yes. But David Maraniss, a colleague of ours, wrote the book on Vince Lombardi.

TRUMP: Yeah.

BW: *When Pride Still Mattered*. Right? What Vince Lombardi did, he got to the point of winning by building a coalition of 11 players on the field. He couldn't have a guard in a tackle who were not part of the team.

TRUMP: I agree with you. Ultimately, I will build a coalition. I think it's too soon. I really do. I think it's too soon. Now, I may be wrong. But this isn't something I needed to do. This is something I want to do. I want to give back, and I'll do a fantastic job.

BW: So we have on the media, which you are quite critical . . .

TRUMP: Media treats me very unfairly, and very inaccurately.

BW: Okay, and the question is, why? And if I may,

Richard Nixon, something he said that I think Bob and I agree with. He said the media looks in the mirror instead of looking out the window . . . and gather facts and listen to other people— they're more interested in themselves. Is that part of the problem?

TRUMP: Well, I think they're more interested in hits. I did a thing the other day with—on CNN—with Anderson Cooper.

BW: Yes.

TRUMP: I don't know if you saw the rating. Give him the ratings, if you have it. Do you have the ratings?

RC: We saw it.

HICKS: You have them, sir.

TRUMP: They were through—I just got this. They were through the roof. Here. Mine was through the roof, meaning my hour was through the roof. Now, that's good and bad. The bad is they want to cover me too much, and they write things that maybe they shouldn't be writing. But those were phenomenal. Won the evening, beat everybody, etc., etc. My segment, not the other segments. The other segments did all right, but my segment was one of the highest-rated shows in a long time and beat everybody on television that night. So that's good and it's bad. The bad is they want to do nothing but cover me. They write stories that are—that don't even make sense. I'm just saying, I wish I could be covered accurately and fairly by the media.

BW: But why, then? Is this ideology, is it partisanship, is it laziness? What is it?

TRUMP: Well, it could be some laziness. Today they want the clicks. In the old days they wanted the ratings, or they wanted to sell newspapers. Today they see if somebody clicks. So they do a story on me and they get clicks all over the place. They do a story on somebody else, it doesn't matter. All I can say is this: I wish I could be treated fairly by the media. And if I was treated fairly by the media, I think you would see a very big difference in coalition and coalition building and a lot of things. I can only say this: my whole life has been about winning. My whole life. I've won a lot. And one little example? This building. This was one of the most sought-after buildings in the history of the General Services Administration— best location in Washington. Right between the Capitol and the White House.

BW: Great building.

TRUMP: The best location, best building. The walls are four foot thick of solid granite. Amazing how they were able to lift it up. I mean, frankly, amazing. This is before they had cranes as we know them today. Unbelievable place. And it will be one of the great hotels in the world. Everybody wanted it. Every hotel company. Everybody. Pritzker wanted it. Who's closer to Obama than Pritzker? Hyatt wanted it. They had the Jewish Museum all lined up. They had everything all lined up. The reason I got it was because I have an unbelievable balance sheet and because they wanted to make sure it got done—and because of the fact that I had a great concept.

BW: But let's . . .

TRUMP: But think of it: I got it in the Obama administration.

COMMENTARY: I'm sure Trump's balance sheet is unbelievable. The government awarded the lease to him because he agreed to provide $200 million in restoration, in addition to paying monthly lease fees. But by not disclosing his loans of more than $1 billion, his balance sheet looked much, much better than it actually was.

TRUMP: And people say to me, Bob, how the hell did you get the most sought-after real estate asset perhaps in the history of the GSA?

BW:	But here's what's going on, we think. And it has to do with psychology. And one of the things you learn, being a reporter, being a builder with your background, is that everyone is concerned about themselves. These people feel disrespected. They feel that they've not been given their dignity.
TRUMP:	They will be loved. At the right time, they will be loved.
BW:	And they want in.
TRUMP:	Yeah, I know.
BW:	And what, to use your term, you've built a wall to a certain extent. You've said, I am the Lone Ranger. I am doing this on my own.
TRUMP:	No, at the right time I want them in.
BW:	Okay, but . . .
TRUMP:	I just think it's early.
BW:	Okay, but suppose you needed to do that sooner. Because . . .
TRUMP:	I'd be capable of doing it. I just think it's . . .
BW:	Will you call us the day it starts?
TRUMP:	I will. These people want in. And I'm taking them in. They're going to come in. One thing I'm going to do, a lot of people are saying, oh, the judges . . . To me, the judges—because there's going to be a lot of them in these next four years.
BW:	Yeah.
TRUMP:	We've got one already that was unexpected in Scalia. So the judges are going to be important. You're going to have either super-liberal judges, or you're going to have conservative judges. So important. They don't know me well enough. Well, what kind of judges? I'm going to do something. It was my idea, and I think it was a good idea. And I'm getting names. The Federalist people. You know, I mean some very good people. The Heritage Foundation. I'm getting names, and I'm going to submit a list of about 10 names, 10 or 12 names, as judges. I'm going to announce

that these are the judges, in no particular order, that I'm going to put up. And I'm going to like, you know, I'm going to guarantee it. I'm going to tell people. Because people are worried that, oh, maybe he'll put the wrong judge in. Like people— my sister is on the court of appeals. Very smart. She's a very smart, very highly respected person. Very smart.

BW: People keep trying to get her to talk, and she won't.

TRUMP: You know what?

BW: Does she have a nondisclosure agreement? [*laughter*]

TRUMP: She's fantastic. She's the exact opposite of me. People say, is she really your sister? She's a brilliant person. Highly respected. When the press calls, I say, listen, they want to do a great story. They actually had a nice story about her in *The Washington Post* recently. But she doesn't want to talk to the press, because she feels as a judge she should not be speaking to the press. Something very nice about that. She's right.

BW: I disagree, but . . .

TRUMP: As a judge. No, but as a judge.

RC: As a reporter, he disagrees.

TRUMP: Oh, as a reporter. No, but there's something nice about that. She feels . . .

BW: But it's not just the individual calls, it's the message of inclusiveness, that it doesn't come through.

TRUMP: Bob, I've been hit very hard.

RC: Here's the problem I think you may face.

TRUMP: Go ahead.

RC: You start an inclusive message, you turn that corner—let's say you're the nominee and you say, you know what? I'm going to tell Woodward who I called. I'm going to start being a unifier. But maybe so many bridges have been burned

	within the party that not everyone's going to be willing . . .
TRUMP:	It's possible, but I don't think so. Don't forget, I've been hit hard. I went in one of 17 and they hit me harder than anybody. Okay? And I hit back very hard. Harder than they hit me. Jeb: low energy. Little Marco. You know, uh, names that were devastating. I think the low-energy Jeb. I mean, all of a sudden you see him running down the street to try and show he's got high energy. And it wasn't him, and it became worse. I hit back very hard. I am telling you, almost all of these people that you would never think would ever— will want to come on board. But I've got to win first. That's why I told you that Vince Lombardi story. Because I think it's a great story. Anyway, I have to go. Let's do it again.
BW:	Okay. When? Should we do it tomorrow? [*laughter*]
TRUMP:	Just treat me fairly. Treat me fairly. Will you clean it up so there's no repeating?
BW:	Thank you so much. You want to do it tomorrow?
TRUMP:	I could do it, but I think I'm in New York tomorrow.
BW:	We could come.
TRUMP:	He wanted to sit in. I know he respects Bob, but this guy is like—even you are impressed.
BW:	Is there a question that we didn't ask that we should have?
DONALD TRUMP, JR.:	Oh, I don't know, I think these days I've heard all the questions. I'm not sure there's any more original thoughts running around D.C.
RC:	I just think it's so important.
TRUMP:	Actually the truth is these were very interesting. Nobody has asked me these questions.
RC:	Because you really are right now on the cusp of possibly being president of the United States . . .

BW:	Thank you, sir. Okay. We'll see you soon.
TRUMP:	You're going to see it, and you're going to know about it.
BW:	Thank you.
TRUMP:	A great honor, man. Thank you . . . .

COMMENTARY: Trump surprisingly defeated Hillary Clinton in the 2016 election. Three years later, I went to interview Trump at the White House.

INTERVIEW 2:
Rocket Man

TRUMP: I said, did you ever hear of the song "Rocket Man"? He said, no, no. Did you ever hear of Elton John? No, no. I said, I did you a great favor. I called you Rocket Man. He goes, you called me Little Rocket Man.

COMMENTARY: On Thursday, December 5, 2019, House Speaker Nancy Pelosi announced the House would move forward with articles of impeachment against President Trump.

PELOSI: If we allow a president to be above the law, we do so surely at the peril of our republic.

Trump was being impeached for his head of state call with Ukrainian President Zelensky. The President had asked Zelensky to investigate his political rival, then former Vice President Joe Biden, and his son Hunter in exchange for security aid from the United States.

A few hours after Pelosi's press conference, I entered the Oval Office to interview President Trump.

Senator Lindsey Graham, Senior Political Counselor Kellyanne Conway, and two of Trump's aides—Deputy Press Secretary Hogan Gidley and Chief of Staff Mick Mulvaney—were also present.

It's important to try to answer the question why Trump would agree to do these interviews with me. One reason was that Lindsey Graham told Trump he was confident I would not put words in Trump's mouth but would report accurately what President Trump said.

BW:	I'm doing book number two.
TRUMP:	Good.
BW:	But we're going to talk.
TRUMP:	I like it much better. So we should've talked on the first one. You know that Bob was going to do a book about me 25 years ago.
GRAHAM:	He told me that he went by with his cohort, Bernstein—
TRUMP:	Long time.
GRAHAM:	—and ya'll were going to do a book. They found you interesting 25 years ago.
TRUMP:	We sat at a table and we talked. I remember it well.
BW:	And Carl said, this guy is really interesting. Now, let me be honest, I said, but not in politics. [*laughter*]
TRUMP:	Yeah. That's right. Who knew? Right?
CONWAY:	Carl Bernstein.
TRUMP:	One for one.
BW:	Did you know?
TRUMP:	Well, I always thought about it, but I never did it. And I did it, and it worked out nicely. I think— did you see the polls that just came out? We're way up, with this crazy impeachment stuff. And it is crazy, by the way. It's crazy. Over a phone call. And you know, did you see the famous sentence with the "us"? Okay? The word was "us," not me. You know, they were saying me, I want you to do "me" a favor. I didn't say that. I said, I want you to do us a favor. And I talk about the country. This is what they're impeaching on?
GRAHAM:	My first impression was it wasn't him on the phone call, because there was no cussing. [*laughter*] And it made perfect sense.
TRUMP:	No, he called up. He said, I didn't know you

were this nice. [*laughter*] You know what this is, though, Bob? These are all judges that I'm signing. Look.

BW: This is on the record for the book.

TRUMP: That's fine.

BW: For next year.

TRUMP: Fine.

BW: Quite frankly, sir, the later it comes out, the better. Other words, September, October.

TRUMP: Ok. I trust you. I have a lot of respect for this guy.

GRAHAM: I wouldn't be here with him if I didn't think he—

TRUMP: And we blew it, because I would've met him—but somebody didn't—I actually called and apologized to him, but it was too late. Somebody—nobody told me about it. And maybe Kellyanne, maybe—I don't know how this whole thing happened, but I would've met with him. Now I don't meet with others. My general policy is if somebody's going to do it, you meet, but it's almost getting—it's hard to meet when you're president, for two reasons. Number one, you're president. You can't meet with everybody. And number two, you don't have enough time. I just met with all of the major ambassadors from the major countries over at the UN. And it was fascinating. You know, really fascinating. From China. From Russia. From all the major countries. And it was great. But I wish I met with you for the last book. But we'll make it up, we'll make it up.

COMMENTARY: When he said this, I was absolutely stunned—as stunned as I had ever been in trying to understand the actions of a president.

My first book on the Trump administration, *Fear*, published in 2018, covered the first year of his presidency and by all accounts it was a devastating portrait.

I had concluded in *Fear* that Trump was an emotionally over-wrought, mercurial, and unpredictable leader. Members of his staff had joined to purposefully block some of what they believed were the president's most dangerous impulses. To do this they stole documents off his desk so he wouldn't see them, and he could not sign them, and could not issue orders. I called it a nervous breakdown of the executive power of the most powerful country in the world—the United States.

Maggie Haberman of *The New York Times* wrote that my book *Fear* "depicts the Trump White House as a byzantine, treacherous, often out-of-control operation," and that the book "unsettled the administration and the president in part because it was clear that the author has spoken with many current and former officials."

I ended *Fear* with a quote from Trump's lawyer John Dowd because in the man and his presidency, Dowd said he had seen the tragic flaw. What Dowd had concluded but could not bring himself to say to the president's face was: "You're a fucking liar."

Now as we met in the Oval Office, Trump was trying to make a sale. He was trying to urgently sell himself to me.

The president sat in a burgundy chair behind the Resolute Desk. He had all his props set out on the desk in front of him.

There was a stack of judicial appointment orders in the center of the desk. Then on one side there was a binder of letters Trump had exchanged with North Korean president Kim Jong Un. And on the other side were large photos of Trump standing next to Kim shaking his hand and smiling.

I had interviewed presidents Carter, Clinton, George W. Bush, and Obama in the Oval Office. All sat in the standard presidential seat by the fireplace and did not have props.

Trump then pivoted to the issue of appointing judges. He had 105 federal judicial vacancies when he took office.

TRUMP:	This is driving them nuts. You know?
GRAHAM:	More coming.
CONWAY:	A hundred and eighty.
TRUMP:	I'll have 182 shortly. We've signed 167. And that doesn't include two Supreme Court judges.
GRAHAM:	[*background talk . . .*] by the way, from South Carolina.
BW:	So I really am here—
TRUMP:	Because Obama left me—

BW: —to listen to your case. And I want to do policy. Because having done nine presidents, you're the ninth—

TRUMP: Okay.

BW: —going back to Nixon—the policy is what matters. It's the spine and definition—

TRUMP: I agree. I agree.

BW: —for the public, for history.

TRUMP: Sure. Policy can change, also, though, Bob, you know? I like flexibility. Some people say I change. I do. I like flexibility, not somebody that has a policy and will go through a brick wall for that policy when you can change it very easily and not have to go through the wall.

BW: You're talking about momentum, sometimes just carries you into—

TRUMP: Momentum. Momentum. That's a very important word, momentum. Having the right momentum. Lindsey called me up many years ago, because I always did sort of okay with certain networks. And he said, could you give me a reference of a certain thing. Remember? Long time ago. I mean, you might not even remember that.

GRAHAM: I just remember you—

TRUMP: But then we ended up in the heat of battle. And it was now between Cruz and Trump. And he said, I have to take either the snake or the poison, and I'll take the poison. I was the snake. [*laughter*] And he said—And then the poison lost. [*laughter*] And then he endorsed me. I don't know if I—

GRAHAM: No, you said I won't . . . Calling me Dr. Kevorkian.

TRUMP: I viewed that as being, you know, pretty far down the pack.

GRAHAM: You called me, the Dr. Kevorkian of endorsers. Everybody I endorsed died. [*laughs*]

TRUMP: Yeah. Anyways, so it worked out. And now he's a great guy. He's been a great friend. So—

BW:	So, foreign policy.
TRUMP:	Yeah.
BW:	Wanted to start with North Korea.
TRUMP:	Okay.
BW:	Because I think that's so important.
TRUMP:	Okay.
BW:	And I would ask you—my wife, Elsa, always talks about the girls' version—
TRUMP:	Right.
BW:	—which is the long version. We know what that is.
TRUMP:	Right.
BW:	Where are you with Kim Jong Un?
TRUMP:	So let me—
BW:	What happened? And what does it mean to you?
TRUMP:	Sure. Let me just tell you what—where we are.

COMMENTARY: Trump had already met with North Korean leader Kim Jong Un three times. His first meeting was on impulse, catching his secretary of state, his secretary of defense, and national security adviser completely off balance. Because Kim Jong Un at that point had a growing nuclear arsenal, the national security team was deeply worried that Trump's impulsive and combative diplomacy could trigger a nuclear confrontation.

And 54 years earlier, as a 22-year-old ensign in the United States Navy, I was part of a two-man team that had custodial control over the nuclear authentication codes that would be used by a president to launch nuclear weapons. I was stationed on the USS *Wright* that was designated as the National Emergency Command Post Afloat that a president could use in crisis or possible nuclear confrontation. I witnessed firsthand the dangers and vulnerabilities in the system for controlling launch and authentication orders for the use of nuclear weapons. I have followed this issue closely as a reporter for decades. Based on what Trump had told me so far about his relationship with Kim, I believed North Korea and the potential for a nuclear crisis could be the big story for my forthcoming book.

| TRUMP: | One of the only times I ever met with Obama— that was because it was mandatory. We were |

sitting in those two seats at the very end. And he said, as you probably know, he said the single biggest problem you have is North Korea. And if he stayed a little bit longer, assuming he were able to, or if Hillary got in—let's assume her position would be the same—you would've absolutely been in a war with North Korea. Possibly nuclear. Would've happened very shortly after.

BW: Did he say that?

TRUMP: He said it's the single biggest problem. Yeah, I mean, he didn't have to say that. I think his basic stance, you'll end up going to war with North Korea shortly. So I said, did you ever try calling him, talking to him? He said no, but the answer was 11 times, yes. And they couldn't get to him. They couldn't speak to him.

COMMENTARY: As you'll hear later, this was not true. In fact, Obama made no attempts to speak with Kim Jong Un himself.

Here Trump gives a monologue on what a diplomatic genius he thought he was to try to forge a partnership. Though Obama had not predicted war as Trump claimed, he had predicted that North Korea would be Trump's biggest problem.

At the time, Obama's worry was shared by all the national security leaders in the Trump administration. Two days before this interview, tensions were high. North Korea had ominously warned Washington of a "Christmas gift" if President Trump did not change his tone.

TRUMP: What happened is, if you go back and look, the rhetoric and all was unbelievably beyond what anyone's ever seen before. And because of that, we ended up getting along.

BW: Right.

TRUMP: And we met. We had a great relation—great thing. And we signed a deal. It said, denuclearization will take place. And then we met again. That was in Singapore. We met again, as you know, the

second meeting. And the second meeting didn't
go as well. We got along great. We've always
gotten along great. I said, did you ever hear of
the song "Rocket Man"? He said, no, no. Did you
ever hear of Elton John? No, no. I said, I did you
a great favor. I called you Rocket Man. He goes,
you called me Little Rocket Man. You know, he
looks at me—[*laughter*]

BW: He knew?

TRUMP: Oh, he knew that. He didn't like Little Rocket Man.
Rocket Man was okay, but he didn't like—

BW: But just to go back with Obama. I mean, having
done some reporting on that, President Trump—

TRUMP: Yeah.

BW: —what didn't come out is how badly it was
going for Obama. And not just for Obama, but
for George W. Bush. The experts I talked to say
for two administrations, both George W. Bush,
Obama, we had feckless policy and a real inept
way of dealing with this. And so I know you use
the English language—it was a shitshow.

TRUMP: It was not good. They didn't have a clue. This is a
different kind of a guy. And I hit him very hard. I
said, we'll blow them to smithereens. I did things
I would normally—People said, he's going to get
us into a war. Remember they were screaming?

BW: Yes, my nuclear button is bigger than yours.

TRUMP: That's right. I said—yeah, he talked about the
button. Right. He said about the button on my
desk. I said, my button's bigger than yours, and
my button works. Yours doesn't. You know, stuff
like that. And it was—I mean, I had friends of
yours saying, he's going to get us into—this is
terrible. So the rhetoric was unbelievable. I made
the first speech at the United Nations, where I
talked about fire and fury, he'll burn in hell, bah,
bah, bah. And then he'd send something back.
And they write things—

BW:	And is this all designed to drive Kim to the negotiating table?
TRUMP:	No. No. It was designed for whatever reason, it was designed. Who knows? Instinctively. Let's talk instinct, okay? Because it's really about—
BW:	Yes, sir.
TRUMP:	—you don't know what's going to happen. But it was very rough rhetoric. The roughest.

COMMENTARY: There was no strategy or plan. It was all determined by Trump's feelings and instincts. This is precisely what worried all of his national security advisers.

TRUMP:	You couldn't be any—
BW:	So what's he like? What's Kim—
TRUMP:	Well, let me just tell you.
BW:	Yes, sir.
TRUMP:	So what happened is the first sign was the Olympics. And then I get a call from South Korea. They would like to see me with the highest delegation. They come in to see me. And they say, Kim Jong Un would love to meet you. Because of me, the Olympics became a great success. Nobody was going to be there. They didn't want to have a nuclear weapon hit the middle of the stadium during an ice-skating event. [*laughter*]
GRAHAM:	That does drive the ticket sales down.
CONWAY:	[The shot put].
TRUMP:	So what happened is I get the word he wants to meet with me. And I'll tell you the funny thing. They go out and announce it to the fake news, which is standing outside. Right? And nobody could believe it. Even stupid CNN, where I got Jeff Zucker his job. I got that bum his job. But what happened is they go out, they announce it, and for a few hours, it was this is the most incredible thing. Then they wake up in the morning and they say, oh, anybody could've—

Nobody could've done it. Obama called 11 times. They showed me the records in Korea. I'm very close to this man. Very close. The ambassador of Russia was just here, along with the ambassador of China and probably 17, 18 ambassadors from the United Nations. It was some—it was Security Council people. But the top people. And they told me—and it's true—I'm the only one he wants to deal with in the world. He doesn't want to deal with anybody but the United States under Trump. And if Trump doesn't win, he's actually—well, you saw what he said about Biden. He is too stupid. He's a stupid—these guys put out the toughest rhetoric. They make you look like a little baby, okay? You know that? You know what I mean.

GRAHAM: I'm trying to up my game.

TRUMP: They put out rhetoric that's brutal. You know what I'm talking about.

BW: Yes, I do.

TRUMP: They said about Pence is this and that—I'm not going to say it. But Pence is this—Pompeo is this—Like, but the president is a great man. It's the craziest thing.

BW: Now why is that though? Do you have an answer?

TRUMP: And China and the Russian ambassador just—no, I just have a relationship with him. You saw when I went—

BW: You haven't met him yet, in the—

TRUMP: Yeah. In fact, I'll get you something that nobody's seen. I'll get you something that's sort of cool. [speaking into a phone?] Bring me some pictures with Kim Jong Un and myself, crossing the line.

BW: Yeah. Yeah.

TRUMP: [speaking on the phone] You have those pictures, right? Yeah. You can bring the smaller ones, I don't care. Just bring me some of them. Those nice color ones that I just saw, right.

BW: But the CIA says about Kim Jong Un—you know

they do all this analysis and reporting—that he's cunning, crafty, but ultimately stupid.

TRUMP: I disagree.

BW: But you know—I'm sure they tell you that—

TRUMP: I hope you write that, and I hope you write my answer. I disagree. He's cunning. He's crafty. And he's very smart. And he's very tough. You know—

BW: Why does the CIA say that?

TRUMP: Because they don't know. Okay? Because they don't know. They have no idea. I'm the only one that knows. I'm the only one he deals with. He won't deal with anybody else. Okay. So here's— he never wrote a letter, right? You know they have historians that study.

BW: Yes.

TRUMP: Here's a series of letters that he wrote. Your Excellency—he calls me Your Excellency. I am thankful your personal letter—

BW: Can I get copies of these?

TRUMP: No, I can't give you copies, but I'll let you read them, if you want to look at them real fast. Then you could see them.

BW: Okay. I'll look at them after we talk, if I may. I'll read them into my—

TRUMP: But these are like 10 or 12 letters that he sent me. He's never sent a letter in his life.

COMMENTARY: This is not true. North Korean Leader Kim Jong Un had written letters to other presidents and world leaders.

TRUMP: And you know how they're sent? Through courier. They're dropped off at the border to an American colonel and the colonel flies back to the United States. He won't send—you know, the whole thing. But I have these, the originals of those. That's the interpretation of—

BW: Do you get a sense he's wooing you?

TRUMP: No, I get—

BW:	Or building a relationship of trust?
TRUMP:	—a sense—I get a sense he likes me. I think he likes me. Okay. So you know he's got a great piece of land. He's in between Russia, China, and South Korea. In the real estate business we'd say, great location. You understand?
BW:	[*laughing*] I do.
TRUMP:	And I—he would love to be able to do something with it. I have him convinced. Remember when I did that thing and I showed condos all over his—
GRAHAM:	Oh yeah.
TRUMP:	Right? You know what? Had a huge impact on him.
BW:	It is chilling to report on North Korea. I've looked in depth at this. The secretary of defense sleeps in his gym clothes because he has an—do you know this?—an alarm and a light in his bathroom in case he is called to an emergency conference.
TRUMP:	We're talking about his secretary of defense?
BW:	No, we're talking about the American secretary of defense.
TRUMP:	Which one are we talking about?
BW:	Mattis and the current—I mean, it's—anyway—
TRUMP:	Mattis was the world's most overrated general.
BW:	I know, you've said that.
TRUMP:	Oh, just terrible.
BW:	You know, when he started testing those missiles, ICBMs, they were scared to death. They would watch them arc up over the Home Islands—
TRUMP:	Sure.
BW:	—north Japan—
TRUMP:	Right. Yes.
BW:	—calculating the aim point.
TRUMP:	[*DJT shuffling though photos*] This is me and him. That's the line, right? Then I walked over the line. Pretty cool. You know? Pretty cool. Right?
BW:	Yeah.
TRUMP:	You see them, Linds? They just came out.

BW: Do I get to keep these?

TRUMP: No, but I'll give you a couple—you can have some
               of these.

BW: Good.

GRAHAM: Did you ever think you'd live to see this? The
               North Korean guy inviting the [*unintelligible*]—

TRUMP: No, nobody's ever been—see that? See that?
               That's the line between North and South Korea.
               And Bob? See this?

GRAHAM: [*unintelligible*] Look at that.

TRUMP: Look, Bob. That's the line. That's North Korea
               and South Korea. That's the line. That line is like
               a big deal. Nobody has ever stepped across that
               line. Ever.

GRAHAM: To live to tell about it.

TRUMP: Except me. Because what I did is I did it. I said,
               would you like me to come in? He said, yes, I
               would like you to come in. Nobody's ever done
               that. I mean, they're cool pictures when you—you
               know, when you talk about iconic pictures, how
               about that?

COMMENTARY: Trump was the first American president to cross
the North Korea/South Korea border, but by no means was he the first
person to do so.

BW: But it's still a dangerous relationship. Would you
               agree?

TRUMP: Yeah, but it's less dangerous than it was.

BW: Okay. Fair point.

TRUMP: Because he likes me. I like him. We get along.
               That doesn't mean I'm naïve. That doesn't mean
               that I think, oh, it's going to be wonderful. He's a
               very tough cookie. And he is smart, very smart.

BW: You're convinced he's smart.

TRUMP: Beyond smart. Look, he took over when he was 25
               years old, a volatile place where the people are very
               smart. Same as South Korea. They're the same.

	Okay? Same people. Very smart. He was violent and vicious and smart. Now, I don't care if you're like portrayed as a godlike figure, doesn't matter. If you're stupid, they throw you out. It's over pretty quickly. He took over as a very young man when his father died. You had the grandfather—
BW:	I know the whole—
TRUMP:	He had great respect for the [*whispers*] grandfather. Tells me everything. I know everything about him.
BW:	So what does he want—what does Kim want out of this relationship?
TRUMP:	But when you do that—I'm saying—he killed his uncle and he put the body right in the steps where the senators walked out. And the head was [*whispers*] cut, sitting on the chest. Think that's tough? You know, they think politics in this country's tough.
BW:	You know how he—
TRUMP:	Nancy Pelosi, who's a dope.
CONWAY:	Praying for you.
TRUMP:	Nancy Pelosi says, oh, let's impeach him. You think that's tough? This is tough. Look, I'll show you. Go ahead. [*laughter*]
BW:	He's tough. I just want to ask you this, President Trump—
TRUMP:	Look, did you ever see him smile?
BW:	—as I'm sure you know—
TRUMP:	Did you ever see him smile before?

COMMENTARY: Trump is showing me pictures of himself and Kim smiling and shaking hands.

BW:	But the NORTHCOM commander—
TRUMP:	Right.
BW:	—in Colorado Springs is presidentially designated to shoot down a missile that might hit the United States homeland.

TRUMP:	That's correct.
BW:	—from North Korea.
TRUMP:	Yeah. We're all set. Because you have to be set. I mean, I'm not a person that said, oh—but I will tell you, anybody else would've been in a war. They would've been in a war. They wouldn't have had a choice. Here's my daughter. I took my daughter to—
BW:	So you're comfortable with that delegation of authority to NORTHCOM?
TRUMP:	Sure. Well, you have to be prepared.
BW:	Because you can't live 24/7 waiting for—
TRUMP:	No, no, no. I don't wait for anything. I don't wait for anything. Nothing bothers me. I don't wait for anything. If it did I would've been not here a year ago. They've been trying to impeach me now for three years. No, more. They've been trying to impeach me from the day I came down the escalator, okay, you want to know the truth. They've been trying to get me from that time. Look, nice picture. But—no, the relationship is good.
BW:	Okay.
TRUMP:	Yeah, you can give Bob some of these. Bob—let's see those, too.
BW:	So, hard question, President Trump.
TRUMP:	Yeah.
BW:	I understand we really came close to war.
TRUMP:	Them?
BW:	With North Korea.
TRUMP:	Very.
BW:	Pardon?
TRUMP:	Much closer than anyone would know.
BW:	Yeah. I realize—
TRUMP:	Much closer.
BW:	—one more ICBM test, and—
TRUMP:	Much closer. You know. He knows it better than anybody.

BW: Did you tell him?

TRUMP: I don't want to tell you that. But he knows. I have a great relationship, let me just put it that way. But we'll see what happens. But now—so we had a great meeting.

BW: And why did we not have that war?

TRUMP: Because it's now three years—until just recently—and there has been no nuclear testing, by the way, for that whole time.

BW: Yes, I know.

TRUMP: You know people say—

BW: And no ICBMs.

TRUMP: Here's the thing that—somebody said, what did you learn most being president? I said, I knew the press was fairly dishonest, but I had no idea how much. And they really are. You know, I can't tell you what the end is going to be yet, how it's going to end. For three years, we've had no nuclear tests. He's tested short-range missiles. Which, by the way, every country has short-range missiles. There's no country that doesn't have. Okay? It's no big deal. That doesn't mean that after January he's not going to be doing some things. We'll see what it is. But I have a great relationship. You know what you can do? When we're finished I'll let you sit down and look at a couple of those.

BW: I will. I will.

TRUMP: But you'll see the level of the relationship in the letter. And again, he never wrote a letter to anybody.

BW: The best North Korean expert I know, a man named Bob Carlin, who's served forever, refers to the situation as the tapestry of doom. Very pessimistic.

TRUMP: You mean—

BW: That this is going to spin out of control.

TRUMP: It's possible.

BW: This relationship.

TRUMP:	Sure. But it would have spun out of control with other presidents immediately.
BW:	Okay. I accept that. But—
TRUMP:	Possible.
BW:	—you're in the driver's seat now.
TRUMP:	Uhhhhh.
BW:	No?
TRUMP:	Well, I'll tell you why. Because when I took over— Lindsey can tell you this better than anybody— when I took over this country, I had Mattis come to me. And I said, you better be ready for North Korea, because it looks like we're going to have to do something. Very good possibility. And he said, sir, we have no ammunition. Did you know that?
GRAHAM:	Oh no, I did. A hundred percent.
TRUMP:	Obama was—we had no ammunition. We have places in Guam that are big warehouses. They had nothing. They had nothing.
GRAHAM:	[They're running out of?] a lot of that stuff in the Mideast.
TRUMP:	So we're much better, because now we have more ammunition than we've ever had. [*laughs*] Two and a half trillion dollars I spent. We had no ammunition, Bob. That was the statement by Mattis. I think he might admit that, actually. But I said, no president should ever—two things. No president should ever have this bullshit happen to him, and no president should ever take over and has no ammunition. I will say that.

COMMENTARY: This is not true. They had enough ammunition. Secretary of Defense Mattis was so worried about the possibility of nuclear war that he went privately to the National Cathedral in Washington DC to pray and prepare himself for the possibility of having to use nuclear weapons against North Korea in order to defend the United States.

Mattis described how difficult it was to have a discussion with the president. An intelligence briefer could barely get through a couple of sentences before Trump went off on what Mattis irreverently called "those Seattle freeway off-ramps to nowhere." You could not take the president to 30,000 feet, Mattis said. You could try, but then something that had been said on Fox News or something more salient to Trump would grab the president's attention and he'd shoot off on to another subject. The facts would be dismissed.

Mattis didn't see any way around the president's lack of attention span. "You just had to deal with it," he said. "You're sitting there, and it's not deference at that point. It's grasping for a way to get it back on subject. And it was just very hard. There wasn't a lot of time for it."

BW:	Have you given Kim too much power?
TRUMP:	No.
BW:	Because if he's defiant, if he shoots one of those—
TRUMP:	Doesn't matter.
BW:	—ICBMs, what are you going to do, sir?
TRUMP:	That doesn't—let me tell you, whether I gave it to him or not, if he shoots, he shoots. And if he shoots, he shoots.

COMMENTARY: This cavalier attitude about nuclear weapons, "if he shoots, he shoots," terrified his national security team, particularly Secretary of Defense James Mattis. Nuclear deterrence is designed to make the use of nuclear weapons unthinkable, an absolute last resort. But Trump's advisers knew that one miscalculation in the seesawing relationship between the young North Korean despot and Trump could launch the U.S. and the world down an escalation pathway to nuclear war that would be very difficult—if not impossible—to get off.

TRUMP:	And then he's got big problems, let me put it that way. Big, big problems. Bigger than anybody's ever had before. You know, I'm getting credit. Most people thought I'd be in a war within the first seven days of my presidency.
BW:	Yeah.
TRUMP:	And they're actually finding out that I'd rather not be. I have built a weapons system that nobody's ever had in this country before. We have stuff that

you haven't even seen or heard about. We have
stuff that Putin and Xi have never heard about
before.

COMMENTARY: The U.S. military possessed some powerful weapons systems, and was continually developing new ones, but I could
never establish conclusively what Trump was talking about here.

This exemplifies the casual, dangerous way that Trump treats the
most classified programs and information, as we've seen now in 2022
in Mar-a-Lago, where he had 184 classified documents, including 25
marked "Top Secret."

TRUMP:	Bush was using our military all over the place. He didn't know what was happening. I don't care what you say on that, Lindsey, that's one thing I disagree with you on. The Middle East. Should've never been there.
BW:	You know by giving Kim all of this—you've given him a lot of power.
TRUMP:	I don't think I have. We haven't taken the sanctions off. Right? The sanctions are stronger now than they ever were.
BW:	And that's what he wants. He wants them off.
TRUMP:	All he wants.
BW:	What did you say?
TRUMP:	That's a big thing. I said, can't do it, sorry. But listen—
BW:	Why?
TRUMP:	—we haven't taken the sanctions . . .
BW:	Why not?
TRUMP:	Can't do it.
BW:	Because you've got this new relationship—
TRUMP:	No, but I can't do it. I said, give me a deal. We'll do it fast. I would like you to treat that with respect. Because I don't need a book coming out where I'm—because I have a lot of respect for him and get along with him. This isn't games.
BW:	Yes. A lot of artillery.

TRUMP: Artillery. Did you ever see the scene on the beach
              where he must've had 3,000 like Howitzer-type
              guns sitting on the beach firing into the ocean?
              Now, unless that was computer generated—and
              they say it was impossible, that was the biggest
              display—

BW: And you've got that—

TRUMP: Do you agree with that, Lindsey? I have never
              seen anything like that.

GRAHAM: There are 14,000 artillery pieces pointed at Seoul
              right now. He doesn't have . . .

BW: Thirty miles away—

TRUMP: So you have 32 million people. We think New
              York is big. We have nine million people. Thirty-
              two million people living in Seoul—

BW: I was there a couple of months ago. It's a
              beautiful,—

TRUMP: Yeah.

BW: —magnificent city.

TRUMP: Wouldn't be beautiful after about an hour. And
              they have them in the mountains. You know, they
              can be knocked out, but it'll take two weeks on
              average to knock them out. Okay, two weeks. But
              in the meantime, Seoul is gone. That's without
              nuclear.

BW: Okay. Do you have a channel with Kim—

TRUMP: Yeah. [sighs]

BW: —if there's some confusion that your military
              people come in and say—

TRUMP: The only one he'll talk to—

BW: —there's a missile coming from North Korea. Can
              you call him—

TRUMP: No. Not calls. Because they only have one phone.
              They only have one phone.

BW: Yeah. It's the intel phone.

TRUMP: In the House of Communism. I don't deal—I deal
              with him a different way. I deal with him really
              through letters. And those letters are fascinating.

When you read those letters, you'll see the
relationship. Now look, I don't want to be naïve
and tell, oh, I have a great—stupid people, right?
I have a great relationship with him. What does
that mean? Maybe nothing. Maybe it means a
lot. But it's worth—so when these guys come in,
Trump has given up so much. He's given—what
did I do? You know what I did? One thing. I met.
Big fucking deal. It takes me two days. I met.
I gave up nothing. I didn't give up sanctions. I
didn't give him anything. Okay? Didn't give him
anything. He was—

BW: So you don't sleep in your gym clothes?

TRUMP: No, I don't even—

BW: Like the secretary of defense.

TRUMP: No, I don't.

BW: And worry about—

TRUMP: He—the secretary of defense. I don't think he did
either, okay, you want to know the truth? I think
it's another good story. It's a yarn.

COMMENTARY: I had learned from the Pentagon and Mattis's staff
that Mattis regularly slept in his gym clothes. So he was ready in an
emergency or crisis to come to a secure call, a National Event Conference as it was called, to deal with a nuclear threat. For example, if
North Korea launched an ICBM, Trump had delegated the authority
to the secretary of defense to shoot down a missile that threatened the
United States.

TRUMP: For three years they haven't tested nuclear
weapons. Almost since I'm here. In other words,
once I started the talks. They haven't tested. That
doesn't mean they won't, and they might.

BW: And they have 40 of them at least, I understand.

TRUMP: And they're the real deal. He's got the real deal
stuff. They don't have a transportation system yet.
But you know they have to travel 8,500 miles.
And I don't believe they can do that yet, but

	we'll see what happens. But I think we're doing
	fine with him. Okay? I think we're doing well.
	We might be doing great. He wants to meet. You
	know, he's trying to send a signal. He wants to
	meet with me. Now I left the last meeting, I said,
	you're not ready to make a deal. I told him. I said,
	you know, you're my friend, but you're not ready
	to make a deal. See he's—
BW:	What'd he say?
TRUMP:	He couldn't believe it. They say he killed all of the
	people that were there. And I will say, I've been
	dealing with those people. I haven't seen them
	recently. So you know—[*laughter*]. We haven't
	been dealing with them. We've been dealing with
	a different group.
GRAHAM:	Now, you do know you can't do that.
TRUMP:	But you look, look at that picture. He's having a
	good time. You know? Nobody's ever seen him
	smile. Look. Look at him smiling. He's happy. He
	feels happy. But he's very smart. Remember this—
	when you take over—and I really mean this too,
	you take over a country and you're 25 years old
	and you survive? You've got, you know, millions
	of people that are all smart as hell and energetic?
	You know the energy's incredible.
BW:	They show you the reports about those camps in
	North Korea.
TRUMP:	Oh—
BW:	President Bush once told me about Kim's father,
	Kim Jong Il, he said, I loathe Kim Jong Il because
	of what he's doing to his people. And for—
TRUMP:	And you know what? That attitude got
	him nothing. In the meantime, they built
	a huge nuclear force during those last two
	administrations. They haven't done it during me.
	Now you know you hear reports that they'll start
	again. But for three years, I gave nothing.
BW:	Has he given you—

TRUMP:	You know, they'd say, President Trump agreed to meet. What the fuck? It's a meeting. I agreed to meet? What? You mean instead of sitting home reading your book, I met?
BW:	Did you think it's kind of Nixon to China?
TRUMP:	No, I don't want to—You know, I don't want to even talk about Nixon to China.
BW:	Okay.
TRUMP:	I think Nixon to China—I think China's been a horrible thing for this country. Horrible.
BW:	We'll get to that.
TRUMP:	Because we've allowed them to build a monster that now I'm doing a very good job—I'm taking in billions and billions of dollars. What these presidents have allowed China to do to our country. The way they sucked money out of our country. Five hundred billion dollars a year, for many years. Was crazy. Go ahead.
BW:	Intellectual property theft on a level that's staggering.
TRUMP:	Intellectual property theft. At least $300 billion a year. That's estimated by people that do that. That's hard to estimate, but that's what they say. I'm sure you've heard those numbers.
BW:	But after North Korea, a lot of people in this world say managing the relationship with China is the most important thing you've got to do.
TRUMP:	Yeah. It's very important. It's important in two ways. I have a very good relationship with President Xi, but it's somewhat strained right now [*laughter*], as you can imagine. Because we're taking in tens of billions of dollars. We never took in ten cents. We're taking in a tremendous amount of money. Get these for Bob, give me those, Bob.
BW:	You're still a tariff man with China?
TRUMP:	Oh, I'm the king of tariffs, yeah. Because it's the only thing that has any impact. Yep. It's the one thing they don't want. Here.

COMMENTARY: Independent analysis showed that Trump's trade war with China cost the U.S. economy $316 billion by the year 2020. It cost Americans 300,000 jobs. The federal reserve found U.S. companies lost $1.7 trillion in the price of their stock as a result of the U.S. tariffs imposed by Trump.

TRUMP:	Give him that one. Give him those two. Nice. Nice. You get three nice pictures. Here, if it's a good book, if it's a bad book I wasted $10 on photographs. But it should be a good book. Because you know why it's a good book? Because I'm here less than three years, and nobody has done what I've done in the first three years of a presidency. Whether you like it or not, nobody's come close. I've rebuilt our military. We have the strongest economy we've ever had. Nobody's done what I've done. And I've done it with these crazy Democrats, these lunatics, trying to concoct all sorts of bullshit between Mueller and Russia and all of the stuff. And I've done it with a cloud, where I have a cloud always, you know—from the day I came down the escalator, I've had that. Nobody's done what I've done. I even brought—I brought you some stuff that you can look at and do whatever you want with, but you can have it. Okay?
TRUMP:	Get those pictures. Maybe if you get them fast, I'll give them to him right now.
BW:	One of your closest confidants said something interesting, said, I am absolutely sure President Trump does not want a war. Is that true?
TRUMP:	No, I don't want a war. No. Because I'm intelligent. Okay? War is no good. War is no good.
BW:	Is there some—
TRUMP:	That doesn't mean—that doesn't mean—
BW:	internal mechanism in you—
TRUMP:	No. No.

BW:	—that restrains you?
TRUMP:	Well everyone thought I'd be in war the first day of my presidency, right?
BW:	Yes. A lot—that was the conventional—
TRUMP:	They thought we would be in World War I within 24 hours.
CONWAY:	[and a recession?].
TRUMP:	And now they're really shocked. As an example, on Iran, they shot down a drone, unmanned. So I said, okay. Not very valuable. I was all set to—you know, I could've done whatever I wanted. And they shot off a second one, they hit Saudi Arabia. You know Saudi Arabia, by the way, Saudi Arabia is paying us billions of dollars. They never paid us any money. I said to the king, King, you got to pay us for protection. But nobody has ever asked. I said, but I'm asking, King. If it weren't for us, you wouldn't be there for two weeks.
BW:	That is true. Did he pay?
TRUMP:	I said, King, have you ever flown commercial? You know, he's got a brand-new 747. Beautiful, most beautiful plane you've ever seen. I said, no, you've got to pay. But he said, but nobody has ever asked. That was his only problem. Because they have nothing but cash.
BW:	And did he pay?
TRUMP:	Already paid. Paid us a billion dollars the other day.
GRAHAM:	They're paying a lot in Syria. They've done more in Syria in the last year than—
TRUMP:	I said, you've got to pass $15 billion.
BW:	Now, can I shift to—
TRUMP:	And he's already paid a lot of money, so—
BW:	—politics for a moment?
TRUMP:	In other words, wait a minute—we have countries paying—I went to South Korea. Nobody knows this. Nobody would write it anyway. It costs us $10 billion a year to protect

South Korea, which is stupid. They've been
paying us $500 million.

BW: But as you know, the military people always tell
you that's the best bargain we make. It's—

TRUMP: The military people are wrong.

BW: —a great investment.

TRUMP: I wouldn't say they were stupid because I would
never say that about our military people. But if
they said that, they—whoever said that was stupid.
It's a horrible bargain. We're protecting South
Korea from North Korea, and they're making a
fortune with televisions and ships and everything
else. Right? They make so much money.

BW: You say in meetings, you kind of say publicly,
we're suckers when we do that.

TRUMP: Suckers. We're suckers. Even Abe—you know,
he's a good friend of mine. I say, Shinzo, you
gotta pay. They're all starting. What happened
with South Korea, I said, you gotta pay. And they
were at the end of their term, the budget term. I
said, give us $2 billion to start. No, no, no, we . . .
they're very tough to negotiate with. Among the
toughest. They don't appreciate what we're doing
for them. We're keeping them from war with
North Korea. And I said, you've got to pay. And
they said the same thing as the king. They said,
but nobody has ever asked us. I said, that doesn't
matter. I can't help it if people were stupid. And
that's the story.

[*BW's cell phone rings.*]

TRUMP: That's probably Bernstein.

[CONWAY]: I didn't know he had it?

BW: It's not—

GRAHAM: Don't know how that got in here. [*laughter*]

TRUMP: Do you want a Coke, Bob? Anything? You want
something to drink.

BW:	No. Can I ask a political question?
TRUMP:	Sure. [*sighs*]
BW:	And that is, looking at this through the lens of a reporter who wants to look at the whole story, you've changed the Republican Party. You realize that?
TRUMP:	Ninety-five percent approval rating. Nobody's ever been at—you know Ronald Reagan was 87. He was—
BW:	Okay. Is this a movement?
TRUMP:	No. Ah—that I can't tell you. I can tell you—
BW:	What do you think?
TRUMP:	It's the party of strength and common sense, both. You know?
BW:	And who's the heir?
TRUMP:	I don't say—
BW:	Who's the heir?
TRUMP:	And I'll tell you what—the heir will have to be determined. That's to be determined. But, but I—okay, as an example. The Republican Party has always been known for disloyalty to each other. Okay, they always broke up. They always broke up. You had many Mitt Romneys. Let's see if he's disloyal. Let's see. Right now, he couldn't be elected dog catcher in Utah. He couldn't run—if he ran, he'd be fifth in a primary, just like happened to little Bob Corker. And just like happened to Flake. They wanted to be senators for the rest of their lives. They were in clover. And Flake attacked me before I ever heard of him. I said, who's this guy named Flake? He's really a nasty son of a bitch. Right? I never even heard of him, but he attacked me. Then I attacked him. He was that way. Bob Corker, I got along with him. But then all of a sudden he hit me a couple of times. And I went after him. He went from 57 to four in Tennessee, and he was fifth in the primary. He wouldn't have even

had a primary. But he couldn't keep his mouth
shut.

COMMENTARY: This is probably not true, and I could find no evidence to support what Trump had said.

TRUMP: So it's the party of really strength and common
                    sense. And what happened is the other day they
                    took a vote. A vote on this situation. The House.
                    Never happened before—197 to nothing. To zero.
                    That's impossible.

COMMENTARY: Exactly 195 Republicans and two Democrats voted
against impeaching Trump.

TRUMP: I will say this, and this isn't a threat, because
                    it's not a threat. But if they went against me,
                    they'd all lose their election. Even if they lost five
                    percent of my voters, because nobody has a base
                    like that.
BW: Okay, now, why do people love you?
TRUMP: I don't know.
BW: Why do they like—
TRUMP: Because I'm real. Because I love them.
BW: Here's my anecdotal—talked to people, and why
                    are you for Trump? And they'll say—one answer
                    you get more than anything: he's not politically
                    correct. They don't like political correctness.
TRUMP: I don't think of it that way. I don't think—
BW: You think that's—
TRUMP: They say I have the strongest base in the history
                    of politics. Remember the statement? I could—
BW: Who said that?
TRUMP: Everybody. They say it now. I don't think there's
                    ever been a base like this. And because I love
                    them, they love me. I mean, it's just a great base.
BW: Why among Democrats—I talk to lots of
                    Democrats—they are on fire about you.

TRUMP:	Yeah. But they—really?
BW:	There is anger.
TRUMP:	How come I had so many votes for me in the last election? And I'll have it again.
BW:	But you listen to them, and if you heard some of the—I mean, Lindsey says it's grievance. But people are just beside themselves. Why?
TRUMP:	Why did I have so many vote for me? So you—
BW:	But why are they—let's talk about—
TRUMP:	Well, wait—but—
BW:	—those that are angry—
TRUMP:	No, I can't, because I'm more popular now than I was then. A lot of them don't want to say. I don't know if that's an insult or a compliment—
CONWAY:	Compliment.
TRUMP:	Do you know why the exit polls were wrong, Bob? Remember I was going to lose the election big, it was over, about five o'clock it was over. You know, the exit polls like at five o'clock.
BW:	I know. I remember.
TRUMP:	You know why? Because there was a group of people—the largest they've ever sampled—that said, F-you. They call them the F-you people. You know what that stands for, right?
BW:	Yes.
TRUMP:	It means, it's none of your business. So they'd walk out. Who are you voting for? Fuck you. Boom. Who are you voting for? It's none of your business. It's none of your business. Okay. Thirty-four percent of those people said—they never had that. Usually it's like five percent. Every one of those votes came to us. They didn't count those votes. That's why the exit polls—
BW:	President Trump, fair point. But there is anger out there.
TRUMP:	There is, but there's also—
BW:	And the question is, you're sitting here in the Oval Office. Why? Why all that anger? It's so—

	look, I've done this almost for 50 years. I've never heard—people come to my house and they're in responsible positions, and I almost have to give them a valium to calm them down.
CONWAY:	[?]
TRUMP:	Okay, I think it's for a number of reasons. I understand what you're—
BW:	Okay.
TRUMP:	But before I—before I—before I—
BW:	You understand the importance—
TRUMP:	—agree to even answer that question, okay?
BW:	Okay.
TRUMP:	I have to say this: there's also many Democrats that silently will vote for me. And it happened last time. The Obama Democrats that came out—I was going to say Barack Hussein, but I figured I wouldn't say that today, because I want to keep this very nice. The Obama Democrats who came out and they voted for me, and it was a tremendous percentage. And the Bernie Sanders Democrats, they voted for me. Now the Sanders did it because of trade. They like—you know. Okay.
BW:	The question is, why are so many people on fire about you? Why are they so angry, sir?
TRUMP:	Because I've accomplished more than any other president, and it's driving them crazy. And because they don't think they can beat me fairly and squarely in the election. I really believe that.
BW:	David Cameron, when he was prime minister of Great Britain—
TRUMP:	Okay.
BW:	—met Obama as president. I asked him at a breakfast, said, what do you think of Obama? And he said, oh, I like him, I love him, he's so smart. Pause. But no one's afraid of him. Is that fair?
TRUMP:	I don't think he's smart.
BW:	Because I think people are afraid of you.

TRUMP:	I don't know. I don't think Obama's smart. See? I think he's highly overrated. And I don't think he's a great speaker. Oh, he's so—you know, hey look. I went to the best schools. I did great. I had an uncle who was a professor at MIT for 40 years, one of the most respected in the history of the school. For 40 years. My father's brother. And my father was smarter than he was. It's good stock. You know they talk about the elite. Really, the elite. Ah. They have nice houses. No. I have much better than them. I have better everything than them, including education, including—so here's the thing—
BW:	So at this moment where they are about to—
TRUMP:	I mean, Obama, Obama, good speaker. So . . . Nobody ever says this, but how come every time I speak—for instance, if I say let's go to Florida tomorrow and I'll speak, and I only have one requirement. Right? That requirement is get me the largest stadium available. And they get me NBA arenas that hold 20,000 people. And I have them filled up, and I have 25,000 people standing outside trying to get in. In one day. So we had elections recently. First of all, I didn't run in '18. And there's a big difference between—but they had elections—
BW:	This is an important moment in history, where they're going to impeach you, the House is going to impeach you—
TRUMP:	Yeah.
BW:	—and we're sitting in the Oval Office here. And you are content, happy, proud.
TRUMP:	Sure.
BW:	Any angst?
TRUMP:	No.
BW:	Any sense of, Jesus, what's going on?
TRUMP:	He knows. He knows. It's okay, don't worry about it.

AIDE:	We've got about five minutes, gentlemen, before the—
TRUMP:	Okay, well—I love this guy.
CONWAY:	He'll come back. Soon.
TRUMP:	Even though he writes shit about me. That's okay.
BW:	What?
TRUMP:	Go ahead. Go ahead.
GRAHAM:	They thought they were going to win. I thought they were going to win.
TRUMP:	I didn't. Because I saw the crowds.
CONWAY:	—the only person on TV saying that, though, so—
TRUMP:	No, no. I saw the crowds.
GRAHAM:	Everything they wanted to do has been undone. You have done a great job of taking the eight years of Obama and rolling it back.
CONWAY:	[?]
TRUMP:	I have disassembled 82 percent of what he did. Okay?
BW:	That's a new number.
TRUMP:	Including his health care, because I got rid of the individual mandate. Obamacare, the whole thing was the individual mandate.

COMMENTARY: The individual mandate was a requirement that individuals purchase insurance or face a tax penalty. While the individual mandate was repealed by congress in 2017, millions of Americans are still on Obamacare.

TRUMP:	Here's the thing that gets me. Number one, I've dismantled almost everything he's done. And that's a killer. Okay? When you ask why. But the other thing are the judges. Because I have two Supreme Court judges. I'll have 182 judges.
GRAHAM:	But here's the point. I told you, and I told him, if Mueller had found something, you've lost me. This is all bullshit. From day one, this has been bullshit. This is Schiff and Nadler, it's the first

	impeachment in the history of the country driven by partisan people—
TRUMP:	All of them.
GRAHAM:	—not by outside counsel.
BW:	But you never know where that—once that train starts, you don't know—
GRAHAM:	Oh, I know.
BW:	—where it's going.
TRUMP:	Okay, Lindsey knows this.
GRAHAM:	I know where it's going.
TRUMP:	They spent on Mueller $44 million. They had 18 Trump haters, all Democrats. Mueller was used, but he wasn't a Trump guy anyway. But he was used, okay? They issued 2,500 subpoenas. Interviewed—listen to this—500 people. And they found nothing. I guarantee I could find something on you. I guarantee it with that. You understand? With one-half the firepower. And I had to go through that for two years. And don't forget, you know, we have a very calm White House. But people would say, oh, the White House. If you go to office and in your first day you have a guy named General Flynn, who people respect—35 years in the armed services, right?
BW:	Mm-hmm.
TRUMP:	And I understand—he walks in. He's almost crying. He's under investigation. From almost the first day in office, they were trying to do an overthrow of this administration. And look what we did. And let me go one step further. When you say there's dissension out there, sure.
BW:	No, anger.
TRUMP:	But you had—
BW:	People are on fire. You know that. You—
TRUMP:	You had the same anger against Barack Hussein Obama. Except it was politically incorrect for people to express their anger. But you had the

same anger for Obama as you do now, except it
was the opposite. Come on in, Mike.

COMMENTARY: Vice President Pence came in.

TRUMP:	You know Mike Pence.
PENCE:	Mr. President. Welcome home.
TRUMP:	Hey, Mike.
BW:	Sir, Bob Woodward.
PENCE:	Of course. Good to see you. Good to see you.
BW:	Good to see you. Good. We're talking—somebody told me in November, when you interviewed Mattis to become secretary of defense, that Ivanka was there and she asked him, when are you going to rewrite the ISIS strategy and how long is it going to take you? Is that right?
TRUMP:	That's right. Ivanka was very much into it. She hated the terrorists. Hated terrorism. Ivanka is—
BW:	How did she learn—
TRUMP:	Ivanka's been a tremendous—Ivanka's done a great job here. Gets no credit for it. You know she's very smart. Top, top student. Top talent.
BW:	But how interesting, I thought, that she would say, how long is it going to take you—
TRUMP:	Yeah, it's interesting. Just a second on Mattis. You know Mattis when I hired him, his real nickname was Chaos.
BW:	Yeah.
TRUMP:	And I said, is your name Mad Dog? Your nickname?
BW:	He didn't like it.
TRUMP:	He said, no, sir. What is it? Chaos. I said, I don't like that name. He said, well, that's my name. I said, I thought it was Mad Dog. No, that's so-and-so. And he told—that's some other guy. I said, all right. Do you mind if I change your name to Mad Dog? He goes, you can sort of do whatever you want. This was at the beginning, before I hired

	him. I said, Mad Dog Mattis. That works out great. But he wasn't. He was just a PR guy.
BW:	I was surprised you weren't able to work with him better.
TRUMP:	I'll tell you what turned out—
BW:	What happened?
TRUMP:	He was a Democrat who was an Obama guy, and he got fired by Obama.
BW:	Yes, he did.
TRUMP:	And for good reason. Because—just didn't work out. You understand. But he got fired. And pretty viciously by Obama. And I viewed that as a good thing, but ultimately he was an Obama-type guy. He was—you know, that was his mentality. No, it was just a mistake. It's okay. Not a bad guy, but he was highly overrated. I took out ISIS 100 percent. When I came in, when we came in, we had—
BW:	They say 99 percent.
TRUMP:	Well, I don't care what they said. They can say whatever. But it was a mess. It was all over. I defeated ISIS. Then remember, I said, all right. I've got 98 percent. I'm getting out. And everyone went, no, do 100 percent. And that's when I went to Iraq, and I met with some generals and it was all an interesting thing. But we took it over, and we did a great job. We cleaned it out. That's another—I don't even put that down, but that's another—I said, Mike, nobody has ever done more in less than three years than what we've done in this administration. And it's not even close. Nobody. No other administration. Even close. First three and a half years. And I've been under a cloud. I told him, from the day I came down on the escalator with our beautiful first lady of the future, but our beautiful first lady—who by the way, people love. Did you see how many retweets she had?

BW: Why did you have this pull and tug with Mattis on allies and the military alliances, like NATO?

TRUMP: Because Mattis has no concept of money, and I do. Because everybody took advantage of the United States. Look, when we defend Saudi Arabia—it's a wealthy country. Nothing but cash. I said, why are we doing this without at least working out a deal with them?

BW: And how much money did you get, or are we getting?

TRUMP: They've given over—they've given a billion dollars, just recently. We asked them two, three months ago. Said, gotta pay, gotta pay. They got hit.

BW: Does it go into the U.S. Treasury?

TRUMP: It goes into the—just standard treasury, yeah. And they'll pay 15 billion. You know who else is going to pay? Japan. South Korea.

BW: So what's the Trump-Pence strategy to win over in the next 11 months the persuadable voter?

TRUMP: Well, number one, I think we're winning anyway. Okay? Did you see the poll that just came out? I'm at 52 percent. And they say you can add 10 points to every poll. Do you agree with that?

BW: I don't—I have no—I think polls are BS, President Trump.

TRUMP: I don't know. You know what? I'll tell you what the Trump-Pence strategy is. You know what the Trump-Pence strategy is? To do a good job. That's all it is. It's very simple. It's not a stra—I don't have a strategy. I do a good job.

BW: Can I come back—

TRUMP: Yes.

AIDE: Yes.

BW: —and we take Iran—

TRUMP: You can come back as many times—because—let me tell you why you can come back, unlike others that I just can't see. [*laughter*] Because I respect you. This man was in my office—I hate to say—

	it's probably more than 25 years ago, but 25 years ago, with Bernstein. They were in my office because they found me an interesting character and they wanted to do—I was very successful, I did a great job.
BW:	I thought you were interesting, but not in politics.
CONWAY:	Not in politics. [laughs]
BW:	I live in—
TRUMP:	And when I announce, when I give my financial statement you'll see how well I did, too. Because I want to give it out, but I want to wait until before the election.
BW:	Why don't you give me your taxes?
TRUMP:	[Tsk]
BW:	No, seriously.
TRUMP:	I would, except for one problem. Bob—
BW:	I asked Sherry Dillon to do this during the campaign.
TRUMP:	I know. I know.
BW:	And we would spend a week—
TRUMP:	Bob, I would. I would except for one problem I have: I'm under audit. And I've been under—no, seriously, it's a problem. If I'm under audit—and everybody in the world—I don't want to do that.

COMMENTARY: Presidential candidates and presidents have routinely released their taxes. Audits are no reason for Trump to not release his. Every president from Jimmy Carter through Barack Obama released tax returns that were under audit.

TRUMP:	Now you have to understand, I have a big company. Much bigger—you saw the filings.
BW:	Yes.
TRUMP:	It said—what did we make? What did we make according to—
BW:	I would love to have your taxes.
TRUMP:	—what did they make last year according to the filing?

BW:	I would love to have your taxes. I would spend a week—
TRUMP:	Do you know what I made last year?
BW:	Pardon?
TRUMP:	Do you know what I made last year, according to the filings?
BW:	No.
TRUMP:	You know we had to file.
BW:	Yes, I know.
TRUMP:	Which is much more detailed than the tax return, by the way.
CONWAY:	That's correct.
BW:	That's true.
CONWAY:	One hundred and four pages, and then 400 last year.
TRUMP:	Four hundred and eighty-eight million or something like that. I made 488—and that's because I'm not there. Meaning [*laughs*] I would've done much better. Four eighty-eight. I built a great company. And all that stuff you read about is such bullshit.

COMMENTARY: Trump earned $427 million from *The Apprentice* and its associated licensing deals over 16 years—based on parts of his tax returns obtained by *The New York Times*. This was his biggest income stream by far. But like all other Trump financial and tax questions, the bottom line is just not clear. I brought up Trump's impeachment trial.

BW:	You know, they always talk about the split screen. What's going on in Capitol Hill, Nancy Pelosi and all of this. And I—it's as if you had won the biggest lottery ever.
TRUMP:	I did. Every day I won it. Look—
BW:	What's the best part about being president?
TRUMP:	—Nancy Pelosi—I don't know if you've seen my—Nancy Pelosi has driven my poll numbers through the roof. And she comes out with, I pray for our president. She never prayed for me in her life. And she uses prayer—

BW: Do you pray for her?

TRUMP: No, not at all. Nor would I, okay, because I
           don't like her. So I would not pray for her, no. I
           wouldn't. And she doesn't pray for me either. And
           I told people a year ago when she said, no, no, no,
           impeachment is a big move. No, no, no. I said,
           she's going to do it.

CONWAY: You did say that.

AIDE: Yeah. Yeah.

TRUMP: Now, what I didn't think she'd do was on a phone
           call—

CONWAY: Nothing.

TRUMP: Over nothing. You read that call, it's like—it's two
           calls. It's two calls, by the way. Nothing.

BW: In a sentence, what's the job of the president?
           What is your job as you see it?

TRUMP: I have many jobs. But among those jobs—

BW: But I think it's figuring out what the next stage of
           good is for a majority of people in the country—

TRUMP: That's good.

BW: —and then saying, this is where we're going, and
           this is the plan to get there.

TRUMP: Correct. But sometimes that road changes. You
           know a lot of people are inflexible. Sometimes a
           road has to change, you know? You have a wall
           in front and you have to go around it instead
           of trying to go through it—it's much easier. But
           really the job of a president is to keep our country
           safe, to keep it prosperous. Okay? Prosperous
           is a big thing. But sometimes you have so much
           prosperity that people want to use that in a bad
           way, and you have to be careful with it. And a
           little bit that's what's happening now. That's why
           they come up with the wealth tax and you know
           the different things that are going on right now.
           By the way, could I ask you a question?

BW: Yes, sir.

TRUMP: So you're a total pro. Who do you think is going
           to get the nomination?

BW:	I have an awful track record on this.
TRUMP:	Yeah? Most people—
BW:	And I did say that I thought you might win and people laughed at me, so—but—
CONWAY:	Did you say it again?
TRUMP:	That's—
CONWAY:	Would you say it a second time? After they laughed?
BW:	[*laughs*] We'll see. We'll see.
TRUMP:	Well, we're in much better shape. You know why, though, Bob? Because—
BW:	Who do you think is going to be your opponent? And remember, this is for next year, for the book.
TRUMP:	I'm being honest with you, I'm being honest with you. I think it's a terrible group of candidates. It's an embarrassment. I'm embarrassed by the Democrat candidates. I may have to run against one, and who knows? It's an election. And I'm looking pretty good right now. But to me it's a terrible group of candidates. And to be honest with you, as an American, I'm embarrassed by those candidates.
BW:	But if you tune into their debates, it's as if it is—
TRUMP:	It's hard to watch.
BW:	I know. But it's like the Senate subcommittee on health insurance having a markup.
TRUMP:	Yeah.
BW:	It is—[*laughter*] Now, what do presidents do? My final, bottom line on this, presidents are talent scouts.
TRUMP:	Well, to a certain extent.
BW:	That's your biggest job. Pick—
TRUMP:	To a certain extent. And we have a great Cabinet.
BW:	Would you agree with that?
TRUMP:	Yes, very much so.
BW:	What's your best pick?
TRUMP:	I've had a lot of good picks. Some of them are quiet. You don't even know who they are. And if I

	tell you, I'm going to insult a lot of other people. But I have three or four people that I think have done an outstanding job. The problem, if I say it, then I got 200 people that will be upset.
BW:	But isn't that true? You can't do all this stuff—you've got to find other people to do—kind of simple management 101.
TRUMP:	You do. Yeah. You do. But we have a—I think we have a great Cabinet.
CONWAY:	We do.
TRUMP:	We've done very well.
CONWAY:	Mr. President, you put out your list of judges, and it helped you. Hillary wouldn't answer the question.
TRUMP:	That was a big thing. You know, Bob, putting out the list of judges, the 25 judges, was a very important thing as it turned out. So come back. Digest that.
BW:	Did you use the autopen on this? Judges?
TRUMP:	No, I used this.
MAN:	No, he doesn't.
TRUMP:	So I use this—Here, Bob.

COMMENTARY: With a flourish he handed me the pen he used to sign the judicial appointments as if he was giving me some trophy.

I left feeling that I'd experienced Trump to the tenth power. What a wild ride. I was still not sure what the story or the book might be. But the grave risks about North Korea were still at the top of my list. I also realized I had to make sure I focused my questions better because Mattis was right: Trump could take you off on a freeway to nowhere in an instant, making it almost impossible to get him back onto the topic I wanted to discuss. Trump was one of the toughest interview subjects I'd ever faced.

INTERVIEW 3:
Nothing Scares Me

Oval Office, The White House
December 13, 2019

TRUMP: Nixon was under a table. [*crosstalk*] Nixon was a mess. I'm not a mess. Do you know what you said to me the last time? I told my wife. I told a few people . . . You said, you act like you just won the election. You're under impeachment. You said that to me. I thought it was a cool line.

COMMENTARY: I interviewed Trump at the White House around 2.30 p.m. in the afternoon of Friday, December 13, 2019. Deputy Press Secretary Hogan Gidley and Deputy Chief of Staff for Communications Dan Scavino were also present. I wanted to see how Trump was handling impeachment. The House Judiciary Committee had voted to impeach him 23 to 17 along strict party lines. The president seemed unbothered, even cheery, and had time for a one-and-a-half-hour interview in the Oval Office.

BW: Sir, you're so nice to let me come by on this day.

TRUMP: You still look good. This guy doesn't change. [*laughter*]

BW: So do you. Yes, I do.

TRUMP: So here's—for you.

BW: Oh, it's the picture. Okay, good.

TRUMP: Sort of cool. Yeah, sort of cool.

BW: You and I sitting, everyone else standing.

President Trump gave Woodward a photo of their previous interview conducted in the Oval Office on December 5, 2019. Also pictured, from left to right, are Acting Chief of Staff Mick Mulvaney, Counselor to the President Kellyanne Conway, Principal Deputy Press Secretary Hogan Gidley, Woodward, and Vice President Mike Pence.

TRUMP:	Everyone else—that's the way it's supposed to be. [*laughter*]
BW:	Okay. That's great.
TRUMP:	You know what, [?]. Take one over here. Bob, come on over here for a second. We're going to get one. One normal one.
BW:	The clean desk.
TRUMP:	Yeah. I always—have you ever seen my other room?
BW:	[*laughs*] Thank you.

[*An aide fixes Trump's tie. They take a photo.*]

TRUMP:	I like the long ties where you can—where this thing goes in the back. Don't you hate it when it flies?
BW:	Yes, that's right.
TRUMP:	I'll show you something, Bob. Come on back. You've been back here at some point in your life.
BW:	Oh, yes sir.

TRUMP:	Over the years. I'll show you. Where you do the work, right?
BW:	Oh, yeah, this is the dining room.
TRUMP:	So this is . . .

COMMENTARY: Trump took me on a tour of his hideaway office, the spot where President Clinton had secretly met with White House intern Monica Lewinsky. The "Monica Room," Trump called it, and gave a knowing smirk. We returned to the Oval Office for the interview. He wanted to give me some photographs taken at our last meeting.

[They leave the room and are inaudible; they return.]

BW:	Oh, you gave me a bunch.
TRUMP:	I wanted to show you—do we have any of the big ones? Okay. Did you read those letters?
BW:	I've got them. Listen—
TRUMP:	Oh, you didn't read them?
BW:	Oh, of course I read them. I marked them up. I thought about—
TRUMP:	It's something, right?
BW:	See, this is the—this is my job now: to piece together what really happens.

COMMENTARY: Trump is referring to the eleven personal letters Kim Jong Un had written to him. Trump had given me what he called "exclusive access" to Kim's letters. He handed me some photos of himself with the North Korean leader.

TRUMP:	So look at these, Bob.
BW:	Look at those. Oh, yeah.
TRUMP:	Nobody else has that.
BW:	Huh. Look at that. Huh. Can I take one?
TRUMP:	Yeah.
BW:	Okay, good. That's what I need.
TRUMP:	Here let me give you a good one.

COMMENTARY: Trump was riffling through photographs of himself and Kim Jong Un.

TRUMP:	See, he's happy there. Now look. He doesn't smile. You never saw him smile. He's happy with me. You understand that, Bob?
BW:	These are big pictures. Yes, sir. Yes, sir.
TRUMP:	He's happy.

COMMENTARY: My google search showed Kim smiling with many others, including South Korean President Moon.

BW:	Look at that. Listen, those letters—now, what I need—
TRUMP:	You did look at them right, and read them?
BW:	Listen, read them, I memorized them. About the fantasy film? He said the next meeting's going to be a fantasy film. What'd you think of that?
TRUMP:	Nobody else has them.
BW:	Okay. I hope that stays.
TRUMP:	Nobody else has them. But I want you to treat them with respect. I haven't [shared them] with anybody.
BW:	Understand. Understand.
TRUMP:	And don't say I gave them to you, okay?
BW:	Okay. I—
TRUMP:	I think it's okay. Normally I wouldn't—I wasn't going to give them to Bob, you know. What'd, you make a Photostat of them or something?
BW:	No, I dictated them into a tape recorder.
TRUMP:	[*laughs*] Really?
BW:	Yes. And my assistant—
TRUMP:	But you were surprised by them, right?
BW:	Yes, because—
TRUMP:	I never saw these pictures.
BW:	—there were 11 of them, and it shows an evolving relationship of being tough and—
TRUMP:	Yeah, he wants to get along with me.
BW:	—opening. Yes.
TRUMP:	They say—Putin told me. Xi told me. I'm the only one he wants. He doesn't want to talk to anybody else. You know it's a hermit kingdom.

COMMENTARY: As you listen to this interview, remember that Kim Jong Un is an autocrat with a merciless record of systematic torture, assassination, and political imprisonment. Hundreds of thousands of people are held in gulag-style prisons and forced labor camps. There is no freedom of speech, no independent media.

BW:	So I have to—
TRUMP:	It's a beautiful day.
BW:	—because of this day, I would like to start to ask—
TRUMP:	Go ahead, tell me.
BW:	—for the book, sir, what's your relationship with Mitch McConnell?
TRUMP:	Very good.
BW:	Probably the most important relationship in Washington in the next couple of months, or maybe year.
TRUMP:	So it's a very good relationship. And people are surprised, because we're sort of opposites. We've put in more judges—you know, judges at a record level. Record. We have every record, other than George Washington, who has a higher percentage. He had 100 percent, but he only had 16 judges. Okay? I'm going to be up to 167 judges. And it'll be 182 before normalization.
BW:	Yes, you mentioned—
TRUMP:	A hundred and eighty-two judges.
BW:	So what does McConnell say to you, President Trump, about what's going on on the Hill and what the Senate's going to do?
TRUMP:	So we talk. You know, this is not a legal process, this is a political process. Right?
BW:	I've noticed.
TRUMP:	And you've seen his statements.
BW:	Yes, right.
TRUMP:	I mean, rather than what he says to me, he says to me the same thing he says to television—
BW:	He calls you? Talks to you?
TRUMP:	I speak to him about it. And I—

BW:	Tell me what he said and what—
TRUMP:	Look, number one, I did nothing wrong. Legitimately.
BW:	I understand your point.
TRUMP:	Nothing wrong. I had a conversation with a guy. You're going to impeach the president of the United States for having—as I say, because it saves a lot of words—a perfect conversation with a man who's a new, young president who ran on a whole corruption thing, right?

COMMENTARY: Trump is referring to Ukrainian president Zelensky.

TRUMP:	And then they take the conversation, and you have a corrupt politician named Adam Schiff who made up my statement.

COMMENTARY: Democratic Representative Adam Schiff of California was then the Chairman of the House Intelligence Committee.

BW:	I've gone through it, sir. So what does McConnell say to you and what do you say to him? What's the—if I were listening in, what's the back and forth?
TRUMP:	I believe that Mitch feels that I've been treated very unfairly.
BW:	He says so to you?
TRUMP:	I think he says it to television. I think he says it to you, if you talk to him about it.
BW:	I will.
TRUMP:	And as you saw last night, he said there's not even a zero percent chance that he ever leaves office because of this hoax. So he said it last night on television, so I'm just—you could quote him—
BW:	And that's what he says to you?
TRUMP:	Well, he doesn't have to say it to me. And the reason he doesn't, 'cause I know all the senators. I get along unbelievably with all of those people.

	Other than Romney. And even Romney I think knows a certain fairness, okay? Romney for different reasons. You know, someday I'll explain that to you. But I get along very well with them. They're all friends of mine. I have a great relationship. Other presidents don't have a great relationship. Nixon, they hated him.
BW:	Oh, I know.
TRUMP:	Because he was arrogant and, you know, very difficult. You know that story much better than me. The last one I'm going to talk to about that is you. But they walked up, they couldn't have been happier. With me it's just the opposite. Every one of them's a friend of mine, practically. You know? Same thing with the congressmen. Look, nobody's ever seen congressmen, Republicans, fighting like they fought yesterday. But they've been fighting that way for three months. You know, some have become major stars because of it. But you look at them against the Democrats, it was like the New England Patriots playing your high school football team.
BW:	Okay. Here's my hypothesis.
TRUMP:	My point is about Mitch. I think Mitch thinks I'm being very unfairly treated.
BW:	And you talk to him regularly?
TRUMP:	I do. I get along with him great.
BW:	Okay. I think it's the most important relationship—
TRUMP:	You know what Mitch's biggest thing is in the whole world? His judges.

COMMENTARY: McConnell's public comments about Trump did not always convey the level of disdain he shared privately with his Republican colleagues in the Senate.

For instance, in 2017, the State Department had strongly denied that Secretary Rex Tillerson had called Trump a "moron."

"Do you know why Tillerson was able to say he didn't call the president a 'moron'?" McConnell asked his colleagues in the Senate cloakroom. "Because he called him a 'fucking moron.'"

I returned to the topic of North Korea. I wanted to know what Trump had written to Kim.

BW:	Can I get your letters to Kim?
TRUMP:	I'll let you read the letters. Just treat them respectfully.
BW:	Okay. Here's my policy assumption in doing this book. Your predecessors, George W. Bush, Obama, didn't figure out how to deal with Kim.
TRUMP:	They couldn't—they called him all the time.
BW:	And you came in—and this I need an answer to—you threw him the ultimate curveball. Other words, I'll meet with you. I'll treat you with respect.
TRUMP:	But before I did that, Bob—there was never tougher rhetoric in the history of our country.
BW:	I know. For the first year. You know, just blasting away at each other.
TRUMP:	Blasting. Okay. Without that, it wouldn't have ever happened.

[*Trump starts thumping the desk*]

BW:	Okay. So how did you develop, and with whom—
TRUMP:	So we met each other—
BW:	—or is this Donald Trump by himself saying, we have to change the game? I will dare to go praise him, he's my friend, let's meet. I'll come to your house. Because that's what happened. How did you get there?
TRUMP:	So we had very, very tough, volatile rhetoric. I called him Little Rocket Man.
BW:	Almost a war. Almost a war, as we talked about.
TRUMP:	There were those that said, please don't go there. Please, please, please. You know.
BW:	Yeah.
TRUMP:	But you had no choice. It was a very bad situation, actually. You know? He said I've got

a button on my desk. And I said, I have a bigger button, and my button works. You know. Yours doesn't. That was one of the kinder things.

BW: Why did you take the—

TRUMP: You do say that nobody's ever received letters like that from the family?

BW: Well, of course. Yeah.

TRUMP: He doesn't write letters. [*thumping table*]

BW: But you changed the direction of—if you will— history, by saying let's meet this guy. Let's treat him with respect. Let's embrace him. Let's go to the DMZ as you did.

TRUMP: He didn't respect Obama. Didn't like him, didn't respect him. Thought he was an asshole. Okay. Bush was too stupid to know what was happening. Bush has no clue. Okay? That's why we ended up in the Middle East and we spent $8 trillion there. When I did this, I said, what do we have to lose? You know, my famous expression with African American. What do we have to lose?

BW: And what comes through—

TRUMP: You know? I haven't taken sanctions off.

BW: —if he realizes how important it was to him. He keeps telling—Your Excellency, Your Excellency, this is going to go down in history. This is going to be—

TRUMP: And you've seen what he called Obama. What he called others. He didn't call them Your Excellency.

BW: I understand that. And you see there's a pivot in the strategy, or the approach, and I'm trying to figure out where it came from.

TRUMP: So—

BW: Is this you alone?

TRUMP: No.

BW: Is this Lindsey Graham?

TRUMP: So, okay, it's very complicated. No.

BW: Is this McMaster?

TRUMP: It's very complicated.

BW:	Who? Great.
TRUMP:	This is me, but it's very complicated. Because I always ask the one question, why are we defending South Korea? See, I have that, you know. Why are we doing this? And I said to South Korea—I told you about the $500 million, right?
BW:	Yes.
TRUMP:	They're paying $500 million more. It took me one day. I said, we're defending you, and we're losing a fortune. And you're paying the same thing for 30 years, which is nothing. You pay almost nothing. You've got to pay. And they've agreed to $500 million. Now I'm asking for billions more. But I say—you know, it's a rich country. I say, so we're defending you, we're allowing you to exist. Why are we doing that? Why do we care? We're 8,500 miles away. Why do we care? Why do we have our 32,000 soldiers over there, willing to fight for you? And you're not paying us? Why?
BW:	Moon is saying to you, ah, but we're under siege because we've got North Korea. Right?
TRUMP:	Moon is saying because you've always done it. They have the same—Abe has the same—I ask all these countries, why are we doing this? I ask Abe. He's a friend of mine. I say, why are we defending Japan? You're a rich country. Why are we defending you and you're paying us a tiny fraction of the cost?

COMMENTARY: Moon was the president of South Korea. Abe was the Japanese Prime Minister.

BW:	And the establishment of course hates that. The—
TRUMP:	The establishment hates that question, which shows you how stupid the establishment is. Okay?
BW:	So how do you pivot—
TRUMP:	And by the way, Bob, they're willing to pay.
BW:	But the outreach—

TRUMP:	You know how bad the Japan deal is? If Japan gets attacked, we have to protect them. If we get attacked, Japan doesn't have to protect us.
BW:	I understand. Well, they—
TRUMP:	So I said, Shinzo, we have to change that.
BW:	So tell me in your own words, your first meeting in Singapore with Kim.
TRUMP:	Okay.
BW:	What happened?

COMMENTARY: The first meeting between Trump and Kim Jong Un was held on June 12th, 2018, at a summit in Singapore.

TRUMP:	So what happened, if you know the big thing, the big breakthrough was South Korea had the Olympics.
BW:	Yes, we talked about that.
TRUMP:	There was unbelievable hostility. They weren't selling tickets. All of a sudden, Kim lets through his people—through me, through Switzerland, etc., etc., let's meet. They would love to help with the Olympics. I said, what's that all about? This is right in the middle of horrendous dialogue. So anyway, that was the beginning. And then a delegation came over from South Korea and said that Chairman Kim would like to meet with you. I said, great, let's meet. Now, you know Obama—
BW:	What did your advisers think?
TRUMP:	Just so you know, Obama and Bush were dying to meet. He didn't want to—this is a man, you talk about an inch all your life, this is a man—when I had the pictures that I showed you, walking on the border, nobody else—I mean, I set that meeting up in five minutes through social media. I said, hey, I'm going to South Korea. Do you want to meet? Because you can't, you know, talk to him—
BW:	So what happened at Singapore? Are there notes? Is there—

TRUMP:	We had a great relationship.
BW:	Yeah. I want to take readers to that moment.
TRUMP:	By the way, it was the most cameras. You know it was the most cameras? I've seen more cameras—
BW:	I want to find out—
TRUMP:	I think I've seen more cameras than any human being in history. Okay? You understand? I go to the helicopter, there's like hundreds of them.
BW:	[laughs] Because they know you might give an interview and make news.
TRUMP:	Well, whatever. I always . . . It's free. I get it for free. It costs me nothing. It's called earned media. And you do earn it. [laughter]
BW:	You figured that out? You figured that out.
TRUMP:	They say I spent 25 percent what Hillary did, but I got $6 billion worth of earned media.
BW:	I believe that.
TRUMP:	And earned, you do earn it.
BW:	So how'd—Tell me as best you can recall what happened in Singapore, and what was going through your mind. Hey, I'm meeting this guy. Hey, he's—
TRUMP:	The Singapore event was a monster. They had a thing set up for the media the likes of which you have never seen. Okay?
BW:	I understand.
TRUMP:	And this is all of Asia. All of the United—I've never seen a thing like it. Thousands. Thousands.
BW:	I accept that.
TRUMP:	Do we have any pictures of that? If you could see—
AIDE:	I'm sure we can probably get them, sir.
BW:	You—but I want to see what you thought of this man.
TRUMP:	Okay. Are you ready?
BW:	I mean, he's not exactly Clark Gable.
TRUMP:	No, but he's very smart.

BW:	We've talked about that.
TRUMP:	He's very smart. Remember what you said? You said, bing, bing, and not smart. I said, no. Bing, bing, and brilliant.
BW:	Right.
TRUMP:	When you take over a country at 25—
BW:	Can I tell you this just for your own . . .
TRUMP:	Yes, go ahead.
BW:	People have said that, and then I've gone back to people and I've said, well, wait a minute. Really? Is he not smart? And people who were involved in all this kind of say, well, maybe he is smart.
TRUMP:	Uh, no. He's far beyond smart. You know, he's very smart. Okay?
BW:	So what'd you think when you saw him and started talking to him? And what happened?
TRUMP:	Okay, so we met—okay. So now we're there, and everyone's going crazy. Everything else. Finally we get to meet. We shook hands. You saw that?
BW:	Yes, of course.
TRUMP:	We shook hands. We turned to these cameras. I looked out and even I said, holy shit.
BW:	Okay.
TRUMP:	It was a wall of more than I think I've ever seen. More than the Academy Awards has ever had—
BW:	So what happened?
TRUMP:	Okay, so we shook—that was the first time we ever met. Then we left and we went and had a very long meeting. And we liked each other.
BW:	What did he say that caused you to like him?
TRUMP:	—like we're smart people, but you have people that no matter what you do, you're not going to like and they're not going to like you. I have those people. You know, no matter—we're smart. Like, we're totally the smartest, right? We got along great.
BW:	What'd he say that caused this gravitational pull?
TRUMP:	We talked about his country. And I talked about

the tremendous potential that his country had. I
talked about the fact that I don't want to remove
him. I want him to lead the country to greatness.
That it could be one of the great economic
powers of the world. It's locationally situated
between China, Russia, and South Korea.

BW: Understand.

TRUMP: Think of it. You have on the border—

BW: And so in one of those wonderful letters after the
Singapore summit, he wrote to you, he knows
that you're going to deliver on your promise.

TRUMP: Yeah.

BW: What was your promise to him?

TRUMP: Economic—tremendous economic—not paid for
by the United States. Paid for by South Korea,
Japan, and other countries in Asia. I said, why
should the United States be paying for this? You
understand, right?

BW: Paying for defense, or an economic revival?

TRUMP: No, economic development. Economic
development. I said, you have—you know, I did
sign an agreement. Do you have a copy of the
agreement that I signed?

BW: Yes. Yes, sir.

TRUMP: You know the first line of that says, you will
denuclearize.

BW: Yes, I know.

TRUMP: People forget that. I came back, and the fake news
said, we didn't get anything. We got a lot. He
signed an agreement.

BW: Well, in the letters he says yes, and then he's kind
of back-tracking. He says, let's do it step by step.

TRUMP: He has a hard time with the word
denuclearization. He signed an agreement. He
promised me. But he has a real hard time. He
backs up. It's really like, you know, somebody
that's in love with a house and they just can't sell
it. Okay? You know what I mean.

BW: Yes. Exactly.

TRUMP: And so we had a really good meeting. We really got along. It was a great chemistry.

BW: Right. Okay.

TRUMP: The word chemistry. You meet somebody and you have a good chemistry, and there is a lot of truth to it. You meet a woman. In one second, you know whether or not it's all going to happen. Okay? Did you ever hear the expression—

BW: [*laughs*] Yes, sir. [*laughs*] Yes.

TRUMP: —In one second. It doesn't take you 10 minutes, and it doesn't take you six weeks. It's like, whoa. We had very good chemistry together. We talked a lot. We could've talked for hours, with an interpreter. We could've talked for hours. We then had a lunch. He had people at the lunch. I've never seen anything like it. I've had many lunches with leaders, you know, where they have 20 people on each side. You know, the long table, and they have all their secretaries—he had people. They sat up at the table. Every single person was sitting up. By the way, he's the total boss. You know when you hear, oh, maybe he doesn't control—a general stood up. He snapped to attention, stood up. His chair was—there was no carpet, it was like a nice, beautiful wooden floor.

TRUMP: His chair snapped back 20 feet. Hit the wall behind him.

BW: The general's?

TRUMP: The general. He stood up. It's like, you know, you stand up and boom, his legs hit—the chair went back, hit the wall. I said, holy shit. [*laughter*] And I joked. I said, I want you people to act like these people. You know, kidding to all my people.

BW: Kidding, but not kidding. Because it's not bad to have that kind of tight control.

TRUMP: It was great. It was great.

BW: He doesn't have to deal with the Congress or a Supreme Court.

TRUMP: Look. This general stood up. The chair went smashing back. I said, I want you people to behave like that. Man . . . Did you ever hear of Elton John? He said, no. I said, did you ever hear the song "Rocket Man"? No. I said, I did you a great favor. I called you Rocket Man. Think of yourself on a rocket flying over Japan. You're Rocket Man. And I told you, he said, no, you called me Little Rocket Man. And it was a funny line, you know what I mean? He was—he didn't like that.

BW: He knew it. He knew what you'd said.

TRUMP: He knew. Let me tell you, he knows. He's a very smart guy.

BW: And so you left the meeting thinking what? What's going through the president's head?

TRUMP: When you say I left the meeting, or Singapore?

BW: Singapore.

TRUMP: I left Singapore saying we have a very good relationship. And that was it.

BW: And did you think internally, ah, we've defused the—

TRUMP: Oh, I did defuse. Oh.

BW: Well, it kind of did.

TRUMP: If Crooked Hillary—

BW: Certainly the tensions—

TRUMP: If Crooked Hillary Clinton got in, you would be in war within a month. It was ready to go, and he was totally prepared. And he expected it.

BW: Did he tell you that?

TRUMP: Ah, yes, he did.

BW: He did?

TRUMP: He was totally prepared to go. And he expected to go. But we met. We got along. There was unbelievable chemistry. I have great chemistry with President Xi of China. See we made a China deal today, a big one?

COMMENTARY: The United States and China had reached an agreement on phase one of a trade deal. As part of that agreement, China committed to buy $200 billion in U.S. goods and up to $40 billion in agricultural products. Later, China reneged on the deal.

TRUMP: It's funny: I get impeached on the same day I make a China deal. That's a beauty. [*laughter*] But it's impeachment-light. Do you agree with that? I call it light impeachment.

BW: So the question is, who on your staff—is it Matt Pottinger, or who is the kind of person who helps you? That's what—

TRUMP: Nobody.

BW: Really? It's all in your bailiwick?

TRUMP: I had one thing that really hurt me with him, I have a good relationship with John Bolton.

COMMENTARY: John Bolton was Trump's former national security adviser.

TRUMP: He was interviewed by Sleepy Eyes Chuck Todd on *Meet the Press*, who's a sleepy son of a bitch. And John said, unfortunately, because Kim as I told you is a very brilliant guy, and he knows every word uttered from anybody of importance['s] mouth. And John Bolton said, no, no, what we have in store for North Korea is the Libyan model. That was early on in John's—

BW: Yes. Short tenure.

TRUMP: I said, tell me he didn't say that. Because the Libyan model is where you take Qaddafi, throw him into a sewer ditch, piss on him, and shoot him simultaneously. You know they were pissing on him and shooting.

BW: I know.

TRUMP: He took 200 bullets to the head. There was no head. And they pissed on him. What John meant was—you know, he had a couple of nuclear

weapons. They took it out. When John said that, I
called. I said, tell me you didn't say that.

BW: What'd he say?

TRUMP: He said, I really wasn't referring to the way they
killed him. I was referring to the way they'd—I
said, they only think about—he died a rough
death. So I said, all right. It's done. Maybe he
won't see it. Five minutes later, a thing comes
over the wire services: We will never die like
Qaddafi. We will not use the Libyan model. They
want—and I said, it really fucked me up.

BW: I understand.

TRUMP: Okay? Do you understand that?

BW: But there's no one playing second chair in this.
This is you saying—

TRUMP: So legitimately, you know it better than anybody.
Is it true? Nobody else.

GIDLEY: Nobody could do it.

TRUMP: Nobody else. Okay. Then we had the second
meeting in Singapore.

BW: Yes.

TRUMP: And it was different. And the reason it was
different was . . .

BW: The second was Hanoi. Yeah.

TRUMP: I'm sorry. The first was—I meant in Hanoi. So—

BW: What happened there?

TRUMP: We go to Vietnam. And I land and I make a
statement. That I've just landed in Vietnam. And
that got a lot of ink. Anyway, we then had our
meeting. And I left that meeting. You know, I left.

BW: Yes, sir.

TRUMP: I said, you're not ready to make a deal. We spent
two hours together, with our people. I spent a
little time with him. Something happened. But it
wasn't something—

BW: What was it?

TRUMP: I don't think it was anything. I think he just—
Look, some people have a hard time doing things

	that are different from what they've been doing all their life.
BW:	Amen.
TRUMP:	I said, do you ever do anything other than send rockets up to the air? Why don't we, like—let's go and—let's go to a movie together. You know, I said, kiddingly. Let's go play a round of golf, even though rumor has it he shot an 18 and he's better than Tiger Woods. [*laughter*] Did you ever hear that?
BW:	[*laughing*] No, I didn't.
TRUMP:	That his father, him and his grandfather—you know the three, boom, boom, boom.
BW:	Yes, sir.
TRUMP:	He's the toughest and the smartest of them all. I'm saying that.
BW:	Kim Jong Il was really tough. His father.
TRUMP:	They're all tough. Yeah. His grandfather was tougher, from what I hear.
BW:	Okay.
TRUMP:	[*whispers*] He respects the grandfather the most. He totally admires the grandfather.
BW:	Okay. So what happened here?
TRUMP:	But here's the thing. Nothing happened other than he just—
BW:	You're talking exercises. He's very upset about the exercises.
TRUMP:	Well, he was. But I don't know that that was an excuse or not. Because in the meantime he's testing—did you ever see the guns when they shot them into the ocean, the picture?
BW:	Yes. Oh wow.
TRUMP:	They were not nuclear, but they were a lot of guns. Like the Howitzer type.
BW:	Gets your attention, doesn't it?
TRUMP:	Did you ever see a thing like that? The beach, the whole beach—they must've had 1,000 of them, right, into the ocean. You know, the whole thing.
BW:	What'd you think when you saw that?

TRUMP:	I thought it was pretty good firepower.
BW:	Scare you?
TRUMP:	No. Nothing scares me. You know why? Nothing scares me. If I was scared, I wouldn't be doing an interview with you today. I'd be under a table with my thumb in my mouth. Okay? Like everybody else has been except me, because I'm different. But anyway. No, not scared. No, but I respected the power. There's real power there.
BW:	And so then what happens next? So you get letters from him—I mean, these letters are such a—
TRUMP:	They're very warm letters.
BW:	They're very—he's wooing you—
TRUMP:	You want a—I'll get you a Coke.
BW:	No, I—he's wooing you, you're wooing him. It's like a good date. Right?
TRUMP:	Whatever. I mean, you say it.
BW:	So then what happened? Why has it reached the point—let's fast-forward to where we are now.
TRUMP:	Yeah. I spent time with him. And my whole life has been deals. I've done great. Far greater than people understand. I've done great. You know I'm going to release at some point before the election, I'm going to release my financial statements. I've done phenomenally. I've made unbelievable deals, from very little made great deals. That's what I do. And I make deals. And I realized early into the second meeting in Hanoi, in Vietnam, that he wasn't going to get where we had to go. He was willing to give up one of his nuclear sites—
BW:	Yeah. He's got—
TRUMP:	But he's got five of them.
BW:	Yeah.
TRUMP:	I said, listen, one doesn't help and two doesn't help. And three doesn't help and four doesn't help. And five does help. I said, look, it doesn't help if you give up—But it is our biggest. I said, yeah, it's also your oldest. Because I know every one of the sites. I know all of them, better than any of my

	people I know. You understand that. Better than anybody that works for—you know, my uncle, I told you, he was—Did I tell you? My uncle? Dr. John Trump.
BW:	Yes. Yes. Right.
TRUMP:	He was at MIT for 42 years or something. He was a great—
BW:	No, I don't want anything.

[*BW turns down a Coke and water.*]

TRUMP:	You don't want water?
BW:	No, sir.
TRUMP:	So my uncle—so I understand that stuff. You know, genetically. I have an uncle who was—The top person at MIT came to the office about a year ago. Brought me a whole package on Dr. John Trump. He said he was one of the greatest men. He was brilliant. I get that stuff.
BW:	Did Kim Jong Un, if I may ask this, did he say anything that was threatening? Because—
TRUMP:	Not even a little bit. No.
BW:	And you know he's getting these—
TRUMP:	I just know he wasn't ready.
BW:	—eight-axle mobile missile launchers from China—
TRUMP:	Yeah.
BW:	—that give him—
TRUMP:	But China—look.
BW:	Why's China doing that?
TRUMP:	I have a great relationship there. Well, because I'm breaking China's ass on trade.
BW:	President Xi hates those tariffs, because he has to find employment for 10 million people each year.
TRUMP:	Those tariffs are [*whispers*] destroying China.
BW:	Pardon?
TRUMP:	They're really destroying—they're hurting China so badly.
BW:	Yeah. And he's mad about it.
TRUMP:	Nobody else understood how to negotiate— Look—

BW:	And somebody said that's why he's given North Korea these mobile missile launchers.
TRUMP:	No, it's not that. Because you know what? He doesn't want them to be nuclearized either.
BW:	Well, they are.
TRUMP:	He's a lot closer to us. I know. Well, I know. But he doesn't want it.
BW:	He's playing a game, both sides.
TRUMP:	He is—look, I get along with him great, but he's for them, I'm for us, and that's the way it goes, I mean, you know, whether we like it or not. I tell him that. I say—and I don't blame him. I say look, these presidents that allowed you to get away with this for so long, it's crazy what they—they were taking $500 billion a year—billion with a "B"—out of this country for years and rebuilding China with the money they were taking out of here.
BW:	What does Xi say when you say that to him?
TRUMP:	Oh, oh. Do you understand? It's like, what does he say? You read it. Okay? You read it. He knows it's true. I was giving a speech—real fast. I was giving a speech in China, 5,000 people. You know, the so-called elite. And I'm giving the speech and I'm talking about how China's ripped off our country. And Xi's sitting right next to me. Right? And I'm saying, man— and he's looking down and he's sort of angry. And I said, hmm, I got a problem. I've got all these people—I've got him. He's fuming. Because I'm talking about how China—I said, but China—and I mean this. I said, but I don't blame China. I wish our people did what he did. What I really blame is our presidents for allowing this to happen. For 25 years, they've been ripping the hell out of this country. Okay.

COMMENTARY: Trump returned to talking about North Korea.

TRUMP: I had a meeting. I wasn't there very long. We did something amazing. You'll see it if you want to check it. We had a press conference. He's never done that before. He was good. He was really good. And these crazy fake news maniacs came in, screaming. What do you think? What do you think about this? What do you—And they asked him a couple of questions. And he gave great answers, but very quick, short answers. And then he goes, enough. Enough. I said, so you don't have this problem, do you? He didn't even know what—he'd never saw anything like this. His press is a little bit different. You know, when I went—I don't know if you know—their security guards, when I went to that step in North Korea—you heard about it.

BW: Yeah.

TRUMP: His security guards took the *Times*—they threw them—they're big, strong—[*makes throwing noise*] It was like a sea opened up. They were all on their ass, every one of them. Oh, they just pushed them. You know. There was a whole big thing about it. You'll read about it.

BW: Yeah.

TRUMP: But here's the thing. So we're in Vietnam and after like a little while—because that's what I do. Deals. Whether it's this or that. You know, it's deals. Deals are deals. And I said, you're not there. What do you mean? You're not ready to make a deal. I said that. I said, I've got to leave. You're my friend. I think you're a wonderful guy. But we've got to leave, because you're not ready to make a deal.

BW: Why's he not ready to make a deal?

TRUMP: And he never heard that before. Because nobody ever left him. And then they say because I don't know if it's true, but nobody's ever seen these people. That the people that set that deal up were [*whispers*] executed. You know that.

BW:	Yes. At least the key person.
TRUMP:	Well, they've never seen people that were around, have never [*whispers*] been seen again. Sorry. So anyway. So what happens is, I say, you're not ready. And he never heard that before. Not ready? But he wasn't. He was willing to give up something but not enough.
BW:	Did you think—this is not—
TRUMP:	And I didn't see staying there would help. You know, it's supposed to be like for two or three days, and I left after the first day. I said, look, you're not ready.
BW:	And he wasn't ready because he wouldn't fully denuclearize?
TRUMP:	I just don't think he would have. That's correct. I don't think—
BW:	And is this an acquired negotiating tactic from New York, if I may ask?
TRUMP:	No, I think negotiating is a natural ability. Just like sinking a three-foot putt or just like hitting a home run. I really do. I think— I've seen guys, they study negotiation. No, I think either you can nego—I don't know. I think a lot of things in life are—
BW:	But did you think, this is not a man who's going to shoot a nuclear weapon or an ICBM at my country?
TRUMP:	I didn't think they had the technology yet. It's 8,000 miles away. Getting closer—
BW:	Yeah. Flatter trajectory and they could do it. Right?
TRUMP:	Getting closer. Yeah. Getting closer. But I don't believe. Look, you have to understand. I always went in with one question: why are we doing this? Why is the United States defending a wealthy country, losing a fortune to protect a really wealthy country from a hostile neighbor? And the wealthy country is in Asia, 8,500 miles away. Why are we doing this?

BW: But you're aware that the possibility he might
            shoot that missile—

TRUMP: There is a possibility, yeah. I think—

BW: —drove the military crazy. Out at NORTHCOM,
            I mean, they have to—we talked about this last
            time—they delegate the presidential authority
            down to a two-star general to shoot down with an
            interceptor a missile—

TRUMP: They're always prepared. They have to be
            prepared. You have to be prepared.

BW: So they conduct—when it looked like a missile
            was coming up, they—

TRUMP: I don't think it happens. I don't think he wants to
            mess with us. I think he likes me, a lot.

BW: Yeah. He could like you and still feel he's in a
            pinch.

TRUMP: Well, I know, but I don't—Look, you read the
            letters.

BW: I know. And that's why the letters are—

TRUMP: That changed your mind a lot I bet, when you
            read.

BW: Yes, because—

TRUMP: The level of effusiveness.

BW: Well . . . What it does, it's—everyone says oh, you
            break all the norms. Right? I've always thought
            you were elected to break the norms, weren't you?

TRUMP: Maybe. I was—

BW: Not maybe.

TRUMP: —elected, I think for a lot of reasons.

BW: Okay. [laughs]

TRUMP: I was elected for a lot of reasons.

BW: But one of them was to break the norms. And
            what you did is you broke the norms in this
            relationship.

TRUMP: Yeah.

BW: Which is the one that drives the intel community
            and the military crazy. Right?

TRUMP: Okay, so let me tell you where we are now.

BW: Yes. Where are we now?

TRUMP: Because this isn't as good a story. So I shook his
           hand. I said, you're just not ready. We'll talk when
           you're ready. And in a very friendly way, I left.
           Now, I didn't realize it, but I heard he was furious
           at his people, not at me. For allowing this meeting
           to take place where I left. But I left on good
           terms. I've spoken to him indirectly and through
           this since. But now we're in a state of never-never
           land.

BW: You said it.

TRUMP: Huh?

BW: We really are.

TRUMP: No, no. We're in a state now where he wants to
           meet. You know, in a certain way he's demanding
           a meeting.

BW: I can see from the letters. He's begging. I'm sorry,
           he's begging.

TRUMP: And communication is unbelievably difficult
           because there are no telephones. All right?
           He reads all of my social media. You see the
           statements I put out. You saw the one I put out a
           week ago, right? A few days ago.

BW: Yes.

TRUMP: That was meant for a party of one. Okay?

BW: To him?

TRUMP: Yeah. He sees all of that. That's the primary way
           of communication [laughs] which is a little—
           because I've got so many, hundreds of millions of
           people. But, but—

BW: And this is the one, December 8, "Kim Jong
           Un is too smart and has too far much to lose,
           everything actually, if he acts in a hostile way."

TRUMP: Yeah. That was only meant for him. I call it a
           party of one. Even though tens of millions of
           people are seeing it. Right?

BW: Understand.

TRUMP: I have a tremendous Twitter following. You

know I actually have—hey, ask Dan to come in please? Dan?

COMMENTARY: Dan Scavino, Trump's Deputy Chief of Staff for Communications and Director of Social Media, enters.

BW:	Okay, so where is it now? What's the next step?
TRUMP:	Wait a minute, I just—hey Dan, you know the great Bob Woodward. This is Dan Scavino.
SCAVINO:	Yes, I do. How are you, sir?
BW:	How are you, sir?
SCAVINO:	Nice to meet you.
BW:	Nice to see you.
TRUMP:	So on my Twitter site, plus the other sites, plus Facebook, Instagram, what do I have?
SCAVINO:	A hundred seventy-six million total right now. Twitter, Instagram, Facebook. You have @realDonaldTrump, @teamtrump—
TRUMP:	Well that way I can fight the fake news. It's the most—I had dinner with Zuckerberg the other night at the White House, okay?
BW:	Yeah.

COMMENTARY: Mark Zuckerberg is the CEO of Facebook and its parent company Meta platforms.

TRUMP:	And he sits down. I said, you're not treating this world fairly. Anyway, he sits down and he goes, congratulations Mr. President. I said, what? He said, you're by far number one on Facebook. I said, that's good. I said, who's second? He said Modi of India. I said, yeah, but he's got 1.5 billion people. [*laughter*]
BW:	Yeah.
TRUMP:	But he said that. You heard that?
SCAVINO:	I was right there.
TRUMP:	He said you're number one. It's in the list, but you're number one. Said number one on Facebook.

SCAVINO: Since 2015.

TRUMP: By far.

COMMENTARY: In early 2020, with 80 million followers, Trump had the ninth-most followed Twitter account behind former president Barack Obama and several celebrities. His Facebook page also ranked below dozens of other celebrities in terms of likes and followers.

TRUMP: So it allows me to fight these fakers, these terrible human beings that are in the media that people think are legitimate but they're not. And you and I might disagree.

BW: I know that—I know this world, obviously, and I think there's a lot more good faith than you understand.

TRUMP: I think it's a much worse world than you remember from back in the day. I do think—

BW: Okay, but I think there's a lot of good faith.

TRUMP: I think there is some very evil—I know, but there's some very evil people.

BW: This is why transparency works. I want the story of how—what the system is. How do you do this? How do you do Putin? How do you do Iran?

TRUMP: I've done more—and I have a great relationship with Putin. I could have—we could do such great things with Russia, but because of the phony Russia investigation—started falsely and corruptly and illegally now as it turns out—but because of that, you know, we're held back. And he knows that, too. Putin said to me in a meeting, he said, it's a shame, because I know it's very hard for you to make a deal with us. I said, you're right.

BW: Yeah. This has been—

COMMENTARY: Special Prosecutor Robert Mueller, the former FBI Director, investigated allegations of collusion between Trump, his campaign, and Russia. Mueller's final report amounted to an investigative crack-up riddled with ambiguities and contradictions.

Mueller wrote in his final report: "While this report does not conclude that the President committed a crime, it also does not exonerate him."

The headline in *The Washington Post* the next morning read: "Mueller Finds No Conspiracy."

Mueller never recommended any criminal charges against Trump, though he cited ten instances of Trump obstructing the investigation.

BW:	This is important—
TRUMP:	Go ahead.
BW:	—particularly this week. The Horowitz inspector general investigation—
TRUMP:	Right. Right.
BW:	—of what the FBI did in Russia has started a massive shift in public opinion.
TRUMP:	I know.
BW:	You realize that?

COMMENTARY: The so-called Steele Dossier was a controversial document assembled by former British intelligence agent Christopher Steele that alleged Trump cavorted with prostitutes in Moscow years earlier. I had publicly said it was a garbage document because it was paid for by Democrats, its sourcing was weak, and its sweeping allegations were unsubstantiated. A trusted source of mine had also told me the document was basically a fraud.

Despite its unreliability, the FBI used the document as a basis for wiretapping Carter Page, a minor foreign policy aide to Trump during the 2016 campaign.

Michael Horowitz, the Inspector General of the Justice Department, found the FBI had insufficient basis for the wiretapping, and the Steele Dossier was eventually discredited.

Trump had latched on to the FBI wiretaps on Carter Page, a minor FBI mistake, and was building a case in his own mind and to me that this amounted to a conspiracy of spying.

TRUMP:	Horowitz in all fairness was appointed by Obama. If he weren't, it could've been much worse. And, you know, he—look, when you see the Lisa

	Page—the two great lovers, right—and Strzok. When you hear those emails between—
BW:	Yeah. I know.
TRUMP:	—the two stupid lovers—they're dumb as— you know what happened? They were having an affair, so they didn't want to put it on their private servers. So they put it on the public FBI server. So the first thing we do is subpoena the server, and we've got all these texts. But when you see that and then Horowitz says there was no bias? Okay. But he got—you know, there was plenty in there. Right? Plenty in there.

COMMENTARY: Trump refers to FBI lawyer Lisa Page and FBI Special Agent Peter Strzok who had exchanged emails that revealed a stunning anti-Trump bias.

BW:	Sir, for 47 years I've done this. I've looked at the FBI. And I think it's the first time since J. Edgar Hoover and Watergate when there is a chance for real FBI reform. Do you—you see that?
TRUMP:	So Comey, I call Comey a poor man's J. Edgar Hoover.
BW:	Yeah. Yeah.

COMMENTARY: Director of the FBI James Comey was appointed by Obama in 2013. Trump fired Comey on May 9, 2017.

TRUMP:	He wanted to be J. Edgar Hoover, but he wasn't smart enough. And he got caught.
BW:	Remember when they gave you that briefing, and I said publicly the Steele Dossier's a garbage document?
TRUMP:	I remember. I remember.
BW:	And you tweeted a thing, thank you, and everyone piled on me. How can you say that? This is a holy document.
SCAVINO:	It's a disgrace what went on.

COMMENTARY: Dan Scavino then weighed in.

SCAVINO:	Five hundred and fifty days I spent on the campaign trail with him, never once heard the word—ever—Russia.
BW:	But sir, it's about the FBI's procedures and this hair trigger to start counterintelligence investigations and other investigations.
TRUMP:	Well, I'll go a step further. You know the way stupid people say, oh, if you didn't fire Comey, this wouldn't have happened? Just the opposite. If I didn't fire Comey, I probably wouldn't be here right now talking to you. Maybe I'd be talking to you from a different location, like New York. If I didn't fire Comey—I was being set up, you know? That was a whole set up.
BW:	I don't know whether it's—look—you know—
TRUMP:	What happened is, when I fired him, that was like throwing a rock into a hornet's nest. They all went crazy. They all started ratting each other out. Everybody—you'll see. This is nothing. What you saw there is nothing.
BW:	You know they start counterintelligence investigations [snaps fingers]. Because, oh, we've got an anonymous phone call.
TRUMP:	Yeah.
BW:	And are you familiar with counterintelligence investigations?
TRUMP:	A little bit.
BW:	Do they brief you on them?
TRUMP:	No. No.
BW:	Do you know all the—
TRUMP:	Yeah, I get a lot of briefings, but—
BW:	But do you get—
TRUMP:	But you know what they should've done? When they first heard, they should've come to me and said, sir, this is what we're hearing. They didn't do it. They went to Dianne Feinstein when she

had a Chinese guy that they thought might be a spy. They went to other people. They never came to me. Because they were looking to do a number on me. And if I didn't fire that—

BW: You've made your case.

TRUMP: —if I didn't fire that scumbag, it would've been— it was a great move I made. And now people are saying it. The smart people, they're saying if you didn't fire him—oh, they were just starting.

BW: But the FBI—but the opportunity—

TRUMP: And we wouldn't have known—wait—we wouldn't have known about Strzok and Page and McCabe and all these creeps.

BW: If it wasn't for Horowitz. Horowitz is the guy who uncovered all that.

TRUMP: No, if it weren't for my firing Comey, because that started—the whole thing blew up. That's when it blew up. Otherwise it would've gone along, along, along. Don't forget, this started before I fired Comey. Because they went after Flynn. They went after Page. They went after all these people. I will consider this one of my greatest achievements: getting the scum out of government. And it's scum. It's the lowest form of human garbage, these people. And I don't mean FBI people. I mean top people in the FBI. Because this thing was run amok. And don't think that Obama didn't know—

BW: And Barr agrees with you. Your attorney general.

TRUMP: Barr. Don't think that Obama didn't know everything that was going on. He knew everything that was going on.

BW: —the awesome power to investigate someone—

TRUMP: Right.

BW: You're an FBI person, I can investigate you. And take you to the cleaners. And they do it. And they're crime-fighters. And what's interesting about somebody like Barr—

TRUMP:	He's a great attorney general.
BW:	Well, we're going to see. We're going to see.
TRUMP:	But he's doing a—people think he's doing a very, you know, great job in many ways.
BW:	Well, he has lots of critics, as you know.
TRUMP:	He's got critics and he's got fans, too. He's got tremendous fans. He's a strong guy, and we're going to see. Smart guy. We're going to see what happens. But I'll tell you what, had I not fired Comey, it would've been not good. And by the way, I fired him—
BW:	I know.
TRUMP:	How about my instinct? Do I get credit for instinct?
BW:	It was an earthquake.

COMMENTARY: Our time was running out. I wanted to move to foreign policy.

BW:	In Bob Gates, his memoir, 2014, he said of Obama and the Afghan war, "Obama doesn't believe in his own strategy. Doesn't consider the war to be his. For him, it's all about getting out."
TRUMP:	Yeah.
BW:	Is it the same for you?
TRUMP:	So it's a situation that we should be there in an intelligence form, but not in a military form. We made tremendous progress, because we've gotten rid of ISIS. You know I got rid of ISIS in Syria and Iraq. But now you have ISIS there.
BW:	But they convinced you, you had to keep some troops there?
TRUMP:	Well, that hasn't been proven yet. We'll see.
BW:	But you're willing to keep some troops there?
TRUMP:	We'll be down very shortly to 8,000 troops.
BW:	Yeah. Okay. In Afghanistan? Yeah.
TRUMP:	And from then I'm going to have to make a decision. I think it's good to have intelligence there,

because it does seem to be a web of development. It's a development web for terrorism.

BW: And as you know, I mean, they'll tell you, if you pull out of Afghanistan and there's a 9/11-like attack—

TRUMP: So the first thing the generals tell you when you want to pull out, they say, Sir, I'd rather fight them over there than fight them over here. And if you're sitting behind this beautiful desk, the Resolute desk, and you have four guys that look like they're right out of Hollywood saying, yes, sir—they'll do whatever you say. I say, what's your opinion, General? Sir, I'd rather fight them over there than fight them over here.

BW: Which general said that?

TRUMP: Well, different generals. Different generals.

BW: Dunford? Mattis?

TRUMP: I've had four generals say almost the exact same words, including—

BW: Tell me, for history.

TRUMP: —including, frankly—I like my new head of the Joint Chiefs of Staff very much—

BW: Milley?

TRUMP: Yes. And Mark is a very strong guy. But I believe that he feels that, too. I believe Esper, who's doing a very good job, feels that, too. And that's a hard line if you're sitting here and you have to make that decision, when you have guys that you respect making that statement. I've had numerous of them say that.

COMMENTARY: Mark Esper, Trump's latest secretary of defense, replaced Jim Mattis. Esper kept a low profile but was one of the most experienced defense secretaries in modern times. Shortly after the 2020 election, Trump angrily fired Esper.

BW: Do you think there's too much concentration of power in the presidency now?

TRUMP:	No.
BW:	I'm astounded, going back—I've done nine presidents, sir.
TRUMP:	Right.
BW:	And power grows, from Nixon to you. And I wonder is there too much power concentrated?
TRUMP:	No. I think you have a lot of checks and balances. I think that you have to be smart. Look, you have to be smart. Not easy to be president, you know? I went through 15 debates. I won every one of them. I went through everything and—you ever see the debate, the polls on debates? I won every single debate. You've got to know what you're doing. You have to have a position where somebody can make a decision, Bob. Otherwise you're just going to be a rudderless ship.
BW:	Yeah.
TRUMP:	Oh, I see—so you think that the presidency is more powerful now than it ever was?
BW:	Oh, yes, sir. Particularly—.
TRUMP:	Is that because of the person?
BW:	Because I think this is true—both the left and the right, Democrats, Republicans—
TRUMP:	They fight each other?
BW:	—they have a reverence for the exercise of presidential power, particularly if it solves big problems. And that reverence leads them to, oh, okay, the president has decided—we're going to— Now, people fight you on things, but—
TRUMP:	Well, you've seen Mitch say he's not going to take up a bill unless he has the approval of the president. Did you see that? This is Mitch, and Mitch is a pro. We're not dealing with a baby, right? But Mitch has said oftentimes—and I've seen other senators say— you know, they're against something. They'll say, I'm only going to approve it if the president says to approve it. So I don't know—is that respect for me or is that respect for the office?

BW:	What's your answer?
TRUMP:	I don't know. I have no answer. But I know it happens.
BW:	When you come in here, you realize you have extraordinary power?
TRUMP:	Do you mean because of the office or because of me?
BW:	Both. They've converged, haven't they?
TRUMP:	I don't know. I think the wrong person wouldn't have much power as president, and I think the right person possibly would. Meaning a certain type of person possibly would. But I understand what you're saying.
BW:	What do you feel when some of the generals tell you about Iran? That well it's really a pissant problem and it's not something that we have to worry about?
TRUMP:	I don't view Iran as a problem like I do others. Look, I think—we can have a very good relationship with China, but then on the other hand I look at them building an airplane a day and a ship a week and I say, this is a behemoth. What I'm doing with tariffs has crippled them. Crippled them. It's not the same country. What I did to Iran, I mean, Iran is not the same. Once I terminated that deal and I put the strongest sanctions in the history of the country on—they have no money. They want to borrow money. Now Obama made a horrible deal. Don't forget, that deal ends in four years. If that deal—what kind of a deal is that?
BW:	That's another thing I want to walk through with your people. Who's your—again, in the second chair—
TRUMP:	You can speak to Robert O'Brien, very good guy.

COMMENTARY: Robert O'Brien, a lawyer, author, and former international hostage negotiator, was Trump's fourth national security adviser.

BW:	Yes, okay, your new national security adviser.
TRUMP:	He's a very good guy. You know why I like him?
BW:	I'm going to quote you to him.
TRUMP:	He was a great hostage negotiator—38 and 0.
BW:	Yes, he did that, didn't he.
TRUMP:	I mean, I'm 38 and 0 with him. We got every hostage. Zero, we never paid a cent. But anyway, no, Robert's good. Robert's somebody I think you could speak to.
BW:	Okay. I'm going to quote you to him.
TRUMP:	I think you could speak to Mike Pompeo. Doing a good job.
BW:	Yes. I want the full story.
TRUMP:	Yeah. No, Mike is good. But—
BW:	You know what the historians talk about? History's clock. Have you ever heard this term?
TRUMP:	No. No.
BW:	And Barbara Tuchman, back doing the book on World War I and the causes and how it was an accident, wrote that "The old order was dying. On history's clock, there was a new order coming in." You ought to put up history's clock here, because history—and I say this all the time—history's clock was kind of ticking along in 2016. No one knew where it was going. The old order—
TRUMP:	Yeah.
BW:	—the Democrats and the Republicans did not come up with a plan or a strategy. And you knew who came along and stole history's clock? Donald Trump.
TRUMP:	I guess—yeah. I, you're looking at him.
BW:	Donald Trump.
TRUMP:	Well—
BW:	And I say that, and people don't like that. I say, look guys, that's what happened.

COMMENTARY: I wanted to know Trump's view on nuclear weapons.

BW:	Doesn't it give you the chills when they come in and say, here are the options, Mr. President?
TRUMP:	Yeah. Yeah. You only hope you don't have to use them. You're talking about people.
BW:	Yeah. God help us.
TRUMP:	You only hope you don't have to use them.
BW:	After you'd been in office a year, NSC meeting, and you're complaining about the allies and all the money we're spending.
TRUMP:	Right.
BW:	And Mattis, according to the notes, is quite upset about this. And you're saying, why are we doing this? Right?
TRUMP:	Yeah. On numerous occasions about different places.
BW:	Yes. Always. It's a constant refrain. And he finally says, Mr. President, we're doing this in order to prevent World War III.
TRUMP:	Mm-hmm.
BW:	What'd you think about that?
TRUMP:	I don't remember him ever saying that. He may have thought it, and he may have thought it was good—
BW:	I think he said it.
TRUMP:	But the problem—
BW:	At least it's in notes.
TRUMP:	Yeah. I don't think it helps in preventing World War III, but when you have wealthy countries that laugh at us behind our back because we're paying for their military, I think it's ridiculous. They respect us more now than they've ever respected us. These same countries—look, I raised $530 billion over the weekend. You know that? NATO.
BW:	Yes. Right. [laughs]
TRUMP:	A hundred and thirty now. And $400 over the next two years. $400 billion. Not—
BW:	Do you think money makes that much difference in politics now?

TRUMP: Yeah. Which way? You mean running for office?

BW: Yeah, and getting all this free media. It's not
               as if—

TRUMP: So, so they said 97 percent of the stories on the
               news now are Trump or Trump-related. Ninety-
               seven percent. If a plane goes down someplace
               with 500 people on board, they don't even cover
               it anymore. It's all got to be Trump or Trump-
               related. Look, Hillary Clinton spent four times
               what I spent. And we beat her, okay? So who's
               going to get the nomination? A tough one.
               Toughest one you've ever—

BW: Isn't it interesting?

TRUMP: It's a tough one. Nobody knows. I mean, when I
               see Buttigieg [*pronounces it Bood-edge-edge*] he
               looks, I say, Alfred E. Neuman, right? But when I
               see him—somebody said they think he's going to
               make it. You know, you sort of dream about that.
               Like, nothing. He's like nothing.

BW: Okay. Now here's, last question, big—

TRUMP: Be very interesting. When you have an idea, let
               me know?

BW: —the big, big important thought. I'm looking
               at how you operate, and I say one of the keys is
               that—

TRUMP: Oh, this just came out, look.

BW: What's this? Latest poll?

TRUMP: Just came out.

BW: Plus nine in Wisconsin, huh.

TRUMP: Look at these, how nice. Look at that. That was
               over the last week. This just came out yesterday
               or today.

BW: Yeah. But these polls mean nothing. You know
               that. Because that's not—

TRUMP: No, but you know what they are? I know, but
               they're swing states.

BW: What matters? November.

TRUMP: No, no, I know that. But still.

BW:	Yeah. It's interesting.
TRUMP:	I went up how many points? Look how much. They were—
BW:	The biggest thought is, how's President Trump doing his foreign policy?

COMMENTARY: At that time this is what I believed the focus of my book would be.

TRUMP:	The single biggest mistake we made in the history of our country was going into the Middle East. We've spent $8 trillion—
BW:	Yeah. That's Steve Bannon's number. That's inflated.
TRUMP:	I believe it.
BW:	Yeah.
TRUMP:	I believe it. I don't think they report the real numbers, okay, you want to know the truth. But we spent $8 trillion. It was seven when I first—it's $8 trillion. Millions of people have been killed. Now, on our side, less. But overall millions of people. We've changed the face of Europe. [*laughs*]
BW:	Through immigration.
TRUMP:	Those people left the Middle East and they walked into Germany. And Angela was very nice, and she made the biggest mistake in the history of Germany when she took millions of people.
BW:	The Iraq war in many ways defines where we are now.
TRUMP:	Well, it wasn't the Iraq war. Don't forget, the Iraq war, which was a big mistake—it was a big mistake because in Iraq, they killed terrorists. Okay? Saddam Hussein killed terrorists. He had control. All of a sudden we're spending massive amounts of money, and it's totally—you know, just a mess. And I also think, why are we defending extraordinarily wealthy, successful nations for nothing?

BW: So is the Rosetta Stone in this for you, instinct?
                    Because that's what you said last—
TRUMP: Maybe—well, well, instinct is a very important
                    ingredient in something, you know? I watched Bill
                    Belichick kick a field goal when the team was dead,
                    and they were like on the seven yard line, fourth
                    down. And the score was I think 28 to three. And
                    the first half was just about over. And Bill, I like
                    him because he endorsed me strongly, okay?
BW: Yes, I noticed.
TRUMP: But Bill Belichick kicked a field goal instead of
                    going for—when you're 28 to three, 27, 28 to
                    three with 10 seconds left, you've got to give it
                    a shot. Most people would say, he kicked a field
                    goal instead of trying to get a touchdown. You'd
                    think he'd need a touchdown, right? He gets
                    the field goal. So now he's six. So it's 28 to six.
                    And I say, what kind of a call was that? And then
                    they tie the game, and they win the game, right?
                    That was two years ago, three years ago, against
                    Atlanta. Okay? And I say, that was instinct. That
                    was great instinct. Because—
BW: Did you tell him that?
TRUMP: Well, I tell him—he's a friend of mine. Look, he's
                    a great guy. He endorsed me. You know I have
                    often said, if you go to war, you take a great guy
                    like a Belichick or you know, people that win.
                    Because strategically, it's not as different as you
                    think. Do you understand?
BW: I understand.
TRUMP: And you get the generals, and you explain it to
                    these guys that have to win on Sunday, otherwise
                    they're out of business, right? And some have
                    done it for years. And some haven't lasted for
                    three weeks. Right? But, no, I think a lot of
                    things are based on instinct. I'm here because of
                    instinct. Because if you go with the things I said,
                    everybody said I was wrong. When I said what do

you have to lose to the African American audience
as I read worst on crime, worst on housing
ownership, worst on education, worst on this,
worst on that—

BW: Maybe the title of my book should be, what do
we have to lose?

TRUMP: —then I said, vote for me. What do we have to
lose? Maybe. [*laughs*] Yeah, what do we have to
lose? Don't use that. Don't use it. [*laughter*] I
don't like it.

BW: Okay. You're great to give me this time.

TRUMP: No, but that is instinct. You know my people said,
oh, that's a terrible thing. No, but it was great.

BW: History's clock.

TRUMP: Yeah. No, that's very interesting.

BW: History's clock.

TRUMP: Where did you hear that? Where is that—

BW: It's in Barbara Tuchman's book. It's a great book
about World War I. Begins in 1910. Edward the
Seventh has died. And there are nine kings coming
to the funeral. And she writes, and Big Ben struck
9:00. And she said, but on history's clock, the old
order was dying in a blinding flash. And it did.

TRUMP: Can I be honest? It's true. And you know who
some of—

BW: It's true. And the question is, is that what
happened in 2016?

TRUMP: Well, you know who some of the worst people
are for me to deal with? If you said I just put in,
I'll have 182 judges and appellate judges and two
Supreme Court judges in less than three years,
right, and if you put somebody else's name as
president—anybody else—all of these lowlifes
that are Republicans, the few remaining Never
Trumpers. There aren't too many. They're on
artificial resuscitation. Or they're just—they can't
get over their sickness of some kind, you know?
I don't like to use the word jealous, because why

should I say jealous? But if you said Bill Smith
was the president and did all of the things I've
done, they'd say he's the greatest president that
we've ever had. But they can't say that because
the hatred is so great. And I find that the Never
Trumpers, in many cases, are worse than the
Obama people and they're worse than the—And
just to finish, and then we'll go on—

BW: And I asked you last time, you didn't want to
answer—why do so many people hate you? Why
are they so angry?

TRUMP: Well, the love is equal to the hate, though.

BW: Okay. Fair point. Fair point.

TRUMP: I have the love that's equaled—you know, the
famous Fifth Avenue statement. Boom. Right?

BW: [laughs] Where'd that come from? Was that
instinct?

TRUMP: Just—it was pure instinct. And it was well
received, but not so well—But now they write it's
true.

COMMENTARY: At a 2016 campaign rally in Iowa, Trump said:

TRUMP: *I could stand in the middle of Fifth Avenue
and shoot somebody and I wouldn't lose any
voters. Okay? It's like incredible.*

BW: You know we have two Americas out there. You
realize that? You are president of two Americas.

TRUMP: Yeah, that's true.

BW: They are divided.

TRUMP: That's true.

BW: Is it, in the end, not your job to try to bring them
together?

TRUMP: I would like to be able to do it. I would like to be
able to do it.

BW: Isn't it your job now? Job one—

TRUMP: I think the biggest problem I have—

BW:	—bring them back together.
TRUMP:	I think the biggest problem I have for doing that—I would love to do that. Because I've oftentimes said that—you remember when I put out the Christmas greeting where I said, Merry Christmas to all, even the haters? You know. But I would love to be able to do it. But the biggest problem is the media. The media is unbelievably dishonest. And it's hard when you have a dishonest media. Because if that report didn't open up people's eyes, then nothing will. You understand that. The report from the incident.
BW:	Listen, that's a great moment. But it's not going to get you elected next year. But it's a great moment to reform the FBI. It's a public service, to come in and say, we've got to fix this.
TRUMP:	It's a systemic problem, but it starts from the top. And it started with Mueller. And it started with Comey. And it's with that whole group. Mueller was—by the way, how about Mueller's performance in front of Congress? That went poof. [laughs] For two and a half years, right? And then—
BW:	You know what they always said about Mueller is if he finds that you did something quite trivial, he will indict you. If he finds something really serious, he can't get there unless he's got the goods. Unless he has tape recordings, unless he has—
TRUMP:	Let me tell you. There isn't a man of substance in this country, maybe in the world, that if you gave them 18 haters—haters, that are very smart, haters—and gave them an unlimited budget—turned out to be $45 million—Cost much more than that because what it did to the country cost billions, okay? Billions. But if you gave them $45 million, you've got 18 brilliant haters—many of whom worked for the opposition, Crooked Hillary Clinton. There are few people in the

	world—They went through everything, including my tax returns, my financial statements—
BW:	Which I'm still waiting to get. I really would like to have them.
TRUMP:	No, but you know Mueller went through them. You know Mueller has seen them, okay?
BW:	You're sure of that?
TRUMP:	Sure, 100 percent. He spent $45 million investigating me, and he had the right to go—
BW:	Maybe, maybe not.
TRUMP:	He went through everything.
BW:	It's not clear.
TRUMP:	He went through everything.
BW:	It's not clear.
TRUMP:	If you gave me you. You're an honest guy. If you had 18 geniuses watching you—every single move you've made, every paper, every check you've signed for the last 30 years, I guarantee you I'd find—they found nothing with me.
BW:	But you know what they said of Mueller was if he discovers you've ripped a mattress tag off, he'll prosecute. You remember on the mattress tag it would say, if you rip this off, you'll be prosecuted.
TRUMP:	Right. Right.
BW:	And they said if he caught you doing that, he would indict you. But the big cases—
TRUMP:	Bob, he found nothing. Think of it.
BW:	Well, you've said publicly, sir, you've made it very—you've said the Mueller report was the best thing that ever happened to you.
TRUMP:	No, but think of it. With all the thousands of checks I signed—I sent—when I went—Poom, poom, poom. Thousands of checks. Thousands of—hundreds of deals, all—He found nothing. There's nobody in the country where that could've happened. He spent $45 million. Had 18 guys. Had 49 FBI agents. I had 2,700 subpoenas, I believe—

BW: And you're sure he looked at your tax returns?

TRUMP: Looked at everything.

BW: I mean they've told you that?

TRUMP: Well, I don't want to get into it, but he looked at everything. There's not a man in the country that could've survived that, and he found nothing. He found nothing. Think of it. I'd get calls—Bob, I get calls from—

BW: So do you still think it's the best thing that happened to you?

TRUMP: No, I don't. I think it's a terrible thing. It should never happen to another president.

BW: Well, that's where reform of the FBI is the future, isn't it?

TRUMP: It should never happen to another president.

COMMENTARY: For me, reform was an obvious conclusion because of what the Justice Department Inspector General had found in the Horowitz report about the willingness of the FBI to use a flawed document like the Steele Dossier as the basis for a wiretap. What I'm arguing here is that the FBI institute more accountability over their procedures when they seek court authorized wiretaps. They have since done so to protect the rights of all citizens.

TRUMP: Nobody else would be able to take it. Your friend Rush, I told you what he said, right? Rush Limbaugh. He said, there's not a man in the world that could've taken what Trump has taken and been a great president.

COMMENTARY: Rush was not my friend. I'd never met him, and he'd said many, many critical things about me and my work.

TRUMP: It's true. I know other guys—

BW: So what's the plan for bringing the two—

TRUMP: Look, you know Nixon. Nixon was under a table.

BW: Yeah. Yeah.

TRUMP: Nixon was a mess. I'm not a mess.

BW:	He had a tape-recording system.
TRUMP:	You know what you said to me the last time? I told my wife. I told a few people. I shouldn't say that, but I told a few people. You said, you act like you just won the election. You're under impeachment. You said that to me. I thought it was a cool line.
BW:	Yeah.
TRUMP:	But things work out. Things always work out. You have to be smart, but things work out. I have a great attitude. Anyway.
BW:	So Karl Rove, who used to work for Bush, I remember seeing him up here in the West Wing when we were talking about the Iraq war—
TRUMP:	Yeah. He's come a long way for me, by the way. He used to be really negative. He's very positive.
BW:	You know what he said? He said, it all depends on outcomes. And it does. This depends on outcomes. China. Russia. The Middle East. And that's what I want to chart—
TRUMP:	Well, you're right, but if nothing else, spending no money, giving nothing here. Three years of peace. Three years of no nuclear tests. We haven't had a nuclear test in three years.

COMMENTARY: Trump is referring to North Korea.

TRUMP:	Three years of no rockets, other than—
BW:	And he says he doesn't need to test because he's got all he needs. [*laughs*]
TRUMP:	Fine. Look, they haven't had a test in three years. And we do have a signed document saying that he's—you know, you have to—that document from Singapore, you have to take that document and study it. It said that he will denuclearize.
BW:	You've been kind. I'll come back. I'm going to— —let me introduce myself.
DEERE:	Bob, I'm Judd Deere.

BW: Hi. How are you? Nice to meet you. I'm going to
                 go through—

TRUMP: He's a legend.

DEERE: I know that.

TRUMP: We're both legends.

BW: —Iran—

TRUMP: What people don't know is he came up to my
                 office in Trump Tower. He wanted to do a book
                 on me 30 years ago. And here we are.

BW: No, Bernstein did. I said—

TRUMP: Oh, Bernstein. Boy has he gone off the way. By
                 the way, there's some nice pictures of you there,
                 by the way.

BW: That's great. I hope—I need to work on my
                 posture.

COMMENTARY: Trump presented me with a large, poster-size picture of himself with Kim Jong Un.

TRUMP: Don't fold it.

BW: I'm not going to.

TRUMP: Do you have a round thing for this so he can take
                 it? Or even a rubber band or something. Because
                 you can't fold it, you'll ruin it.

BW: I'm not going to.

TRUMP: That's a pretty top picture.

BW: I love that picture.

TRUMP: I don't even know why I'm giving it to you. That's
                 my only one. That's all right.

BW: Well look, he's smiling. That's your point.

TRUMP: By the way, you ever see a picture of him smiling?
                 He never smiled before. I'm the only one he
                 smiles with. You know that means something.

BW: Those letters—now, you've got to let me read
                 your letters to him. So I have—

TRUMP: I'll let you do it.

BW: I've got half the puzzle. Right?

TRUMP: Okay. I'll let you do that.

President Trump meets with North Korean Leader Kim Jong Un. Both leaders are smiling. Trump gave Woodward a large, poster-size copy of this photo. It was most likely taken during Trump's meeting with Kim Jong Un in Hanoi, Vietnam, on February 27, 2019.

BW: Okay. Good. That's great. That's key. Great. You got something to put that on?

[*Recording ends*]

COMMENTARY: Trump's relations with the North Korean leader and his transactional dealings with other countries were a frightening case study of how Trump conducted foreign relations. He wanted to do it alone. Based on personal instinct and natural ability. And with a stunning disregard for his CIA experts and military generals.

Staunch allies, crucial to maintaining stability and the U.S. place in the world, were treated like unwanted, disposable burdens. Trump personally demanded that South Korea pay billions for continued U.S. military protection. He said:

TRUMP: So we're defending you, we're allowing you to exist. Why are we doing that? Why do we care?

This is about as demeaning a statement that any president could make about another country, let alone a longstanding and important ally. Autocrats, however, who lavished Trump with praise and played to his ego were respected, even admired. Trump remembers that Putin said he was brilliant. He remembers that Putin and Xi told him Kim Jong Un only wanted to talk to him.

TRUMP: I'm the only one he wants to deal with in the world.

Trump says that only he understands North Korea's five major nuclear facilities, not because he studied them in-depth but because his uncle worked at MIT. Trump told me,

TRUMP: So I understand that stuff. You know, genetically.

Trump's foreign policy is dangerously and unpredictably dictated by his own self-adulation and instinct. Nobody is tougher than him, nothing scares him, and nobody knows more than him. Only me. Nobody else. This is what terrified his national security advisers.

INTERVIEW 4:
It Ended in Dust

Mar-a-Lago, Palm Beach, Florida
December 30, 2019

TRUMP: Getting along with Russia is a good thing, not a bad thing, all right? Especially because they have 1,332 nuclear fucking warheads.

COMMENTARY: On Monday, December 30th, 2019, I was sitting in the reception area of Trump's Mar-a-Lago home in Palm Beach, Florida. The club area, originally built as a private home in 1927, was opulent and luxurious in an Old World way, like a gilded, candle-lit version of the Wizard of Oz's castle. A 16-inch plaque stood prominently on the receptionist's table. It read: "Donald J. Trump. The Mar-a-Lago Club. The only six-star private club in the world."

This would be my third interview with Trump this month. A highly unusual opportunity with a sitting president.

I wanted to review with President Trump Mueller's Russia investigation and Trump's impeachment by the Democratic House of Representatives twelve days earlier on December 18th.

The daily story was still impeachment.

I watched Mar-a-Lago club members stream in for dinner at what a Secret Service agent told me was "the regular evening soiree."

Trump appeared in suit and tie with billionaire Nelson Peltz in tow. "Oh," Peltz said, "he's doing great things for the economy. It's all him." Trump pointed to the gold leaf on the 20-foot-high ceiling. "Look at that," he said to me. "See that? See that?"

Trump then escorted me back to a conference room. We sat next to each other at a large table.

Music blared in the background. In the audiobook, we have processed the interview to remove the music for copyright reasons. Deputy Press Secretary Hogan Gidley was also present.

TRUMP:	Well—
BW:	I'm going to turn this on. On the record for the book. Unless you modify—
TRUMP:	For the book only, right? Only for the book?
BW:	Book only, yeah. I'm not—
TRUMP:	Okay. For the book only. Right?
GIDLEY:	Right. No stories coming out, no nothing.
TRUMP:	I didn't know Rosenstein, but I got to know him.

COMMENTARY: Rod Rosenstein was the deputy attorney general who oversaw the Russia investigation because the attorney general Jeff Sessions had recused himself. Trump was absolutely furious at Sessions's decision to take himself out of the case.

TRUMP:	I couldn't fire him because I didn't want to be Richard Nixon, who fired everybody. And being a student of history—I like learning from the past. Much better than learning from yourself and mistakes. So one of the best things that I did, and I did a great job by doing it, drained the swamp, is firing Comey. Not keeping him.
BW:	Yes, we talked about this.
TRUMP:	Right. If I would not have fired him—I don't know, maybe I would be—because this was a coup, this was spying, this was a lot of things. Okay. And that was before Mueller. When I hired Jeff Sessions, I did it because he was the first senator to support me. He came to see me four to five times. He wanted it so badly. I didn't want to have him, but I'm a loyal person. He had a position in Alabama prior to being a senator that was, you know, a law enforcement position. And I agreed to do it. And when I hire a secretary or an attorney general, I hire somebody that's

supposed to go out and get great people to work for them. And for the most part I have had very good people. I've had a good Cabinet. You know I really have had a good Cabinet. And if I don't, I change them. I don't mind changing people at all. When I hired Jeff Sessions, he had six deputies that he could've hired. And he had Rosenstein. I didn't know any of them. But I knew five of them were solid. I knew a couple of them, I should say, but I didn't know who—I expect all of my people to hire good people.

BW: But Rosenstein took control of this investigation. Under the rules, Mueller was just like another U.S. attorney. And so he could monitor and control him. So Rosenstein had the Russian inquiry, traditionally the deputy—

TRUMP: Yeah. Which by the way, it now found out that they should have exonerated me in the first 24 hours. Because if you look at what happened with the report, the IG report, that just came out. They knew 24 hours after this whole thing started that Trump did nothing. It went on for two years, or whatever the period of time, but it went on for two years.

BW: It did, it went on for two years. But Rosenstein's got the handle on this.

TRUMP: Yeah.

BW: Controls the Russia investigation. The deputy has the FBI. Your relationship with Sessions was gone, so Rosenstein could step in. And at the end of the inquiry, he resigned this year and he sent you a love letter saying that you had great conversations, you showed humor, it was, look, everything we accomplished. He told people privately that—this is interesting—that Trump is bulletproofed for 2020 now.

TRUMP: This is recently?

BW: Did you know that?

TRUMP:	No. When did he say this?
BW:	He said this over the summer, after he resigned.
TRUMP:	Yeah. And what does that mean, though? You're asking me about Rosenstein. In what sense? Are you asking me that he was an evil guy, or a strong guy?
BW:	Did you know that he had this kind of—no—Did you know he had—
TRUMP:	I mean are you saying that he was on my side?
BW:	—this control? Yeah, was he on your side? And he'd learned early from Mueller that they weren't going to find anything.
TRUMP:	Yeah.
BW:	Did he tell you that? Or did he tell the White House counsel?
TRUMP:	So—so I obviously can't reveal all my conversations.
BW:	But help me for the history, Mr. President.
TRUMP:	I got along with him—Yes. Let me just explain. I didn't know—you know, I didn't know him at all, never met him. Came from Baltimore, which is a Democrat area.
BW:	Right.
TRUMP:	Elijah Cummings stood up and said what a great choice he is to head—after Sessions left, on the first day, the first day, after he recused himself. I had a choice. I could've fired everybody, or I could grin and bear it. I decided to do the second, because I watched a person that you know better than I do fire everybody. How did that work out, right?
BW:	Not well for Nixon.
TRUMP:	And if you see where I am now—because that's all done—if you see where I am now, that was a very smart thing to do. Because it all went into—
BW:	But did you know early, comparatively early on, that Rosenstein knew that Mueller had nothing—
TRUMP:	No.

BW: —on Russian conspiracy?

TRUMP: Nobody ever told me that, no.

BW: I see. When did you find out, then?

TRUMP: Well, I knew early on that he had nothing because
             I never dealt with a Russian. I knew early on that
             I never made a phone call, I never—you know, I
             have millions of calls. Right?

BW: Yes, sir.

TRUMP: There wasn't one phone call to or from Russia. So
             I knew from the standpoint of I know, because I
             never dealt with a Russian.

BW: It's you. Right.

TRUMP: Just a quick little—so I would hear, even before
             Mueller, little stories about Russia. Do you know
             anything about Russia? Like there was something
             percolating.

BW: Yes. Right.

TRUMP: You may know what I mean. And I kept saying,
             oh, no. And I never even thought of it because
             I never thought—you know, it was like, have
             you heard stories about Russia? And here's the
             story. I'd say, no, no, no. After five or six or
             seven people asking me over a period of months
             [about it?], I said, what's this stuff with Russia? I
             keep hearing—because I have nothing to do with
             Russia. Okay. With Rosenstein. So he took over
             early. Because Jeff Sessions recused himself. Jeff
             Sessions should've told me—

BW: Yes. I know. I know.

TRUMP: —he was going to recuse himself prior to—

BW: You've made that clear.

TRUMP: —going in. And it would've been a whole
             different thing. But he didn't. He took the job,
             but then he recused himself the following day, and
             Rod Rosenstein was the deputy.

BW: But here—President Trump—

TRUMP: I learned—I knew they had nothing because there
             was nothing. But I didn't know—

BW:	But as you know, they can find things, they can dig things up.
TRUMP:	Sure.
BW:	And this went on for two years.
TRUMP:	Two years, and they had nothing. Well, I'll tell you—
BW:	And the question is, when did you feel relief? And did you get some information—
TRUMP:	I never felt relief.
BW:	Why?
TRUMP:	I never felt relief. Because that was the way it was being played. They were dirty cops.
BW:	So what Rosenstein said to Mueller was, let me know if you find anything that shows coordination or conspiracy. It never came.
TRUMP:	Yeah.
BW:	And he knew this earlier this year, before the report came out. He said he bulletproofed you for 2020, which is—
TRUMP:	Big statement.
BW:	—pretty important bulletproofing.
TRUMP:	That's a big statement. Now, that's a big statement.
BW:	Did you know that?
TRUMP:	I didn't know that. No, I never heard that.
BW:	Have you talked to him since?
TRUMP:	I have not.
BW:	After the—
TRUMP:	I have not. But I left him in charge, as opposed to removing him. And I let them run it. And let me tell you something, I did something that some would do and some wouldn't do. But I did something that was—I think it was probably wise in the end. I didn't have to. I could've gone right in there and taken over. I let them do whatever they wanted to do. And because I didn't want to have fingerprints, I didn't want to have—I had an absolute right to get involved if I want to.

BW: Oh, you could've fired—

TRUMP: I could've fired—

BW: Listen, within Mueller's operation, all these lawyers, the people you didn't like, it was kind of like a closed, balanced aquarium. And every time you tweeted or said something, they said, we're finished. And they felt if they—

TRUMP: What does that mean, we're finished?

BW: That you'll fire them all. Fire the whole team. They—

TRUMP: I think if I would've fired them, there would've been bedlam in the country.

BW: I think you're probably right.

TRUMP: I think I would—oh—I think if I would've—

BW: And you asked people to try to get rid of him.

TRUMP: If I would've fired Mueller, if I would've fired the group of, as I call them, 13 angry Democrats— which turned out to be 18 angry Democrats. If I were to fire them, I think there would've been bedlam in this country. Even though I knew that I did absolutely—I had nothing to do with Russia.

BW: And they thought, within Mueller's team, that if they subpoenaed you, they'd be fired for sure. And so they wouldn't do it.

TRUMP: Yeah. They were wrong.

BW: That's one of the reasons—

TRUMP: I would not have fired them.

BW: You would not have fired them?

TRUMP: No.

COMMENTARY: In fact, Trump did try to have Mueller fired. Former White House Counsel Don McGahn testified before Congress that in 2017, Trump asked him to tell Rod Rosenstein to remove Mueller. When McGahn refused, Trump backed down.

TRUMP: I would've fought it out, but I wouldn't have fired them.

BW: So John Dowd, your early attorney—

TRUMP:	Good man.
BW:	—was right to tell you, don't sit for an interview with Mueller. That it's a perjury trap.
TRUMP:	So John Dowd is a good attorney. An old-timer, old-school.
BW:	Yes, very.
TRUMP:	John Dowd is a man who was so committed to this, and he was so upset because he thought within the first few weeks this case should've been ended. And he would tell me, oh, this case is ending very shortly. They have nothing. And at the end, it took—it was like a year and a half. It went on forever. He almost had a nervous breakdown. He was so committed. He thought it was the most unfair prosecution—when you talk about malicious prosecution. He said it was the most unfair thing he's ever seen.

COMMENTARY: Dowd was the lawyer I quoted at the end of my book *Fear*, published the year before this interview. Almost certainly Trump had not read my book. Dowd said he had seen Trump's tragic flaw. What Dowd concluded but would not say to the president's face was: "You're a fucking liar."

BW:	Rosenstein was your friend, it turns out. When he took over the investigation—
TRUMP:	Who told you that?
BW:	—he thought—
TRUMP:	But who told you that?
BW:	President Trump, I've talked to everyone, and I've got—
TRUMP:	Okay. I'm glad to hear that. But—
BW:	He initially said, hey look, this investigation is about the Russians, not about Trump.
TRUMP:	Yeah.
BW:	And that was his focus. And it turned out—
TRUMP:	People have said that. But what happened is, I'm not sure that Comey—Comey was a bad person,

is a bad person. You know, he tries to pretend
like he's a pious, wonderful—he's a bad guy. And
I'm not sure that Comey had that in mind at all.
I think he had the opposite. I think he had a lot
of bad thought in mind. I think he's a sick man. I
think Comey's sick. There's some mental problem
that he's got. And I think some of the people that
worked for him are very sick.

TRUMP: One thing.

BW: I just want to make sure—

TRUMP: The IG was good.

BW: Yes.

TRUMP: But he never quite gets there. Because he was an
Obama appointment. Now, in one way—

BW: No, it's because he didn't want to ascribe motives
to the behavior. It was unacceptable.

TRUMP: Okay, ready? When you have Page and Strzok
saying we're going to take him down, saying if
she loses we have an insurance policy—To me, the
greatest of all was that. That's the most important
email of any of them, and we have some beauties.
See, they made a terrible mistake. They put their
lovers' notes on the public server, on the FBI server.

BW: Yes, I know. When this was all over, did you talk
to Rosenstein at all?

TRUMP: I haven't spoken to him. I want to stay away
from everything until it's all over. By the way,
this is very different from me. I had a choice. I
could've gone the exact opposite. I could've fired
everybody. Could've done whatever I wanted. I
guess they say that the president of the United
States is the chief law enforcement officer. You
understand?

BW: Some people do, yes.

TRUMP: Okay, chief law enforcement officer. I didn't want
to put the country into a position where—I just
think if I did it the other way, it would've been 10
times worse than anything that's happened thus far.

BW:	One of the interesting things about Nixon, after he resigned, he gave these interviews to David Frost.
TRUMP:	Right.
BW:	And one of the things he said, it's quite eloquent, he said, I gave them a sword, to take me down.
TRUMP:	Yeah.
BW:	And a lot of people in my business, as you know, thought the Mueller investigation was the sword.
TRUMP:	Was going to end—yeah.
BW:	Was going to—
TRUMP:	And it ended in a whimper. It was pretty amazing. It ended—you know what I said? It ended in dust.
BW:	Amazing, and that's why—
TRUMP:	It all ended in dust. Look, the big thing on the Mueller, the words—two simple words: no collusion. Because see, it's all about collusion.
BW:	No coordination, no conspiracy.
TRUMP:	That was the key. Now, phase two, well, there was no collusion. And then all of a sudden we started getting all these great text messages and finding out all about the conspiracy and all the bad things that happened. So you realized it was an illegal investigation. It was a totally illegal investigation. And therefore—and then Bill Barr made a determination, so you had no obstruction, you had no collusion. But the big word was really no collusion. Because the big thing was, was he at all colluding with Russia? And the answer was no. They were two very big words. And then Bill Barr, he ruled on the no obstruction. There was no obstruction. There was no obstruction. But the collusion was the thing that people—a lot of people said, well, wait a minute, it's an illegal thing, and you're talking about obstruction.
BW:	So the bulletproofing, I'm telling you, this is the first you've heard of?
TRUMP:	Yeah, I have not heard that. I have not heard that.

	I felt it, because I knew I never had anything to do with Russia. Now Putin did call me yesterday. Do you know that?
BW:	No, no. He did?
TRUMP:	Oh. So we found—we helped them. Terrorists were assembling to blow up a big portion of Saint Petersburg. And we found out about it. And I said, notify them. They notified them. And Putin's people went in and got them, probably 24 hours before they were going to do it. It was going to be a major terrorist attack in Saint Petersburg, Russia, which is a beautiful place. I was there a long time ago.
BW:	Yeah.
TRUMP:	And they were going to blow up a big, big important section of Saint Petersburg. And I got a call yesterday morning from President Putin, who I get along with very well. That's a good thing, not a bad thing, by the way.
BW:	I know. [*laughing*] I understand.
TRUMP:	Anyway, he called me to thank me that they were able to capture these terrorists—they were terrorists—prior to this event taking place. I thought it was very, very good, very good. That's the way we should work. When are you putting the book out?
BW:	I don't know. When I get done. And, you know, there's just lots of work—
TRUMP:	Since I saw you last, I have approved $738 billion for Space Force, for the Wall—
BW:	I saw that. Yes. Now, I want to go back to the Syrian situation.
TRUMP:	By the way, excuse me, 70 years ago, we got the Air Force.
BW:	Now we have Space Force.
TRUMP:	Now we've got Space Force, Joint Chiefs of Staff. I created a branch, the sixth branch, of the United States military. That's a big story. That's a big

thing. And by the way, very important, because that's where it's going. It's all going up to space. Hard to believe. When you look at the great, sophisticated military equipment now, you will see that it's all controlled by space. Very important. So we have Space Force.

BW: Everyone—

TRUMP: Would you say that's a pretty good achievement? That's just one of many. One of many, my Bob.

BW: And so you're going to be—

TRUMP: Should've done the book—30, 25 years ago, he came to my office.

COMMENTARY: Again, Carl Bernstein and I had gone to interview Trump in 1987. We didn't end up doing a story or a book, but Trump always recalls the meeting.

BW: What's so interesting here is, how does this all end?

TRUMP: What all end?

BW: The situation next year with the reelection. Everything's about reelection, don't you think?

TRUMP: I think the impeachment hoax is playing very badly for the Democrats. And I see it two ways. In the history of politics, there's never been fundraising like I'm doing. Hundreds of millions of dollars of cash is pouring into the campaign. And much of it is because of the impeachment hoax. That's number one. Number two, my poll numbers are through the roof.

TRUMP: Since I last saw you, we killed al-Baghdadi. Since I last saw you, we killed the second, who was going to be the first. And we have the third on the— *shhh*—you know.

BW: I saw that. Okay. The question about the Syrian situation is, I've found, and my assistant, that you have what they call kind of a shadow system on the phone of calling people where the intel

people don't know and it pisses them off. Is that
correct?

TRUMP: I don't know if it pisses them off.

BW: Okay, but you do have a shadow—

TRUMP: But I get better intel the way I do it than I can
ever get from other people.

BW: And with Erdogan in Turkey, seven calls my
assistant has found that you had with him before
you finally announced you were pulling out,—

TRUMP: No.

BW: —which led to the Mattis resignation.

TRUMP: Now, let me tell you, it had very—that did not.
Mattis left because he knew I didn't want him. He
was one of the world's most overrated generals.
And his name was not Mad Dog. I gave him that
name. His name was Chaos, okay, and Chaos I
didn't like. I said, you know what—

BW: Did you work the system—

TRUMP: And Mattis turned out to be—he was a nice guy,
Mattis. I thought he was a nice guy. I actually
got along with him okay. But he didn't do what I
wanted him to do.

BW: But did you work out with Erdogan—I just, I'm
trying to see about this shadow communications
system you have.

TRUMP: Let me just tell you.

BW: Okay.

TRUMP: Where I talk to him more than any other time
was—and I think it worked out great, and
I think—do you ever see—You know, I use
the analogy, and it's probably a little strange,
sometimes you have two kids in a playground.
They hate each other. Sometimes you let them
fight for a minute, and then you break them up.
That's what I did. They fought for a few days, and
it was vicious. And then I told them, you don't
stop, because I've created an economic wonder.
The United States has far—

BW:	And did you tell Erdogan—
TRUMP:	You know what we're up? We're up many trillions of dollars. China's down many trillions of dollars.
BW:	Understand. I just want to get this one detail nailed down, President Trump.
TRUMP:	Go ahead. Go ahead.
BW:	Did you tell Erdogan, look, it's all yours, we're done, and then four days later you tweeted it and announced it?
TRUMP:	No. No. Well, you saw the letter I wrote. Didn't you see the very strong—
BW:	Yes sir. [*laughs*] Very—
TRUMP:	No, I didn't say that.
BW:	"Don't be a fool."
TRUMP:	I said, don't do it, but we're leaving. But I don't think you should do it.
BW:	Yeah. But you do have a shadow communication system, that's correct?
TRUMP:	He decided—well no, I get along with world leaders. Excuse me, NATO. I just—you know I just raised $530 billion.
BW:	Yes, sir. I know.
TRUMP:	Which nobody in the newspapers write about.
BW:	But you do have a shadow communication system.
TRUMP:	I get along with people. I talk to people. Yeah, I mean, I do.

COMMENTARY: This was an important acknowledgement that there might be transcripts, reliable accounts or even audio recordings of his phone calls. But various investigations initially did not uncover anything conclusive.

BW:	The intel people and a lot of people in the government don't like it.
TRUMP:	I don't know if they like it. I just want them to do their jobs.
BW:	I know they don't like it, because they told me. [*laughs*]

TRUMP: Okay. I want them to do their jobs. If you think
                      I'm happy with intel after what I went through
                      with Comey, who's a—stupid guy, a very stupid
                      guy. But when I have Brennan, I have Clapper, I
                      have Comey.

COMMENTARY: Trump is referring to former CIA director John
Brennan, Director of National Intelligence James Clapper, and Director of the FBI James Comey, who all served under Obama.

TRUMP: I have this scum that I have to deal with. That the
                      remnants of it—and there are many other people
                      I could name, but I won't bother naming them
                      right now—and then I'm supposed to say how
                      wonderful our intelligence is? I don't think so.
                      That's not going to happen.
GIDLEY: Excuse me one second. What is a shadow
                      communications—he's the president of the United
                      States. If he makes the call, that's the call.
BW: No—I understand. But it's on a system that
                      doesn't necessarily involve the NSC or the—
TRUMP: No, I have no secrets. I have no secrets from
                      anybody in our government. But Brennan who's
                      absolutely in my opinion a garbageman—
BW: Yeah.
TRUMP: But if you think I'm supposed to be in love with
                      intelligence, you're wrong.

COMMENTARY: Trump's former director of national intelligence,
Dan Coats, believed the greatest threat to the U.S. national security
apparatus, was that Trump wanted to ignore any kind of process that
went through experts—people steeped in certain issues or certain
parts of the world.

    The president believed he could pick up the phone and call any-
body he wanted. Trump's attitude was: "I can solve all these problems." He didn't care for expert, professional assessments or options.
He thought he could get better intelligence on his own. Coats knew

that key leaders such as Putin, Xi of China, and Erdogan of Turkey would lie to Trump. They played Trump skillfully. They would roll out the red carpet for him, flatter him, then the leaders would do what they wanted.

TRUMP:	Hey, I told you the story. I came to Washington. I didn't know anybody. I was here 17 days. My entire life, never stayed over at night. Never once. Maybe one night, who knows? I don't know, you'll find one night I stayed over, but basically I was here 17 times in my entire life. Right? And all of a sudden I'm running this vast country.
BW:	Going back to Mattis again. He had such stature, in your eyes.
TRUMP:	He did. He had stature in my eyes, but I did change his name—
BW:	Yes, I understand.
TRUMP:	His moniker.
BW:	And one of the things he said on this issue—
TRUMP:	But he was fired by Obama.
BW:	Yes, he was. Your relations with Kim Jong Un, which we talked about, which in the end you've said it's instinct. Instinct.
TRUMP:	What did you think of the letters? Let me ask you—it's all instinct. It's all relationship.
BW:	And so one of the things Mattis has said—
TRUMP:	Let me ask you real fast. You looked at the letters. I showed them to nobody. Nobody. Nobody has seen those. You looked at them.
BW:	I know.
TRUMP:	What did you think? Pretty amazing, right?
BW:	Astonishing. Because at one point, he talks about a fantasy film, that you're going to be in a fantasy film if you meet again after the first meeting. [*laughs*]

COMMENTARY: This is an excerpt from the letter that Kim sent to Trump on December 25, 2018, Christmas Day:

"Your Excellency, It has been 200 days since the historic summit in Singapore this past June. The year is now almost coming to an end. Even now I cannot forget the moment of history when I firmly held Your Excellency's hand at the beautiful and sacred location as the whole world watched with great interest and hope to relive the honor of that day. As I mentioned at the time, I feel very honored to have established an excellent relationship with a person such as Your Excellency.

As the new year 2019 approaches, critical issues that require end-less effort toward higher ideals and goals still await us. Just as Your Excellency frankly noted, as we enter the new year the whole world will certainly once again come to see, not so far in the future, another historic meeting between myself and Your Excellency reminiscent of a scene from a fantasy film."

BW:	What'd you think of that?
TRUMP:	Well, he wants to meet. He wants to meet now. That's no normal relationship, right? You know, you have people, historians that study him, his father and his grandfather. They study them. You have Asian historians that really study him. He's never written a letter to anybody. You saw—how many, 10?
BW:	Yes, I know. But it's going to be a fantasy film. What'd you think when you read that? For history, for the book.
TRUMP:	I think—
BW:	Because that's an astonishing—
TRUMP:	I think that Kim Jong Un and I have a good chemistry together.
BW:	Yeah. See, even—
TRUMP:	Wouldn't you say that, when you see what you've read? Shocking.
BW:	Yes, and one of the things Mattis has said is that there was a little magic—his word—that you had with Kim, Erdogan, Putin, and Xi. Is that right?
TRUMP:	Magic is an interesting word. It's called chemistry. I have good chemistry with a lot of people. And I have—

BW: Mattis has called it diplomacy by theatrics.

TRUMP: Well, I don't know. I think his first definition maybe is better.

BW: Magic?

TRUMP: But I don't think—I'd say—I'll tell you this. If I weren't president, we would have—perhaps it would be over by now, and perhaps it wouldn't— we would've been in a major war with North Korea. And when I met with Barack Obama—I don't know if he'll tell you this—

BW: Yes. Oh, we've gone through this.

TRUMP: —but Bob, I'm telling you, he told me—he essentially told me that he thinks—and he did try to call them, many times, and he was unable to get—

BW: But at one of these meetings about Kim, and as you're developing your relationship with Kim, in the notes, Mattis says to you about Kim, he lies through his teeth to you. Do you remember that?

TRUMP: Not specifically, no. Look, he said a lot of things. We had nothing to lose. I have a meeting. I gave nothing. The sanctions are at their all-time high right now. Bob, what did I give? When the fake news reports Donald Trump is meeting, he's given so much, I keep saying, what did I give? I gave nothing.

BW: Well see, this is the conventional, old-Washington, establishment view that you don't do this, you have to build up and send—

TRUMP: It's bullshit.

BW: —diplomats and so forth. So even Mattis said—

TRUMP: I had—I'll tell you what, I had a good relationship with Kim Jong Un from the first moment I met him.

BW: And so one of the things Mattis said is actually the relationship that the president had with Kim probably gave Kim a reason not to do something nutty. So he's giving you credit.

TRUMP:	I know that. He felt it was amazing, actually. I don't know that he'd say that, but he felt it was amazing.
BW:	Well, here he says it kept him from doing something nutty. Of course, that's the big fear.
TRUMP:	Well, excuse me, so far you haven't seen any Christmas surprise. You know, Christmas is three days ago, okay?
BW:	Understand. And everyone was writing these stories—
TRUMP:	And everyone was very worried, except me. I'm not saying it doesn't happen, but I'm saying, what do we have to lose? Hey, for three years we've had peace. For three years we haven't had a nuclear test. For three years we haven't had a ballistic missile. Now, that doesn't mean it's going to continue Bob, but what the hell have we lost? We gained three years, okay? We haven't lost anything. And a lot of things can happen. A lot of things can happen.
BW:	Are you optimistic about this next year with Kim?
TRUMP:	No, but I'm not pessimistic either. I can't tell you.
BW:	Are you going to meet again?
TRUMP:	He would like to.
BW:	Another episode of the fantasy film?
TRUMP:	Don't forget, don't forget—the last meeting, I said, you're not ready. He wanted to close two, probably, of the five plants. I said, even if you close four, that's not good.
BW:	Yeah. You want all five.
TRUMP:	I said, you're my friend, but you're not ready to make a deal. I said, I'm going home.
BW:	Well, he's not ready to denuclearize.
TRUMP:	Well, but he saw—you've got to look, you gotta look. He signed a document, and my first—it said he's going to denuclearize. The press keep saying, he never—well, he signed a document that said he is going to—well no, I know, but that's all I can have.

BW: Yeah. But he's not—if you were him, you
             wouldn't—those nukes are his leverage, are his
             status symbol.

TRUMP: It could also be the end of his country.

BW: Yeah. Well, of course that's the threat.

TRUMP: You know? Can also be—I told him. I talked to
             him very openly. Look, I did something when
             I walked on to his land. I said, you want me to
             walk on? He said, I would love to. Then I was
             supposed to just do a step, but—

BW: I need to get—

TRUMP: We'll be okay time-wise.

BW: —all those letters you sent.

COMMENTARY: I am asking for Trump's letters to Kim Jong Un. I
had Kim's letters to Trump.

BW: Because this relationship, when—I've got Mattis
             saying, well, actually, it kept Kim from doing
             something nutty, that's pretty—

TRUMP: So, Bob, when I first got in office, the rhetoric I
             used was probably the toughest rhetoric ever used—

BW: I know. [laughter]

TRUMP: —by a president in this country at any time.

BW: It was staggering.

TRUMP: There's nobody that's tougher than me.
             Nobody's tougher than me. You asked me about
             impeachment. I'm under impeachment, and you
             said you just act like you just won the fucking
             race. Nixon was in a corner with his thumb in his
             mouth. Bill Clinton took it very, very hard. I just
             do things, okay? I do what I want.

BW: Do you feel now looking at it—and again, this
             is for serious history, President Trump—that you
             wound up with Zelensky in that phone call, you
             gave them a sword?

TRUMP: It's a perfect phone call. No. I don't. I didn't give
             them a sword.

BW: You don't think you gave them a sword?

TRUMP: Let me tell you what they did. They failed in
                 Russia. Failed horribly with Mueller. And then on
                 top of it, Mueller testified and he was a disaster.
                 And that was their words, not mine.

BW: Understand. Understand.

TRUMP: Their biggest, stupidest spokespeople said oh, my
                 God, he was a disaster. That's a quote. They said,
                 they used the word he's a disaster. Now, as days
                 went by—

BW: Did you watch any of Mueller?

TRUMP: Sure I did. Who didn't watch it? Let me just tell
                 you about Zelensky. They never in a million years
                 thought I was going to release the call, number
                 one. Number two, they never in a million years
                 thought that we had it transcribed. I want my calls
                 transcribed.

BW: Understand.

TRUMP: I never in a million years thought I'd have to use
                 it. If I didn't have that call transcribed—someday
                 I'll be given great credit for that. I wanted that.
                 All my things. Here's the reason.

BW: Is it—President Trump, just for a second, please—

TRUMP: If I didn't have that transcribed, they made up my
                 call. Look—Schiff—

BW: No, it's the transcript that's the sword for them.

COMMENTARY: It was my belief that the transcript was the proof,
far more compelling than the whistleblower report.

TRUMP: No. Okay.

BW: You can argue against it—

TRUMP: Let's assume I didn't have a transcription—

BW: No, I'm just saying—

TRUMP: —then I would've lived with a false report by a
                 whistleblower saying that it was a terrible call.
                 There was nothing wrong with those calls. There
                 were two calls, not one. Two calls.

BW: I understand. I've looked at them all. I've looked
           at them all.

TRUMP: And it said, it talked about us. It talked about help
           us, comma, the country. Our country.

BW: Can I ask you this, President Trump?

TRUMP: And then I talked about see the attorney general.

BW: As a matter of policy, would you want the
           president of the United States to be talking to
           foreign leaders about investigating anyone,
           particularly some—that's just bad policy, isn't it?

TRUMP: Let me explain. Let me explain.

BW: You understand what I'm—as a matter of policy,
           do you want the president of the United States—

TRUMP: I think it's fine. But there's no—well, let me
           tell you—

BW: You do?

TRUMP: When we're giving vast amounts of money to a
           country, I think you have to say if they're corrupt,
           where is this money coming from? Why is it that
           there's such corruption when we're giving it?
           And you know, there's another thing that I also
           talk about. And I talk about why isn't Germany,
           France, the European nations who are much more
           affected by Ukraine than us, because Ukraine is
           like a massive wall. Think of it as a wall between
           Russia and Europe, okay?

COMMENTARY: This is an important statement since Putin later
demolished that wall by invading Ukraine in early 2022. I then pro-
ceeded to question Trump on the impeachment issue. Since he never
testified at his impeachment trial it is the only time he was aggres-
sively questioned—even interrogated—about it.

BW: Will you allow me to persist with I think this is
           the important, core question in this?

TRUMP: There wasn't a thing—excuse me, Bob, there
           wasn't a thing wrong with that call.

BW: Well—

TRUMP: And those people—now here's what was—

BW: Do you want the policy of the United States to be
              that the president of the United States can talk to
              foreign leaders and say, investigate? I want you
              to talk to the attorney general about investigating
              somebody who's a political opponent?

TRUMP: No. No. No. I want them to investigate
              corruption. What he did was corrupt. I want them
              to investigate corruption. And I didn't say, call my
              campaign manager. I said, the attorney general of
              the United States—

BW: Right. I know that.

TRUMP: And I didn't say we. Now, when the Democrats—

BW: And it's been misreported by saying oh, you asked
              a favor. That was about CrowdStrike.

TRUMP: No, no. They talked about, will you do me a
              favor? They always say that. It's not me. It said,
              will you do us a favor, comma, our country—ba,
              ba, ba.

BW: I understand the defense. I'm asking the policy
              question.

TRUMP: No, but I'm just saying this. When the Democrats
              talk about that call, they always quote, do me
              a favor, do me a favor. You see it hundreds of
              times. We don't let them get away with it. And
              you have to say one thing: no, I want corruption
              investigated. And how can we investigate
              corruption in a foreign country? How can
              we do that? We can't do that. We can't do it
              because we're not—you know, we don't have
              access. We're giving billions of dollars away to a
              foreign country. Yes, we should have the right to
              investigate corruption.

BW: I understand the points you're making. I'm asking
              the policy question, is this a good policy for the
              president of the United States, to be talking to
              foreign leaders about—

TRUMP: Okay, ready?

BW: —investigating anyone—

TRUMP: Corruption. Yes, corruption.

BW: Well, but naming a political opponent.

TRUMP: If the political opponent is corrupt, they can let us know. Look, his son—

BW: Do you think that's the president's job?

TRUMP: His son—

BW: Is that the president's job? I'm sorry to persist on this, but—

TRUMP: The president's job is to investigate corruption.

BW: Yeah.

TRUMP: If there was corruption, we're giving billions of dollars to a country, that country should let us know if there's corruption.

BW: You don't see the other side on this at all?

TRUMP: I don't see it at all, no.

BW: Zero?

TRUMP: No. If there was no corruption—but there was corruption. And when you look at that tape of Joe Biden, quid pro Joe, they call him. Quid. Pro. Joe. When you look at that tape, Bob, that's—that's the ultimate quid pro quo. Okay? It's the ultimate.

BW: Okay. I just wanted to ask, I wanted—

TRUMP: I'm only saying this. Look, I'm only saying this. That conversation I had with him was perfect. But here's what happened. You had an informer who now disappeared. You had a second whistleblower who now disappeared. You had the first whistleblower who reported the call. He reported it totally different than—there were eight quid pro quos. There was that statement that Schiff dishonestly made. Don't call me, I'll call you. I didn't say that. I didn't say quid pro quo. There was no quid pro quo. I didn't say, if you don't do this, we're not going to do that.

BW: I understand your defense, sir.

TRUMP: There was none of that. No, no—

BW: I understand the defense.

TRUMP:	Well, how can you have a better defense?
BW:	Would you want the next president of the United States to be talking to foreign leaders about investigating political opponents? Would that—
TRUMP:	I would want the next president of the United States to investigate corruption. And in fact, we have a treaty signed with Ukraine, because it is a very corrupt country in the past. Hopefully the new president will do something about it, but we have a treaty that we actually have to do it.
BW:	You see why I'm asking these questions?
TRUMP:	Look, look, what happened here is very interesting.
BW:	Indeed it is.
TRUMP:	They made up a phony conversation, and it sounded terrible. The reason I released—
BW:	When you released that transcript, you gave them a sword, President Trump.
TRUMP:	No, the opposite.
BW:	Yes, you did. Well, I know you say you—
TRUMP:	Look, let me ask you a question.
BW:	Sure, of course.
TRUMP:	Wait, wait. I had a very innocent conversation with the leader of a country. Not one, two conversations. You've got a report. The first one was hello, the second—talking about do us, as a country. Okay, you ready? If I didn't have that transcript, I would have a very big problem right now.
BW:	No, sir. You would not.
TRUMP:	Excuse me. I had a whistleblower—
BW:	There's a kind of clarity in a transcript—I know this going back to the Nixon tapes. As soon as you have a transcript, even though it's not, you know, entirely perfect, verbatim, as soon as you have that, that's what everyone focuses on.
TRUMP:	The whistleblower wrote this horrible thing. And it was out that the whistleblower said with, I think

	certainty, all of these horrible things that took place in this conversation, Bob. If I didn't have a transcript, I would've had a big problem.
BW:	But it just would've been a whistleblower report.
TRUMP:	They made up—
BW:	Okay.
TRUMP:	Bob, Bob, they made up a story.
BW:	You understand why I'm asking the question, I hope.
TRUMP:	The transcription, this transcribed report, was perfect. Nothing was wrong. If you read the whistleblower report, you would've said that's the most horrible thing that a president has ever said.
BW:	But it has very fuzzy status, because it's just a whistleblower report. The transcript—
TRUMP:	Ready? The whistleblower report—
BW:	You know—
TRUMP:	Okay, before I do the transcript—
BW:	—me well enough to know that I'm—
TRUMP:	I know. I know. And I think—
BW:	—I'm neutral.
TRUMP:	—I think you believe it, but I think you're wrong. Ready? The whistleblower report, before you ever heard of a transcript, it was given to Congress.
BW:	It doesn't have any standing.
TRUMP:	It blew up.

COMMENTARY: The whistleblower report was written by Lt. Col. Vindman, who reported on the call and alleged that it was improper. Vindman was a member of the National Security Council staff.

TRUMP:	It blew up. We were getting—and all we had, it was going to be a disaster.
BW:	But it's not proof.
TRUMP:	It was a false report, written by a guy whose lawyer is a scumbag, okay, a real scumbag. Look at the background of these people. The whistleblower report was a fraud. If I didn't put

out this very innocent conversation I had with
the president of Ukraine, who then confirmed the
conversation saying there was no pressure put on
him whatsoever—

BW: Okay. You're willing to have this conversation,
and you know me well enough, I'm—I really want
to understand in a comprehensive way—

TRUMP: Let me ask you, so I have an innocent
conversation. Do us, the United States, a favor.
Then I say, our country—

BW: I understand.

TRUMP: —I don't say my campaign, I say our country.
And then I say the attorney general of the United
States. Okay? If I didn't have that very accurate
transcription—and now it's been proven to be
accurate because even these lieutenant colonels
agreed that it was accurate. Okay, so you know—I
don't know, I think it would've been a disaster.

BW: I'm going to tell you something from my
experience.

TRUMP: Go ahead.

BW: Because you've been very—

TRUMP: Nobody more experienced.

BW: Well, you're willing to have this—as you know in
the Nixon case, I always said afterwards—

TRUMP: By the way, this is a much different case.

BW: Yes. I'm the first to say that. It's massive.

TRUMP: This is peanuts compared—

BW: But as soon as the Watergate burglars were
caught, if Richard Nixon had gone on television
and said, you know, I'm the man at the top.
I'm indirectly responsible for this. I'm sorry. I
apologize. It would've gone away. You don't
think so?

TRUMP: I would never have done it here. Yeah, Nixon
should've done that. But I shouldn't have done,
because I did nothing wrong. I did nothing
wrong.

BW:	Have you ever found that you did nothing wrong, but apology is the path to ending the issue?
TRUMP:	I wouldn't apologize if I did nothing. Can't do it.
BW:	You can't?
TRUMP:	No. If I did something wrong I could apologize. I mean, but I wouldn't—
BW:	I think on this—I mean, again, I'm telling you from too many decades of experience in cases like this. If you apologized, it would go away.
TRUMP:	I think if I apologized, it would be a disaster.
BW:	Mm-mm.
TRUMP:	Because that would be admitting I did something wrong, and I didn't.
BW:	Well—
TRUMP:	I didn't do anything wrong, Bob. I had a very good conversation with a very nice man who— who, by the way, when we did finally meet at a news conference—
BW:	I think they used it against you because—
TRUMP:	Because they failed with Mueller.
BW:	No, it's a simple definition of, oh, he's on the phone. You clearly wanted the Bidens investigated. And—
TRUMP:	No. No. I want corruption investigated, Bob.
BW:	Okay. I understand your—
TRUMP:	Bob, I want corruption. We're giving them.
BW:	—defense. Okay.
TRUMP:	And you know what else was in there that they didn't talk about? The Merkel statement. I said, why isn't Germany? Why isn't France? Why aren't these other countries putting up money? Why is it always the foolish United States?
BW:	I know it wouldn't fit with your persona to apologize.
TRUMP:	I would totally apologize if I did something wrong.
BW:	I—it's just—it's bad policy. And that's what they—
TRUMP:	It's not bad policy to investigate corruption.

COMMENTARY: I believed what Trump had done was wrong. But I knew from our past interviews once Trump dug in he'd be immovable, especially in the middle of his impeachment trial. I was trying to get him to instead look at it from a different perspective. And I wanted to engage him with the broader policy question. Was it good policy for a sitting president to ask a foreign leader to investigate his political opponent?

BW:	Mr. President, that's what they—
TRUMP:	Why should we be giving money to a country that's going to use the money in a corrupt fashion? We actually—you have to do this—
BW:	You know lots of our money—
TRUMP:	We have a treaty. I think it's 1999 or something. We have a treaty with Ukraine, talking about corruption. We don't have those treaties with other countries, that I know of, for the most part, because Ukraine was very corrupt. We actually—I actually have an obligation—
BW:	Who's the person you trust most in the world?
TRUMP:	[*long pause, then Trump chuckles*] That's an interesting question. I don't know. I don't want to get into it, because I have so many people—I have great family. I trust my family members.
BW:	Okay. Ask them if you should apologize.
TRUMP:	I think they—I think if I apologized—I think if I apologized for something that I did nothing wrong—I believe—
BW:	It's a question of—
TRUMP:	[*deep sigh*] How can I apologize for making a decent statement? A very appropriate statement?
BW:	And I appreciate your indulgence. I am telling you my experience, and my conviction, my reportorial belief, you gave them a sword when you released that transcript. Now—
TRUMP:	I have such respect for you. And I so disagree with you. [*laughter*]
BW:	Okay.

TRUMP:	I think if I didn't have a transcription—if for some reason it wasn't made, let's say. You know we have these very professional people, and it was very accurate. And now that's been—the one thing that really came out good—the lieutenant colonel said, one thing, could you mention—but people now agree that it was accurate. I think this. If I didn't have a transcription, they would have made up a story that was so phony, and I would've had no defense.
BW:	Okay. I met Ivanka coming in.
TRUMP:	Good.
BW:	I'm just saying this from—take her for a walk around this lovely place.
TRUMP:	I'll ask her.
BW:	And say, would an apology, carefully phrased, end this or put it in a context?
TRUMP:	It would be a disaster. You know, I have this reputation of not being willing to apologize. It's wrong. I will apologize, if I'm wrong. This conversation—
BW:	Yeah. When's the last time you apologized?
TRUMP:	Oh, I don't know, but I think over a period—I would apologize. Here's the thing: I'm never wrong. Okay. [*laughter*] No, if I'm wrong—if I'm wrong—I believe in apologizing. This was a totally appropriate conversation. We have an agreement with Ukraine.
BW:	I understand.
TRUMP:	We have all these things.
BW:	I understand all the background.
TRUMP:	But what I said—what I said—I use the word perfect. It was perfect.
BW:	Yeah.
TRUMP:	And again, if I did something wrong, I would apologize. Okay?
BW:	Understand. And look, let me say—
TRUMP:	I just told you that I—I went through hell for

	the good of the country. I went through hell in the Mueller report because instead of firing everybody—which could've been a much easier solution—I said I'm not going to fire anybody. I'm going to let this go through and through and through. And they kept it going much longer than they should have. And it turned out then Mueller was a disaster. You know the whole thing.
BW:	You're Job. You're Job. From the Bible, do you realize that? [*laughter*]

COMMENTARY: I said this ironically. As frustrated and defensive as Trump got, he never showed anger. He let me push him and push him and his answers were reduced to one simple declaration, namely that the call was "perfect."

TRUMP:	What I did, and it was the wrong thing they did to me, it was a wrong thing they did to my family. They hurt my family very badly.
BW:	—Hogan has asked me to leave. [*laughter*]
TRUMP:	You go ahead. I like [him]. [I don't even know if I have anything].
BW:	You said something that really grabbed me. We were talking about Kim Jong Un and North Korea and instinct.
TRUMP:	Yeah.
BW:	And you said, parenthetically, but it was one of those things that came from the heart, "I'm here because of instinct."
TRUMP:	Yeah, that's true.
BW:	Elaborate. I mean, that's an important part of the Donald Trump story. And when you said that and the way you said it, "I'm here because of instinct."
TRUMP:	I never thought of it until you and I talked. But I said that. I remember saying that. And I said, hmm. Yeah, I'm here because of instinct.
BW:	Explain it.

TRUMP:	So when I—you mean why I'm president? In other words, how I made the decision?
BW:	What instinct operated to—
TRUMP:	So I had many professional people that said it's impossible for a non-politician, because it's never happened, unless you're a general.
BW:	Right.
TRUMP:	It's only been a general or a politician, but 90 percent have been politicians, right? Plus there's a certain expertise, plus it's what they've been doing, plus a lot of things. Right? But many people said that it's impossible to win. And I felt that winning would be easy.
BW:	Why?
TRUMP:	Because I've dealt with politicians all my life. I've dealt with a lot of people. I've dealt with a lot of people. And even the first time, you know, with Romney, a poll came out that I was leading Romney at the beginning. I couldn't do it because I was signed with NBC, with *The Apprentice*, I was building two big buildings that were very expensive, very great buildings and I had to finish them. I didn't—my kids were younger, etc. So there were reasons. But I always felt if I ran—the only time I ever thought about it was the previous four years before with the Romney run. It was just very hard because I had contractual obligations.
BW:	But you know in the campaign, the 2016 campaign, you said some very tough things.
TRUMP:	Yeah.
BW:	And you said some outrageous things, too. Right?
TRUMP:	Well, obviously they worked.
BW:	Was that instinct?
TRUMP:	It was instinct. It was common sense. And it was from the heart. And I said them because it's good for the country. For instance, in my original speech, when I came down the escalator, I made the speech. I talked about rape.

BW: Yeah, I know.

TRUMP: I used—that's a very tough word, rape. Yeah,
             I think I'm here because of instinct. I think if I
             would've listened to everybody—you know, most
             people said you can't do it.

BW: I watched those debates. And you were tough. I
             mean, is it that people are looking for somebody
             who's tough? And the only way to prove that
             you're tough is to go over the line a little bit, as
             you did a number of times. I think you would
             acknowledge?

TRUMP: I don't know. I'm not sure. You know, it's funny
             with the debates. I don't know if I mentioned it,
             but you know my whole life has been a debate,
             but I never debated professionally or anything.
             But I said, huh. And I checked. And you know,
             Ted Cruz was the national debate champion. I
             don't know if you know that. Princeton top—

BW: Yeah. I know.

TRUMP: Harvard. And he was national debate—and many
             of these guys always wanted to be politicians.
             They were—you know, that's what they do.
             I debated with instinct more than I did with
             vast knowledge. I think I've developed a vast
             knowledge.

BW: Did you realize that it was instinct operating?
             Because it was—

TRUMP: I don't know. Let me tell you what I realized. I
             don't think, oh gee, it's my instinct. Because I
             think if you do, you no longer have instinct. Do
             you understand?

BW: Really?

TRUMP: When you start thinking about oh, my instinct, I
             think it's got to be—it's gotta happen—

BW: It's got to come from the gut.

TRUMP: It's got to flow. But here's the thing. I never left
             center stage. So anyway, I think Bob that instinct
             is a very important thing to have—if you have

	a good instinct about things. You have a lot of things coming at you. You have a lot of things coming at you.
BW:	I think it's because people wanted someone tough.
TRUMP:	Maybe. Do you know that Obama campaigned harder against me than Hillary Clinton?
BW:	I know you said that. I'm not sure that's true.
TRUMP:	Yeah, he did. And he also campaigned very dishonestly against me. Okay?
BW:	How did Barr decide to open this Durham investigation?
TRUMP:	You'd have to ask Barr.
BW:	Did he tell you he was doing it?
TRUMP:	Well, he told everybody he was doing it. I think it's going to be big leak.
BW:	Could be.
TRUMP:	There's tremendous corruption.

COMMENTARY: Attorney General Barr appointed Connecticut U.S. Attorney Durham to investigate if there was wrongdoing in the opening of the Russia investigation in 2016. Trump hopes that it will find evidence that his campaign was spied on. Dan Scavino then enters the room.

TRUMP:	Ask him how many people. How many people do I have?
SCAVINO:	I actually did it today, 176.2 million people on Twitter, Facebook, Instagram, LinkedIn.
TRUMP:	It's six different sites. Now that's—by the way, so when I have—that's more than all of these people put together. My wonderful, dishonest media. Listen—
BW:	Do you agree—
TRUMP:	Do me a favor. Hey, Dan. That's on six different sites—
BW:	—with your new national security adviser? I talked to him the other day.
TRUMP:	Yeah. Nice man.

BW: We had a very good talk. And he said the core of
               national security now is how to deal with a rising
               China and a declining Russia.

TRUMP: No, I don't agree. I don't think Russia is
               declining.

BW: You don't?

TRUMP: No, not at all. I think Russia is a smaller economy,
               but I think that they're a strong military. I think
               they have vast natural resources. And they have
               a lot of pride in themselves. No, I disagree with
               that. I didn't know that he said that. That's his
               opinion.

BW: He said—he was very emphatic.

TRUMP: No, no, that's wrong. He's wrong.

BW: He said what happened, China likes to live in the
               future. Trump—you, President Trump—pulled the
               Chinese out of the future, into the here and now.

TRUMP: Well, they had the worst year they've had in—
               now 68, it was 57, now it's 68 years. This is the
               worst year they've had, because of what I've done
               with the companies and with the tariffs.

BW: Yeah.

COMMENTARY: Trump has publicly claimed vastly different statis-
tics on China ranging from the worst year in 27 years to the worst year
in 61 years.

TRUMP: I think Russia though has a great opportunity for
               success. And by the way, nobody's been tougher.

BW: All these people think, like I think Mattis thinks,
               all roads lead to Moscow.

TRUMP: Yeah. Nobody's been tougher than me.

BW: And Dan Coats thinks—Dan Coats thinks all
               roads lead to Moscow.

TRUMP: Is that because of me?

BW: Yeah.

TRUMP: Oh, you think Dan Coats was negative to me?

BW: Yeah, on this. That you were—

TRUMP: Well, that's a big thing.

BW: That you had this affection for Putin and
                    Moscow.

TRUMP: Excuse me. I like Putin. Our relationship should
                    be a very good one. I campaigned on getting
                    along with Russia, China, and everyone else.

BW: I remember.

COMMENTARY: Rex Tillerson, who had headed ExxonMobil,
the largest publicly traded oil and gas company in the world over an
eleven-year period, had become Trump's first secretary of state, the
top cabinet post. Russia's largest oil exploration area in the world was
with Exxon.

    Tillerson, who met regularly with Putin, told Trump: "Putin feels
like we treat Russia like a banana republic." Tillerson recalled for
Trump how in 2015 he had been tooling around the Black Sea on
Putin's yacht. "And Putin said to me, 'You Americans think you won
the Cold War. You did not win the Cold War. We never fought the
Cold War. We could have, but we didn't.'" Tillerson said the comment
sent chills up his spine.

TRUMP: Getting along with Russia is a good thing, not
                    a bad thing, all right? Especially because they
                    have 1,332 nuclear fucking warheads. And it's
                    so stupid to be—and they work. It's not like
                    gee, maybe North Korea's work, maybe they
                    don't. They have tremendous nuclear power, but
                    maybe it works, maybe it doesn't. Getting along
                    is a good thing, Bob. Not a bad thing. But the
                    relationship was hurt by the Russian fraud, by
                    the Russian hoax. It was hurt.

BW: Understand. You're going to be surprised what I—

TRUMP: And by the way—

BW: —found out about the Mueller investigation.

TRUMP: I love that.

BW: They did not—they—first of all, it was a rushed
                    job. The report. And they didn't realize they were
                    putting inconsistencies in where they said, we

don't exonerate the president, and then they said but this report does not conclude the president committed a crime.

TRUMP: I never even spoke to Russia. I have nothing to do with Russia.

BW: I know. But they contradicted themselves.

TRUMP: Well, Bob, the biggest thing you can do? Nobody ever has been tougher on Russia than me. I'm the one also that brought up Nord Stream. Nobody even knew what Nord Stream 2 was. That's the big pipeline. You'd never heard of Nord Stream until I came along.

BW: So does Putin get mad at you when you do these things?

TRUMP: No, Putin respects me. And I respect Putin. I think Putin likes me. I think I like him. But here's the—I do like him. Do you know that Putin—and I spoke to him about this on our last call, he wants to do a nonproliferation agreement. He wants to make far less weapons. So do I. I'd like to—

BW: Well, then, do it.

TRUMP: I can't do it unless they agree. I can only do it if they agree. I'm the one that broke up, on top of everything else, I'm the one that ended the agreement. You know why? Because they weren't living up to it. But wait a minute, Bob, just before you leave. He—I did far more to Russia—look at the tariffs, look at the sanctions. Look at all the stuff. Now at the same time, getting along with Russia is a good thing. Now, they just had a great prison swap, right?

BW: O'Brien says we can't have good relations with Russia if they are invading the neighbors, like—

TRUMP: Well, I don't like that. No.

BW: —Ukraine, Georgia—

TRUMP: But if you look at, because of us, they just did a big prison swap with Ukraine. A lot of things are happening, Bob. A lot of things. And nobody's—

	Nord Stream. You take a look. It was never mentioned. Take a look at all of the things that I've done. Look at Ukraine. Obama sent them pillows. I sent them tank-busters. Okay?
BW:	Will you have that walk with Ivanka? And get her to call me?
TRUMP:	I will, but I disagree with you so much. It wouldn't matter what she said.
BW:	I know, but what would you do if she says—
TRUMP:	It wouldn't matter what she said.
BW:	—Dad, I think—
TRUMP:	He thinks—
GIDLEY:	He's way off.
TRUMP:	He thinks that my call was less good with Ukraine. I said it was a perfect phone call. I talked about the United States.
BW:	No. Bad policy. Bad policy.
TRUMP:	And he thought—and I'm saying, investigate corruption. Okay? He thinks I should apologize. And I said, the problem is, it was a perfect call. I have nothing to apologize for. I think if I apologized, it would be a disaster. I don't know.
[SCAVINO?]:	A hundred percent. The media would kill—
TRUMP:	Dan, show him this thing. Turn that off for a second.
BW:	Yes, sir.
TRUMP:	You won't even believe this. Watch this.
BW:	Okay.

COMMENTARY: I shut off my tape recorder as requested.

Dan Scavino opened his laptop to show a clip of the president's 2019 State of the Union speech. Instead of Trump's words, hyped-up elevator music played as the camera panned for extended shots of senators and members of Congress watching and listening to Trump.

The first shot was of Senator Bernie Sanders of Vermont, who looked bored.

Trump was watching over my shoulder and was agitated. He was so close I thought I could feel his breath on my neck.

"They hate me," the president said. "You're seeing hate!"

I peered at the screen.

The camera stopped on Senator Elizabeth Warren, the Massachusetts liberal. She was listening and had a bland, unemotional look on her face.

"Hate!" said Trump.

A shot of Alexandria Ocasio-Cortez (AOC) was next. She had no expression on her face.

Then Kamala Harris. Next year she would be chosen as Biden's vice-presidential running mate. Harris had a bland, polite look on her face.

"Hate!" Trump said so loudly within inches of my neck that I jumped. "See the hate! See the hate!"

I didn't see it. Many Democrats, of course, did hate Trump. They were vocal and angry opponents of his presidency. But his insistence that what I was seeing was "hate!" was unsupported by the images of Democrats on Scavino's computer.

It was a remarkable moment. A psychiatrist might say it was a projection of Trump's own hatred of Democrats.

To me, this Trump response was both unforgettable and bizarre.

INTERVIEW 5:
Those Are So Top Secret

Phone Call
January 20, 2020

COMMENTARY: Out of the blue Trump called me at home about 1:30 p.m. on Monday, January 20th. It was Martin Luther King Jr. Day—a federal holiday. It was a long weekend and I had just walked in the front door with my wife, Elsa.

Elsa is also a book author, former *Washington Post* reporter, and staff writer for *The New Yorker*. She has worked on and edited all of my Trump books. It was the only occasion I did not have my tape recorder ready.

My account of this call is based on my handwritten notes. "Do you have time for President Trump?" the White House switchboard operator asked. Yes, I said. Trump came on the line. Elsa later checked the phone's call log and verified the call came in at 1:23 p.m. and lasted for 25 minutes. Trump had been president exactly three years.

"These two sleazebags who wrote this book about me—it's unbelievable. It won't do well," Trump said. He was referring to the book *A Very Stable Genius* written by my two *Washington Post* colleagues Philip Rucker and Carol Leonnig. The book was highly critical of Trump. I asked Trump whether he'd read it. "No," he said. "I just read a review of it."

Trump returned to the latest polling. A Rasmussen poll showed he had a 51 percent approval rating among likely voters as of January 16th, 2020. He said it was wonderful. And when I pressed on whether he believed the polls, he backtracked, "I don't. I don't believe them," he said. Polling had widely predicted a Hillary Clinton victory in 2016.

I asked him for the letters that he wrote to Kim Jong Un because I had only the letters Kim had written to him.

"Oh, those are so Top Secret," Trump said. "But I'll let you see them. I don't want you to have them all." I said, well, I want to quote from some of them.

Recent investigations revealed that Trump kept these letters along with other sensitive and top-secret documents at Mar-a-Lago after he left office. The National Archives retrieved the letters from Mar-a-Lago in January 2022.

Trump seemed worried. "You can't mock Kim. I don't want to get in a fucking nuclear war because you mocked him," Trump said.

I assured him I was not going to mock the North Korean leader.

Trump returned to the Rucker/Leonnig book. He particularly did not like a scene in the book which suggested that he did not seem to know much about Pearl Harbor. This was revealed during a private tour of the USS *Arizona* Memorial. Rucker and Leonnig reported that his then-chief of staff John Kelly was stunned that Trump did not know the history of Pearl Harbor and needed to have it explained to him.

"They said I don't know about Pearl Harbor," Trump told me. "I know everything about Pearl Harbor. How can they say I don't know?" He then accurately recited some of the history.

Trump claimed it was all made up. I said, look, reporters have sources. This is a good-faith effort. They are excellent reporters. Trump said, "Well, 70 percent of it is made up. Well," Trump joked, "I have Russia and Sean Hannity with me."

I asked Trump what he thought of the *New York Times* editorial page endorsement of Senator Amy Klobuchar and Senator Elizabeth Warren for the Democratic nomination for president. "I so dream about running against Elizabeth Warren," Trump said, loudly and with apparent sincerity.

Trump was pleased that Henry Kissinger had been in the Oval Office recently and told him how great he looked given impeachment. "During all of Watergate and Nixon's impeachment investigation, he was a basket case," Trump alleged Kissinger had told him.

I pushed Trump, once again, to help me talk to Matt Pottinger, his deputy national security adviser. Trump said, "Yeah, call Matt. Tell him to talk to you."

After this unexpected call from the president, I started to leave handheld recorders around my house within easy reach of the phone. There was one by my bedside table, in the kitchen, by the front door, in the den, and in my office.

INTERVIEW 6:

Favorite Dictators

Phone call
January 22, 2020

BW:	What happened, sir?
TRUMP:	I saved his ass. That's what happened.
BW:	You saved whose ass?
TRUMP:	MBS.

COMMENTARY:

WALSH: Hi, this is Elsa Walsh, Bob's wife.

On the evening of January 22 at around 9 p.m., the phone rang at our house. I picked it up.

"Is Bob there?" a man asked.

I didn't recognize the voice so I asked, "May I ask who's calling?"

"Donald Trump," the man said.

"Hello Mr. President," I responded, and I handed the phone to Bob.

BW: I put Trump on speakerphone and Elsa continued to listen, as she did in many of these calls.

Again, it was an unplanned call, but this time I had a recorder.

Trump had just returned from Davos, Switzerland, where he had spoken victoriously about the American economy at the World Economic Forum. This was an exclusive gathering of international financial leaders. The president seemed in high spirits.

Earlier that day I had interviewed Deputy National Security Adviser Matt Pottinger about the letters Trump had received from North Korean president Kim Jong Un. I was still pressing to get the letters Trump had written to Kim.

I will warn you that the audio quality is rather poor for this recording.

BW:	I'm going to ask my wife Elsa to pick up and introduce you on the phone, if that's proper.
TRUMP:	Good. Okay.
WALSH:	Hi, Mr. President. How are you?
TRUMP:	How are you? Nice to talk to you.
WALSH:	Good. Are you keeping warm in Davos?
TRUMP:	Well, I just got back. I literally just landed. I walked in, I heard that Bob called. So I'm just returning his call. But literally just got back. It was a great success. We had everybody there. I think you probably saw it was really a great success. Good place. It was a good meeting with a lot of people.
WALSH:	Always fun to be in Switzerland.
TRUMP:	Well, you sound excellent. Thank you. You help your husband a lot, I'll bet, in a lot of ways.
WALSH:	I do. [*laughs*] You know, these things are always a team.
TRUMP:	Well, that's true. And he's a great gentleman, he really is. I wish I worked with him on the other book. But Bob knows what happened. They tried to—
BW:	Well, I was over talking to Matt Pottinger today, President Trump, and we got going on looking at all the Korean situation and development.
TRUMP:	Good.
BW:	And he has said we'll spend an evening going through the whole chronology.
TRUMP:	Good. I think it's actually important to a certain level. I just would like you to be careful, because I'm not looking to insult him.

COMMENTARY: By "him," Trump is referring to North Korean leader Kim Jong Un.

TRUMP:	You know, I took a couple of people with me. One of them was Tucker Carlson, who's a nice guy,

treats me good. And he left, and he said terrible things about him. He said terrible things, that he's in bad physical shape and he looks terrible. [*laughs*] I mean, it was really a disaster, if you want to know the truth. And you know it's tough to bring somebody in, and then he leaves and says how horribly out of shape you are and all of that stuff. So it was pretty bad. But—

BW: Well, I want to get the details. And Matt's going to help me. And I want to talk to—

TRUMP: Good. I think that's great. You know, in the meantime it's been three years without a war. There's a very good relationship.

BW: And the other one I want to do a full excavation on, the development of policy, is Iran.

TRUMP: Okay.

BW: Because clearly that's important. And I talked to Ambassador O'Brien about China, and I'll talk to him more about things.

TRUMP: Okay. China, by the way, is now an extraordinarily good relationship. The deal is extraordinary. They're going to be spending $250 billion in the United States. And we have a great relationship.

COMMENTARY: Trump's China deal is now largely considered a bust, but Trump regularly and publicly declares it the greatest trade deal ever.

TRUMP: And you know, it's a very important thing to have a good relationship if you can with these countries, because—I mean, you would know probably better than anybody, but outside of religion, trade is the most dangerous thing there is. Very dangerous, I feel.

BW: And if you were looking at this and you're living it and you're the decision-maker, what else in foreign policy or domestic policy should I look at to do the comprehensive book, September,

October of this year to say to people, this is what happened. This is the results and so forth.

TRUMP: Yeah. Well, let me give you just a couple of little quick things. So Idlib . . .

COMMENTARY: Idlib is a city in northwestern Syria.

TRUMP: . . . they were going to go to war there two years ago. They were going to blow the whole town up. Three million people live there. I was in Ohio at a big rally. And a woman, a very substantial woman, she's Syrian, I guess. And she was backstage, and she was crying, crying. Her parents live in Idlib with her sister. I had said, what's your problem? She goes, they're going to kill everybody in Idlib. Which is true. And I said, no they're not. The world is watching. You can't—it's not like the old days. Right? But things sometimes, they're not so different, maybe. And I get back and I pick up the terrible *New York Times*, and I open to page, like, 14. It was just—And I see Idlib. First time I had heard of it. This is two years ago. And it said Idlib and then Russia, Iran, and Syria have surrounded the city of Idlib, with three million people, and they're going to blow the hell out of it. They're not discriminating like us. We go from door to door, and people lose their legs and their arms doing that. They bomb it and they worry about it later. It's a very tough thing. Millions of people die. But they don't do it the way we do it. We do it the nice way, but we lose a lot of boys. We lose a lot of limbs. A lot of arms, lot of legs, etc. That's one of the reasons we haven't—Anyway. I put out a social media statement: you better not do it. And they stopped. Russia, Iran, and Syria, they stopped.

COMMENTARY: Initially public pressure from Western leaders did stall a full-on offensive by the Syrian government forces backed by

Russia and Turkey in Idlib. However, airstrikes later resumed, killing hundreds and displacing hundreds of thousands of Syrians.

TRUMP: That's one thing. Okay, so now we'll see. And we're still doing it, and we're working a little bit with Turkey on that. I get along very well with Erdogan, even though you're not supposed to because everyone says what a horrible guy. But you know, for me it works out good. It's funny, the relationships I have, the tougher and meaner they are, the better I get along with them. You know? Explain that to me someday, okay. But maybe it's not a bad thing. The easy ones are the ones I maybe don't like as much or don't get along with as much.

COMMENTARY: Recep Erdogan, the 68-year-old strongman leader of Turkey, consolidated power over 19 years and is widely considered one of the world's most notorious autocrats.

BW: So what else would you look at, President Trump?
TRUMP: Well, let me tell you a quick one. So for five years, Egypt—the Nile, right? The great Nile. Egypt has a large army. And you know Egypt, Sudan, and Ethiopia. Ethiopia built one of the largest dams in the world. I think the largest dam in Africa, but one of the largest. A massive dam. Hundreds of millions of dollars. And just massive. When I say hundreds of millions, $4 billion. It's extraordinarily big. And they've been building it for years. And they've been negotiating with Egypt. Sudan is involved, too. Sudan has no money, but they're sort of right in the middle. Very warlike.

COMMENTARY: Trump is talking about the Grand Ethiopian Renaissance Dam, the biggest in Africa. Egypt and Sudan had been in fraught negotiations with Ethiopia for years about how the dam would affect water supply.

TRUMP:	So for five years they've been negotiating. This took place two weeks ago. And Egypt is threatening to go to war. They're going to blow up the dam. The dam is not built yet, but it's starting to hold back water. And what would happen is the Nile would literally not have water. Not too good, right? Not fair, either. So I'm friends with el-Sisi. So they send a delegation into Washington to meet with Mnuchin, secretary of treasury. And el-Sisi called me to say how bad it is. And they, you know, he sort of indicated it's going to end up being war.

COMMENTARY: Trump had previously referred to Egyptian president el-Sisi as his favorite dictator.

BW:	And when was this, Mr. President?
TRUMP:	This was one month ago. So they've been negotiating five years. They got nowhere. Zero, nowhere. And it was getting more and more difficult. And now the water's being blocked more and more as the dam gets built. It'll be done in a year and a half. It'll be done in two years. So I get a call, and I knew that they're here. That all of the representatives are here. The top representatives of the countries, the three countries. So I tell Steve Mnuchin to bring them into the White House. I said, hello. And then I said, okay. How much aid do we give you, Sudan? She said, you give us—it was a woman. She said, you give us $500 million. No, I said, we give you $541 million. That's a big difference. So mark it down. How much aid do we give you, Ethiopia? He said, $1.1 billion. I said, no, we give you $1.19 billion. It's a lot of money. And how much aid, Egypt, do we give you? Don't even tell me, because it's $1.3 billion. I know that one very well, because they're always looking for their money. I said,

	are you ready? Within one hour—They've been negotiating for five years, Bob.
BW:	Yes, sir.
TRUMP:	I said, within one hour, come back to my office and tell me you have a deal. And if you don't have a deal, I'm going to cut off all aid to all three countries. No, no, no, sir, you can't—I said, that's okay. You've got plenty of time. One hour. I sent them into the Roosevelt Room, right across the hall from the Oval Office. Forty-eight minutes later they came back in. Sir, sir, we have a deal. We have finally made a deal after five years. I got a call from el-Sisi. He said, I've got to tell you, I cannot believe it. He called me to see would it be possible for me to see it because they were going to have to blow the dam up. You can't turn off the water for the Nile, okay? You know, I mean—So instead of going to war—and Ethiopia has a massive army. Tremendous.
BW:	So this has never been reported?
TRUMP:	No, nobody will report it. So what happens is I get a call from el-Sisi. Tough guy, right?
BW:	Yeah.
TRUMP:	He's—you know, the general. He's the boss over there. And he says to me, it's a miracle. I cannot believe it. He said, I called not thinking you could do it, but knowing you were the only man in the world that could do it. I said, it was easy. It was very easy.

COMMENTARY: It appears that a lasting deal was never reached, and Trump's role was never clear at the time. But months later Trump publicly suggested Egypt might blow up the dam. Ethiopia's foreign ministry accused Trump of trying to incite a war between Egypt and Ethiopia. The former prime minister of Ethiopia said of Trump: "The man doesn't have a clue what he is talking about."

TRUMP:	Then today, I don't know—did you see my news conference that I gave today?

BW:	Yes, sir.
TRUMP:	I talked about the European Union in pretty harsh terms. I said, the European Union is worse than China. They're much tougher to negotiate with, and they've been ripping us off for years. But I wanted to finish China. I didn't have to take on Europe and China at the same time. But now that China's all done—you know that deal's all signed and done?
BW:	Yeah, I saw.
TRUMP:	Bob, we're going to take in $250 billion. And I left the tariffs on. I get 25 percent of $250 billion. They can't even believe it. Even China can't believe it. And now I can use the tariffs, in other words, as a negotiating thing for phase two whenever we—
BW:	So why did they make that deal, sir?
TRUMP:	Because—why? [*Trump draws out the word: Becauuuuuuuuse, why?*]
BW:	Yeah.
TRUMP:	They really wanted to make a deal. I mean, you know—
BW:	Why? Why?
TRUMP:	Unbelievable deal for us. You have to make it . . . You know why, Bob?
BW:	[?]
TRUMP:	Their supply chains were being broken up. Everybody was leaving. They were going to different countries. They weren't going through China anymore. You know, I had all the cards. I heard that the World Trade Organization, which is ripping us off like crazy for 25, 30 years, the head of it was there and he wanted to meet me, say hello. So I called him. I said, Roberto, you treat us very badly. The United States is, like, considered this very wealthy place, and China is considered a developing nation, and India's a developing nation. If you're a developing nation, you get

things that nobody else will get. I said, we're going to be a developing nation. And he said, no, no, no. I said, here's what I'm doing: I'm pulling out of the World Trade Organization.

BW: I know. You threatened that for a long time.

TRUMP: And I said, unless we make a new deal. No, no, sir, please, please. So he's coming to New York. We'll make a deal. And I actually brought him into my news conference, because it was right before I left. I said, come on, I'll introduce you. So I introduced him. He's a nice guy. We'll make a deal. But here's the best: So the European nation has been ripping us off for years. We're losing $150 billion plus every year for many years. It was formed to screw the United States. So Mexico, I finished. Canada, I finished. Great deals, by the way. Nobody can even believe it.

BW: Look at the world—

TRUMP: No, no, I made all these deals, but nobody wants to talk about them!

BW: Okay, well, you know I—

TRUMP: I created the greatest economy in the history of our country! And it was announced last night. They talked about the impeachment bullshit, which is going nowhere. They talked about the impeachment horseshit for 97 percent of the time. I hope your wife isn't on, because I don't want to have her hear. Because I know her ears must be very beautiful and very—she doesn't hear bad language. But they talk about the impeachment thing 95, 96 percent of the time. They talk about the economy less than one percent, and it's the greatest economy in the history of the country.

COMMENTARY: While Trump talks like the chief financial officer, he is vastly exaggerating the situation. The economy was doing well, but it was not the best in the history of the United States.

Unemployment had fallen to near historic lows, but growth in Gross Domestic Product remained low compared to previous presidents. The federal budget deficit also widened during Trump's presidency even before the pandemic.

BW: So how do you feel about impeachment now? Have you talked to Lindsey Graham recently?

TRUMP: I feel very good about it. I think the Republicans are very strong. Strong as they've ever been. I just signed my 187th federal judge. It's a record, 187 judges in less than three years, Bob. And two Supreme Court judges. Never been done before. The only one that has a better percentage is George Washington, because he appointed 100 percent. But my percentage is, you know, like, ridiculous. A hundred and eighty-seven—

BW: And there were a couple of those judges.

TRUMP: I'll end up with—when I get out, I'll probably have more than 50 percent of the federal judges in the country appointed under Trump.

BW: And Lindsey Graham has said that there were a couple of those judges that he himself didn't care for and rejected them. Are you aware of that?

TRUMP: Yeah. And other senators, too. When they don't like them, I don't put them in. You know, I don't want—

BW: Cause that's his committee, and they—

TRUMP: Yeah, no, if Lindsey and other people don't like them, I don't put them in. You know why? Why do we want to buck the system, you know? They don't like them because they may be, in some cases they're not conservative or they don't believe or they came out with a couple of bad decisions on something. So—

BW: And it's interesting. Lindsey Graham is worried that the judiciary is going to become too partisan. Do you agree with that? Do you worry about that?

TRUMP: Well, it depends. Yeah, it's very partisan right now, basically. It's always a party vote. I mean, look, the whole country right now is a partisan vote. Look at the seven articles that they put up. It's been 53 to 47 all seven times, right?

BW: Yeah, except once Susan Collins changed.

TRUMP: Yeah, on one unimportant one. No, we're doing well on that. It's a hoax. Schiff is a—you know. Can you believe that guy? I think he's having a nervous breakdown. I thought his presentation was so bad. But they get out there right away: oh, he was great, he was great. You know, it's spin. Right? It's spin. Like Ronald Reagan, they used to get out and spin. He was great. He was great. Oh, really? Great.

BW: So now do you see this story about the Saudis intercepting Jeff Bezos's phone?

TRUMP: Yeah.

BW: Now what do you—

TRUMP: I just read it. I don't know anything about it. I mean, I just don't know.

BW: I mean, that's extraordinary.

TRUMP: Well, you know. I'm not a Bezos fan. I think he stinks.

BW: I know you're not. Elsa and I are. We've known him for 20 years. So—

TRUMP: You know what I did with him? We had dinner, like, six months ago, with the top four guys. You know, all your killers.

BW: Yes, right. You had them all.

TRUMP: I had them all. Probably seven, eight months ago, at the White House. It was a great dinner. Everybody had a great time. Couldn't have been better. And then at the end I pull Jeff aside. I said, you know, Jeff, you don't have to treat me good. But just treat me fairly. When I do something great, say it's great. When I do something good, say it's good. And when I do

something bad, knock the hell out of me. He
said, oh, I never get involved. I said, what do
you mean you don't get involved? You're losing
$250 million a year, of course you get involved.
And I see the relationship you have with these
guys. I said, you're practically holding hands. He
said, well, no, I never get involved.

BW: Mr. President, that's true. It really is.

TRUMP: Hard to believe.

BW: Yeah. Well, I mean—

TRUMP: Well, if I really knew it was true, I'd treat him
much differently. Because I haven't been very nice
to him, you know. But if I really felt—if I really
believed it was true. It's just hard for me. Maybe
it's a different personality. But it's hard for me to
believe that he buys *The Washington Post*—they
treat me so badly. Like these idiots that wrote the
book. Phil Rucker and "the Le-ong" [Leonnig],
the other one.

BW: I know you're—I haven't read it yet.

TRUMP: No, no, but think of this. Think of this. It's
not leaks, by the way. There might have been a
couple. You know it's not leaks. It's fiction. They
make up stories. Let's see, what can we do to
demean? So how about—

BW: Well, we've talked about this.

TRUMP: —how about the one—Bob, you know me—

BW: You know, I know them. To the best of my
knowledge they don't make up stories.

TRUMP: Oh, they do.

BW: They have sources—

TRUMP: Phil Rucker is a bad guy. He's a sleazebag. But
listen, Bob, Pearl Harbor. Oh. What's Pearl
Harbor? What's—I have the movies memorized
from the time I'm a kid. Like, the greatest movies
ever. You know, the original Pearl Harbors are
better than the modern ones that look like they
were done by a computer. I mean, can you
imagine? I studied Pearl Harbor. I talk about it all

the time with Abe. I talk about kamikaze pilots. I talk about all that stuff. They write in there that I wanted to know what exactly is Pearl Harbor. Now you know how insulting that is to me? It's so false. They made it up. That's not a leak, Bob. That's they made it up.

BW: Well, I'm going to dispute you on that.

TRUMP: All right. That's okay. I don't mind. Look, it's nice [crosstalk]—

BW: Because I know them, and if they ever made up something—

TRUMP: Tell Phil Rucker he's a sleazebucket. I know him well. He never writes good. Look, look, I kill al-Baghdadi and they make him into a great religious [unintelligible audio] hero.

BW: No, no. Everyone knows that had to be done. Bezos and the people at the Post are upset about the Khashoggi killing. And that is one of the most gruesome things.

TRUMP: Yeah.

BW: I mean, you yourself have said.

COMMENTARY: Jamal Khashoggi was a Saudi-born, U.S.-based journalist and dissident who was brutally murdered in the Saudi Consulate in Turkey in 2018. The CIA said in an assessment that Saudi crown prince Mohammed bin Salman, MBS, ordered the assassination. At the time of his death, Khashoggi was a contributing columnist for The Washington Post.

TRUMP: But Iran is killing 36 people a day, so—

BW: I know, but that's our guy. And how do you come out on MBS's role in the Khashoggi killing? Because that's important.

TRUMP: Well, I understand what you're saying. And I've gotten involved very much. I know everything about the whole situation. But I also know that—as you know—Saudi Arabia spends $400 billion every couple of years in our country. Millions of jobs. They pay us, you know, I don't know if you know. The troops that were sent over that you probably—they're paying for it. You know, they're paying. It's no longer freebies, stupid freebies, given to the richest countries in the world that wouldn't be there if it wasn't for us. So I understand it very, very well.

BW: So what happened, sir?

TRUMP: I saved his ass. That's what happened.

BW: You saved whose ass?

TRUMP: MBS.

BW: Yeah. By?

TRUMP: They were coming down on him very strongly. But I was able to get Congress to leave him alone. And it wasn't easy, because that was a hot subject at the time.

BW: How were you able to do that?

TRUMP: Well, I was able to get them to stop. They were going after the country. They didn't want to trade with them. I said, oh, I see, good. Let them trade with Russia instead. Let them buy a thousand planes from Russia instead of the United States. Right? Let them go to China and buy all of their military equipment instead of the United States. I said, fellas, you've got to be smart. And over a period—You know, I'm very friendly with those guys.

BW: Which guys? The Saudis?

TRUMP: Congress. I'm very friendly with Congress. Look, I won 195 to nothing in the House. And as you probably hear, I'm doing—I have a very good relationship with the senators, too. I'm a relationship person, believe it or not.

COMMENTARY: The 195 to nothing refers to the total Republicans who voted against impeaching him.

BW: No, I—

TRUMP: By the way, the things I told you, like with

Ethiopia? I'm not getting a Nobel Prize. Obama got one in the third week he was president. He didn't even know what the hell he got it for.

BW: Okay. I'm going to scope all that out. I'm going to be over there, banging on the door of Ambassador O'Brien and Matt Pottinger and say, let's go through this.

TRUMP: Okay, good.

BW: Good.

TRUMP: I could give you ten other things. North Korea. I stopped a war. I stopped a war.

BW: Listen, I've got all the letters—

TRUMP: I'm having a fight—I'm having fights with South Korea, Bob, because look, I said, you got to pay. They hadn't paid. They don't pay. And so I said, you've got to pay. With respect, you've got to pay. And they agreed to pay $500 million a year to the United States of America. I said, that's not enough. You've got to pay more.

BW: I know. You want—[laughter]

TRUMP: No, but isn't that better than a guy that just let this country go to hell?

BW: Well, you know, and the Pentagon tells you, look, we can't bring all of our troops home from South Korea. What, 32,000 of them? Where are we going to put them?

TRUMP: Well, there's truth to that. You know why? Because when I was a great real estate developer, and I was great, every week I'd get a listing for an Army base or a military base. I mean, they sold these bases. We used to have hundreds more bases. I used to get listings all the time of military bases. Great properties, by the way, many of them. You know, some were in the ocean. Some were legendary properties.

BW: Let me go back to MBS and Saudi Arabia. What did you say to him?

TRUMP: Look. To me he will always say that he didn't

	do it. He says that to everybody, and frankly I'm happy that he says that. But he will say that to you, he will say that to Congress, and he will say that to everybody. He's never said he did it.
BW:	Do you believe that he did it?
TRUMP:	No, he says that he didn't do it.
BW:	I know, but do you really believe—
TRUMP:	Well, I don't want to get into that. It's not my— but he says very strongly that he didn't do it.
BW:	Okay, but that's—
TRUMP:	You know. Bob, they spend $400 billion over a fairly short period of time. And you know, they're in the Middle East. They're one of the few people that we have that relationship—you know, they're big. Because of their religious monuments, you know, they have the real power. They have the oil, but they also have the great monuments for religion. You know that, right? For that religion.
BW:	Yes. And they—Listen, all those countries are vulnerable unless we provide protection.
TRUMP:	They wouldn't last a week if we're not there, and they know it.
BW:	From my reporting, sir, I think Iran is afraid of what the U.S. military could do to their oil refineries.
TRUMP:	Only lately. Only lately. Only since I'm here. They weren't afraid of Obama at all. They treated him like garbage.
BW:	Yeah. But, I mean, they're vulnerable. You could take them out—
TRUMP:	No, no, they're very concerned with me. And you know what? They better be. . . . So anyway. No, they want to make a deal. I think they might want to wait until after the election. Don't forget, everybody said China was going to wait until after the election. China went out, hired the best pollsters in the country, and they said

Trump's going to win in a landslide. They said, might as well get it over with. Right? Anyway, so—

BW: So and the last question is—you're really kind to spend some time doing this—

TRUMP: Okay. I find you very interesting, actually.

BW: Well, but President Xi of China, what's his personality and what's your strategy for dealing with him?

TRUMP: Okay. Well, first of all, his personality is incredible. His strength, his mental and physical strength, is great. He's very, very smart. He's very cunning. I get along with him fantastically well. We had some rough patches during this time, because I walked out of a former meeting. I don't think that's ever happened to him. It happened to Kim Jong Un also. Nobody ever walked out of a meeting. He didn't know what it meant. I said, listen, you're not ready to make a deal. I'm leaving.

BW: I know.

TRUMP: So my relationship with Chairman Xi is great. It was strained very much during the deal. We heard China—you know, China's had the worst year they've had in 67 years.

COMMENTARY: Publicly he had said 27, 52, 54, and 35, all in the space of a few months.

TRUMP: We've gone way up, and we've gone trillions of dollars up, and they've gone trillions of dollars down. So we're now the number one country by far. If Hillary would've gotten elected, we would've been long the number two. Long. We would've gone way, way, way down because of the whole thing with regulations and taxes and everything else. It was a disaster. But our country is rocking now like it hasn't rocked—

BW: Okay, so how do you deal with Xi? Because he wants China to be number one, as you know.

TRUMP: Well, I said one thing. So he's got China '25. You know China '25.

BW: Yes, sure.

TRUMP: I said that's very insulting to me. He said, but what does that mean, what does that mean?

BW: What'd he say?

TRUMP: I said, when you say China '25, that means you want to be number one in '25. Well, that's very insulting to me that you would say that. Because I'm running things here, and I want to be number one, too. I don't want you to say China '25. Because that means too many bad things. I don't like it.

COMMENTARY: President Xi's ambition was to make China the world's largest economy by 2025.

BW: So what'd he say?

TRUMP: By the way, you know what he did?

BW: What?

TRUMP: Didn't say another word. It disappeared.

BW: Really?

TRUMP: Yup. Disappeared. Remember that? It was a big thing. China '25.

BW: Yeah, but they're still working on it.

TRUMP: Oh, look, look. Their ambition is unbelievable. I said, take your wife out to dinner. Just relax.

COMMENTARY: I wondered how President Xi had responded to that.

BW: Elsa, say hello.

TRUMP: So I look forward to meeting you! Come over and say hello to us sometime. Come to a meeting.

WALSH: [*laughs*] Me?

TRUMP: Yes!

BW:	We will do that.
TRUMP:	I'm such a fan of your husband. So your husband, as I'm sure you know, but your husband was in my office in Trump Tower 25 years ago. Like, I don't know.
BW:	Yeah . . . going to do that book.
WALSH:	I remember when he went.
TRUMP:	He was over—he was in my office. He was going to do a book. And I was so honored, because I think the world of him. Not the other one, the other guy—I called him the lightweight, although he's actually the heavyweight in another way. But he was the lightweight. Mentally the lightweight. But he was going to do a book. I remember sitting around the table with you in my office. And that would've been a great honor, but somehow that didn't happen. And that's fine. But then—Bob, who would've thought—
BW:	I said, why would we do a book on—this is this New York real estate developer.
TRUMP:	Right.
BW:	And we try to write about politics and presidents.
TRUMP:	Well, maybe you were going to do one when we sat in the hotel that I was building down the road, right, which turned out to be very successful. You were going to do one then. Remember we sat there?

COMMENTARY: He is talking about when Robert Costa and I interviewed him three and a half years earlier, in 2016.

TRUMP:	But that one I was uncomfortable with because it was too soon. I mean, I just got in. And I hadn't been able to have the successes. You know, if you look at all the things we've got completed now, it's incredible. Including, by the way, making *The New York Times* and *Washington Post* and cable television successful. Because they were all going

down the tubes. But they'll be gone. When I
leave, they're all going down. They're going to be
gone.

BW: You know, I hope that's not the case.

TRUMP: Well, I hope so, but it's going to be the case.

BW: Because I think it's really important that we have
the First Amendment. You know that. I'm not—

TRUMP: You know that Sulzberger came to see me about
six months ago.

BW: Yes. You—

TRUMP: I said, okay, so you want me to stop saying "fake
news." Because that was a term I came up with,
and now it's almost a—it's in the vocabulary,
right? I said, so you want me to stop saying that?
No, no, no. I don't care about that. I want you
to stop saying that the media is the enemy of the
people. It's killing us. I said, but you are the enemy
of the people, because you're so dishonest. And he
goes no, no, no.

COMMENTARY: Sulzburger has publicly confirmed the meeting
with Trump and said in a statement, "I warned that this inflammatory
language is contributing to a rise in threats against journalists and will
lead to violence." Sulzburger added: "I implored him to reconsider
his broader attacks on journalism, which I believe are dangerous and
harmful to our country."

TRUMP: And my biggest thing is, who is worse? Who's
more dishonest? *The Washington Post*, which I
know you hate to hear that, but—*The New York
Times* or *The Washington Post*? And I'm surprised.
In one way I'm happy about it, but I don't know.
I find—maybe you don't know. Hard to believe
that Jeff Bezos is not controlling what's happening
at the—

BW: Listen, I know those people. Elsa and I have
known Bezos for 20 years.

TRUMP: That'll be a competitive business someday,

though. Because if you look at what's happening with Walmart and a lot of the great chains, they're all going that way.

BW: Okay. Now, the biggest thing you could do for me—

TRUMP: So, Bob, let me ask you—so you think that—why don't you tell the *Washington Post* guys, treat Trump fair? What's wrong with having low taxes, a great military—you know, all the different things. I don't get it. Someday they'll explain that, because it's ridiculous.

BW: Okay, but, sir, the best thing you could do to help me is call in your national security adviser, O'Brien, and Matt Pottinger tomorrow and tell them we've gone through these lists of things that you've done, like with el-Sisi and Egypt and so forth. And that I want to get chapter and verse on them.

TRUMP: You may want to speak to el-Sisi, which he'll do if I ask him to.

BW: Yeah, sure. I'd love to.

COMMENTARY: My strategy here was to get word out around the White House and the administration that I was visiting often and talking regularly to Trump and to his senior officials. I wanted to shake the trees and open as many doors as possible so his staff would talk more to me.

TRUMP: Why don't you give me a list of the people you'd like to speak to. I'll call them and say fine. Is that okay? Like el-Sisi, as an example.

BW: Yes.

TRUMP: Oh, here's the funny thing. So the head of—I shouldn't really say it, but let's just say one of the countries that we just talked about is going to get the Nobel Prize. You know the dam, right? You know the dam we're talking about?

BW: Yeah.

TRUMP:	So the head of, frankly, Ethiopia—So the head of Ethiopia is getting the Nobel Prize. It was just announced.
BW:	Yes, he did. Yeah.
TRUMP:	And without me, there'd be a war. Okay? I get nothing. I get nothing. But that's okay, Bob.

COMMENTARY: Ethiopia's prime minister was awarded the Nobel Peace Prize in 2019 for his peace deal with Eritrea.

BW:	I need more information—
TRUMP:	Do me a favor. If you guys could create a list— come in. I'd love to say hello to your wife. Come in and say hello, the Oval Office.
BW:	Okay. But—
TRUMP:	I would love that.
BW:	—the more I need—I need your side and Pompeo, I want to talk to him. And all of the people at the White House. And we're going to go through and we're going to find out—if you've read any of my books on Bush or Obama or Clinton and so forth, and they're very detailed. This is what happened. This was the debate. This was the strategy.
TRUMP:	I know. Okay. I'll do it. Nobody's done what I've done, Bob. Tell you what, you mentioned Obama. Ninety percent of the things he's done, I've taken apart. And so you tell me. He left me 142 judges, Bob. Nobody would believe it. If you leave one, you know, they're considered gold.

COMMENTARY: Republicans had controlled the Senate for the last two years of Obama's presidency, making it very difficult, if not impossible, for Obama to get judicial appointments approved.

| TRUMP: | A hundred and forty-two judges. And Bush didn't know what he was doing. So you come in, we'll spend some time. We'll see if we can actually get a fair book. |

BW:	Great. I'll call Molly tomorrow and we'll get—
TRUMP:	Good. Yeah. Tell Molly I said, and she'll see me. We'll do that. Bring me lists. Okay?
BW:	Will do, sir. Thank you. Have a good evening.
TRUMP:	Okay, you both take care of yourselves. Have a good night. I'll see you.
WALSH:	Bye.
TRUMP:	So long. Bye.

[*Recording ends*]

Phone call
February 7, 2020

TRUMP:	When you're running a country, it's full of surprises. There's dynamite behind every door, and—
BW:	Huh.
TRUMP:	—you want to say good. But then something happens.

COMMENTARY: On February 5th the Senate acquitted Trump on two articles of impeachment. Chief Justice Roberts, who was presiding at Trump's impeachment trial, announced the verdict to the Senate and to the country:

ROBERTS:	*It is therefore ordered and adjudged that the said Donald John Trump be and he is hereby acquitted of the charges in said articles.*

The vote was 52 to 48 on abuse of power and 53 to 47 on obstruction of Congress. Senator Mitt Romney of Utah was the sole Republican who voted to convict.

Two days later, Trump won a lawsuit about whether he had profited illegally from foreign and domestic officials who stayed at his DC hotel and other businesses. As he left the White House, Trump stood in front of reporters waving a copy of the ruling:

TRUMP:	*We just won the big emoluments case. It just came out a few minutes ago so I'll be*

> *reading it on the helicopter, but it was a*
> *total win.*

   Later that day, Trump called me out of the blue at home around
9 p.m. It was Friday, February 7th. I was watching the televised Democratic debate among the party's possible presidential candidates,
including Biden. I expected Trump would be in a good mood.

OPERATOR:	Mr. Woodward, the President.
TRUMP:	Hi, Bob.
BW:	President Trump, how are you?
TRUMP:	How are you? Lindsey said, give you a call. I just spoke to a couple of people. I said I just came back from two speeches, and I said I got to call the man. What's going on? You're doing okay.
BW:	Well, I am. I was watching the Democratic debate. I thought you would be watching.
TRUMP:	I am. I just turned it on. I have Tivo—the world's greatest invention. So, ah, it does give you a little leeway, right, to put it mildly. But no, I'm watch—I just watched the very beginning of it. It's boring as hell, but I gotta—it's almost like an obligation to watch; it's called debate prep.
BW:	Well, what I'm trying to do, and I'm turning my recorder on here as I always do just so I have a good—I make sure I get everything right.
TRUMP:	Ok.
BW:	I'm trying to focus on all the policies—
TRUMP:	Right.
BW:	—because I think in the end, by September or October, that's what people are going to be voting on.
TRUMP:	Could be. No, I think they're going to be voting on a lot of things, including the economy, which is phenomenal. We've had a lot of victories this week [*laughing*], it's a lot. We've had a lotta good stuff happen.
BW:	But you've made a lot of news.

TRUMP: Yup.

BW: How do you feel about all that now?

COMMENTARY: I am asking about the State of the Union address on
February 4th, three days before this interview.

TRUMP: Good. I think good. It's, ah . . . We had a great
                speech. Some people thought it was a phenomenal
                speech. Got very good reviews. For the most
                part, I got tremendous reviews. You saw that. The
                one . . . the State of the Union. Good day, won a
                big court case today. Big one in the DC Circuit.

BW: I saw that.

TRUMP: Lotta, lotta things—went to North Carolina today
                to—good job. And then I came back, and I just
                spoke before the governors of the country, the
                governors, and they come to the White House on
                Sunday night, you know, for the big governors'
                deal. The Governors Ball, I think they call it.

BW: What I'm trying to do is explain to people what
                you've done and what you're doing on—

TRUMP: Okay.

BW: —North Korea, China, the Middle East, Russia,
                the economy, health care. And I want to—

TRUMP: That's good.

BW: And let me be direct with you. There are people
                over there at the White House who are helping
                me. Some are dragging their feet. I'm not sure—

TRUMP: Some don't know the answers because I don't tell
                everybody what I want to do. For good reason. I
                don't tell everybody. You know, I have people that
                work here that I don't tell them what I want to
                do. It depends. Who are you speaking to?

BW: Ambassador O'Brien, Matt Pottinger, people on
                the NSC staff—

TRUMP: Some of them don't know, and some of them
                don't know what they're supposed to be saying in
                terms of, you know, how much are we supposed

	to be telling one of the great writers of all time, right?
BW:	Well, I hope everything—
TRUMP:	Yeah, well—
BW:	—and as you and I have talked, it's very important—
TRUMP:	I mean, you can't give away your strategy. Like, if I have a certain military concept or a strategy, I can't tell you what that strategy is because when you write it, it's like Bolton. You know, Bolton can't do a book and, you know, he leaves the White House and he does a book. You can't do that kind of stuff.

COMMENTARY: John Bolton, Trump's national security adviser for 18 months in 2018 and 2019, finally published a book, *The Room Where It Happened*, which really was an exposé of Trump's mishandling of foreign policy.

BW:	But I want to look back. Also, you've had three years of policy and I want to explain it to people in detail—
TRUMP:	Tremendous success. We're down low with the troops in Afghanistan—out of Syria other than we kept the oil. You know, I kept the oil, by the way. I hope you know that.

COMMENTARY: Trump publicly has made this claim many times that he "kept the oil." Not true: The State Department downplayed this language completely, clarifying that U.S. forces were fighting to secure the oil fields against ISIS, but they were not there to extract the oil. If the U.S. were to take oil without permission from the government of those countries, legal experts on all sides said it would amount to pillaging—which is a war crime under international law.

Trump was obsessed with getting the natural resources from other countries, including Afghanistan.

In my first book on Trump, *Fear*, I described how Trump was infuriated because he thought the Chinese were getting copper out of

Afghanistan while the U.S. was sitting idly by on its ass. His aides
said they were running all these decisions through a National Security
Council process. "I don't need it done through a fucking process!"
Trump yelled. "I need you guys to go in there and get this stuff. It's
free!"

BW:	So what's the biggest economic issue you think people are going to be voting on at the end of the year?
TRUMP:	Well, I think the economy, just the economy. You know, the issue is the economy. There are lots of little things that go into making a great economy. But when you add it all up, it's going to be THE economy.
BW:	OK? What are those little things, if I may ask? Because, well, that's what people are connecting to. I mean—
TRUMP:	The trade deals are the biggest thing. We're going to be taking in . . . by the time the election comes around . . . Now, we got a little bit of an interesting setback with the virus going in China, you know, because we signed this massive China deal. But right now they are very focused on that. And I think that goes away in two months with the heat. You know, as it gets hotter—
BW:	I saw that, yes.
TRUMP:	—that tends to kill the virus. So, you know, you hope. But so that should be in good shape. I spoke to President Xi last night. We had a great talk for a long time.
BW:	Yes, now tell me about that. What was on his mind—
TRUMP:	I have a good relationship with him, actually. I have, ah—
BW:	Though you've been tough on him at times, too.
TRUMP:	Oh yeah, we've had some arguments, but we have a good relationship. I think we like each other . . . a lot. I think I like, you know, most of the leaders

I get along with very well. People wouldn't
understand that, and they respect this country
again. They didn't respect us. They were taking
advantage of us. That includes our allies.

BW: And so what was President Xi saying yesterday?

TRUMP: Well, we were talking mostly about the, ah, the
virus, and I think he's going to have it in good
shape. But, you know, it's a very tricky situation.

BW: Indeed it is.

TRUMP: It goes—it goes through air, Bob. That's always
tougher than the touch. You know, the touch. You
don't have to touch things, right, but the air, you
just breathe the air and that's how it's passed. And
so that's a very tricky one. That's a very delicate
one. It's also more deadly than your, you know,
your, even your strenuous flus. People don't
realize we lose 25,000 to 30,000 people a year
here. Who would ever think that, right?

BW: I know. What are you able to do—

TRUMP: It's pretty amazing. And then I say, well, is that
the same thing? [*crosstalk*] This is more deadly.
This is five per, you know, this is five percent
versus one percent and less than one percent. You
know, so this is deadly stuff. And—but he's got
it. I think he's going to do a good job. He built,
you know, a number of hospitals in record-setting
time. They know what they're doing. They're
very . . . they're very organized. And we'll see.
We're working with them. We're sending them
things, you know, in terms of equipment and lots
of other things. And the relationship is very good,
much better than before, you know, before it was
strained because of the deal, but before that they
were just taken advantage of, you know, like, if
you go back to Obama, Bush, and every other,
you know, and everybody else.

BW: I want to make it clear what I'm trying to do. You
and I talked about this in December. What are

people thinking? They're saying: ah, what's the next stage of good?

TRUMP: Well, in December, they said I'll never be able to get a great deal or a deal with China. And not only did I make a deal, I made a great deal. It's a great deal for this country. It's a great deal.

BW: And I want to get exactly how it worked.

TRUMP: Well, I mean, I got it done. I got it done. How it worked is that I told people that this is the deal and you got to sign it.

BW: I understand that, Mr. President, people are going to say, what's in this vote for me, right? Don't you think—

TRUMP: What's in what vote? You mean the vote of the president?

BW: No, when they vote in November—

TRUMP: November 3rd, okay.

BW: [crosstalk] And they're going to say, what's in this for me?

TRUMP: I think when they see that kind of—Well, first of all, look at the numbers—225,000 people today, far higher than anticipated by—

BW: Understand, understand.

TRUMP: —you know, most of these great geniuses.

BW: And I want to explain how you got there. And then I want to look forward and tell people in a comprehensive way, this is what Trump will do for you. This is what whoever [static noise] is going to be on the other side. It might be Nancy Pelosi who will be running against you.

TRUMP: Oh, I don't know. I think she's a highly overrated person. I think she's highly overrated. No, she's given us 10 points. Yeah. Get me something. Yeah [speaking to someone else], she's highly overrated. Look, we kicked her ass, and she's terrible. She's—she doesn't know what she's doing. I think they'll overthrow her

	eventually. Hey, my polls went up 10 points, Bob. You saw it—
BW:	I've seen that you're—
TRUMP:	I've got the highest numbers now—
BW:	And people are going to say, what's in an extension of the Trump presidency for me?
TRUMP:	—more success, more safety, great military. I mean, look, I've rebuilt the military. I've rebuilt our police forces. I've helped our police forces. They were getting drained; our military was depleted. I've done all of these things. And as far as women are concerned, women want safety. Watch how well I do with the women vote. I see that the rallies—I go to a rally, there's Women for Trump signs all over the place. Same thing they did last time, Bob. Remember last time? Oh, the women . . . ! I did great with the women. I'm doing record-setting African American numbers. Now let's see what happens. But, you know, we have the best economy. We have all these great numbers. And if you look at the polls, you see polls that are in the 30s, nobody's ever been in the 30s. A Republican.
BW:	Understand. And the question is, what's the plan for the next eight to 10 months?
TRUMP:	Just do well, do well, run the country well, Look—
BW:	Help me define well—
TRUMP:	When you're running a country, it's full of surprises. There's dynamite behind every door, and—
BW:	Huh.
TRUMP:	—you want to say good. But then something happens, something happens. Boeing happens, as an example. Boeing was the greatest company in the world, and all of a sudden it has a big, big misstep and it hurts the country. General Motors goes out on strike. They shouldn't have gone, they should have been able to work that out,

	but they couldn't do it. They go out on strike. Hundreds of thousands of people aren't working and, you know, all of this stuff happens, Bob. But it happens. But you have to do something with it, and you have to make it good.
BW:	Understand that. But you can still have a plan and a strategy.
TRUMP:	Oh, I have so many plans. I have military plans. I have . . . you know, the vets? I got Veterans Choice passed, Bob. But you know what, Bob? Here's the story. Look, I left early for North Carolina. I made two speeches. I got back at seven o'clock and I said, good, I'll go home now. It's, you know, enough. And they said, sir, no, you have to go to the big auditorium where you have the governors of the United States and many of their guests and make a speech. I said, oh, that's great. That's great. I just came in three minutes ago. I just wanted to call you and say hello, I didn't really want to do a whole big interview, to be honest.
BW:	[*crosstalk*] Oh, you're kind, I appreciate that— And I'm pressing on. I need your help.
TRUMP:	OK, no you and I will meet? Let's meet where I can give you the proper time.
BW:	OK, good.
TRUMP:	Just came in, I've got, like, 20 calls. And on top of it, I didn't know I was supposed to make a speech tonight and I did. I did a nice job. You would have been proud of me, but I had the governors of the country and over at some big auditorium. And so I just did that. So I just got in. But we'll meet sometime soon. When do you want to meet, Bob?
BW:	Good, great. And what you need—you could help me with, sir, is who were the key people?—
TRUMP:	OK.
BW:	—I need to talk to. I need to talk to Ambassador O'Brien.
TRUMP:	Yeah.

BW:	You see what I want to do? I don't want somebody to pick up this book when it comes out and say, well, I don't know what's in it for me.
TRUMP:	When are you coming out? What's your date for this?
BW:	You know, September or October right before the election, to say, here's . . . here's the story.
TRUMP:	Good, Bob. I like it. I have great confidence in you. I'll get some—
BW:	I'm going to start pushing the buttons on those Cabinet Office—
TRUMP:	—because nobody else can do what I do. Nobody else can do. You saw the letters from the gentleman. OK, you saw that; nobody else has that.
BW:	That's only—
TRUMP:	They couldn't even talk to them on the phone. You know, it's a hermit kingdom. Nobody could speak to him on the phone. Remember, I said, did you ever hear of Elton John? No, no, I didn't. You know, it's a hermit kingdom, truly?
BW:	Yes. What's the status of that relationship with Kim?
TRUMP:	Well, it's fine, you haven't seen anything, you know, you kept hearing about a Christmas present, you haven't seen that yet, have you?
BW:	No, maybe it'll be—
TRUMP:	It's fine, it's fine. It's better than being in war. If we had Obama, we would have been at war— and it would have been a bad war, too, you know, would have been a rough war. We gave him nothing, other than I gave him a couple of meetings.
BW:	Those letters, as you know, no one has ever seen them.
TRUMP:	Nobody's ever seen them, except me and you. Most people that work here other than the very top, and even most of them haven't.

BW: I wouldn't give them to Matt Pottinger, but I gave him the list of twenty-nine major letters between you and Kim and Kim and you. If you look at this and you put the chronology together and your tweets and statements from Kim, you see what happened? You see the evolution—

TRUMP: Good.

BW: —of a policy—

TRUMP: And the relationship, the very good relationship in a certain way. You know, it's pretty amazing, actually. But I'll see you sometime shortly. Okay?

BW: Thank you. Okay, thanks. Good evening.

TRUMP: So long, Bob. You, too, Bye.

[*Recording ends*]

COMMENTARY: I had seen a few news reports about the virus in China. China had reported more than 800 deaths from the virus, mostly in the province of Wuhan, home to more than 9 million people. Wuhan had been under strict lockdown for two weeks to stem the outbreak, which later became known as the "2019 novel coronavirus" or COVID-19.

The Centers for Disease Control and Prevention had announced the first confirmed coronavirus case in the U.S. on January 21st. President Trump responded in an interview with CNBC in Davos the following day.

TRUMP: *It's one person coming in from China, and we have it under control. It's going to be just fine.*

In early February, like most Americans I was not focused on the virus. I'd heard no one calling for any change in Americans' behavior other than not traveling to China. There were around 12 confirmed coronavirus cases in the United States and no deaths at that point. The CDC was watching all of this closely. Our nation's top infectious disease expert, Dr. Anthony Fauci, said:

FAUCI: *The risk right now, today, currently, is really relatively low for the American public, but that could change.*

During our phone call, Trump said President Xi knew what he was doing.

TRUMP: He's got it. I think he's going to do a good
                job. He built, you know, a number of hospitals
                in record-setting time. They know what
                they're doing. They're very . . . they're very
                organized.

Like many Americans, I continued to travel around the country, unaware the virus was a threat here. Instead, my reporting was focused on Trump's foreign policy and his dealings with foreign leaders.

The day after this interview, I started trying to get details of his phone call with President Xi, and, preferably, I wanted the full transcript. I had been told by a longtime source that if I heard Trump's private conversations with foreign leaders it would "shake the pillars of the republic."

Going back to the Nixon Tapes or the Trump-Zelensky transcript, I knew that verbatim accounts of a president's conversations have an evidentiary purity that could significantly aid my inquiry.

INTERVIEW 8:
I'm Number One

Phone call, Air Force One
February 19, 2020

TRUMP: There has been no president even close that has
             done what I've done in three years. You know it
             and so does everybody else. Let's see whether or
             not you're willing to write it.

BW: Okay, well . . .

COMMENTARY: I reached President Trump by phone at 1:45 on
Wednesday, February 19th.

OPERATOR: Mr. Woodward, you're connected to the Air Force
             One operator.

BW: How are you?

SECOND OPERATOR: Great, sir. One moment for President Trump.

BW: Thank you.

COMMENTARY: He was on Air Force One, flying to Arizona for a
campaign rally. It was ten months before the election. The coronavirus
remained no more than a sidebar in everyday life, national news, and
my own reporting.

I was fully focused on getting the full story of Trump's foreign policy decisions: North Korea, Russia, China, Afghanistan, and Iran in
particular. I wanted to know what was going through the president's
mind when he was making these decisions. What did it mean for the
United States' role in the world? What did it mean for our national
security when the president shunned allies and wrote personal letters

to dictators? This was the danger scenario I was focused on for the United States at this moment.

We didn't have a great phone connection during this call. It's clear that Trump can't hear me very well. He talks over me . . . more than usual.

BW:	Hello?
SECOND OPERATOR:	Go ahead, Mr. President. You are connected.
TRUMP:	Hi, Bob!
BW:	Sir, how are you?
TRUMP:	Hi.
BW:	Good.
TRUMP:	I'm good. I'm on the plane. I'm going to Arizona. We gave them about two days' notice. And we have 30,000 people lined up to see a speech tonight. I'm going to a fundraiser first and then a speech I give tonight. And tremendous crowd in Arizona, like beyond. And then tomorrow I do the same thing in Las Vegas. I go tonight to Las Vegas, and I do the same thing in Las Vegas. Then I come home. I told Jared to speak to you, and I believe he has.
BW:	Yes. I—
TRUMP:	And I just told him a little while ago that if you would do me a favor, Jared, and coordinate a little bit with Bob so that Bob can speak to anybody he wants to, Jared will handle it. Very capable guy, Jared. You can't get people like this.
BW:	We talked once.
TRUMP:	One smart cookie.
BW:	I'm scheduled to see him—
TRUMP:	If you could deal with Jared a little bit. See me whenever you want. Lindsey Graham just walked into the room. The room is Air Force One, so—[*laughter*] we're flying over to Arizona from Nevada. But if you could, see me any time you want, but if you could deal with Jared, Jared's got a whole list of whatever you need and people that you could speak to and everything good.

BW:	That's great. I was talking to—
TRUMP:	And if you could also, because I gave you access to those letters that nobody else has ever seen, nobody else, even those that were written. If you could treat those with great respect.
BW:	I appreciate that. And I talked to Matt Pottinger at length yesterday. We're going to talk again.
TRUMP:	Right. Good.
BW:	And what I have asked him to check with you on is I would like to get the notes of your meetings with Chairman Kim, because that's where the rubber meets the road, obviously. And I think people—
TRUMP:	Now, I didn't make notes. It's possibly, somebody did. You know, I had dinner with him. I met with him, you know, on three occasions. But I had dinner with him, a long, beautiful dinner with him. I had lunches with him and stuff. But I don't have guys sitting there writing notes.
BW:	Okay. Well—
TRUMP:	Only Bolton would write notes. He's, you know, a schmuck. And Chairman Kim didn't want Bolton at the meeting. Chairman Kim said, I cannot allow him to be at the meeting. Because he was the one—I told you the story. When he made the statement about "Libyan model," that really set us back.
BW:	Right. Well, and of course—
TRUMP:	And Chairman Kim would not allow him in the same room with us.
BW:	And Bolton was—
TRUMP:	He'll probably have notes anyway, because, you know, make them up. [*laughs*]
BW:	—calling for regime change.
TRUMP:	Anyway—
BW:	Well, I appreciate that.
TRUMP:	Bob, it could be that somebody has notes. I'll tell

	you that. I'm sorry, excuse me, go ahead, Bob, what did you say?
BW:	Yes. No, I would love to see those notes. Matt said he thinks that he had some and maybe there's some officially.
TRUMP:	Okay, good. [*to someone else*] Would you tell Matt Pottinger, would you tell Matt to speak to Bob and to tell him about the meetings, and if he's got some notes he can tell him pretty much what he has to tell him about the meetings that we had with Chairman Kim? [*to BW*] I mean, the third meeting he offered us to close one of his big nuclear sites. And I said, no, you're not ready to make a deal.
BW:	Yes. Right, I know—
TRUMP:	And I respectfully left.
BW:	I mean, that's—
TRUMP:	But that was the third meeting. Basically there were two meetings and then we had a meeting at the line. You know, the line that nobody ever crossed [*mumbles*] until I crossed it.
BW:	Yes. That's right. That's right. Well, good. I'd love to get those, and I'm—
TRUMP:	Anyway. Jared will work—[*to someone else*] and tell Matt Pottinger to work with Bob. And that will be fine. He can see me if he'd like. [*to BW*] And, Bob, I'm available when you need me. I'm pretty busy, to tell you the truth, but I'm available.
BW:	Okay. What I want to do is, I want not to waste your time. I want to get lined up what I can find from other people and from notes, and as you know, people keep diaries—
TRUMP:	Good.
BW:	And then come to you and say—
TRUMP:	Good.
BW:	—okay, here's what I've got. Basically the question is, what was going through your mind as

	you said what you said or made whatever decision
	it was on a range of issues—
TRUMP:	Okay.
BW:	—in foreign policy, China, North Korea, Russia—
TRUMP:	Fine. You let me know when you're ready. We'll
	set aside some time.

COMMENTARY: I was convinced at the time the important story was Trump's relations with those countries.

TRUMP:	Look, we've done a great job, Bob. Now in the
	meantime, there's no war with North Korea.
BW:	I've noticed that.
TRUMP:	Iran is behaving nicely. We'll see if that continues.
	It might not. You know, it might not. I'm a very—
	I'm like you. We get it. We get the world, okay?
BW:	I'm going to turn my recorder on—
TRUMP:	Soleimani was a very big event.

COMMENTARY: Trump is referring to his decision to have the head of the Iranian Quds Force killed in a drone strike on January 3rd.

TRUMP:	The head of Pakistan, the prime minister of
	Pakistan, Khan, said *the* biggest event of his
	lifetime. I had no idea. Other people have said the
	same thing: it was an earth-shattering event.
BW:	So what's this with Attorney General Barr going
	on now? I know—
TRUMP:	It's a false rumor, false statement. It's a false
	statement. Well, he made the statement about
	Twitter. It just feels like—it's not Twitter, it's
	social media. Because I don't call it Twitter, I call
	it social media. Without social media, number
	one, I wouldn't have won, and number two, you
	know, I'm number one on Facebook. Zuckerberg
	came to the White House two weeks ago. Sort of
	a group of people.
BW:	So what's going on between you and the attorney
	general, sir?

TRUMP: Said congratulations, you're number one on Facebook.

BW: This is all for the history—

TRUMP: And I'm number one on Twitter. That's public information. And if I didn't have—so even though they may be against me—maybe they're not—but even though—When you're number one and when you have hundreds of millions of people, whether they're against you or not they still read what you say because you put out a statement. I don't need commercials.

BW: [laughs]

TRUMP: When you're number one, you don't need commercials. And number two is Modi, but he's got 1.5 billion people. I have 350. You know? So it's a little different.

BW: So tell me about the—this is all for the serious history, Mr. President.

TRUMP: Social media—I wouldn't probably be talking to you right now if it weren't for social media.

BW: I understand.

TRUMP: At least not in this capacity.

BW: I understand that.

TRUMP: In Air Force One, beautifully riding to the great state of Arizona. You know? I wouldn't be talking to you, probably. So it's very important.

BW: Sir, what's—

TRUMP: It's just fake news that he's quitting.

COMMENTARY: Trump returned to my question about Attorney General Barr. Six days earlier, Bill Barr had blasted Trump in a remarkable television interview:

BARR: *Public statements and tweets made about the department, about people in the department, our men and women here, about cases pending in the department, and about judges before whom we have cases make it impossible for me to do my job.*

TRUMP:	Fake news.
BW:	Okay, but what did he say to you—
TRUMP:	You know, someday—
BW:	I mean, this again is for serious—
TRUMP:	—everybody leaves.
BW:	—history. You know, it's got a lot of people all in a twitter about it, to use that term.
TRUMP:	Good, that's what I like.
BW:	[*laughs*] You like—
TRUMP:	That's what I like. I like that everybody's in a twitter. That's okay with me. Keep them that way.
BW:	Well, it's working—
TRUMP:	In the meantime, I've got great polls. We've got internal polls that we're beating everybody. I put out a statement on that today, I don't know if you saw. The internal polls, we're beating everybody. But the fake news is at it again. They like to put in polls where I'm not.
BW:	Okay, now, sir, anyone who knows the Constitution realizes you as president have authority over every department, including the Justice Department.
TRUMP:	Yep.
BW:	And—
TRUMP:	That's right. Total. And I haven't exercised that authority. I've let people run it.
BW:	Okay—
TRUMP:	I've let people run it. But listen, Bob, just so you know—
BW:	Lots of people think you shouldn't do that. I think if you asked—
TRUMP:	—this was the greatest crime, political crime in the history of our country. They spied on this campaign. The opposite party, in control of the nation, spied on their opponent and their opponent's political campaign. They caused tremendous injustice. They caused tremendous damage. And they destroyed many lives.

BW:	Listen, I've looked at—
TRUMP:	And they got caught.
BW:	I'm looking at that really closely. It's going to be very interesting to see what this U.S. Attorney Durham comes up with.
TRUMP:	Well, let's see what he comes up with. They got caught. And frankly, with all the information that's out there that's public. They got caught. This was a treasonous act. This was a terrible act. And if this were Obama sitting in the seat where I am right now instead of me, these people would've been in jail. For 50 years they would've gone to jail. They would've spent 50 years in jail, meaning they would've died in jail.

COMMENTARY: There was no evidence that Obama spied on Trump's campaign.

BW:	Okay, Mr. President—
TRUMP:	And this is a disgraceful—
BW:	—let me ask you this question while—
TRUMP:	And frankly it's something that should—
BW:	Ask Lindsey Graham what does he—
TRUMP:	—never be allowed to happen in our country again. And should never happen to another president again. They spied on our campaign—
BW:	I know you—
TRUMP:	And after I won—They tried to make it so I couldn't win, and I did. Then after I won, they tried to take me out. And we stopped them.
BW:	I wonder—
TRUMP:	And the biggest, one of the most important things I did was firing the sleazebag named Comey, because if I didn't, all of—
BW:	[laughs] I've heard your views on that six times, sir. The question is, ask Lindsey Graham whether he thinks it's a good idea for you to be saying publicly and get in a fight with the attorney

	general about your authority. Is that a good thing for you to do?
TRUMP:	All I did—no, but see, it's because it's the fake news. They only put the part on, I have the authority. I didn't say that. I said, I have decided not to use it.
BW:	Yes, I saw that—
TRUMP:	But I do want everyone to know that I do have the authority, but I've decided not to use it. They don't show that. They just say I do have the authority. Do you understand?
BW:	I do—
TRUMP:	They cut it up and they slice it up. You don't see the real deal. Anyway, Bob—hey Bob, call me when you're ready. I'm asking Jared to deal with you. There has been no president even close that has done what I've done in three years. You know it and so does everybody else. Let's see whether or not you're willing to write it.
BW:	Okay, well—Jared told me about—
TRUMP:	Jared just walked in. Bob's legit. He wanted to do a book about me 25 years ago, Jared. [*crosstalk*]

COMMENTARY: Earlier in February I had spoken with Jared Kushner, the president's son-in-law, who was often deployed personally by Trump as an out-of-channels special project officer. Kushner's view of the world was a declaration of optimism about Trump, the presidency, and Trump's reelection chances. Kushner said he knew that Trump's constant refrain that the economy had never been better in history was an exaggeration. But the economy is really great, Kushner said. "If you have a good issue, controversy elevates message." When the president says it's the best economy in the world and it's only a good economy, that's enough, Kushner is saying. That is the message that comes through to people.

So that's what Trump wanted me to do here: deliver his message. It didn't matter that it wasn't true.

BW:	Can I talk to—is he there?
TRUMP:	Yes. Can you talk to who? Yeah, Jared. Jared's here. You want him?

BW:	Yes, I'd love to say hello.
TRUMP:	You want Jared? Yeah, here he is. Hold it.
BW:	Okay.
TRUMP:	Take care of yourself, Bob. Say hello to your wife. Okay?
BW:	Okay. Thank you, sir.
TRUMP:	Hold on.
KUSHNER:	Hello?
BW:	Jared, Bob Woodward. How are you?
KUSHNER:	Good. How are you?
BW:	Good. Did you hear what he said? That I'm going to come see you. We've got a date scheduled I think next week.
KUSHNER:	Perfect.
BW:	And then you can help me with some of these other people I want to talk to. Is that—
KUSHNER:	Perfect. Well, what I'll do is I'll make a list of other people. What I heard from the president is basically that I now work for you [*both laugh*], so I will make myself available around that schedule and I will make sure I get you a good list. I'll come up with my list, and if you come with your list of wants, I will work to try to make it all happen.
BW:	I want you to know I have no illusions that you work for me. I know you work for Ivanka, right?
KUSHNER:	[*laughing*] Okay, fine, you get it. You get it. That's probably why you're Bob Woodward. That's true.
BW:	I get it. Okay, well, that's great. Travel safely, and I look forward to seeing you. I've got some good questions.

[*phone connection cuts out but BW doesn't realize*]

BW:	Who has what role? What do they do? Do they apprehend—which is my question to your father-in-law, the president, and that is, what does he want to accomplish? What is he trying to do with Kim Jong Un? With China? All of the main countries that we're dealing with in a major way.

And then, you know, what's the plan? As I talked
to you the other day, what's the plan for the
campaign? I think people who go vote are going
to go into that voting booth and they're going to
say, what's in it for me? If Trump's reelected or if
the Democrat, whether it's Bloomberg or whoever
it might be, it's a kind of a kitchen-table way of
looking at why people vote. Is that reasonable?
Hello? I think I lost you.

[*Recording ends*]

COMMENTARY: Jared Kushner's recommendation for understanding Trump was to consider the advice of the Cheshire Cat in *Alice in
Wonderland*. He paraphrased the cat: "If you don't know where you're
going, any path will get you there." The Cheshire Cat's strategy was
one of endurance and persistence, not direction.

Another text Kushner suggested I read to understand Trump was
Scott Adams's book *Win Bigly: Persuasion in a World Where Facts Don't
Matter*. Adams, the creator of the *Dilbert* comic strip, explains in his
book that Trump's misstatements of facts are not regrettable errors or
ethical lapses but part of a technique called "intentional wrongness
persuasion." Adams argues that Trump "can invent any reality" for
most voters on most issues, and "all you will remember is that he provided his reasons, he didn't apologize, and his opponents called him a
liar like they always do."

I was astonished at the time that Kushner would deliver such a
hard, negative assessment of his father-in-law.

Was it possible the best road map for understanding this administration was a novel about a young girl who falls through a rabbit hole
and a book that argued the President could persuade people he was
right, even when he lied?

INTERVIEW 9:
I Wanted to Always Play It Down

Phone call
March 19, 2020

BW:	Was there a moment in all of this, last two months, where you said to yourself, ah, this is the leadership test of a lifetime?
TRUMP:	No.

COMMENTARY: It was a month since I'd talked to President Trump. It was a momentous month, March of 2020. The coronavirus exploded in the United States and in the world.

On March 13th, on national television, Trump said:

> TRUMP: *To unleash the full power of the federal government in this effort today, I am officially declaring a national emergency—two very big words.*

Trump freed up billions of dollars in federal funds. Seventy people had died in the United States from the virus. By the end of March, that death toll had risen to 4,951 in the United States. Trump had appointed Vice President Pence to head a White House Coronavirus Task Force.

President Trump called me at home the evening of Thursday, March 19th. Earlier that day, California governor Gavin Newsom had become the first governor to order residents in the state to stay home except for essential needs. This was the first of a wave of shutdown orders across all 50 states that would eventually lead to tens of millions of unemployment claims and the nation's greatest economic downturn since the Great Depression.

In this interview the president spoke with pride about his leadership during the pandemic. He blamed China and President Obama for the coronavirus, and Trump continued to accept no responsibility for the mounting crisis.

Again, I pushed to understand if he had a plan of action. This was a real crisis.

TRUMP:	Hi, Bob.
BW:	How are you? The busiest man in the world.
TRUMP:	Yeah, I am busy. I am busy. But, I don't know, we have to be busy, Bob. This thing is a nasty—it's a nasty situation, man.
BW:	Well, tell me—I have—and this again is for the book to come out before the election.
TRUMP:	Yeah.
BW:	Maybe you can give me some new insight into what's going on. And what I'd really like to ask first is, how's Melania doing?
TRUMP:	She's doing great. She's doing great. And I just got back up. It's—I think we're doing very well. We have to see what happens. We have it very well shut down. The American people are terrific. You know, what they're putting up with. It came out of China. And they tried to convince people for a little while that it came out of soldiers, American—
BW:	Yes, I saw that.
TRUMP:	That's a beauty. But that didn't work out too well for them. But if we can end this thing, I think we're going to be poised for some very fast growth, if you want to know the truth. Because this wasn't really a financial thing. This was a— not at all a financial thing. This was a medical catastrophe.
BW:	Well, certainly, and of course the economy is taking a hit.

TRUMP:	Oh, sure. Well—
BW:	I've done this for—
TRUMP:	Well, you have no choice. This is the first time in history we are paying people not to work.
BW:	Yes, and—
TRUMP:	When you think—and we have no choice, because otherwise you'd lose millions, potentially, of people. You see what's going on in Italy, where they were late?
BW:	Oh yes, certainly.
TRUMP:	They were so late.
BW:	I wanted to capture the moment when your son Barron asked you about this.
TRUMP:	Yeah?
BW:	Tell me a little bit more about that, because that's very human. And what caused him to ask you?
TRUMP:	Well, he's just turning 14, so he was 13 when he did. And he wanted to know, Dad, what's going on?—
BW:	Where were you, in the White House?
TRUMP:	Yeah, in the White House, upstairs. In his bedroom. He said, Dad, what's going on? What's going on? You know, sort of cute.
BW:	Yeah.
TRUMP:	From a young kid. Smart kid. Good kid. But he goes, what's going on? You know, because it's so abnormal when you look at all of the stuff. You know, you turn on the news and they show a lot of places that got hit—I'll tell you, a very big moment was when I closed it up—
BW:	So to just finish with Barron, if you would, sir—
TRUMP:	Yeah.
BW:	So he asked you what's going on.
TRUMP:	What's going on, Dad?
BW:	Did he cite anything that he had heard or—
TRUMP:	No, but he sees it. He sees it on television. He watches a little television, and he sees it. I mean, honestly, Bob, and you've seen a lot of things and

you've covered a lot of the biggest things ever, but
have you ever seen anything that has gotten—I
mean, it's, it's—there's nothing else even that they
talk about. They don't talk about anything else.

BW: No. And they did on NBC tonight a six-minute
segment about how to wash your hands perfectly.

TRUMP: Yeah, I know. I know.

BW: So imagine that.

TRUMP: Nobody's ever seen anything like this.

BW: So you told Barron, you said, "It's bad, it's bad."
And then—

TRUMP: I said—no, I said, it's a very bad thing, but we're
going to straighten it out.

BW: Did he have any other questions about, like, how
are you going to—

TRUMP: He said, how did it happen? I said, it came out of
China, Barron. Pure and simple. It came out of
China. And it should've been stopped. And to be
honest with you, Barron, they should've let it be
known it was a problem two months earlier. And
we wouldn't—the world would not—we have
141 countries have it now. And I said, the world
wouldn't have a problem. We could've stopped
it easily. And they didn't want to do the—they
waited and waited. Kept it secret, secret. Then we
started hearing things coming out. I told him how
it was working. And I said, and now the whole
world is infected and inflicted with this.

BW: And did he seem comforted by it, or did he—you
know, here you have your dad, the president of
the United States—

TRUMP: Oh, I know.

BW: —saying what you said to him.

TRUMP: Well, and he talks about it with his friends all the
time. Everybody. Bob, that's all they talk about.

BW: Yes, I know. [*laughs*] I've never—

TRUMP: That's all they're talking about. You've rarely
seen—you've covered a couple of the biggest.

	Watergate. You've rarely seen anything like what's going on.
BW:	Nothing. And wars and 9/11 and 2008.
TRUMP:	Part of it is the mystery. Part of it's the viciousness. You know when it attacks, it attacks the lungs. And, I don't know—when people get hit, and now it's turning out it's not just old people, Bob. Just today and yesterday, some startling facts came out. It's not just old, older. Young people, too, plenty of young people—but look at what's going on in [?]
BW:	Yeah. Exactly.
TRUMP:	—what's going on in—
BW:	So give me a moment of talking to somebody, going through this with Fauci or somebody, who kind of, it caused a pivot in your mind. Because it's clear just from what's on the public record that you went through a pivot on this to, oh my God, the gravity is almost inexplicable and unexplainable.
TRUMP:	Well, I think, Bob, really to be honest with you—
BW:	Sure, I want you to be. [laughs]
TRUMP:	I wanted to—I wanted to always play it down. I still like playing it down, because I don't want to create a panic. But think about it. Who was the first one that put up the border? Who was the first one to stop the Chinese? I had 21 people in my office, and of the 21 there was one person that said we have to close it down, I'm sorry. That was very early on. That was weeks—
BW:	And who was that?
TRUMP:	—ahead of when it became fashionable.
BW:	Who was the one person who—
TRUMP:	And I was called by Biden, Sleepy Joe, and I was called by all of these people, including NBC and everybody, a xenophobic and a racist and anything else you could be called because I shut it down. They said it didn't make sense. So—

BW: And who was the one person who wanted—

TRUMP: —that was long before. At the same time, I said, everybody has to be calm. And I would say that a lot. Everybody has to be calm. It's all going to work out. And they viewed that as, like, I didn't take it seriously. I took it more seriously than they did. I closed down our country to China. You think that's easy? And I got calls from China. Don't—

BW: Yeah, what's your relationship with President Xi now?

TRUMP: I think it's good, but I haven't spoken to him in a couple of weeks. But I think it's, you know, look, he knows that I'm for this country and he's for that country. So, you know—but I have a good relationship with him.

BW: So tell me who was the one person—

TRUMP: I have a good relationship with every leader of every country, which people don't understand. I have a good relationship with all of them. But they also know that I'm doing the right thing for this country. But I—if you think of it, Bob, I shut it down—

BW: Can you tell me who was the one person who was for—

TRUMP: —long before—I shut this down long before it was fashionable.

BW: Right. I understand that.

TRUMP: I was called all sorts of names.

BW: You said you had 21 people in the Oval Office and one person wanted to shut down China.

TRUMP: And that was your friend. That was me.

BW: That was you? [laughs] Okay.

TRUMP: Yeah.

BW: Who was opposed?

TRUMP: Everybody—nobody wanted to, because it was too early. So when they said I didn't take it seriously, well, how come I shut down one of the largest countries, our biggest trade, you know, everything—I shut down the biggest country. I shut it down.

COMMENTARY: I later had conclusive evidence from the participants that at least five people were in favor of the restrictions, including National Security Adviser Robert O'Brien and his deputy Matt Pottinger. But Trump continued to say it was him. He alone against the rest.

TRUMP:	They said I didn't take it seriously.
BW:	Why did you do it?
TRUMP:	Now, what I didn't do is run around in a panic screaming, oh, this is terrible. Because I don't want that.
BW:	You can understand my question, Mr. President.
TRUMP:	Yeah. Go ahead.
BW:	Why did you then alone decide to cut off China?
TRUMP:	Because the consequences were so great if I didn't.
BW:	And what were they?
TRUMP:	The consequences was tremendous death. They did something on one of the shows tonight. Southampton University, in the UK. They did a poll that I closed it down unbelievably early and three to four weeks early, earlier than anybody knew it was even a problem. A long time before the time you're talking about. Had I not done that, there would've been massive numbers of deaths by now. It was a big move. Because, you know, we take in thousands of people a day from China. And China was heavily infected.

COMMENTARY: While Trump shut down travel from China on January 31st, thousands from China went to Europe, and from Europe the virus came to the United States. Subsequent detailed investigations have shown that JFK airport was a major open doorway. Friday, March 13th, Trump also suspended travel from Europe. But it was too late. The virus had already taken hold in the United States.

BW: Let me make this real human and real. What was
               it like to take that test for you? To have that—

TRUMP: I didn't like that test. That test—

BW: Yeah. They stick that up your nose, right?

TRUMP: Well, they shove it up your nose, and then it
               hangs a right under your eye. I didn't even know
               you could go there.

BW: How long was that?

TRUMP: Well, what they do—have you taken the test?

BW: No, sir. I have not. I've not had to. No symptoms.

TRUMP: It's not pleasant. No, it's a tough test. What it is,
               basically, is it goes up your nose and then it has
               to make a right turn or a left turn, either way,
               depending on which nostril. It goes up your nose
               and then it makes a right turn under your eye.

BW: Right.

TRUMP: And that's where they take the sample. I didn't
               even know you could go there. Right?

BW: Yeah. And did you feel it?

TRUMP: Yeah, I felt it. I didn't like it, either.

BW: And so then what happened when they took it
               out? How long did you have to wait?

TRUMP: Okay, it was fine. I mean, look, it was the very
               professional doctors. White House doctors, as they
               say. Very professional. The concept is unpleasant.
               It's not like they just touched a little bit of the
               nose. I mean, they went—they go up there.

BW: No, listen, that's one sensitive area. [laughs]

TRUMP: Had you heard that, though? Have you heard
               this? Not an easy test.

BW: Yes, I know. So what's the best idea—

TRUMP: And I only did it because the press was saying, oh,
               you were with the head of Brazil, the president
               of Brazil. Make Brazil great again. He's a good
               guy. And he has it. They said he had it. Well,
               he didn't have it, it turned out. Or that's what
               they announced. I had no symptoms, right, but
               the press was my symptom. Because they kept

	screaming. And then after I took it they said, why did you take it? You had no symptoms. [*laughs*] In other words, you can't win. So they're screaming for me, why are you not taking it? Then when I took it, they said, why would you take it when you had no symptoms? Because you're not supposed to take it when you have no symptoms.
BW:	Okay. So now tell me about the relationship with Fauci. You know, Fauci—as you now say you're a wartime president, and I think that's exactly right, by the way.
TRUMP:	This is a war.
BW:	This is a war. And he's in many ways your Eisenhower.
TRUMP:	Well, he's a very good guy. He's done it before. He's a sharp guy. I think he's 79 years old.
BW:	Yes, he is.
TRUMP:	Very good.
BW:	He's even older than you or me.
TRUMP:	Well, when you compare him—listen, when you compare that to Biden, and when you compare it to a lot of the people we see, right—no, he's sharp. And he's doing a good job. He's a very dedicated guy.
BW:	Have you ever sat down alone with him and gotten a tutorial—
TRUMP:	Yes, I guess, but, honestly, there's not a lot of time for that, Bob. This is a busy White House. This is a busy White House. We've got a lot of things happening.

COMMENTARY: He's talking to me for hours but doesn't have time to sit with the top infectious disease expert? He doesn't have time to sit for a lesson on the coronavirus? I again was genuinely and deeply troubled.

TRUMP:	Look, we had the greatest economy on Earth. The greatest economy we've ever had. And

in one day, this thing came in and we had a choice to make. Close everything up and save potentially millions of lives, you know, hundreds of thousands of lives. Or don't do anything and look at body bags every day being taken out of apartment buildings.

BW: Yeah. Who told you that? What was the brief—

TRUMP: It was me. I told me that. I mean, it was—I just made that determination. It turned out to be right. You know, Italy tried to wait and look what happened. They waited.

BW: I know, listen. Hey, listen, for 100 years, people are going to be writing about this. And I've got this opportunity to ask the decision-maker—you—how you got there. What was the best idea that came from, okay, how to fight this?

TRUMP: Yeah. So we have some very talented people. Fauci is very talented. Dr. Hahn is now new.

BW: Yes, I saw that today.

TRUMP: He's a very good guy. I don't know if you saw with the medicines. They call them therapeutics. Right? But if we—if one of these two things works—and we have other things that we're looking at. But I think one of them is actually, maybe, going to work. And that would be a game-changer, to put it mildly. But so we have people who are really terrific. Dr. Birx, the woman—

BW: Saw that.

TRUMP: She's fantastic. Deborah Birx. She's fantastic. And they're professionals. And they've done it. You know, Dr. Birx was involved with the fight against AIDS, the fight against Ebola.

BW: So what's the best idea—

TRUMP: Beautiful, elegant woman, I don't know if you noticed it.

BW: —in all of this? Other words, if I was a fly on the wall through your whole day over the last month, what would be the moment that would tell me the gravity, tell me how you are deciding, weighing information. No one understands this—

TRUMP: I think the biggest would be that a number of months ago, I was asking, tell me about the gravity. And it was pretty new at that time. They weren't—nobody could be totally sure. But it looked bad, because of what was going on in China. That was Wuhan Province.

BW: Right.

TRUMP: And it looked bad. And I was asking, I probably had seven or eight people, professionals, and we were talking about it. And I said, what is the extent of this danger we're talking about? And all I know is that after the discussion, then more and more people would come. And ultimately there was a lot. Twenty-one, as I told you. Approximately 21 people. But I said, what is the extent? And at the end of them telling me the extent, I closed down our country to China. And Asia. And I'll tell you what, that was probably when I felt we potentially had a problem. But even then, I took a lot of heat because a lot of the—almost all of the news was saying I moved too soon, it was too soon—if I would've done it four weeks later, it would've been a disaster. We would not even be talking about the same problem right now. We'd be talking about something that would be on a different level.

BW: So you think closing down China was kind of the—

TRUMP: That was the big move, yeah. We had just made a trade deal with China.

BW: Yes, I know. Phase 1.

TRUMP: I just made a trade—so now, I make a trade deal, the ink isn't even dry, and I'm saying, all right, we've got to close it down to China. [*laughs ruefully*] It's like—it's not easy.

BW: Have you heard any complaints from Xi or
                anyone about that?

TRUMP: No, I haven't. I have not spoken to him since,
                actually.

BW: Okay. What's the best idea about how to help the
                economy now—

TRUMP: Okay. So—

BW: —that you've heard, or you're implementing.

TRUMP: —this is a very unusual thing. Because we have
                to keep people in their houses. We have to keep
                people separate from people. We have to keep
                people at a distance. So this is the first time in
                history that there's ever been something that they
                call social distancing, where—

BW: Sure, I know.

TRUMP: —we want to keep people apart. So what
                we're doing is spending a lot of money to keep
                people apart. So what we want to do is keep our
                businesses together, not have people fired all over
                the place, give companies and people incentives
                to stick around so that when the virus is gone, we
                will be able to immediately open up. And I think
                if we can do that, it's going to be a V instead of
                an L.

COMMENTARY: A V-shaped recovery means a return to normal. An
L means no return to normal.

TRUMP: You know, we're going to have tremendous—
                [crosstalk]

BW: Now what do you think of Lindsey Graham's
                idea that the federal government has to protect
                people's income?

TRUMP: Well, I think it's fine. But there are lots of ways of
                getting there. You have six or seven different ways
                of getting there. One of them's a cash payment.
                One of them's incentive to the company, where
                the company pays. You know, the problem is

you don't know that the company's going to do that, so I don't like that so much. But there are numerous ways to get there. There are numerous ways, Bob.

BW: But it's key, his point—

TRUMP: But it's a—it's a tragedy what's going on.

BW: —his point really struck me, is if you think, you don't want an inadequate unemployment check. You don't want just a one-time—you want your income protected. If I was out there and had worked in a restaurant or something and I'm out—if somebody can come in and say, we'll protect your income, then all of a sudden, okay, this is going to be easier than I thought. Or at least I can survive. But some of these other ideas seem, frankly, small-bore.

TRUMP: Well, one of the things we can do is a direct cash payment. And there's something very good about that.

BW: Yeah. But if you protect people's income, that's more money—I mean, a lot of people are talking about this is going to cost $2 or $3 trillion at least.

TRUMP: Well, we'll make that back very quickly, Bob, if the economy stays strong and we get rid of the virus. You know, we're taking very strong measures. They're going to be closing down Los Angeles in a little while.

BW: Yeah.

TRUMP: Not only Los Angeles. Excuse me, they're going to be closing down the state of California very soon.

BW: I think you're quite right. Was there a moment in all of this, last two months, where you said to yourself, ah, this is the leadership test of a lifetime?

TRUMP: No.

BW: No?

TRUMP:	I think it might be, but I don't think that. All I want to do is get it solved. There are many people that said that to me. They said, you're now a wartime president.
BW:	Who said that first to you?
TRUMP:	Oh, many people have said that to me.
BW:	Well, help me. I like to make it concrete.
TRUMP:	I don't want to even think about it. I just want to get it solved. I don't like to sit back and think about that kind of thing.
BW:	Why?
TRUMP:	Because I don't have that much time to think about it, Bob. I'm busy as hell. Even making this call with you—
BW:	I understand that. And I thank you—
TRUMP:	I took the call because it's you.
BW:	And I appreciate—
TRUMP:	Anybody else, I don't take the calls. Which is probably a mistake. I get fake news all the time. If I talked to people, it would be—
BW:	Well, you said the news media is doing a good job, and I think you're right. I think they're taking this seriously.
TRUMP:	No, the news media lately has been much more fair. And they're re—look, the poll is coming out tomorrow morning at ABC, which I hear is a great poll, as to the job I'm doing. And they can't—one of those—ABC, at 6:00 they release it, they tell me it's a great poll about the job I'm doing. So who knows? Look, I want to just do the job.
BW:	What I'm trying to do—
TRUMP:	You know, the news conferences I've been doing on a daily basis, because I think it keeps people informed and it's been good, they've gotten very good reviews, but they've also gotten unbelievable ratings. And if I would speak to all the reporters that would call, I'd get the greatest press in the world. But I can't do that. [BW laughs] I wouldn't be able to do my job, Bob.

COMMENTARY: Earlier in the day, Trump had given an 80-minute press briefing in which he controversially promoted the use of the drug hydroxychloroquine as an alleged treatment for the virus. "If things don't go as planned, it's not going to kill anybody," Trump said.

BW:	The most important thing is for a definitive book to come out before the election—
TRUMP:	That's why I'm talking to you. I have respect for you. I wish I talked to you on the last book. I would've had a whole different book. Look, nobody's done what I've done in the last three and a half—
BW:	Okay, now help me with this. How are you going to engage your supporters, because you can't have rallies now, or you're not going to?
TRUMP:	Oh, I don't know. We'll find—hey, I just want to tell you before I forget. So I just signed my 220th judge, federal judge, plus two Supreme Court justices. I have 44 more to sign. I'll be at 260, 270, maybe even 280.
BW:	Uh-huh.
TRUMP:	Maybe even 300 by the end of the first term. It's unheard of, Bob.
BW:	Maybe they'll put a statue of you outside the Supreme Court. [*laughs*]
TRUMP:	Oh, what a good idea. I think I'll have it erected tomorrow. What a great idea. I think I'll use it. I won't—I won't say it came from me. [*laughs*] No, but think of that, Bob.
BW:	Hey, listen, I did a whole book on the Supreme Court and have a—
TRUMP:	Well, you know what that is. I'm going to get very close to 300. I might even hit it. But I'm already at 220 and have 40 in for approval. Forty!
BW:	So what do you think of the health care information coming out of China? Because now they're saying they had not a single infection yesterday. Do you believe that?

TRUMP:	Probably not. But I'm not focused on that.
BW:	Someone said there's some intel coming out that—
TRUMP:	I know. They put out intel. They also said it didn't come from them, it came from American soldiers, so, I mean—
BW:	So you're skeptical?
TRUMP:	Well, I'm skeptical. I don't want to be skeptical, but I'm a skeptical person. Right? I hope it's true. Because that would mean there can be an end to this. Because we're going to be following them. We're a couple of months behind in the sense that it hit us a couple of months later.
BW:	And a lot of people have criticized you for when you said you take no responsibility. And I understand the context of that—
TRUMP:	No, I don't take responsibility for this. I have nothing to do with this.
BW:	Yeah, well—
TRUMP:	I take responsibility for solving the problem.
BW:	Okay.
TRUMP:	But I don't take responsibility for this, no. We did a good job. Look, the testing, we were never set up for testing. The Obama administration, they were obsolete tests. And in all fairness to them, nobody ever thought in terms of millions of people. You know, they had a test that was fine for CDC. But it was a very minor test.

COMMENTARY: Coronavirus did not exist during the Obama administration. The first tests for COVID were created by the Centers for Disease Control in early 2020.

TRUMP:	Now, the other thing is, we're just trying to help out governors and states, Bob.
BW:	Yeah. When you asked Pence to run this, what did you say to him and what'd he say to you?
TRUMP:	Well, I had a choice. I had a lot of people that wanted to run it. And I asked Mike. I said, what

about it? And Mike is very good and he's a good manager. I said, Mike, what about you doing it? And he jumped at the chance. And I think he's done a very professional job. Very good job. What do you think?

BW: Listen, he's there, he's every day. He's calm. He's factual.

TRUMP: Right. He's calm, he's cool. He's done a very good job, a really good job! And we're getting great marks. I mean, take a look at the poll tomorrow. We're getting great marks.

BW: We will see. What do you hear from some of the other leaders? Like Abe in Japan or from South Korea?

TRUMP: Well, let me tell you about the leaders here first.

BW: Okay.

TRUMP: Cuomo is saying great things. Gavin Newsom— and we always, you know, go back and forth. He's been saying great things. You saw what he said today, or you saw what Cuomo said today and yesterday? We're getting very good marks from the governors. We're helping the governors. Because, you know, it's a local problem. You can't solve that federally. But we're helping the governors and we're getting very good marks. Today I had a meeting with fifty governors—

BW: How'd that go?

TRUMP: It was a 10. Nobody—the news was there. They—

BW: And Larry Hogan is out criticizing you. The Maryland governor.

TRUMP: When did he do that?

BW: Oh, he said something—they asked did they get the testing going up fast enough, and he said no, it was a failure.

TRUMP: Well, Hogan is a third-rate guy, in my opinion. I don't think he does a good job. I mean, I really don't. I don't think he does a good job. But he was very good today. I will tell you this.

BW: Can I ask you this? Where you say it's a local
           problem, I think—and the reason I'm bothering
           you tonight when you're the busiest man in the
           world—

TRUMP: No, it's a—I don't say it's a local—But look, Bob,
           federal government can't be running every little
           city and town.

BW: No, of course not, but you set the tone and
           people have expectations.

TRUMP: Well, I don't know about Hogan, but if you
           take a look at Gavin Newsom and every other
           governor—I heard—look, I was—Hogan was
           there today. And Hogan said fantastic things. Take
           a look at what he said today, Bob.

BW: Yeah. Okay. Well, he was picking at you.

TRUMP: Wait a minute. Was it this afternoon? When
           was it?

BW: I don't know. I just saw a clip of him at a podium
           saying that.

TRUMP: See, there's a case of the fake news. So I have
           50 governors on a call. It was a teleconference.
           Every one of them was positive, including Hogan.
           And the fake news finds a problem with Hogan.
           And Hogan's bad news. He's the most overrated
           governor in the country. So that's the story. Okay.
           Well, who cares?

BW: Okay. So what's the plan now—

TRUMP: But that's fake news, Bob. They don't even go
           after a Democrat. There's no Democrats.

BW: Now, help me with this. What are the next steps?
           You must have in your mind a checklist or a
           to-do—

TRUMP: My next step is I've got 20 calls waiting for me on
           this stuff, and I've got to get making them. Okay?
           That's my next steps. My next steps, Bob, is I
           have to do a great job.

BW: Okay. Yes, exactly.

TRUMP: And I have to be very professional.

BW:	This is the leadership test—
TRUMP:	And I'm doing the news conferences and I'm giving the reporters plenty of time to ask all the questions in their little hearts. And I think that people are respecting what's happening. And I think, frankly, since I started doing the news conferences, it's all turned around. Because we've done a great job. And you've got to always say one of the best parts of the great job was the shutdown of China very, very early.
BW:	Okay. I'm going to look at that in detail. I'm going to try—I know Tony Fauci. My wife, Elsa, and I have had him at our house here some time ago. He's quite a—I mean, he's unique.
TRUMP:	He's a very good guy. Say hello to him.
BW:	Well, you see him every day.
TRUMP:	Well, I do. Every day, every other day. But you'll speak to him, if you're going to call him now. But he's a very good guy. He is. He's a very good guy. So anyway.
BW:	Who else—
TRUMP:	When is your book coming out?
BW:	It'll come out in September. Let's hope. The last word is, this is over. If this is over—
TRUMP:	I'd love that to happen. Bob, once it ends— because I'm very good at finance. Once it ends, our country is going to go like a rocket ship. It's going to be great.
BW:	Yeah. But a lot of people are going to be hurting.
TRUMP:	Well, they will be, but they'll gain it back, Bob.
BW:	This is why—
TRUMP:	A lot of your friends have been hurt. But it wasn't—hey, Bob, it was no fault of mine, and it was no fault of anybody's. It just happened. Except maybe China. China, it was China's fault.
BW:	No question, or, well, it was—one of the accidents of nature. Don't you think that's what President Xi—

TRUMP: Well, it came from a place where it could've been stopped.

BW: So of the 20 calls stacked up, what's the next one you're going to make?

TRUMP: Next four are going to be four senators talking about the bill.

BW: Ah, good. Who's leading the charge on this?

TRUMP: Well, all. But I have Steve Mnuchin—smart guy, good guy. He's leading it right now, along with other people. We have some great financial people, though. You know, it's very different. We have a medical problem. And we don't have a financial problem, Bob. We have a medical problem.

BW: Yes, but you—

TRUMP: So in the other days we had the financial problem. Right? This is a medical problem.

BW: Let me be a pest on this question of protecting people's incomes. Take a poll of what's the average worker out there worried about—yeah, they're happy to get a check, they're happy to get, what is it, $322 a week in unemployment insurance. Like, this idea of a stimulus—

TRUMP: Well, we're going to do better than that, Bob. That's not the right number.

BW: Well, I mean, some places that's the number. It depends locally—

TRUMP: No, I know, but we're doing it better than that.

BW: People want their income protected.

TRUMP: We're actually going to make a cash payment. We're going to do it different ways. We haven't exactly finalized it, so, you know—

BW: And the biggest mistake in this, if I may say, having done too many of these things—

TRUMP: Yeah?

BW: —will be if you and I talk in two months and you haven't done enough.

TRUMP: Go ahead. Go ahead.

BW: —you haven't done enough. Doing too much is not a problem. Because—

TRUMP:	Oh, I love that. No, no. Hey, I agree with you. No, we're going big. This is a big—
BW:	And you've got to think about—
TRUMP:	Yeah. We're at $1.3 trillion. It may be higher than that. We can go back for more if we need it.
BW:	Yeah. Yeah. It's just—look, it's a political—
TRUMP:	No, no, we're going big. Look, we have options. We could do the hundred, two hundred, another hundred—no, no. We're going big.
BW:	Okay.
TRUMP:	Absolutely.
BW:	And I tell you, if the workers in two months or three months or six months say, my income was protected. And I know Lindsey, because I talked to him, Lindsey Graham, he said to you, your number one job is to protect people's income.
TRUMP:	Well, no, protect people's lives. And then also protect their income. I've got a double-whammy here. I've got to protect their lives, too. This thing is vicious.
BW:	I agree.
TRUMP:	It's the most contagious virus anyone's ever seen.
BW:	You have—so when my book comes out, people are going to look back and they're going to say, was everything done? I wrote books on 9/11, the terrorist attacks, which you remember vividly.
TRUMP:	Absolutely. Great.
BW:	And always the problem was, are we doing enough? Now what they had to do was take this great espionage establishment that we had and gear it up, and they threw $50 billion to the intelligence community. And we never had another big terrorist attack. A giant accomplishment.
TRUMP:	Yeah. Let's talk about that for a second.
BW:	Yes, sir.
TRUMP:	Since we last spoke, I took out al-Baghdadi. I took out our wonderful Iranian general, right? Soleimani—

BW: Soleimani, yes.

TRUMP: —who was the king of the roadside bomb. The
             king. Ninety-two percent of the bombs planted
             were because of him, directly or indirectly. That's
             Soleimani. I took out the son of Osama bin
             Laden, who was a bad one. And I took out the
             head of three different terrorist organizations.
             That's since we last met. And did plenty of other
             things, too. And, you know, one of the big things,
             you know, I don't want to bore you with it, but
             you know how important it is—are the judges.
             I mean, nobody's ever done the judges that I've
             done. Nobody.

BW: That's right, and—

TRUMP: You know, you have presidents that never got to
             appoint a Supreme Court judge. I've appointed
             two in three years.

BW: Now, listen, I understand that. They always
             thought, well, who's Jimmy Carter going to
             appoint? He got none, as I recall.

TRUMP: I think he had none, yeah. He deserved—

BW: Yeah, he had none.

TRUMP: He deserved none.

BW: [laughs] And it broke his heart. So if I go out and
             talk to 50 people in September before this book
             comes out and I say, how did President Trump
             do? There'll be the medical question, and there's
             going to be the economic question.

TRUMP: Right.

BW: Because even the people who don't get the disease
             are affected in a profound way.

TRUMP: Oh, absolutely. Absolutely right.

BW: I mean, the numbers—even if the worst—

TRUMP: Everybody's affected one way or the other. Some
             people both ways.

BW: It's going to be very interesting to see what the
             scorecard from the person on the street is, if the
             answer is President Trump protected my health, if

	he led, and he protected my income. That's what people—
TRUMP:	Well, you might get a good idea by then. It's going to be a little further down the road, I think.
BW:	Yeah. Well, it's not my idea, I'm just—
TRUMP:	You'll have a pretty good idea by then, Bob, I think.
BW:	Okay. That's great. What else do I need to know?
TRUMP:	Ummmmm . . . [*loud sigh*] I mean, if you asked me the question two weeks ago, I would've said we have the strongest economy in the world. We soon will again, as soon as I get rid of the scourge.
BW:	Yeah. Well—
TRUMP:	Very good management. Very calm. The news is, it's very fake. It's all fake news.
BW:	How's Pompeo?
TRUMP:	Doing a very good job. Solid rock.
BW:	What's his focus now?
TRUMP:	Yeah, he's doing a good job. Smart guy. Number one in his class at West Point.
BW:	Right.
TRUMP:	Smart guy. Number one at Harvard, I understand.
BW:	What's his assignment now?
TRUMP:	The world, you know. He's doing everything. We're having lots of different discussions about lots of different things. He's a very good person. Good guy. Good, solid guy.
BW:	You know, Warren Buffett agrees with you on the negative trade deficits.
TRUMP:	Really?
BW:	Have you ever talked to him about it?
TRUMP:	Anybody that does business, it's ridiculous. I inherited a mess. We were losing $550 billion with China. Did you see the trade deficit's way down with China now, Bob?
BW:	But what's important, and the Buffett point on this is that the transfer of wealth—other words, we're giving China all this money. And we get goods, yes, and the Gary Cohns of the world say,

well, it's an even trade. But Buffett and you and
Lighthizer say, uh-uh. That is a transfer of wealth
to China. They get the money.

TRUMP: Totally! It's a transfer of wealth and it's a transfer
of jobs, okay? The people that don't get it,
sometimes they're called free traders. They really
have to go back to school. There's never been
anything like what happened, and I stopped it.
I've stopped the flow. Hey, Bob, I have to go. I've
got all these senators waiting.

BW: Okay, sir. Good talking to you. I'll be in touch.
Thank you.

TRUMP: Let me know when you're ready. We'll talk. I love
talking—

BW: I've recorded this for my history book, and I
appreciate it.

TRUMP: That's okay. I don't mind. I figured you did. Let
me know when you're ready. We'll talk again.
Thanks, Bob.

BW: Thank you, sir. Bye.

[*Recording ends*]

COMMENTARY: The United States was the first country in the world
to record more than 100,000 cases of coronavirus.

INTERVIEW 10:
Words Cause Wars

Phone call
March 28, 2020

TRUMP: One of the things we're doing is we're testing at such a level, so much higher than any other country, that—you know, like, it shows we have more cases? Well, the reason we have more cases, because we're testing. So we're finding a lot of people with, like, sniffles, and they have it, so that's called a case. You know what I mean?

My next interview with President Trump was the morning of March 28th. The day before, Trump had signed a massive $2 trillion pandemic response bill that had passed the House and Senate almost unanimously. It provided money to individuals, large and small businesses, and local governments.

At a Fox News town hall four days earlier, Tuesday, March 24th, Trump said:

TRUMP: *I would love to have the country opened up and just raring to go by Easter.*

Easter was only 19 days away when Trump made his comment to Fox News.

The audio quality of my call with President Trump is not very good.

TRUMP:	Hi, Bob. Hi.
BW:	President Trump, how are you?
TRUMP:	Hi, good. I'm running a big, big operation. The world is under siege, as you know. It's very interesting. But I think we're doing a good job. We're getting a lot of equipment coming in. It's unbelievable, though, Bob. What's your feeling?
BW:	Well, I mean, we talked, and you know the leadership task that's on your shoulders—
TRUMP:	Yeah.
BW:	—is, as we talked last time, people are going to be looking at this and trying to understand it 100 years from now. How do you feel, and all for the book, I'm recording this again. What are your priorities?
TRUMP:	Yeah, I can't talk too long, Bob, because I have generals downstairs. I have National Guardsmen downstairs that I have to speak before. So I can only give a couple of—look, I think we're doing a really good job. I think we're getting a lot of credit. I think there's a lot of really fake news out there where they try and demean everything. They had a case where CNN was going to interview somebody and the person went over and said Trump's doing a great job, and they refused to put him on the air. You know, it's a very respected person, by the way.
BW:	Okay, so the question, though, is what are—because it's on your shoulders, what are your priorities? I'm really interested.
TRUMP:	My priorities are saving lives. That's my priority. That's my only priority. We got a great bill passed.
BW:	Yes.
TRUMP:	Actually $6.2 trillion. It's $4.2 but—it's $2.2, but it's actually $6.2 because you get an extra $4 trillion. It's the biggest bill ever passed. And that takes care of a lot of things. And it's going to really help with the big comeback that we have to

make. We made one comeback. Now we have to
make a second comeback. And it gives us virtually
unlimited money, credit, everything else we have
to do. We're taking care of people that lost their
jobs. We're taking care of jobs not being lost—a
lot of jobs won't be lost because the incentive
is now to keep your workers. And tremendous
things in that bill. I got it done. I got it passed
unanimously.

BW: Thursday you said you talked to President Xi of
China. Would it be possible to get somebody to
give me a summary of that call? I think so much is
gonna hinge on—

TRUMP: No, we had a very good call. And it was a long
call. It was an hour.

BW: Yes.

TRUMP: Yeah, I could have somebody give you a summary.
You know who could give you a summary is Jared.
Jared's a big fan of yours.

BW: That's great. And you said—

TRUMP: Yeah. Jared Kushner was on that call, along with
Mike Pompeo, along with a few other people.
And Jared could give you—tell him I said it was
okay. Jared could give you a recap. It was a very
good call.

BW: You had said you discussed with President Xi kind
of how this began. Did he have an answer?

TRUMP: Right. Well, I did, and I discussed it. And then
I said, look, it's no longer relevant right now.
We'll talk about it after it's all over. Because in
the meantime we have to fix what's here. But
there's no reason to get into a big argument
about that now.

BW: Understand.

TRUMP: Sometimes you just sort of say, okay, let's talk
about that sometime later. They're very defensive,
as you would be.

BW: Of course. Well, you have the weight of the world

	on your shoulders, and I'm going to acquiesce to the responsibility and not even ask you any more questions. For the first time in my life. [*laughs*]
TRUMP:	Well, thank you. Are you feeling good? Don't go out, right? Just relax, you know?
BW:	Yeah.
TRUMP:	Relax.
BW:	When we talked in February, I was fascinated. You said there's dynamite behind every door. And this is before all of this accelerated, and I wonder if at that point did you have some inkling or intelligence that, my God, we've got this storm coming?
TRUMP:	Well, nobody knew that a thing like this could happen. The best decision I made was Europe and China, closing our doors. We would've had a much bigger problem, like many times bigger than we had. We would've had unbelievable amounts of death. You know, one of the things we're doing is we're testing at such a level, so much higher than any other country, that—you know, like, it shows we have more cases? Well, the reason we have more cases, because we're testing. So we're finding a lot of people with, like, sniffles, and they have it, so that's called a case. You know what I mean? So we're testing at a level—but we're really trying to keep it under one percent. And we're under one percent. We're one of the lowest. We're just about the lowest, actually.

COMMENTARY: Trump is defensive about case numbers and clearly concerned with how the numbers make him look rather than how the virus is rapidly spreading. Already over 147,000 people in the United States had contracted the virus and the death toll was climbing rapidly toward 3,000.

BW:	I see on the internet that Fauci is predicting we may have 100,000 deaths in this country?

TRUMP: He thinks that could be—it could happen. And if we didn't do what I'm doing, you would've had a number many times that. Can you believe that?

BW: Well, we—listen, let's get the history right. The history of where this lands in your relationship with China and on the trade and military issues—

TRUMP: As I've been saying for a long time, and one of the reasons I got elected was China. You know, China's taken advantage of this country for a long time. And we've done too much with China. China was not a good thing for us. We didn't need to buy pencils, Bob, for two cents. We could've made them ourselves, you know? We didn't need 10,000 pencils for every child. You understand?

BW: How's Xi's mood? Because they've been clobbered also. I understand from the intel that there's—

TRUMP: They've been clobbered far worse than you read.

BW: Yeah. And I understand that it shows in North Korea they're being clobbered also.

TRUMP: Like you wouldn't believe.

BW: Yeah.

TRUMP: Oh, I got another letter from him, by the way.

BW: Oh, good. Well, I've got those 29 letters—

TRUMP: I'll show you. Yeah. Very good letter.

BW: —and we'll get that history right.

TRUMP: Very good letter. It's just a letter. So, you know, it's interesting timing. For all those people that say, well, he hasn't made the deal. Well, what's not making the deal? I'm in for three and a half years, and we haven't had a war. Okay? And then you have something like this. And this stops wars, because they've got their own war now. You understand that, right?

BW: Oh, listen, somebody told me that the virus is just blazing through North Korea.

TRUMP:	Yeah. A big problem. Iran is an unbelievable problem. Iran is an unbelievable problem.
BW:	Well, it's good you can talk to President Xi of China. Was he angry with you at all?
TRUMP:	Well, they accused our soldiers of doing it, because they're worried—
BW:	Yes, I saw that.
TRUMP:	And I said, look, you can't do that. And you know, we had a little bit of an argument. But, basically, we—in the end I said, look, we'll talk about that later. In the meantime, we have to get to work.
BW:	And so you've got that channel open? Because that's clearly important.
TRUMP:	Oh, it's clearly important. Because you can— things can cause wars. When stupid people say stupid things, it can cause wars, Bob. You know? Words cause wars.
BW:	Absolutely. Accidental—
TRUMP:	I had a couple of guys—you know, I called it the Chinese virus. That's not easy for them to handle, okay?
BW:	Yes, I know.
TRUMP:	But I had guys that all of a sudden became emboldened, and they start—they were hitting China so hard. You've got to be careful. You can't do that shit. I stopped them, fast. And I told him that, and he was happy about that.
WALSH:	Hitting China.
TRUMP:	But you know, we're not dealing—I wish you could hear a tape of the call. I mean—
BW:	Yeah, that's what I'd love to do.
TRUMP:	It was so incredible—there's nobody that can describe that call. Call lasted for over an hour. There's nobody that can describe that call but a tape. Bob, I've got to go back to work.
BW:	Okay, sir.
TRUMP:	Listen, you take care of yourself. . . . I'll talk to you soon. Call Jared, okay?

BW: You take care. Will do, sir. Have a good day.
[Phone call ends]
WALSH: Such a better interview—such a totally different
                     person there.
BW: Yeah.

[Recording ends]

INTERVIEW 11:
What Is the Plan?

Phone call
April 5, 2020

TRUMP: I think we'll never get credit from the fake news media no matter how good a job we do. No matter how good a job I do, I will never get credit from the media, and I'll never get credit from Democrats who want to beat me desperately in seven months.

COMMENTARY: On April 3rd, when the Centers for Disease Control issued new guidance recommending that Americans wear masks, Trump said at the Coronavirus Task Force briefing that day:

TRUMP: *This is voluntary. I don't think I'm going to be doing it.*

The death toll in the United States had reached 7,000 and the number of new cases was rising by a staggering 30,000 each day.

I had spent the past three weeks intensely interviewing the medical experts as the virus exploded in the United States. My questions were directed at what needed to be done. It was apparent to me that Trump did not have a strategy or a plan.

I had talked at length to Dr. Fauci, the country's top infectious disease expert, and Dr. Robert Redfield, the Director of the Centers for Disease Control and Prevention. Redfield had the responsibility of protecting the health of all Americans. He had 23,000 people, including contractors, working for him all over the world.

I was told by multiple sources that the president was not listening. Dr. Fauci said the president's attention span during crucial briefings was "like a minus number." This dramatically echoed Mattis's point about Trump taking the freeway offramps to nowhere during national security briefings. Privately, Fauci said Trump's leadership was "rudderless."

If there was one theme, the experts said tackling the virus required a coordinated effort led from the top.

I had the president's attention now. The question for me was how to use the information I was gathering from his top advisers. Trump seemed to be more patient listening to me than to his experts, who were really disillusioned with his failure to organize an aggressive campaign against the virus.

My goal was to cover all of their priority areas in our interview and find out what Trump thought and might have planned. Given the risks and hazards from the virus, this could not be a regular interview. I wanted to lay it out as starkly and candidly as I could. Was he organized? Was there a plan? Did he know what the main issues were? Was he paying attention? It reminded me that I had personal responsibility beyond just being a reporter.

The president had given up on his plan to open the country by Easter. He sounded resigned, almost chastened, with a solemn tone unlike any I had heard from him in our previous interviews.

"The plague" he said when I reached him on April 5th.

TRUMP:	It's a horrible thing, what's going on. It's unbelievable. You know it just hit its 182nd country. Can you believe it?
BW:	Is that right now?
TRUMP:	It's now up to 182, yeah, as of this morning. It's hard to believe. It moves rapidly, Bob. It moves rapidly and viciously. If you're the wrong person and if it gets you, your life is pretty much over if you're in the wrong group. You know what I mean. It's a tough deal.
BW:	Is there any way to tell what that group is yet?
TRUMP:	Yeah, well, the group is older and people with a condition especially. I mean, older with a

condition, big trouble. Big trouble, if you have a combination of the two.

BW: Well, that's our age group, isn't it, sir?

TRUMP: It's—well, hopefully we're much younger than that, Bob. You look younger. But it's our age group. You know? Older, especially 80. Well, you're not anywhere near that. What are you, Bob? Just out of curiosity.

BW: No, well, happily I'm only 77.

TRUMP: Okay, good. Well, yeah. I'm 73.

BW: Here I want to ask you a series of questions.

TRUMP: Yeah, you go quick, Bob.

BW: All for the book. I know you're pressed for time.

TRUMP: A little pressed. I've got about 12 generals downstairs waiting for me. But that's okay.

BW: Okay. [*laughs*] I appreciate that. The central question is, in doing some reporting on briefings that people have given and so forth—

TRUMP: Right.

BW: —are we going to go to full mobilization? People at least I talk to say they want that feeling of full mobilization.

TRUMP: Well, I think we're at—other than we can call up additional military. As you know, I've sent in military doctors, surgeons, nurses, first responders, over a thousand to New York yesterday. You know that.

BW: Certainly.

TRUMP: And I'll tell you what is happening is what I said is going to happen. So far it's been true in every case. They're not needing the kind of things they think. For instance, you look at the ventilators. So far they've had the ventilators. You know, you have no idea, Bob, but ventilators are a big deal. You know, it's like building a car, okay? You know it's a very expensive—

BW: Sure. I heard you yesterday—

TRUMP: No, well it is. It is. You can understand. That's not like—gee whiz. Now we have millions of face masks that have come in and, you know, but that's a whole different thing. You're not hearing about that much anymore. You're not even hearing about the gowns very much anymore, the protective gowns.

BW: No, we've talked about this question, which is at the core of this: and that is to make sure you do everything. You know, no one in history is going to come back and say—

TRUMP: No one's going to say Trump did too much, you mean? Yeah.

BW: Yeah. There's never too much.

TRUMP: I agree.

BW: And I've found 16 things with my reporting, real quickly. On the testing, people out in the field, Fauci in private briefings and so forth is saying we aren't there yet. And do you—

TRUMP: But Bob, Bob, the test—well, first of all, we have great new tests. We inherited a broken test. But just so you understand, the states are really supposed to be doing the testing. You know? We got put into a position, and I didn't like that position. We're helping the states, but the states are supposed to be doing the testing and they have from the beginning. And really they are doing it. If you go to California, if you go to most states—the only ones that complain are the ones that aren't doing a good job, frankly.

BW: Okay, but still, a lot of people are saying we need a Manhattan-like project. That's, you know, the project to beat the—

TRUMP: Bob, this will be gone before you—we have done that, Bob. We have done that. We've got—you know I made the big center that we built, and the military wasn't thrilled with it. They built 3,000 beds in the Javits Center, right? That was for regular, you know, surgeries, et cetera. That was for regular patients, not COVID patients.

BW: Do you think you have a Manhattan—

TRUMP:	All COVID facility. And that was, that is being operated by the military. I don't know if you know that. Do you know that?
BW:	Yeah. Certainly. The question is—
TRUMP:	But you know that's a big deal though, Bob. I mean, that's a big deal.
BW:	No, a lot of big things going on. The question is, are you happy? Is it enough?
TRUMP:	Uh—okay. The answer is this: if a Democrat governor—for the most part. A couple of others, too. But if they're looking for 1,000 ventilators, right, and I said, no, no, no, I'm going to send you 10,000. They'll be so nice. Thank you, Mr. President, you're the greatest. When the news speaks to them or when they're on a show or something: How's the president doing? He didn't send us enough ventilators. Okay?
BW:	Sure. Listen, I understand the back and forth.
TRUMP:	There is nothing I can do to have a Democrat say good things. Now, despite that, you have Democrats saying good things. Like Gavin Newsom. Not—
BW:	Sure, but if you come out and say this is full mobilization, this is a Manhattan Project. We are going—pardon the expression—balls to the wall, that's what people want.

COMMENTARY: I am referring to the enormous scale of the 1940s collaborative project between the U.S. government, scientific, and military sectors to build the atomic bomb.

TRUMP:	Yeah. Well, okay.
BW:	And people want to feel that that's—
TRUMP:	I think maybe then I'm doing a bad job of not saying it. You know, I go to these news conferences—I'll probably, possibly do one today. I'm going to a task force meeting right now. Literally.

BW: Yes, right.

TRUMP: Been speaking to people all day. Been calling up governors, been calling up everybody. And hey, look, Cuomo asked us for 40,000 ventilators. Okay? Think of it. You don't have to know too much—

BW: Okay, but Cuomo is not the issue.

TRUMP: No, no, I know. But 40,000.

BW: I'm just saying—

TRUMP: I told him, you don't need anywhere near that amount.

BW: Mr. President, as a reporter—

TRUMP: Now it's turning out that we're right.

BW: —we've talked about—you are the one. This is a question about your leadership. And I just want to know how you feel about it. Second thing is the medical—

TRUMP: I feel good. I think we're doing a great job. I think we'll never get credit from the fake news media no matter how good a job we do. No matter how good a job I do, I will never get credit from the media, and I'll never get credit from Democrats who want to beat me desperately in seven months.

COMMENTARY: COVID-19 had now killed 12,182 people in the United States, four times the U.S. deaths from the 9/11 terrorist attacks. The disconnect between what the doctors were outlining and what Trump was saying was about as large as it could be. From my position as I watched Trump's response, it reminded me of the responsibility to yell "STOP!" when somebody is about to step in front of a bus.

BW: If you go out and say this is full mobilization, we are—

TRUMP: I've done it. I have done it.

BW: —Manhattan Project—

TRUMP: Well, yeah.

BW: —state. Anyway. The medical supply chain.

People I talk to say they still aren't satisfied
with it.

TRUMP: [*loud sigh*]

BW: They wonder whether you're going to federalize
            that. Is that possible?

TRUMP: We're getting very few complaints. Now, I am a
            big fan of the hydroxychloroquine.

BW: I know. I know.

TRUMP: It may not work, by the way, and it may work.
            If it does work, I will get no credit for it, and if
            it doesn't work, they'll blame the hell out of me.
            Okay? But that's okay. I don't mind that. But
            we've ordered millions of doses of the hydroxy.
            We've ordered millions. We have millions. We're
            stocked.

BW: Okay, third area, sir—

TRUMP: The governors—now you have some governors
            that were totally opposed to it that are really
            wanting it, and we're able to take care of them.

COMMENTARY: Hydroxychloroquine is an anti-malarial drug that
has dangerous side-effects. Trump was widely criticized for ignoring
the advice of his scientific and medical experts for promoting the drug
as a COVID cure. None of the doctors had mentioned hydroxychloroquine to me.

Here is Fauci's response when asked at a press conference if the
drug is an effective coronavirus treatment:

FAUCI: *The answer is no.*

When Trump returned to the microphone, he said:

TRUMP: *I disagree. I feel good about it. That's all it is,
                just a feeling, you know. I'm . . . smart guy. I
                sure as hell think we ought to give it a try.*

Hydroxychloroquine has never been shown to be an effective treatment for COVID-19.

BW: The third area, sir, is the unemployment benefits and the cash payments. Is there really in place a system where this is going to work? People I talk to—

TRUMP: Okay, ready? I was totally opposed to the distribution of the money the way the Democrats wanted it. They wanted it to go through unemployment insur—you know, centers. But many of them have 40-year-old computers. I said, it'll take a long time to get there if you do that. The money is sent. It's up to the states to deliver it.

BW: Okay. The fourth area is the small business loans. I know you said—

TRUMP: That's going really well, Bob. I mean, that—you know, I don't know if you saw. It was opened on Friday.

BW: I understand. But some of the banks are not participating because they say that—

TRUMP: Well, if they don't participate we're not going to be happy with them. But Bank of America, JP Morgan Chase, they had to get their own stuff straightened out. It had nothing to do with us.

BW: They say the interest rate is too low and they're reluctant to participate in full.

TRUMP: Well, didn't we sell $13 billion in one day?

BW: Whatever it was, yes. But the number has got to be up to, what, $300 billion. $377.

TRUMP: We're probably going to have to raise it, because we're going to need—which is a good thing not a bad thing. No, it's going out very fast, Bob. And the banks are doing it. And the biggest thing are the community banks are doing it. You know?

BW: Fifth area: shelter in place.

TRUMP: It's been very successful, anyway. Go ahead. What?

BW: Does it need a national order? I know you're reluctant to do this. I'm just telling you as a reporter—

TRUMP: Bob, 93 percent—almost 95. I think 95 percent closed. We have a couple of states. There are a lot of constitutional reasons, there are a lot of federalist reasons. And those states are all in good shape, Bob.

COMMENTARY: A "stay at home order" was in place, which meant only businesses deemed "essential" could continue to operate. For instance, schools went online, restaurants transitioned to take-out and delivery only, other businesses closed their doors for good.

BW: Sixth is the food supply. Are you confident that the food supply is going to get out to people?

TRUMP: Yeah. You haven't even heard a complaint about that, Bob. I mean, it's going great. I had a big meeting with all the big suppliers on Thursday. The biggest in the world, all of them. We also had meetings with all the big department store types and all of them—from Amazon to Walmart to all of them. And they're all doing well. And they're also, they have long lines going to stores because we're keeping them six feet away in the line.

BW: Okay. Seventh area, international coordination. Did you see Henry Kissinger's piece in *The Wall Street Journal* saying—

TRUMP: I did not, no. What did he say?

BW: —there needs—Do you have somebody who will be the focal point of coordinating with all the other countries involved in this?

TRUMP: I do. I do. We have a secretary of state named Mike Pompeo.

BW: And he's focused on this?

TRUMP: Oh yeah. He's very focused on it. We have more than him, but we have a secretary of state, we have—the entire State Department is focused on it. But honestly Bob, it's more of a local problem from that standpoint.

BW: Next area. What's the definition of an essential worker? People feel it's—everyone's defining it the way they want to define it. Do you have a definition or does the federal government—

TRUMP: We have a specific definition. I can give it to you if you want. But we do have a very specific definition.

BW: Well, it seems loose and vague to people. I'm telling you this—

TRUMP: Okay, well, I'll put it out. Maybe I'll talk about that today.

BW: —as a reporter.

TRUMP: Yeah. I'll do that. Essential. Yeah. You know, we had a case where the churches are saying it's essential. It's a very interesting question.

COMMENTARY: An essential worker was someone who was needed to maintain critical infrastructure and continue critical services—this included healthcare providers, police officers, firefighters, utility service crews, and grocery store clerks. All non-essential workers were required to stay home and people were advised to only leave their homes for essential needs like grocery shopping, medical appointments, and outdoor exercise.

TRUMP: The churches are saying they're essential.

BW: How about air travel? Some people say you're just sending planes with four people on it from one city to the next—

TRUMP: Right.

BW: —and that is jeopardizing people. Is there a national policy which—

TRUMP: They're mostly closed down. We have to keep some flights open for emergency purposes, but they're mostly closed down. The airlines are doing checks. We're doing checks. But they're mostly closed down, Bob. But they do have some routes. If you do what some people—you need to have at least a semblance of, a little bit—now, we check people going on, getting off. And it has not been a problem.

BW: Do Fauci and Dr. Birx, do they say this is enough?
            Or this is a leakage—
TRUMP: Well, they haven't complained. I mean, you
            know—maybe I'll ask them that question, but
            they have not complained either.

COMMENTARY: George Kennan, the renowned Soviet scholar and
author of the containment doctrine, had said that presidential aides
and cabinet officers too often failed to tell presidents what they really
thought. Kennan called this, "the treacherous curtain of deference."
Over the decades I had seen and reported on this countless times. Of
course, Trump was also not hearing complaints as he routinely dismissed advice.

BW: Okay. Now who's in charge of the effort and I've
            talked to some people—
TRUMP: [deep sigh]
BW: —who are doing very aggressive, imaginative
            work on vaccines and antibodies.
TRUMP: Right.
BW: Who's in charge of that?
TRUMP: NIH. National Institute, which is phenomenal.
            And they are doing it. They're in charge of it.
            We have a lot of potential vaccines, especially
            probably Johnson & Johnson.

COMMENTARY: Producing multiple COVID-19 vaccines with
life-saving effectiveness years ahead of the regular schedule was an
area the Trump administration did well.

TRUMP: You know, NIH is doing the work, but we also
            farm it out to many, many companies.
BW: Have you talked to Bill Gates at all? Because—
TRUMP: No, I have not. He—But I think I'm going to be
            meeting him very shortly, yeah.
BW: He's the expert. He spent billions of dollars of his
            own money on this. And he says we only get out
            of this when we have vaccines. And so again, I'm
            just reflecting what—

TRUMP:	Well, we're doing great on vaccines. The problem with a vaccine is a vaccine will take 13 to 14 months once you have it. Because you have to test a vaccine. As opposed to the hydroxy, you have to test it. Because the hydroxy's been out there for 25 years. You know, on another disease, okay? On another problem.
BW:	Next area is China on the wet markets. I think Fauci is saying privately in briefings we've got to get China to close down their wet markets.
TRUMP:	Yeah, some people are saying that. And that one I have not done yet. You have to understand, I just signed a massive trade deal turning everything— because China's been ripping us off for years. Like ripping us like you've never seen, economically. Destroying our country.
BW:	No, I—listen, Mr. President, I understand all of that. The question is, you've got some experts like Fauci—
TRUMP:	Well, I don't know. Fauci also said that this wouldn't be a problem, so—this disease was not going to be a problem. I was in the room when he said it, okay? So you know—
BW:	How about the small government Republicans in your own—
TRUMP:	No, but—people have said—people, experts now that are all into it have said this was not going to be a problem. It's going to be easily put out. And some of the people that you mentioned. And you know, they turned out to be wrong on that. So you know, they can be wrong too, Bob. Right?
BW:	Absolutely. I think—I'm telling you as a reporter, I'll emphasize this again. They want a sense of World War II mobilization. President Trump up there saying, these are the 12 areas—this is the person who is going to come before you and tell you—
TRUMP:	All right, I got you. I understand. I got you. I think we're doing a very good job, but I've got

	exactly what you're saying. Now in New York the deaths have fallen for the first time.
BW:	I saw that. Saw that.
TRUMP:	That's a big step.
BW:	How about the small government Republicans who, you know, are real leery of all this spending of trillions of dollars?
TRUMP:	Sure. But they're allowed to their views. I mean, you know, if I did that I wouldn't have closed the country.
BW:	Are they obstacles?
TRUMP:	If I, you know, listened there I wouldn't have closed the country.
BW:	Okay. How about the intelligence agencies? How's Gina doing telling you what's going on in the world?
TRUMP:	I meet with her every day, practically. Her or her people.

COMMENTARY: I was asking Trump about his CIA Director Gina Haspel.

BW:	And do you feel that you know what's going on in the world?
TRUMP:	Better than any president's known in 30 years.
BW:	Okay. And the question—
TRUMP:	I meet with them every day. I have a meeting every single day with them and others, by the way. Defense, et cetera.
BW:	You know, just from 50 years of doing this, sir—
TRUMP:	I know. No, I'm listening to every word you're saying.
BW:	—what is the first person who made you see how serious this was going to be?
TRUMP:	China, when I saw how many people were dying.
BW:	But wasn't that in early February, when you talked to President Xi?
TRUMP:	No! No! It was earlier. Look, I did the stop I

think in January some time, toward the later part of January, Bob.

BW: Yeah. I suspect if you say, sir, full mobilization, we're at Manhattan Project level here—

TRUMP: No matter what I do, they'll always tell you bad.

BW: Okay, but you know what?

TRUMP: I don't care.

BW: —I think people want—even people who don't like you, people who are opposed to you—want this country to succeed on this.

TRUMP: Well, no. I think there are some people that would rather have it not succeed. Okay? That's a big statement. Right?

BW: I hope not. I mean—

TRUMP: Okay. Well, there I disagree with you. There are some people that would rather have it not succeed so that they could possibly beat me in the election. All right?

BW: But they're irrelevant.

TRUMP: No. They're significant, and they're lying, and they control some of the media. Not all of it. I'm doing fine in much of the media. But there's a lot of really fake news out there, Bob.

BW: Listen, we've—I'm looking at this—

TRUMP: You have people that would like us not to succeed, I will tell you that with straightness.

BW: Say that again sir?

TRUMP: You have people—many—there are people on the radical fringes and the left that would rather have us not succeed.

BW: Well, God will never forgive them, then.

TRUMP: Well, maybe that's true. I will never forgive them.

BW: Okay. But you have—

TRUMP: Anything you ask those people—It's like I told you. We need 1,000 ventilators. Here's 10,000. And then they'll tell the press that's not good enough. Okay.

BW: Okay, but—

TRUMP:	It's happening all the time.
BW:	—but if you go to full mobilization—
TRUMP:	I am.
BW:	—and you tell the world and the country that's it, these are the people who are in charge of testing, of unemployment benefits, loans, the food supply, international coordination, air travel, the vaccines, China, the intelligence world, if that's clear to people—
TRUMP:	Right.
BW:	See, if I may bring this up—
TRUMP:	Go ahead.
BW:	During the Nixon case—
TRUMP:	Right.
BW:	—Nixon did not understand the goodwill that people feel toward a president. You know that is a problem now in this country, the polarization, no question. But—
TRUMP:	Yeah, but the ones that like me like me a *lot*, okay?
BW:	But people know this is a survival issue. People are talking about their kids, and they're saying, what kind of world are we going to give to our kids? And—
TRUMP:	They're right. But Bob, when you talk about that—Nixon was an unpopular guy. I have great support out there, Bob. You don't see it, probably, but—
BW:	No, no, I understand that.
TRUMP:	All you have to do is take a look at the polls. I'm getting—I just got a 69 percent or 68 percent for the approval rating for this, and that's despite the fact that you're fighting an uphill battle with these people you're fighting with all the time.
BW:	Okay. Listen, I understand.
TRUMP:	I have great support out there, Bob.
BW:	I'm asking you a series of questions—
TRUMP:	Yeah, I know.

BW:	—based on my reporting.
TRUMP:	Bob, what I have is—I have to—if I'm going to do what you would like me to do, which I'm doing—
BW:	No, no, that's not—
TRUMP:	—I have to go.
BW:	—my job. My job is to tell you—
TRUMP:	Because I've got people waiting downstairs in a big meeting, and I have to go. I'm talking to you.
BW:	Okay. Okay.
TRUMP:	But if I'm going to do what I'm doing and—you know—
BW:	I'll listen at five o'clock if you're coming on, and I appreciate your time.
TRUMP:	Give me the list of the things you said. Did you write them down, or not?
BW:	Yes, I wrote them all down.
TRUMP:	Okay. Give me that list of those things. I'm going to talk to my—
BW:	Okay, what I'll do is send them to Jared, or you want me to—
TRUMP:	Just read them out. Go ahead, read them.
BW:	Okay. The first is testing. It's got to be a Manhattan Project. Number two, the medical supply chain has to be made as perfect as it can be. Experts say you may have to federalize that.
BW:	Number three . . .
TRUMP:	Go ahead. [*fades under the commentary*]

COMMENTARY: I was intentionally channeling the deep frustration felt by Fauci, Redfield, and others. I read Trump the list again. I wanted to make available to him what his experts were saying to me. I could see the breakdown in communication between Trump and his experts was almost total.

BW:	. . . oh, okay, the interest rate is—
TRUMP:	Okay, I got it. Let's move it along. Okay.
BW:	Number five, shelter in place. That there needs to be a national order. I know you don't want to

	wear a mask. The experts are saying—I hear the briefings, sir.
TRUMP:	All right, go ahead.
BW:	Six is the food supply. Number seven, international coordinator who's made it clear this is the person who reports to President Trump and has that responsibility.
TRUMP:	Okay.
BW:	The definition of what is an essential worker. So everyone can know. The next one is air travel. It's not working. Talk to the experts about it. They'll just say for four people going from Detroit to New York—
TRUMP:	I got it. Go ahead.
BW:	Next is the vaccine antibody czar. Somebody who's in charge—
TRUMP:	Vaccines. I got it. I got people in charge. Go ahead.
BW:	Next is China and the wet markets and that whole relationship. Next is how do you accommodate the small government Republicans who are— you know, you make that clear. You're trying to balance something. But this, small government doesn't work. You have signed a bill for $2.2 trillion. That's all you've spent on the defense of this country in the first three years. It's a giant amount of money for a good, necessary cause.
TRUMP:	Right.
BW:	Next is the intelligence. That you're getting it, your people are getting it. There is an assessment of where we are on this globally. And another one is people really need a sustainable income stream. Or an income stream that they can say, okay, at some point I'm going to get this money—whether it's unemployment benefits, cash payments, some sort of loan. This has got to be done—you want people—sorry, that's what people are telling me. They want somebody—

TRUMP:	That's good. I'm glad you told me. Many of these things are done or in great shape. But I'm glad you told me. That's cool.
BW:	Okay, great. This is—
TRUMP:	I will talk to you tomorrow or something, Bob. Okay? We'll find some time.
BW:	Okay, sir. Thank you. You have a good day.
TRUMP:	Thanks, Bob.
BW:	And thank you for letting me be so aggressive.
TRUMP:	No, I like that. I like listening to smart people, okay?
BW:	Thank you, sir.
TRUMP:	Thank you very much. Bye.
BW:	Bye.

[*Phone call ends.*]

BW:	What do you think?
ELSA:	You were really shouting at him.
BW:	I was. To get in a word edgewise.
ELSA:	Your shouting, though, was really loud.
BW:	It's okay. It's okay.
ELSA:	You want to get more information from him, not—
BW:	I know. Like this. I agree.
ELSA:	—telling him what he needs to do.
ELSA:	You kind of sounded like you were telling him what to do.
BW:	Yeah. Well—
ELSA:	You don't want to do that.
BW:	Okay. But we're in a different world now, sweetie.

COMMENTARY: I hung up feeling distressed. Trump never did seem willing to fully mobilize the federal government and continually seemed to push off problems to the states. He clearly didn't see the virus as his responsibility. There was no real management theory of the case on how to organize a massive enterprise to deal with one of the most complex emergencies the United States had ever faced. But without question the aimlessness and absence of leadership at the top was contributing to the nation's inability to respond.

That same evening, Lindsey Graham spoke with Trump by phone.

Graham, who had talked repeatedly with the president during the crisis, also worried that Trump didn't want to own the coronavirus problem.

"He's got one foot in and one foot out," Graham said, describing their call. "He wants to be a wartime president, but he doesn't want to own any more than he has to own."

Graham told Trump he thought it was Trump's job to fix problems, "even if it's not your fault."

Graham told the president he needed a plan. "You need to explain to the country, we're not helpless against the virus," Graham said. "Here's the game plan to beat the virus. You need theater commanders like you've got in Iraq or in Afghanistan. Somebody in charge of testing. Somebody in charge of vaccines. You need a Petraeus to regain your footing. You've lost the momentum."

While Trump's job approval rating had reached the highest level of his presidency the week of this interview, it was beginning a downward slide as the crisis drew on. "You need to peak in October," Graham told Trump. "You need to have the economy showing signs of life. A vaccine on the horizon. Drug therapies that work." Biden would be a rough opponent, Graham told Trump, but his opponent—his real opponent—was the coronavirus.

"That's probably true," Trump answered.

Graham pressed: "If you fuck it up, there's nothing you can do to get reelected. If you seem to manage it well, you're pretty much unbeatable. You keep the body count down, people will see you as somebody that was successful."

The next morning, April 6th, I noticed the president began the day on a cheery note. He tweeted, all in caps: LIGHT AT THE END OF THE TUNNEL!

One of Trump's allies, United Kingdom prime minister Boris Johnson, came down with the virus and was moved into intensive care.

On April 7th Trump said publicly of the virus: "It will go away."

On April 11th the death toll from the coronavirus in the United States climbed above 20,000. The U.S. surpassed Italy as the country with the most virus fatalities.

On Sunday, April 12th, Fauci was asked whether Trump had been too slow to act on the virus. Fauci said:

FAUCI: *If we had right from the very beginning shut everything down, it may have been a little bit different. But there was a lot of pushback about shutting things down back then.*

Hours later, Trump retweeted someone's tweet that suggested Fauci should be fired, sparking widespread speculation and worry about Fauci's fate.

INTERVIEW 12:
You Have Options

Phone call
April 13, 2020

TRUMP: You wrote four books. Bush took—I heard that he took a lot of time with you. He was not a bright man. How he ever got to be president is mind-boggling to me. Mind-boggling.

COMMENTARY: I reached Trump at the White House about 10 p.m. Monday, April 13th. I wanted to follow up with some questions on the areas I had described that needed to be tackled when we had gone over them a week ago. He did not want to talk about the policy details of his administration's virus responses. He wanted to talk about Mueller, impeachment, and the news media.

Trump held a White House coronavirus press briefing earlier that evening. And the president played a montage of TV news clips to the reporters in the briefing room set against dramatic music.

The video criticized the media for downplaying the threat of the virus in January, February, and March and tried to shift the blame away from Trump.

Trump then said:

TRUMP: *When somebody is the president of the United States, the authority is total. And that's the way it's got to be.*

He had total authority but was not exercising it to solve the crisis at hand. Instead, he put on a show, trying to blame the media.

TRUMP:	Hey, Bob, how are you, Bob? I just got in. What's happening?
BW:	Oh, well, you are at the center of the storm.
TRUMP:	Good. I always like that. For me, it's been good. What did I do? You mean what?
BW:	Well, I wanted to ask you for the history that I'm doing. I mean, what a moment.
TRUMP:	I'm dealing with the fake news. And we have them cold, Bob. Everybody's talking about it. We have them totally cold. These are a bunch of—I mean—I don't know. You're not going to—
BW:	I saw all of this. You know, that's going to be litigated for a long time. And I—
TRUMP:	What is going to be? You mean who's got the power over the states?
BW:	No, no, the question of exactly what happened, what could've been done. You know, this happened with 9/11.
TRUMP:	Well, they all said that I acted too quickly. And we have it down on tape. Every one of them. That stupid Maggie Haberman, who should give back—she got a Pulitzer Prize for calling the Russia investigation wrong. How do you like that? All these guys that won Pulitzer Prizes, they got their ass kicked on Russia, Russia, Russia—
BW:	Okay. I suspect, sir—
TRUMP:	No, but why wouldn't they give back the Pulitzer Prize? They were wrong.
BW:	[laughs] Well, they only—it's going to be such an interesting history. But what I want to ask you—
TRUMP:	Interesting—
BW:	—for the history—
TRUMP:	Hey, Bob, they got a Pulitzer Prize for Russia, and they turned out to be wrong. And wait until you see what's going to happen. But they got a Pulitzer Prize for Russia, and they turned out to be the exact opposite. The Pulitzer organization, whoever they may be, should pull those prizes

	back from every one of them. Including the clowns at *The Washington Post*, who are total fake news also. I'm trying to figure out who's worse.
BW:	The issue is, what are you going to do now? That history—
TRUMP:	About what? About what?
BW:	About the virus. Other words, how do you make a decision—
TRUMP:	Oh, I have a plan, Bob. I mean, you know it is what it is.
BW:	For the—
TRUMP:	It's a terrible thing.
BW:	Of course it is.
TRUMP:	Came out of China, and—
BW:	It's a monster. So as you sit and look at this, where do you get good advice?
TRUMP:	Well, I have a committee that I'm naming tomorrow. It's a number of committees, actually. One on religion, one on business, one on medical.
BW:	I saw that.
TRUMP:	Everybody wants to be on it. Everybody. And I'll be announcing it tomorrow. And it's great names. You know, names that you know. And I'm going to be getting advice from them. But even before I get the advice, I have a pretty good idea what's happening here, what I'm going to do.
BW:	But you're going to listen?
TRUMP:	Oh yeah, I do listen. I listen much more than people think.
BW:	Can I say this to you, sir, and ask this question?
TRUMP:	Sure. Sure.
BW:	Having done this for 50 years, on nine presidents from Nixon to you—
TRUMP:	Right.
BW:	—I often found that presidents think they really don't have options. But actually, presidents have incredible options.
TRUMP:	Mm-hmm.

BW: When Bush decided to—George W.—to invade Iraq, his national security adviser Condi Rice—

TRUMP: Oh, the single worst mistake in the history of this country.

BW: And do you know what she said in her memoir? She said, well, we did it because there was no other option.

TRUMP: Oh boy.

BW: Can you believe that?

TRUMP: There was one other option. Don't do anything. Okay? That would've been a nice option.

BW: Exactly. Exactly. And so I wonder whether you have to think about, okay, I'm going to listen, I'm going to weigh it. It's a decision that our grandchildren will be reading about in the history books.

TRUMP: This is a big one, Bob. Do you agree?

BW: Oh, it's the biggest. The biggest.

TRUMP: This is a war. I call it the invisible enemy. This is truly a war.

BW: Yes. But you have options. I've done—

TRUMP: I do. I agree.

BW: I've looked at what you did in North Korea, for instance.

TRUMP: Right, look what happened. Hey, Bob? We would've been at war—had Obama stayed another year, you know, as an example, or an Obama neophyte come in, we would right now be in war with North Korea, 100 percent.

BW: Well, if it hadn't been—

TRUMP: They expected there to be a war with us.

BW: But I've gotten into the details of the pressure campaign and you were—your military was doing some very aggressive, provocative things—

TRUMP: Absolutely. Absolutely.

BW: —to North Korea and you stepped in and said, no, we're not going to do it that way. We're going to talk to him.

TRUMP: We would've been in war right now. And I can't
            tell you—I will not tell you the end result, but
            you saw letters that nobody else has even seen,
            including most people in the admin—you know,
            in the country.

BW: Right, but see, you exercised that option. People
            were saying, why is he giving Kim Jong Un a
            meeting? That's—

TRUMP: Yeah. Well, you know what happened, Bob?
            Obama wanted—11 times he tried. Kim Jong Un
            told me. Eleven times. But I also see it, you know,
            here.

BW: No, that's not—Kim Jong Un gave you bad
            information on that. I don't think that's true.

TRUMP: No, no, Obama wanted to meet with him. Obama
            wanted to have a meeting with him. Obama
            White House, yeah.

BW: That's in dispute. But the issue—

TRUMP: Whatever. That's what I was told.

BW: —is you have so many options, do you realize
            that, in this?

TRUMP: You're talking about having to do with the virus?

BW: Yes, sir.

TRUMP: Yeah, I feel I have options. Yes.

BW: And you don't have to decide except when you
            want to decide.

TRUMP: I agree. But, Bob, we've got to get the country
            back, too.

BW: Of course. And I understand the—

TRUMP: We can't stay out—this is beyond you and I. The
            country isn't designed, structurally—

BW: But you've got to get the wisest advice possible.
            Who's—

TRUMP: You're one of them. You're one of them.

BW: —for history—no, no, no, that's not my job.

TRUMP: You told me something that's very interesting,
            about options. But you're right, you don't think
            of it. But I agree with you.

BW:	And if you go back to the 1950s, when we were kids—I don't know that you remember this—Eisenhower was president, and there was a Two China policy.
TRUMP:	Mm-hmm.
BW:	Red China and Taiwan. Remember that?
TRUMP:	Right.
BW:	And the Joint Chiefs came to Eisenhower and they said, Taiwan's in danger. It's under threat. We want you to authorize the use of tactical nuclear weapons. And Eisenhower said, hmm, let me think about that. The next meeting, they said, we want authorization to use tactical nuclear weapons. And he said, let me think about that.
TRUMP:	Mm-hmm.
BW:	And it happened time and time again, and finally at the end he said, no. Tactical nuclear weapons will open a whole new window of violence.
TRUMP:	I understand.
BW:	And he said no. And I just think from my reading of this, you've got time. You can get the advice from anyone in the world. You can weigh it. You can be like President Eisenhower saying, you know, I'm going to think about that.
TRUMP:	Interesting story to tell me.
BW:	Isn't that?
TRUMP:	Yeah.
BW:	I mean, it floored me.
TRUMP:	Eisenhower was a good president, right?
BW:	Yeah.
TRUMP:	Would you say better than good?
BW:	Yeah, I mean, he was one of the best.
TRUMP:	I saw where Reagan was a big fan of Eisenhower. Is that correct?
BW:	Yeah. And they're—but this idea that you have choices, and the choices are going to matter and define you.
TRUMP:	You're right, though. It's an important time.

BW: And so the process—

TRUMP: With the understanding that we do have to get back to work, Bob.

BW: Yeah, at some point—

TRUMP: The country structurally is not designed—

BW: I understand that. And people are floating ideas—

TRUMP: —for everybody to be sitting home watching television.

BW: Some people can get back—you know, I don't know. But as somebody trying to write this serious history, which you are letting me write—

TRUMP: Right. I am. I've shown you things that I would show nobody.

BW: That, okay, the president talked to this person, that person. He had this meeting. And he said, okay, let me think about that. [*laughs*]

TRUMP: Yeah. That's very interesting.

BW: And think about it, because there are all kinds of wise people out there. Have you been able to talk to Bill Gates?

COMMENTARY: I believed that Bill Gates, the Microsoft billionaire who had worked on virus eradication worldwide, could help Trump understand the necessity of full mobilization.

TRUMP: He called me a little while ago. What do you think of Bill Gates?

BW: You know, I do not know him. I just know he spent billions of dollars on fighting these diseases, and he's very informed.

TRUMP: But he still gets a lot of money from the U.S. government to fight.

BW: Yes, he does. But he puts up a lot of his own money too, and you know about when somebody puts up money, it means they care. Somebody like that, you need to listen to.

TRUMP: Mm-hmm.

BW: And you can say, okay, I'll weigh that. I will talk to all the businesspeople. I'll talk to the Faucis. I'll talk to the experts. And then out comes the—you know, you never make a perfect decision.

TRUMP: Right.

BW: But out comes the best decision. And you and I have talked about this. The interesting issue is you have full mobilization now of the country.

TRUMP: Right.

BW: And people are trying to say, oh, the mayors are doing this, the governor's doing that—

TRUMP: Very smart people that have said, since I beat that impeachment hoax, it was just a hoax, that that puts me in the most powerful position that any president's been in for a long time. Because you beat back a hoax.

BW: Who said that?

TRUMP: I'd like to tell you. I don't know—

BW: Oh, tell me. It should be in the book. It's part of the—

TRUMP: I will tell you a number of people have said it. Lindsey Graham was one that you could speak to. He said it.

BW: Okay. Yeah, I know Lindsey.

TRUMP: You're more powerful than any other president for many years because you have weathered a storm from this scum. He didn't use that word. I do. Like nobody has ever weathered. And it's true. Look at, how did Nixon end up? Not so good, right?

BW: Yes, but what Nixon did, he fired the special prosecutor.

TRUMP: No, but I learned from Nixon. Don't do that.

BW: Yeah, you didn't fire Mueller.

TRUMP: You don't do that. I learned from him. You don't fire him. Mueller fired himself. When he testified, that's when he fired himself. He was a disaster.

BW: Okay. But you have a series of problems. The

	testing—I know you've made the case millions of people are being tested.
TRUMP:	Yeah.
BW:	The experts say if—
TRUMP:	We have good testing.
BW:	Talk to Gates about it. You will never regret listening to somebody, sir. You never will.
TRUMP:	Uh-huh. I mean, one thing I did hear, Gates, and I saw him on some show, and I read something that he said. And one problem is if it was up to him, he'd keep the country closed for two years and you won't have a country to head.
BW:	It's not up to him. But you know, he's big on testing. He's very—I mean, you've got lots of economic problems about unemployment benefits, those SBA business loans. Yes, you make a case—
TRUMP:	Those are doing great, Bob.
BW:	Yeah, but not enough! There are still—
TRUMP:	Well, we're trying to get more. We're trying to get—
BW:	You know what I was also thinking about? Wanted to ask you about. The vaccines, the antibodies. I know there are dozens of firms and scientists working on that.
TRUMP:	Right. Many.
BW:	You know what the government should do? Should award a prize for somebody. Suppose somebody comes up with the vaccine that works, and people are taking it. And it's the end of the year or beginning of next year. What's the value of that to America?
TRUMP:	I agree. You know the biggest problem? We probably already have the vaccine. Johnson & Johnson. You know the biggest problem though, Bob? You have to test it, so you have to make sure—it kills the virus, but you've got to make sure it doesn't kill the person.
BW:	Yes, of course.

TRUMP:	Can you imagine? You vaccinate 100 million people, and you find out it's poison, right?
BW:	Understand. So you have to go through the procedures. But here it is now 10 o'clock. And you and I are working. [*laughs*] How many people are working?
TRUMP:	Not many.
BW:	Most people are not working.
TRUMP:	No. I just got back. I was—I literally just walked in the door.
BW:	I know that. But people are scrambling at those laboratories. And they can accelerate the process.
TRUMP:	They're working hard. How are you doing, okay?
BW:	I'm—listen, I'm doing—I am living this, and I am committed to looking at your whole presidency. Mueller.
TRUMP:	By the way, did you see all the stuff that's been found out with the FBI? This was an attempted takedown of the president of the United States, Bob. Did you see all the stuff that's come out over the last week?

COMMENTARY: The Justice Department inspector general concluded that the Steele Dossier was so flawed it should never have been used by the FBI as a basis for wiretaps.

TRUMP:	This was a takedown by all these guys. Comey, Brennan. Sleazebags. They're all sleazebags.
BW:	I understand—
TRUMP:	Here's the only difference between me and other people. They got caught. They tried to take me down. They got caught. You watch. This was a takedown. The stuff that they found over the last week is beyond anything. You know who's guilty too?
BW:	Who?
TRUMP:	Obama. Went right to him.
BW:	That's going to be litigated.

TRUMP:	It went right to him.
BW:	Here's what I suspect—
TRUMP:	There's no way they did it without him knowing everything.
BW:	Here's what I suspect. When this, the virus business is over, you as president of the United States are going to appoint a commission to look at virus, to look at Mueller, to look at that Steele Dossier, and to look at impeachment. All of those things need to be examined. And that's what I'm trying to do as a lone reporter.
TRUMP:	Good, I love you doing it. You should call up certain people on that, though. There are certain lawyers that have it cold. You should call up—I could give you some names of people—they have this stuff cold.
BW:	Good, give me some names.
TRUMP:	Okay. Well, you can call Jay Sekulow, is one.
BW:	Yes.
TRUMP:	You can call Pat Cipollone, the White House counsel.
BW:	Okay.
TRUMP:	I'll give you some other names. Why don't you talk to those two, I'll give you some other—oh, you know who you should call?
BW:	Who?
TRUMP:	A guy from Judicial Watch named Tom Fenton [*sic*]. The guy's a killer.
BW:	Oh yes, I see. Okay.

COMMENTARY: He is referring to Tom Fitton.

TRUMP:	The other one you should call is Gregg Jarrett. He knows this stuff. Just tell them I said—
BW:	I say this to you directly: what happened in the past, it's getting in the way, I think, of you doing the job—I mean, ask Melania. Is the past—
TRUMP:	Why do you think that, Bob? I think people tried to—this was a coup. This was an attempted and

	failed coup. Like nobody's ever seen before in this country and they got caught.
BW:	When I'm done with it, I don't think that's what it was. I think it was a series of things that—you know, there's a momentum. I wrote four books on George W. Bush's wars. I went through NSC notes, CIA reports. I spent hours with Bush. All of the people.
TRUMP:	Oh, you did?
BW:	And you know why we went—
TRUMP:	Didn't he come out terribly in those books?
BW:	See, what he did—I mean, the third book was called *State of Denial* because he got into denial.
TRUMP:	Let me ask you.
BW:	Sir.
TRUMP:	He spent all that time with you.
BW:	Yes.
TRUMP:	And you made him look like a fool, okay, in my opinion.
BW:	No, no, no. I made—look, he had his say. He had his say. He didn't object.
TRUMP:	Well, that's the only problem. I hope I'm not wasting a lot of time. Because to be honest, I can think of other things I'd rather be doing.
BW:	I understand. And my job is to find the best obtainable version of the truth—
TRUMP:	Ugh. And in the end you'll probably write a lousy book. What can I say? I respect you as an author. But if that's an example, you wrote four books. Bush took—I heard that he took a lot of time with you. He was not a bright man. How he ever got to be president is mind-boggling to me. Mind-boggling.
BW:	Yes, but they went to war in Iraq. His big, defining decision. It was momentum. They kept telling him, oh, it's going to get easier—
TRUMP:	You know, Bob, that's the worst decision in the history of our country.
BW:	Well, it's—it didn't work out, there's no—

TRUMP:	Didn't work out. We spent $8 trillion as of today.
BW:	Well, that's an inflated number. We spent too much. There's no question about—
TRUMP:	I'm talking about in the whole Middle East.
BW:	Okay, so your big decision now is what to do with the virus.
TRUMP:	Yeah. All right, I'm comfortable.
BW:	That's your decision.
TRUMP:	I know. I'm comfortable, Bob. You won't even know if it's a good decision probably by the time you come out with the book.
BW:	[laughs] Well, maybe we will. Maybe it's going to go—
TRUMP:	Well, maybe it'll go away. But it's possible you won't even know about it.
BW:	Yeah, okay.
TRUMP:	You could have a little bit of a flare-up. You know what it does, it flares up a little bit, but it's much less and you wipe it out fast.
BW:	How many experts like Fauci and Deborah Birx, how many of those other people have you talked to?
TRUMP:	I have others. I have many others.
BW:	Good.
TRUMP:	Well, you know, Fauci got it wrong. Fauci said no problem in late February.
BW:	I understand. I understand.
TRUMP:	Okay, you know, just so we understand. But I like him. He likes me. We have a good relationship. We'll find out.
BW:	You know he's become a symbol to lots of people, so you—
TRUMP:	Well, he is, but don't forget they don't say that he got it wrong. They don't ever print that he got it wrong. If I want, I can do that—but I'm not looking to do that to him. I like him.
BW:	I understand that. So you now, when we talked—
TRUMP:	But he did get it wrong. I got it right. I put up a

wall, basically I put up a ban on China. I banned people from coming in from China. Fauci was against it. So was everyone else. I turned out to be right. Almost everybody was against me.

COMMENTARY: Again, this is not true at all. I had talked to five participants who were present at the meeting and who unanimously agreed that O'Brien, Pottinger, Fauci, and Redfield supported the China ban.

BW:	Okay now—
TRUMP:	Took a lot of heat.
BW:	—it's April 13th, so on March 27th, you said publicly, you said, "My priorities are life and safety, then the economy." And no one reported it. I watched that and I wrote it down. I said, ah, that's the strategy.
TRUMP:	That's my priority today. Nothing's changed.
BW:	Life and safety.
TRUMP:	Life and safety. It's an interesting term, because I said life and safety. But life is very important, because this thing is a killer if it gets you. If you're the wrong person, you don't have a chance.
BW:	Yes, yes, exactly. And so—
TRUMP:	Like, a friend of mine died. Very great real estate developer from Manhattan. He died yesterday.
BW:	I know. Listen, students of mine—I teach a journalism seminar—have written me, have had it. And one of the women said she had it, they said she was cured, and they kept coming back with new symptoms. Strange things happened. She had intense headaches—
TRUMP:	So what happened?
BW:	She's in agony. And they're telling her, oh, you're cured now. You're over it. So this—I mean you've said it, this is a monster—
TRUMP:	This rips you apart.
BW:	—this is a scourge. And—

TRUMP:	It is the plague.
BW:	It is the plague. And—
TRUMP:	And Bob, it's so easily transmissible, you wouldn't even believe it. I was in the White House a couple of days ago. A meeting of 10 people in the Oval Office. And a guy sneezed, innocently. Not a horrible—just a sneeze. The entire room bailed out, okay? Including me, by the way.
BW:	[*laughs*] Really?
TRUMP:	No, the room bailed out. I mean, this is a different—
BW:	Well, you're risking getting it, of course, the way you move around and have those briefings and deal with people. Are you worried about that?
TRUMP:	No, I'm not. I don't know why I'm not. I'm not.
BW:	Why?
TRUMP:	I don't know. I'm just not. By the way, how about the oil deal I made over the weekend that everybody said was impossible?

COMMENTARY: Russia, Saudi Arabia, and the United States brokered a deal between oil-producing countries to cut production in an effort to stabilize oil prices.

BW:	That's interesting. And you've been working with the airlines, too?
TRUMP:	Saving the airlines. The airlines are screwed right now.
BW:	A lot of businesses, a lot of people are screwed.
TRUMP:	How about Boeing? Boeing a year ago was the greatest company anywhere in the world, and then the plane fell out and then they had this.
BW:	Yeah, exactly.
TRUMP:	This isn't exactly good for Boeing. It's not like somebody's going out to buy 50 planes. And that Max plane was not their best.
BW:	[*laughs*]
TRUMP:	Not their best thing, right? Who would've

BW: thought Boeing would be—so Boeing is working with us, and the airlines are working with us. And so how did Boeing screw up on the Max? They screwed up in their process. They weren't listening. The CEO was kind of drinking his own Kool-Aid, and he wasn't going down and walking the floor to find out what was going on. Who tests this?

COMMENTARY: The Boeing 737 Max plane was grounded in 2019 after two fatal crashes.

TRUMP: And they also made a mistake. They shouldn't have taken the 737 and enlarged it. The engines became bigger. They hit the runway, they had to move them in. It became a totally different plane.

BW: And a disaster. So you've got the problem that Boeing had, magnified 10,000 times. As we talked about in March, the leadership test—

TRUMP: Well, in terms of—

BW: —a lifetime.

TRUMP: —in terms of the importance of the decision, certainly—

BW: Yes.

TRUMP: —but Boeing, boy, what they've done to that company, you have no idea. It's hard to believe.

BW: Yeah.

COMMENTARY: I had just said I thought the virus problem was 10,000 times worse than the problem of Boeing. He did not challenge me but wanted to talk more about Boeing.

BW: And so you've got your process—you make a—

TRUMP: [blows a frustrated-sounding raspberry]

BW: —important point. By the time my book comes out, I may not know the outcome. But I want to know the process.

TRUMP: All right. What's your time, what's your timing?

BW: My timing is I want to come out in September or October. I've talked to Jared about getting those transcripts of the talks with Xi—

TRUMP: Now think of it: if it's a bad book, you're right in front of my election. That's a beauty.

BW: Well—

TRUMP: Look, you know I was not a Bush fan.

BW: Understand.

TRUMP: Okay? Not because I dislike him. He's been very nice, actually. But I thought he was, you know, totally unqualified for this job. But he—I never saw anything like it. And I wasn't a big fan. The only reason that the father got a good funeral was because of me. Because they figured by building up Bush, that makes me look bad. You understand?

BW: Sure, no, no, let's hope we all have good funerals, right?

TRUMP: I think it's okay. I don't care.

BW: Yeah, I think here's what I do, if I may share this, Mr. President. I get up in the morning and I say to myself, what's hidden? What don't I know? And I say, these are the six people I have to talk to today. I'm not going to bed until I talk to them. And it's amazing how the—

TRUMP: No, you're relentless, there's no question. You're a relentless man.

BW: And, but that's the way—

TRUMP: We almost did this book 25 years ago, I guess. Right? Who would've thought—did you ever think, sitting in the office in Trump Tower, you'd be talking to a guy that's going to be president someday? [*both laugh*] Who would've thought?

BW: I didn't. I told you—

TRUMP: That's—You know what, that's a very interesting story.

BW: Yes. Bernstein saw it though. I'm sorry. He said, this guy's really interesting. And I said, but it's business, it's not—

TRUMP:	Well, you should say that.
BW:	I've said it. I've told you, I've told—
TRUMP:	No, but I don't mean that. You should say it in this book. You didn't say it in the last book.
BW:	Yeah. That's right. I should.
TRUMP:	Which was horrendous, but that was my fault.
BW:	No, no, that was my—
TRUMP:	That was my fault. I mean, I would've loved to have seen you. But they didn't tell me you were calling. And you know, we were rather busy, don't forget. They were trying to impeach me.
BW:	But this—
TRUMP:	They were trying to get me with the fake Mueller report. They were trying to get me with the fake dossier.
BW:	Do you remember when the dossier came—
TRUMP:	So in all fairness to you, Bob, so when you called up, you want to do a book, it's not like, gee whiz, let's talk to him. Do you understand?
BW:	Understand, understand.
TRUMP:	When you called me on—now it's a much different ballgame. When you called me last time, I was under siege. Okay, so here's a thing that's interesting. I come in, and I learned that I'm being investigated by scumbags that are in the previous administration. And I learned that they are trying to do a number, and I figure out that they're trying to take me down. Now it's very interesting. So then they say, oh, the White House is chaotic. Well, if you had a White House where your chief of staff got three subpoenas on the 10th day, where your many people that you know and deal with got subpoenaed to appear before grand juries with scumbags, if you had a White House where all of this activity was an illegal attempt to take down the president of the United States, I think I probably had the calmest White House in history.

BW:	I'm going to tell you, when I'm all done—
TRUMP:	Because nobody else could've done what I've done, and nobody else—there's no president that's done what I've done in my first three and a half years. No president . . .
TRUMP:	I hope you treat me better than Bush, because you made him look like a stupid moron, which he was. Anyway, Bob, you take care of yourself, okay?
BW:	Okay. Okay. You take care. I'll be in touch. I will contact those people—
TRUMP:	Remember, no president has done what I've done in three and a half years.
BW:	Well, you're going to be—
TRUMP:	I just signed my 242nd judge.
BW:	Sir, you're going to be judged by how you handle the virus.
TRUMP:	I disagree.
BW:	No.
TRUMP:	It'll be a part of it, but I've done a lot of other things, too.
BW:	It's so monumental.
TRUMP:	I agree. It's a war. It is a war. It's like being attacked. You know the term I use is the invisible enemy—
BW:	Yes. Yeah, it is a war—
TRUMP:	—which now people pick up, you know what I mean.
BW:	Yes, right. A scourge. You call it the scourge, and it is.
TRUMP:	I was the first one. I call it the plague. I call it the scourge.
BW:	And when it's all—I mean, this—
TRUMP:	I agree, but I'm not going to be judged entirely by that. But that's okay.
BW:	Listen, the other things are going to be there. This is people's lives. And as I was telling you about my student who had it, who all of a sudden you're cured, you can't be tested again—wait, I'm getting headaches, wait, I've got memory loss.

TRUMP:	It's a terrible—Bob, it's a terrible thing.
BW:	Well, we don't fully understand this. I am convinced—
TRUMP:	I'm telling you, my friend—now he had three problems. He was fat, he was old, and he was very rich. [*laughs*] Okay? And the very rich, he didn't—the scourge doesn't like the rich either, okay? So but he called me up like a week and a half ago, two weeks ago. He said, I tested positive. I said, gee, that's too bad. How do you feel? Well, I feel okay. I'm going to the hospital. The next time I called, he was unconscious.

COMMENTARY: Trump is talking about New York real estate developer and longtime friend Stanley Chera, who died at age 77, two days before this call.

TRUMP:	You take care, Bob. Call me. Let me know.
BW:	Okay, thank you, sir.
TRUMP:	Thank you.

[*Recording ends*]

COMMENTARY: Trump had not grasped his responsibility. I continued to talk to Fauci, Redfield, and other experts who voiced continuing alarm at the failure of presidential leadership. The public coronavirus press conferences showcased a president in denial.

In April, Trump started to tell advisers that he'd had enough of the shutdown. According to my reporting, in a meeting Trump ratcheted up pressure on Drs. Fauci, Birx, and Redfield to endorse a plan for reopening.

"I am not going to sit back and preside over the funeral of the greatest country in the world," Trump said. "You guys have to realize. You're my medical experts. But my job is to look at a lot of different factors.

"I don't know how you're going to do it," Trump said to them. "You guys can do what you want. You know, figure out a way to do it, but we cannot stay closed. We've got to reopen."

The doctors acquiesced. They came up with the guidelines for governors to reopen states when their state showed a 14-day downward trajectory in coronavirus cases. Trump was going to declare the war was almost over.

. On April 16th Trump announced the plan publicly.

TRUMP: *Our nation is engaged in a historic battle against the invisible enemy. To win this fight, we have undertaken the greatest national mobilization since World War Two . . .*

Based on the latest data, our team of experts now agrees that we can begin the next front in our war, which we're calling "Opening Up America Again."

Jared Kushner told me he saw this as his father-in-law taking the country back from the doctors.

KUSHNER: The last thing was kind of doing the guidelines, which was interesting. And that in my mind was almost like Trump getting the country back from the doctors. Right? In the sense that what he now did was, you know, he's going to own the open-up. There were three phases. There's the panic phase, the pain phase, and then the comeback phase. I do believe that last night symbolized kind of the beginning of the comeback phase. That doesn't mean there's not still a lot of pain and there won't be pain for a while, but that basically was, we've now put out rules to get back to work. Trump's now back in charge. It's not the doctors. They've kind of— we have, like, a negotiated settlement.

Clearly Trump had rolled the doctors. Governors rushed to reopen. Trump praised the governors who accelerated and ignored his own guidelines. The virus claimed the lives of more than 50,000 Americans in April alone.

TURNING POINT:
Trump's National Security Advisers

Executive Office Building and phone calls
May and June 2020

O'BRIEN: I think the exact phrase I used was, "This will be the biggest national security threat you face in your presidency." I was pretty passionate about it.

On May 1st, I conducted one of the most important interviews for my book *Rage*. It wasn't with Trump. Rather it was with National Security Adviser Robert O'Brien and Deputy National Security Adviser Matthew Pottinger. I had spoken to them previously about North Korea. But this time I wanted to talk to them about Trump's early decision making on the coronavirus. What happened exactly? I wanted the details, particularly the full transcript of Trump's call with Chinese President Xi on February 6th.

I went to the White House to meet with O'Brien and Pottinger in the Executive Office Building adjacent to the White House. Robert O'Brien, a lawyer, author, and former international hostage negotiator, was Trump's fourth national security adviser.

Matt Pottinger, O'Brien's deputy, was a decorated former Marine intelligence officer, brought into the National Security Council staff by Mike Flynn. Pottinger had lived in China for seven years and been a *Wall Street Journal* reporter during the SARS outbreak. A China scholar, he spoke fluent Mandarin.

Pottinger said he knew firsthand that the Chinese were masters at concealing trouble and covering it up. He had written over 30 stories about SARS and how the Chinese had intentionally withheld information for months about its seriousness and vastly understated its spread—a mishandling that allowed SARS to move around the globe. The *Journal* had submitted Pottinger's work for a Pulitzer Prize.

I conducted and taped hundreds of hours of interviews with Trump officials. I am including parts of my interviews with O'Brien and Pottinger because my discussions with them represented a fundamental turning point in my reporting for the book. Trump had told O'Brien and Pottinger to talk to me.

O'Brien said they were very concerned in January about the coronavirus in China. When I spoke to them now on May 1st, four months later, over 67,000 people had died from the virus in the United States.

O'BRIEN: I was extraordinarily concerned, given what we were seeing coming out of Wuhan and given Matt's experience having lived in China during SARS and us having discussed this, that this thing could spread rapidly and quickly.

O'BRIEN: We saw it spreading in Wuhan. And the other problem is we saw people fleeing out of—and I thought, as this thing gets bad and spreads through China, the Chinese are wealthier than they were 10, 20 years ago in prior pandemics. They're going to get out of Dodge. Their health care's not as great. They're going to try to get to Western countries, get to more rural areas, and they're going to get out of China. They're going to spread this like crazy.

COMMENTARY: Pottinger had launched his own investigation into what was happening on the ground in Wuhan. He was uniquely, almost perfectly qualified to advise the president on the virus outbreak in China.

POTTINGER: Meanwhile, stuff that we weren't getting from the intel community but what we were getting from social media and calling people in China on the ground, we were hearing that the death rate was six times normal in Hubei. Okay? So over the course of a month, that translates to about

> 36,000 extra deaths in one city. So this is what
> we were hearing, this is me calling people . . .

Pottinger began shuffling though several pages of notes. When he
says "PPE" he means Personal Protective Equipment, such as N95 masks.

BW: What are those notes?

POTTINGER: Yeah, ah, just some of the background about what
was going on at this time in the world. I mean,
related to this, but it's not—

BW: Like what?

POTTINGER: The PPE dependency. China, we were learning
that they had bulk purchased all of the PPE from
countries all over the world—like a month or
more before they said—

O'BRIEN: Back in January, they sent purchasing agents
around the world and bought up every bit of PPE
they could.

BW: Really?

O'BRIEN: Yes.

POTTINGER: Starting in December.

COMMENTARY: O'Brien and Pottinger then turned to a President's
Daily Brief on January 28th. The "PDB," as it is called, is a meeting
designed to give and showcase the most useful and sensitive, top-secret
intelligence about national security issues directly to the president.
Here is O'Brien recalling that meeting:

O'BRIEN: The next time it comes up is on January 28th,
in the Oval at the PDB. And I think that was an
afternoon session.

O'BRIEN: So I then jump in, and at that point I think
the exact phrase I used was, "This will be the
biggest national security threat you face in your
presidency." I was pretty passionate about it.

COMMENTARY: I can't even find language to describe my surprise.
In 50 years of reporting and dealing with at least 16 national security

advisers beginning with Henry Kissinger, I had never heard of one giving a president such a stark, dramatic warning.

"This will be the biggest national security threat you face in your presidency." The threat was not from Russia, China, Iran, or North Korea, but from the coronavirus.

O'BRIEN: And so look, my concern is with the massive increase in global traffic over the last 20 years. Everyone being able to get on an airplane. People being able to spread this, you know. Just the interconnectivity of the globe today. Every decade it's gotten more integrated and more global than it was before. I was concerned . . .

BW: But you're literally saying to the president, this will be the biggest national security threat you face in your presidency?

O'BRIEN: I told him. Yes. [*This is crosstalk.*] Yes.

I remembered the president's words to me almost three months earlier on February 7th. He had been aware of the nature of the coronavirus. He said it was transmissible through the air and deadly. But he had not told me he had been warned by his national security advisers that it would threaten the United States, that it would be the biggest threat he would face in his presidency. Instead he assured me that President Xi was handling the situation in China.

BW: When I talked to him on the 7th, he's very informed about this. He said it's a tricky situation and the virus goes through air. That's always tougher than the touch. Other words, he's picked it. And then I say, okay, what's the plan for the next eight to 10 months? It's not clear the virus is going to be the big story. And he said, just do well. And I said, help me define well. Remember your reporting days?

POTTINGER: Yeah.

O'BRIEN: I think he had a sense that this thing could be bad. And look, we were all hoping it wasn't. I was hoping I was wrong.

I asked about Trump's call with Xi the night before.

O'BRIEN: I don't think there was ever a point in time
                where the Chinese came out and said, hey, this is
                terrible, it's a pandemic. The WHO was holding
                off on calling it a pandemic for weeks.
POTTINGER: And we think that was under pressure from
                China, do not call it—they didn't call it a global
                pandemic until it took off in the United States.
POTTINGER: We're always getting better information at the
                ground level with China than we get at the top.

I needed more detail and wanted to talk to Matt Pottinger. I didn't
have a home phone number for him. I riffled through one of my old
contact books, so worn the pages had separated from its spine, and I
happened on a number for the nighttime White House signal operation. It worked. I was put through to Pottinger at his home. It was June
8th, around 10 p.m.

BW: You know, the extraordinary statement O'Brien
                made on January 28th about this is going to
                be the biggest national security threat you face
                in your presidency. I want to understand what
                triggered that for him and you. Can you help me?
POTTINGER: I'm going to tell you that background story
                of what led us to that, because it was an
                accumulation of a few different things, okay?
                That happened in the days prior.
                One, I had spoken to a bunch of contacts.
                Included among them were some of the doctors
                who had treated SARS cases and done some of the
                science on SARS back in 2003. Okay? So people
                in China who I reached out to, and to just get an
                unvarnished, informal take on what was going on.
                And what I was hearing from them was, this isn't
                SARS 2003. This is 1918 again.

Again, I was stunned. The basis for the O'Brien/Pottinger assessment to the president was coming from experts who said this would

be 1918 again. The year the Spanish Flu pandemic began in the United
States that killed more than 650,000 people. Pottinger was using the
Chinese medical underground that he had made connections with in
his years as a *Wall Street Journal* reporter.

POTTINGER: It wasn't speculation on their part. It was based
                   on hard data.
                   The key things were that it was spreading
                   asymptomatically, in a big way, and if you were to
                   go back to the SARS outbreak in '03, only—less
                   than one percent of the cases involved suspected
                   asymptomatic spread. Okay. Less than one
                   percent. In fact, there was only one known case
                   out of like 9,000, okay? So in this case, what was
                   the preliminary data, which was not being shared
                   by the Chinese government, was not being shared
                   with the WHO or by the WHO. This is now, I'm
                   talking about guys on the ground saying, "Here's
                   what the real data says." They said 50 percent, as
                   many as 50 percent of the cases are asymptomatic
                   spread, and therefore it's going to be impossible
                   to screen for it. It's going to take off like wildfire.

Asymptomatic means that a person may have COVID-19 but not
present any symptoms. They are still contagious and can spread the
virus to others.

POTTINGER: The fact that we were being told, again, not from
                   any of the formal channels, not from the CDC,
                   not from WHO, not from Beijing organs, but
                   from people close to the action were saying that
                   there is sustained human-to-human transmission.
                   Meaning it's not just like a husband catches it
                   from his wife because they're cooped up in an
                   apartment together and have lots of exposure,
                   but rather people who are second, third, fourth
                   generation removed from the index case. That
                   was happening, and it was happening far from

Hubei. It wasn't just in Hubei province where Wuhan is. And so that and the fact that it was spreading asymptomatically was like the three alarms of a three-alarm fire. And the fact that when I asked one researcher there, I said, is this going to be as bad as '03? He said, don't think SARS 2003. Think influenza pandemic 1918.

BW: And so then you guys made your presentation to Trump. Did he say anything?

POTTINGER: Well, no, he listened to it carefully . . .

BW: . . . and there was rather spectacular coverage in my paper, the *Post*, and *The New York Times*. And on January 25th, three days before, actually President Xi was calling the emergency "grave" and there were literally millions of people—I mean at that point they had over 50 million people quarantined.

POTTINGER: So that was the beginning of a weekend. And then I just started working the phones and also reading social media. Chinese-language social media, so stuff that was a little bit closer to what was happening on the ground. And I came out of that weekend with my hair standing on end.

BW: I see. And so that really triggered this extraordinary kind of statement to the president?

POTTINGER: Yeah. Yeah. That was O'Brien's statement, and I was standing right there . . . I regret to say it all turned out to be even worse than we'd feared, and a few of us were pretty fearful at that point.

With this new information from Pottinger and O'Brien, I went back through hundreds of pages of transcripts of my interviews with Trump and began to chronologically set out all he had said to me about the virus.

When I began with O'Brian and Pottinger's stark warning on January 28th that a pandemic like the 1918 Spanish Flu was heading for the United States, Trump's comments to me in his early interviews become shocking and explosive evidence of his failure to protect the people of the United States as he had promised. He had failed to take this warning seriously.

Trump had ignored the warning from his national security advisers and then continued to ignore and play down the virus as it began to take off in the United States all during February, March, and April.

It was a painful and solemn moment of realization for me.

Seven and a half weeks away from my publishing deadline, I started rewriting my book *Rage* to focus on the absence of presidential leadership, from Trump's failure to warn the public about the threat of the coronavirus to his inaction and deliberate misinformation in the months that followed.

Three days later on June 11th, I spoke with Ambassador O'Brien.

BW: Thank you for your patience. I don't like being a
               pain in the rear end.
O'BRIEN: No, listen. This is important to the president. And
               it's important to you, so I'm happy to help and
               give you whatever time you need.

I asked if he recalled the president's reaction to his warning that the virus would be the greatest national security threat to his presidency:

O'BRIEN: Yeah, I think he was—I don't want to say he was
               surprised, but he kind of, you know, certainly his,
               you know, his head popped up. He was interested.
               I believe he may have asked a question of the
               briefer or two.

               There were two concerns I had. One was the
               reporting that I was getting from Pottinger from the
               people that he was talking to on the ground, saying
               that this is very serious, and, you know, that we've
               got to get our arms around it.

               You know, look, the first step is to cover up
               for most of these communist, totalitarian
               governments . . . And I was thinking Chernobyl

as well. Between what Pottinger was saying, my experience with the avian flu, and knowing how these totalitarian governments will cover up these natural disasters, or even man-made disasters, whatever they are. My concern is what's going to happen if the Chinese have been covering this up, or if they continue to cover it up. You know, this is going to be hard to get our arms around. It was a combination of those things that caused me to make that statement to the president.

February, there wasn't a lot public that was going on. But behind the scenes we were scrambling to prepare ourselves for this thing. Because it was clear that there was—at least from our point of view it was clear that there was a potential tidal wave that was coming, and we had to be prepared and we didn't have enough masks and we didn't think we had enough ventilators, and we didn't have enough PPE . . .

This was something that I thought, and Matt certainly thought, this was something that could develop very quickly. And, you know, create a major problem for the United States, you know, in the short term.

BW: But I lived through February like you did, but as a reporter on the outside. And as I look back on it—what I was doing and who I was talking to—no one told me, hey, we're about to face the biggest national security or health threat that we ever have. I feel, and, you know, this is my fault. I should have been more curious. I talked to the president a number of times during February. You put all this chronology together, and I think the duty to warn that you gave the president on the 28th is an amazing part of this story. He was warned. I don't think the public was told enough. There was not the feeling

	that the public was warned or given a heads up. That's all.

O'BRIEN: Yeah, look. Again, I'm not—
             I'm just giving you the way that I saw it at the time. [*crosstalk*]

BW: I understand.

O'BRIEN: We weren't sleeping, but I do think there was a lack of understanding. And you had all kinds of politicians and people hoping that it was going to be fine. But I can tell you that during the month of February I was very—like, I was using hand sanitizer like crazy, you know—

BW: Oh, you were?

O'BRIEN: Matt and I at one point, I think it was February, arranged to get masks for the White House.

COMMENTARY: O'Brien and Pottinger clearly weren't sleeping. They were taking the protective steps the rest of the country should have been taking.

I called Pottinger again at home on June 17th.

BW: How are you? I'm sorry to call you at home.

POTTINGER: That's all right. What's going on?

BW: Ambassador O'Brien said that in February you started using hand sanitizer in the White House. Is that correct?

POTTINGER: [*laughs*] I'm sure. I mean, I moved—well, it was later that I moved my office out of the West Wing. But that wasn't until early March. But—

BW: When did you move out of the West Wing?
             Out of that little closet-like office, right, for the deputy?

POTTINGER: Yeah. Yeah. I moved out—

BW: I don't blame you. I go way back to people who've lived in that office. Like Scowcroft, and I think Colin Powell was the deputy once, and—

POTTINGER: [*laughs*] Yeah. Yeah.

BW: —Hadley was once.

POTTINGER: Yeah, Hadley was in there.

BW: There are a lot of ghosts in that room, Matt.

POTTINGER: I know. I can feel them breathing down my neck.

BW: And so do you know what, the exact date you moved out?

POTTINGER: I can find it. It was early March.

BW: And when did you start wearing a mask?

POTTINGER: Pretty soon after that. I think it was right around then that I began asking—not requiring, I wasn't quite allowed to require it—but urging and providing masks to NSC staff who were working in the Situation Room.

I wanted to know exactly how Pottinger got his early on-the-ground information from China.

POTTINGER: That was like 25th through 28th I was making phone calls.

BW: I see, and you did it all by phone calls. And this—someone said this was all supported by the intel.

POTTINGER: No! The intel—whose intel? There wasn't shit from the intel community about it.

BW: No, but about what was going on in China.

POTTINGER: No, that's not intel, that's hearsay and Chinese Twitter—not Twitter, but their version of Twitter [*the Chinese equivalent of Twitter is called Weibo*], WeChat notes and—in other words, that was personal contacts and people who were sending stuff on WeChat, not to me personally, just stuff—little videos that were starting to circulate on the internet. [*WeChat is a semipublic messaging app in China; the closest Western equivalents are WhatsApp or Facebook.*] That wasn't intel.

BW: I see.

POTTINGER: None of this—intel was irrelevant to all of this decision-making process.

BW: Well, that's alarming, isn't it?

POTTINGER: It was. Well, it was. It was. We weren't getting intel about this. This was—you know, people just paying closer attention to what Chinese

	people are saying on their internet, social media accounts, and then me calling some contacts.
BW:	And you were kind of a voracious reader of social media, weren't you?
POTTINGER:	Well, that weekend I was. But I'm not—I don't even have social media accounts. I'm not a social media junkie. I hate social media. But I was certainly paying attention to what friends and Chinese contacts and others were starting to forward. This is open-source stuff, not intel. This is stuff that the press had equal access to, you know? [*laughs*] There was nothing that by virtue of my position in government that I had access to that convinced me of this stuff. It was me being a former journalist who'd covered the SARS epidemic that led me to pay attention to sources that were out there for anyone to look at, and contact.
BW:	Isn't that interesting, though?
POTTINGER:	It's interesting. But it's not a case of we had inside dope on this thing because of classified intelligence. That's completely not true. There was no classified intelligence that was telling us, oh shit, look out.
BW:	Right.
POTTINGER:	In fact, it was steering us toward a more complacent interpretation of things. That is *the* on-my-honor truth, as a journalist and as a Marine. [*laughs*]
BW:	Yeah, okay.

COMMENTARY: Now I went back to what Trump was saying around that time. On February 4th, nearly 40 million Americans had tuned in to watch the president's annual State of the Union address, a constitutionally mandated update to Congress about the most pressing issues facing the country. The speech is the highest visibility moment for a president to address matters of great importance. This was a week after the explicit January 28th warning from O'Brien and Pottinger.

About halfway through the lengthy one-hour-and-18-minute speech, Trump mentioned coronavirus in one short, 20-second paragraph:

TRUMP: *Protecting Americans' health also means fighting infectious diseases. We are coordinating with the Chinese government and working closely together on the coronavirus outbreak in China. My administration will take all necessary steps to safeguard our citizens from this threat.*

Trump did not share with the public any of O'Brian and Pottinger's warning from a week earlier that a tidal wave was coming for the United States.

I called Pottinger again on June 19th.

BW: Here's the question, or one of them, Matt. Why, in early February the president gave the State of the Union address, and he made some very passing reference to working with China and so forth. And I just wonder, why not step up to that moment and say, my national security advisers have told me that this will be the biggest threat to my presidency. If it's a threat to my presidency, it's a threat to the country. And I don't know whether they're right or that's true, but there are mitigation actions that can be taken. I mean, it'd be a first in a State of the Union to say social distancing, wash your hands, avoid large crowds, and let's wait and see. Because this thing—you know, it can be delayed. There's an incubation period.

POTTINGER: Yeah. I think there was still deep skepticism among most people in this country and in other Western countries about how serious this thing was going to get. I think people just didn't believe it.

BW: Yeah, but you—you and O'Brien, who had the

	most information, had the most history with all of this, did believe it and did worry. Right?
POTTINGER:	Yeah. You're saying me?
BW:	Pardon?
POTTINGER:	You said who believed it?
BW:	O'Brien and a guy named Matt Pottinger, you.
POTTINGER:	[*laughs*] Yeah, yeah. Exactly. So we were the weirdos. I don't know what to say. It's like even after it became clearer what a threat it was, it was still difficult for people, including the press, including, you know, I mean, fuck, Boris Johnson and his cabinet got together and they were like, yeah, we'll ride it out. Right?
BW:	Right.
POTTINGER:	Next thing you know, they're all fucking in the hospital. It's just, the thing I'm getting at is, it's human nature and not an intent to withhold information or to ignore a duty to warn. I think it's really hard for people to comprehend a threat from something microscopic that they can't see.

I had another question for Pottinger:

BW:	Do you think the word got out emphatically enough in a way that there was this kind of—
POTTINGER:	Well, I—I mean, I think that—[*laughs*] You know, I don't want to comment on it.

As a foundation for writing my book *Rage*, I used each of the transcripts of Trump's interviews with me. I found the evidence of Trump's failure to lead the country most striking in my March 19th interview with him:

MONTAGE OF CLIPS:

BW:	Was there a moment in all of this, last two months, where you said to yourself, ah, this is the leadership test of a lifetime?

TRUMP:	No.
TRUMP:	Part of it is the mystery. Part of it's the viciousness. You know when it attacks, it attacks the lungs. And I don't know.
TRUMP:	I wanted to always play it down. I still like playing it down, because I don't want to create a panic.
TRUMP:	No, I don't take responsibility for this. I have nothing to do with this. I take responsibility . . .
TRUMP:	It was no fault of mine, and it was no fault of anybody's. It just happened. Except maybe China. China, it was China's . . .
BW:	Fauci—have you ever sat down alone with him and gotten a tutorial—
TRUMP:	Yes, I guess, but honestly there's not a lot of time for that, Bob. This is a busy White House. This is a busy White House.
TRUMP:	We're getting very good marks from the governors. We're helping the governors. Because, you know, it's a local problem. You can't solve that federally. But we're helping the governors . . .
BW:	I wanted to capture the moment when your son Barron asked you about this.
TRUMP:	Well, he's just turning 14, so he was 13. In the White House, upstairs. In his bedroom. He said, Dad, what's going on? I said, it came out of China, Barron. Pure and simple. It came out of China. And it should've been stopped. And to be honest with you, Barron, they should've let it be known it was a problem two months earlier. —we have 141 countries have it now. And I said, the world wouldn't have a problem. We could've stopped it easily.

COMMENTARY: After my draft of *Rage* had been submitted to my publisher, I went to the White House on June 30th to meet with O'Brien and Pottinger to find out when they had learned about asymptomatic spread, a key driver of the pandemic.

POTTINGER: It was the morning of the 28th that I—I don't even want to put that date in there. But it was the 28th, we said 50 percent asymptomatic spread, based on the data from inside of China. And China, to this day, won't admit that. You still have the WHO claiming that there is no real asymptomatic spread. It's crazy.

And it took time for a lot of experts to believe that a respiratory, deadly virus would spread asymptomatically. The orthodoxy—the model up to then—is people who are super-spreaders are very sick people. It's highly symptomatic, and so forth. We now know that the way that this virus got around the world was from pre-symptomatic or asymptomatic spread. And, in fact, the highest viral dose, the time when you are most infectious, is right as you're just beginning to show symptoms. That's when you are most infectious. So it's turned the orthodoxy on its head.

You have to remember the human nature element of this. That people—even really smart, informed people whose job it is to look at this stuff—this virus threw curveballs that put them off their game. Okay? The idea that you would have a respiratory disease, a deadly respiratory disease that's spread asymptomatically, I'll tell you, Tony Fauci didn't believe that when I raised it with him.

That solidified in my mind that O'Brien and Pottinger's warnings to the president on January 28th were a crisis alarm bell, not based on a hunch or speculation, but on the best obtainable evidence at the time.

Trump ignored it. He listened to President Xi. He played it down and refused to acknowledge the crisis for what it was: the biggest threat to his presidency and to the American people.

INTERVIEW 13:
I'm Sure He Said It

Phone call
May 6, 2020

TRUMP:	We're coming back. The country's coming back. I'm also a cheerleader for the country. You know I have to be the leader, but I have to be the cheerleader, too. You know? You can't have a deadhead.

COMMENTARY: Now with the new explosive information about the January 28th meeting from O'Brien and Pottinger, I knew I had to confront Trump. It was the old Watergate question: What did the president know and when did he know it?

I reached Trump by phone at around 7 p.m. on Wednesday, May 6th. It was six months before the presidential election.

TRUMP:	Hi, Bob.
BW:	President Trump, how are you?
TRUMP:	How are you doing with my guys that I have working with you? You working with them?
BW:	I am. Jared's really helping. O'Brien is, Pottinger is. I've got some other people helping. And we're getting to the story. Jared said something the other day I wanted to ask you about. I'm going to turn on my recorder. This is all deep—
TRUMP:	Bob, I cannot spend any time on this. I've got the whole Joint Chiefs of Staff waiting for me downstairs.

BW: Okay, good.

TRUMP: Or at least part of them. So I'm going to have to
             go. But tell me, what did he—go ahead.

BW: Well, he was talking—because I'm trying to get
             the big picture. He was talking about how you
             always discuss the touch on the putting green. No
             two putts are the same. So you get to the green
             and each putt is different. The conditions are
             different. The weather's different. You're feeling
             different. And so you always have to adjust for the
             shot that you have to make.

TRUMP: Right.

BW: I think that applies to what's going on now.

TRUMP: It applies to life. It applies to life, and certainly
             to what's going on now. And I'll tell you, I don't
             know if you see it yet, but there's a great spirit
             with this opening up the country, Bob. There's a
             great spirit.

COMMENTARY: I did not feel anything resembling a great spirit. I
could not hear anyone applauding. The country was paralyzed.

TRUMP: And we would've lost two million people, maybe
             more than that, if we didn't do what we did. But
             there's a great—don't believe the stuff with the
             herd, the herd. If we would've left this open, it
             would've been one of the great disasters of all
             time.

COMMENTARY: Trump's reference to "the herd" is "herd immu-
nity," which occurs when a large portion of a community becomes
immune to a disease either through vaccine or exposure.

TRUMP: Look at what's going on in Brazil and look at
             what's going on in a couple of the countries.

BW: I know there's so much out there.

TRUMP: By the way, look at Sweden. You know Sweden's
             lost 4,800 people as of today. Denmark is at 206.

And I guess Norway is at 406. I just have numbers here. So, you know, you hear these stories, but then you say, well wait a minute, but the facts don't bear them out. Brazil is a disaster. You know, they did the herd. You know what the herd is, right?

BW: And so you have to make the calculation how to measure all the conditions: the weather, how you feel, how you make the adjustments—

TRUMP: Yeah, right. That's right. You've got to figure it all out, Bob, otherwise it doesn't work out so well.

BW: Yeah. How do you feel about that now?

TRUMP: I feel that we're doing well. We have six months to go. I was sailing, sailing. Like, I could show you numbers—

BW: I know. I know.

TRUMP: I was up 10 and 12. I was presiding over the greatest economy in the world.

BW: No, I know. And now people say—

TRUMP: [?]

BW: —the race, presidential race, is a coin toss. Do you think that's—

TRUMP: Yeah, I guess. You know, maybe. And maybe not. I'm up 28 points in enthusiasm. That's a big number. [*BW laughs*] Enthusiasm. You know what I mean, right?

BW: Yes.

TRUMP: My people vote, and they vote seriously. And I don't see it with my opponent, Sleepy Joe. But we'll have to see what happens, Bob. We're doing a very good job. We're not getting credit for the job we're doing. The job we're doing is an incredible job, just like the job I did on the economy before. But I think this: if the economy starts going up and if we get rid of the plague—

BW: This is the toughest job. And one of those calls I talked to Ambassador O'Brien and Pottinger about was in March when you talked to

| | President Xi. You started in the middle of the month referring to the Chinese virus. |

TRUMP: Right.

BW: And that set people off, and apparently it set President Xi off. Do you recall that?

TRUMP: Yeah, sure.

BW: What happened?

TRUMP: Well, I referred to it as the Chinese virus. And they called and very respectfully asked if it would be possible for me not to do that. And I said, I respect that request. There was no reason to do that. So I call it lots of different things. But I respect the request. If somebody calls me and respectfully asks me not to do it—I said, I respect that.

BW: And then some of your people kind of were emboldened and went out saying some things about China which really made you worry about some sort of war, or something getting—

TRUMP: No, no, not war. You know, I've seen a lot of tough people over the years. [BW laughs] And you know what? The toughest people aren't the ones that do the talking.

BW: Okay. This is—

TRUMP: A lot of people talking, they talk tough, even people with me. They—

BW: Who was talking tough that got you disturbed? You were concerned.

TRUMP: Well, a number of people. I mean, people that are with me, 100 percent.

BW: Like who?

TRUMP: But I don't want to—I don't want to embarrass anybody, Bob. I don't want to—Maybe I'll tell you when we're together.

BW: Okay.

TRUMP: We'll do a get-together.

BW: Okay. You see why I want to know that?

TRUMP: But the toughest people—you've seen it as much

as I have. You're one of the few who can say it. I've seen a lot of tough people, but they're usually not talkers.

BW: This is what Jared's point is. He also goes on to say—and this is so interesting. He's helped me a great deal.

TRUMP: Good.

BW: He said, you are the first president to understand the real power of America.

TRUMP: Mm-hmm.

BW: And I thought, what is the real power of America? What is it?

TRUMP: So the people that came before me, how they allowed China and other countries to take advantage of us was just shocking. For 25 years, we've been ripped off. You know we rebuilt China? And I give them all the credit in the world. But our presidents allowed it to happen. And how these guys, whether it's Bush or Obama or any one of them—

BW: And they own all of our—not all, but so many government bonds.

TRUMP: Bob, we gave them the money. They don't—what they own, I don't care about that. We got all—we got such power. Because we have the dollar, and we can do what we want. We have the power. They don't have—and a trillion dollars is nothing, now, to have a trillion dollars. We spent—

BW: So what's their—I know—

TRUMP: We spent $3 trillion on this. So that's not the problem.

BW: So apparently President Xi in that call at the end of March suggested there's a cause-and-effect relationship between the tone of U.S. statements and the degree of cooperation he will give. And so—

TRUMP: Wait till you see—look, I am right now in the process—it's a great chess match.

BW: Yes, isn't it?

TRUMP: And we're right now in the process of seeing.
               But over the next few weeks, we're going to see.
               We're going to see. And a lot of things are going
               to happen over the next few weeks, Bob, in a lot
               of different ways, not only with China. But we're
               coming back. The country's coming back. I'm also
               a cheerleader for the country. You know I have
               to be the leader, but I have to be the cheerleader,
               too. You know? You can't have a deadhead. And
               we're going to be very strong. And we're coming
               back, and I think that you're going to have a great
               third quarter. It's a transition quarter. You know,
               we're transitioning in. And I think the fourth
               quarter is going to be really, really good. And I
               think next year is going to be one of the best years
               we've ever had economically, you watch.

BW: Do you feel that you've reached full mobilization
               yet? We talked about this a couple of times. And
               I think that's critical, that people feel, ah, we're
               fully mobilized. We're committed.

TRUMP: Yeah. Yeah.

BW: Is that your—

TRUMP: Yeah, it's very important to—It's very important.
               And plus, we have tremendous stimulus. And
               there's a pent-up demand that's incredible, Bob.
               There's an incredible pent-up demand. You're
               going to see. We're going to transition. You
               understand. We're transitioning now. But we're
               going to transition in. In the fourth quarter, we're
               going to start to see some decent numbers, and
               next year we're going to have among the best
               numbers we've ever had, you watch.

BW: Well, should that happen, you'll win by
               acclimation.

TRUMP: Well, I think there'll be a little bit of fourth
               quarter in the election. You understand, because
               some of it won't be finished yet.

BW: Who was the first person and when—

TRUMP: People are going to see it. If I can, if I get—just wipe out the plague—and people don't expect total wipe—We're going to have, I call them embers. We're going to have little fires, and some bigger fires, and we'll put them out. We learned a lot about that. But if I can knock out the plague, substantially, so that we handle it pretty routinely—and that will happen. And if we can start going up with the economy, I think Trump's going to be very hard to beat.

BW: For the serious history of this, coming out in the fall, how's your relationship with Fauci?

TRUMP: Very good. No problem. No problem.

BW: Okay? He's used—

TRUMP: Everybody said—look, he's a Democrat, but we have a good—you see that.

BW: Yeah.

TRUMP: If there was a problem, he'd know about it. So would you. No, no problem.

BW: Okay. So who was the first person to tell you in January or February and alert you to, my God, this is the plague, this is going to be the big event of your presidency?

COMMENTARY: I was probing to see if he would bring up O'Brien and Pottinger's January 28th early warning. Trump, however, made no reference to it.

TRUMP: Well, you start seeing it, Bob. You don't have to—you start seeing it. You see what's going on and, think about it.

BW: When did you see it first?

TRUMP: Well, I'd say toward the end of January, if you think about it. Because I put the—I did something that nobody else thought was appropriate.

BW: I know, about China.

TRUMP: I put a ban on China coming into this country.

	Only people allowed in were the people that were citizens of our country, American citizens.
BW:	I understand that you knew—
TRUMP:	They went through a lot to come in, too. They had to go through quarantine, a lot of other things. But I did a ban at the end of January on China coming in.
BW:	I know. Listen, I know. And I understand—
TRUMP:	And Pelosi and Schumer and all these losers are talking at the end of February and March about how this whole thing is going to blow over. And by the way so was Anthony Fauci at the end of February. He's saying it's going to blow over. So you know, so.
BW:	Yes, I know. He said that publicly.
TRUMP:	So that's, you know, that's the end of that.
BW:	Did you ever talk to him about that? Said hey by the way on the ninth—
TRUMP:	He said to me, very specifically in front of a group of people, that President Trump saved hundreds of thousands of lives when he put a ban of China on the border. And let me tell you, I had a room of 20 or 21 people and everyone in that room except me did not want to have that ban.
BW:	Yeah. So I understand—
TRUMP:	Because it was too early.
BW:	—your new national security adviser, O'Brien—
TRUMP:	Right. Well—
BW:	—said to you on January 28, "Mr. President, this virus is going to be the biggest national security threat to your presidency." Do you remember that?
TRUMP:	No. No.
BW:	You don't?
TRUMP:	No, I don't. No, I don't. I'm sure if he said it— you know, I'm sure he said it. Nice guy.

COMMENTARY: He's sure that O'Brien said it, but he doesn't remember it? What a moment. I marveled at the clever, lawyerly dodge. What an amazing underhanded confirmation. It was a classic Trumpian evasion. Because O'Brien and Pottinger had been so specific and detailed, I was confident that the warning had been delivered. Now Trump at least had confirmed, "I'm sure he said it."

TRUMP: Look, on January 29th, or whatever, the end of January, I put a ban. I put a ban on. And the ban was very powerful, and China couldn't come into our country. Then after that, a number of weeks later, I put a ban on Europe coming in. Nobody would've done those two. First time it's ever been done.

BW: Where'd you get the idea of putting the restrictions—

TRUMP: And then Nancy Pelosi wanted people to go at the end of February and dance in the streets of San Francisco. China. Chinatown.

BW: I know. Listen, in early—on January 3rd, there were people looking at this in the world of epidemiology and immunology. Some of the best scientists in the country. On January 3rd, and looked at it and said, my God, there are 44 cases, and they've got 121 quarantined and they say there's no human spread. And they jumped out of their chairs and said, that can't be. Of course there's human spread.

TRUMP: Mm-hmm.

BW: And I've talked to these people. I said, why didn't you call me? Why didn't you call President Trump on January 3rd?

TRUMP: Right. Right. Nobody called us, yeah.

BW: Because they're all in their own little cave.

TRUMP: They never did. And—nobody did. No, when I put the ban on, I did that more from what I was seeing on television and reading in the newspapers. I was reading about China. And I said, wait a minute, we can't have—and I was surprised at how many people come in from

	China. It's a lot, when you add it up. So anyway. Hey, Bob, I have to go. I'll talk to you soon.
BW:	Yes, sir. Good.
TRUMP:	Are my guys taking good care of you, then?
BW:	Couldn't be better, and I thank you—
TRUMP:	The A-plus treatment. The guy is one of the greats, let's give him the A-plus so let's see if he can actually write a good book about somebody. Because I deserve it. So long. Take care. Say hello to your wife, too, Bob.
BW:	Thank you, sir, have a good evening. Bye.
TRUMP:	Okay? Thanks, Bob.
BW:	Bye.
TRUMP:	Thanks. Bye.

[*Recording ends*]

COMMENTARY: Now in my book I had to show the grand scale of Trump's inaction and deceptions in the face of a serious and still mounting crisis. Fifty thousand lives lost would only be the beginning.

INTERVIEW 14:
I Ain't No Bush

Phone call
May 22, 2020

TRUMP: You're probably going to screw me. Because,
                    you know, that's the way it goes. Look, Bush sat
                    with you for hours and you screwed him. But the
                    difference was, I ain't no Bush.

COMMENTARY: At 9:18 p.m. on Friday, May 22nd, I reached President Trump by phone at the White House. It had been two weeks since we last talked. Trump was doing a 180 degree turn from his natural optimism. At the same time, he seemed to be searching for someone else to blame.

OPERATOR: Mr. Woodward, the president.
TRUMP: Hey, Bob.
BW: President Trump, how are you?
TRUMP: I'm good, Bob. I'm good. Busy day. Just got back
                    in two minutes ago. Let's see, what time? 9:18. I
                    had an early night tonight. That's good.
BW: What a time. I need your help.
TRUMP: Yeah. How are my guys doing with you? Good, I
                    hope?
BW: Yeah, look, they're doing great. But you know,
                    these are your decisions. And what I need your
                    help on is, as you're living the sea of daily stories,
                    I want to do the serious history. And O'Brien
                    and Pottinger have been good, but they won't

give me the kind of transcript of those two calls
with President Xi. And if I'm going to do a
serious history here, I can't get caught up in what
happens each day. I've got to focus on the key
relationships.

TRUMP: Let me look at it. I'm going to read them. I'm
going to get them. I have an order out for them.
Let me read them. They're very good calls.

COMMENTARY: I still wanted the Xi transcript to see if Chinese
President Xi provided Trump with a warning about the virus that was
somewhat equivalent to what O'Brien and Pottinger had told him on
January 28th. My presumption was that this call was the basis for
many of Trump's comments to me on February 7th about the virus.

TRUMP: You know, I've very much hardened on China.
BW: Yeah.
TRUMP: So. I'm not happy. Let me tell you, I'm not a
happy camper.
BW: Yeah. What really turned you? What—again, for
the serious history, I've got my recorder going.
TRUMP: We had a great trade deal. And $250 billion—
it's—the ink wasn't dry, and this thing happened.
And you know, I'm going to probably show you
at least what these calls were. And you'll see. I
wanted people to go into China.
BW: Twice you said, my people are ready. You almost
said their bags are packed.
TRUMP: He didn't want to do it.
BW: Yeah. And he—
TRUMP: I was okay with it. You know why? Because I
figured they knew what they were doing. Okay?
And they either did or they were incompetent,
and either one is no good.
BW: But he stiffed you. I mean, when you look
back on—
TRUMP: No, he didn't stiff—let's say—I think he was, you
know, he's a prideful person. And he thinks that

	they were able to contain it. Or not. Okay? You know, there's a chance, or not. You understand that, right?
BW:	Of course. Of course.
TRUMP:	But he thought he was able to contain it. And I think what could've happened, Bob, is that it got away from them and he didn't want to contain it from the rest of the world because it would've put him at a big disadvantage.
BW:	Sure. But I think at that point—this is February 6th, when you talked to him—and it's pretty obvious that there's a giant problem. And, you know, O'Brien and—
TRUMP:	No. Maybe it is, but Nancy Pelosi and Schumer and all these guys were into March before they—
BW:	No, I understand that. And that's why—
TRUMP:	They like to say I wasn't quick. I banned them at the end of January, right? So I was really ahead of schedule. I was—I'll tell you what, I was the only person that wanted to do that. Nobody. Fauci, nobody wanted to do it.

COMMENTARY: This is not true at all. His national security and health experts had advocated for it.

BW:	But you see, if people are going to understand serious history, that I have to have the detail.
TRUMP:	Okay. I will—
BW:	If you—
TRUMP:	I'll talk to you over the next couple of days. I'm going to take a look at it. Okay?
BW:	Okay. Pottinger and O'Brien, I need them. If you don't give them the green light, they're worried that they're going to do something that you won't approve of.
TRUMP:	All right. I understand. Look—
BW:	You know how it—
TRUMP:	—you're probably going to screw me. You know,

	because that's the way it goes. Look, Bush sat with you for hours and you screwed him. But the difference was, I ain't no Bush. Boy oh boy, what a mess. I'm trying to get out that mess that he got us into in the Middle East. And I'm doing it, too. You know we're down to 8,000 soldiers in Afghanistan? Four thousand in Iraq. Getting the hell out of there.
BW:	Right. And somebody told me you want to go to zero in South Korea by October. Is that correct?
TRUMP:	Well, if they don't pay. You know they paid—I got them to pay a billion dollars. And I said, you've got to pay much more. So they're paying a billion dollars. A billion a year. Nobody knows this stuff. Nobody even—oh, you heard that, right?
BW:	Oh, yeah. And I know—
TRUMP:	I said, I'll visit you in a few months, and we'll start talking about more money. They offered me $300 million additional. So that would be a billion three. And I said, I'm not accepting it. The agreement expired. I said, I'm not renewing it. I'm putting you on a month-to-month basis.

COMMENTARY: At the end of 2019, Trump threatened to pull U.S. troops from South Korea if they did not agree to pay $5 billion. That would be a 500 percent increase on the roughly $900 million they paid in 2019.

BW:	Yeah, and—
TRUMP:	They've gotten away with murder.
BW:	What does Pompeo think? Someone told me he's worried that we'll just exit completely, and he's not delighted with that prospect.
TRUMP:	I don't—I think he is. I think he wants them to pay for—they're a wealthy country, and why should we be subsidizing their military?
BW:	I know you've always—

TRUMP: Now we've done it for 80 years. It's ridiculous. It's ridiculous. Why should we be? You know, Saudi Arabia is paying us billions of dollars now, right? Billions.

COMMENTARY: Trump was exaggerating. Saudi Arabia paid the U.S. approximately $500 million for its troop presence in December 2019.

BW: Let me ask you this, and this again, for the serious history in the fall—do you ever get down? Do you ever feel, my God, an avalanche of one thousand problems has descended on me?

TRUMP: This is the good thing, Bob, I'm so busy [*laughing*] I don't have time to get down. Okay? It's crazy. But you know, Saudi Arabia. So you know, they wanted some protection. They didn't have protection when they got shot at eight months, nine months ago, whatever, a year ago. And they wanted protection. I said, yeah, but—I don't mind giving you protection, you've got to pay.

COMMENTARY: Trump is selling protection without seeming to understand the enormous strategic value in the alliances themselves.

BW: Okay. Well, if you can get Attorney General Barr to talk to me, look, he knows me going back 30 years ago.

TRUMP: Okay.

BW: I'm going to take what he says seriously. And if you can give the liberation flag to O'Brien and Pottinger—

TRUMP: I thought they were pretty open with you. I told them—

BW: Yeah, they were, but you know, look, I want to go all the way.

TRUMP: Because I have nothing to hide.

BW: Okay—

TRUMP: I'll tell you what, Bob, we would've been at war
            with North Korea if it wasn't for me. You'd be in
            a war, ending one way or the other, right now.
            But you would've been in a war two and a half,
            three years ago if it wasn't for me. That was a war
            deal. They expected to be in a war. They were
            ready for a war. And there was tough rhetoric at
            the beginning. And the rhetoric is what stopped it.
            But you know, the whole thing with me and him,
            it was public rhetoric. Very public.

BW: Yeah. But you want a serious, real history. And so
            when this comes out, people say, ah, okay, this is
            what—

TRUMP: I want a real history that's the truth.

BW: Yes, exactly. Same here. And I'm—

TRUMP: If people had any idea what I do. Now, if you just
            look at the list—hey, Bob, I'm going to be up to
            280 judges very soon. [BW laughs] Nobody's ever
            had that. Two hundred and eighty. You know?
            Nobody's ever had that. You know what I did?
            You have the judges, a lot of them are older—

BW: I know and—

TRUMP: —and they go on senior leave. And we convinced
            many of them to go on senior leave. And, more
            importantly, Obama gave us 142 judges when I
            came here. This never happened. You never had
            one. If you were a president, you would never have
            any federal—they're like golden nuggets, right?

COMMENTARY: Republicans had controlled the Senate for the last
two years of the Obama presidency and Majority Leader McConnell
blocked most appointments. The Senate confirmed 234 of Trump's
judges by the end of his term.

BW: So I think the whole virus business and the
            relationship with China and your decision-making
            tree—in earnest, so somebody can look at this and
            say, ah, that's authentic. That's what happened.

TRUMP: I'd be inclined to give you the call, but I'm going to have to take a look. I will though.

BW: Great. And let's do it, and let's get it right. And I don't want to be in a position where, well, I can't quite find out this, or this isn't—You know, we've opened the doors on this, and let's go through them all the way.

TRUMP: Nobody's ever done what I've done, Bob. And nobody's ever done so much. When you look at our list of things that I've done, nobody's ever done that. Like even a little thing like getting massive amounts of money from some of these countries that were freeriding us. You know, they were freeriding us. Take care of yourself, Bob. I'll talk to you very soon. Okay?

BW: Okay. Okay, sir. Have a good night. Thank you.

TRUMP: Say hello to your wife. So long.

BW: Thank you. Bye.

[*Recording ends*]

INTERVIEW 15:
George Floyd

Phone call
June 3, 2020

TRUMP: These are arsonists, they're thugs, they're
              anarchists and they're bad people. They're bad
              people. Very bad people.

COMMENTARY: On May 25th, a Minneapolis police officer Derek
Chauvin was caught on camera with his knee pressed into the neck of
George Floyd for nine minutes and 29 seconds, torturing and killing
Floyd, a 46-year-old Black man.

A massive wave of protests erupted in more than 140 cities across
the country on a scale not seen in America since the Civil Rights
Movement and the Vietnam War. "Black Lives Matter" extended its
reach as a rallying cry against racism and police brutality.

On Sunday, May 31st, in Washington DC, a fire was set in the
basement nursery of the historic St. John's Episcopal Church, a thousand feet from the White House. Following the fire, the church had
been boarded up. A city curfew set by DC mayor Muriel Bowser was
scheduled to begin the next day, June 1st, at 7 p.m.

Trump, in a phone call with the governors stressed the need to use
force against demonstrators. He wanted an energetic crackdown:

TRUMP: *You have to dominate. If you don't dominate,*
              you're wasting your time, they're going to run over
              you, you're going to look like a bunch of jerks.

Trump returned my call on the morning of June 3rd.

BW:	Sir.
TRUMP:	How's the book?
BW:	Haha, boy—
TRUMP:	How are you doing, am I keeping you busy enough?
BW:	You give me new chapters.
TRUMP:	Yeah. It's law and order, Bob, law and order. We're right where I want.
BW:	Do you have a few moments to—
TRUMP:	Law and order, Bob. So, anyway. And among other things, by the way. The other thing is your economy is going to start going up very soon. The numbers were much better today. You know, the unemployment numbers were shockingly better— five million better than they thought. States are opening up and they're opening up strong. You look at Florida, you look at Georgia, you look at many of the states that are opening. They're strong. And if I can get this thing going up prior to the election, you will watch—it's happening and it's gonna happen. And the virus, we're doing very well on vaccines. We're doing very well on therapeutics. We're doing very well on cures. And we're going to get ready to send in the military, slash, National Guard to some of these poor bastards that don't know what they're doing, some of these poor radical lefts. Of course, you're a poor radical left to an extent, I guess.

COMMENTARY: I think in his mind this is at least partially how he thought of me.

[BW *laughs*]

TRUMP:	We're going to send in the troops because they don't know. I did it in Minnesota and I put out his problem. And he's been very thankful. He wanted no troops, and I said we're sending them. Because Minnesota was a disaster, Minneapolis.

BW: Can you tell me, just real quickly for the history, I'm turning on my recorder, Mr. President, and that is—

TRUMP: Bob, I'm going to get off the phone real fast. I got about 20 guys. And I'll talk to you later, I don't mind. How are you doing with my guys, though, are they helping you at all?

BW: Good, good. We're doing okay. I want to get the, you know, what happened, step-by-step, in reaction to the George Floyd tape. Did you see it?

TRUMP: Yeah, I saw it. It was terrible. I thought it was a terrible thing. I've said it—

BW: I know you have.

TRUMP: During my speech. My rocket speech on Saturday.

BW: Yes.

TRUMP: Which you probably saw.

BW: Yeah. Of course.

TRUMP: I said it during my China speech on Friday. And I said it the day before yesterday.

BW: Did you see it and, you know, watch the whole thing, or just parts of it?

TRUMP: I got to watch—oh yeah, sure I got to watch it. Everybody did. All you need is a television, it was on.

BW: Where were you and who was with you and—

TRUMP: Well, I watched it numerous times. I mean, mostly I was in the White House, upstairs, because I don't get to watch much television during the day. I mean, upstairs. And I watched it. It's been on, it's been on a lot. No, it's a terrible thing and strong feeling toward it. I don't like it at all. I'm very unhappy about it. And action has been taken and it will be taken, and it will be dealt with. And I think the riots are—I put it out in Minneapolis [*says Min-ee-an-apolis*]. That was the worst one of all. They were ripping down the city. They're all liberal Democrats, every one

	of them is a liberal Democrat. Hard to believe, right?
BW:	And the question is, how did you decide, okay, I'm going to give that law-and-order speech?
TRUMP:	It was very easy for me to decide. Because I looked and there was no law and order. And the radical left Dems and the Democrat—they're all Democrat mayor or governors. I mean, every one of them. Every one of them. Every one where there's weakness is that. So that was an easy speech for me to write. Usually I write them and/or substantially adjust them.
BW:	Did somebody help you?
TRUMP:	Yeah, I get, I get people. They come up with ideas. But the ideas are mine, Bob. The ideas are mine.
BW:	And then—
TRUMP:	Want to know something? Everything is mine. You know, everything. Every part of it.
BW:	And then the decision to go across the street? You know, that's getting lots of attention.

COMMENTARY: It was one of the most photographed and video-taped parades of the Trump presidency and almost everyone at the White House that evening appeared to trail the President on his walk across to St John's Church.

Included in the group walking with him was Defense Secretary Mark Esper and Chairman of the Joint Chiefs Mark Milley.

Esper and Milley were disturbed. They had been called to the White House for a meeting but realized Trump was using them for his political spectacle.

"We've been duped," Esper said to Milley as they walked to the church. "We're being used."

Milley agreed and turning to his personal security chief, said, "We're getting the fuck out of here."

Boarded up and charred, the church and the sprawling scene outside brought the racial unrest convulsing the country to Trump's front door.

Trump stood for about two minutes, holding a Bible uncomfortably and waving it around.

TRUMP:	Yeah, both good and bad. But it's—
BW:	With the Bible—
TRUMP:	Well, read Hemingway's article today. She—it's total bullshit. They didn't use tear gas. Number one, I didn't know if there was anybody—I just said, I think I'll go across the street.

COMMENTARY: Park Police and DC Metro police later confirmed that tear gas and pepper balls were used on protesters in Lafayette Park.

TRUMP:	Well, these nice, wonderful people tried to burn down the church the day before. You know, they were all saying, these were nice people. Well, they weren't nice people. They were rough people. And the day before, they tried to burn down the church. And so now the Republicans are all on my side. By the way, I had a big night last night. We won all of—every race that I endorsed. And I'm 64 and 0 this congressional cycle, 64 and 0 on endorsements. Both wins, and wins in primaries. And many of them were losing before I endorsed.

COMMENTARY: That's a big win and I'm sure it gave him a big boost.

BW:	And so the idea of standing there with the Bible, that's quite a photo.
TRUMP:	It's my idea. And a lot of people loved it.
BW:	Yes. A lot of people did. And I'm sure a lot of people don't.
TRUMP:	Perhaps.
BW:	Why did you decide to use the Bible as a symbol?
TRUMP:	Because I thought it was terrible that they tried to rip down a church that was built simultaneously

with the White House, whose first parishioner was James Madison, who was also the first person in the White House, number six.

COMMENTARY: James Madison was the fourth President of the United States. John Adams, the second president of the United States, was the first to live in the White House.

TRUMP: And I thought it was a terrible thing, and a terrible symbol that they could do such a thing. And made a strong statement, and people loved it. Other than the radical left, people loved it. And by the way, they ought to appreciate it, but they tried to knock it as much as possible. And Mollie Hemingway actually wrote a great piece on it. I hope you read it.

BW: Okay, I will look at it. Did you actually go—

TRUMP: You got to look at. On my Twitter, you'll actually see it on the tweet. Anyway.

BW: Did you go down in the bunker, as they said? In the PEOC?

COMMENTARY: News reports said the president had been rushed to the White House Presidential Emergency Operations Center or "PEOC" the previous evening.

TRUMP: I had a choice. And it was really more of an inspection than anything else. He said, because they wanted me to inspect it. It was a very minor event, and I just went down to inspect it. It was, first of all, it was during the day, where there was no problem during the day at all. You know, when people get rambunctious, it happens during the night. This was during the day, long before there was any darkness. And they said, would you like to inspect it now? Would you like to go down? I said, oh, I'll go down. And then they write a fake piece in *The New York Times*, like I'm sitting in

a bunker. That was during the day and it was the
inspection, the second time I've ever seen it.

BW: And were you there a long time, or just looking
            around?

TRUMP: Uh, fifteen minutes. Just looking around. Looking
            around, came right up—it was during the day!

COMMENTARY: Attorney General Bill Barr later concluded that he
thought Trump was embarrassed to be led down to the bunker and
wanted to project strength with his walk across to St. John's Church.
Barr would later say on Fox News that it was not an inspection.

> BARR: *Things were so bad that the Secret Service*
>   *recommended the president go down to the*
>   *bunker. We can't have that in our country.*

BW: It's not exactly a cozy place, is it?

TRUMP: No, it's just—you know, it was really, you're
            supposed to go and inspect it. And I did. And I
            did it. They said this would be a good time. I said,
            why? They said, well, we got people outside, but
            there's no problem. It was, I think four o'clock,
            five o'clock in the afternoon. It was during the
            day. Trust me, it was beautiful.

BW: Who suggested that you inspect it?

TRUMP: Huh? One of the Secret Service guys said, you
            don't have to do it now—I didn't have to go
            down—it was, I went down as an inspection. And
            they said I went down. And the reason I went
            down as an inspection was, it was appropriate
            to do because I had to go down and inspect it
            anyway. And I got—and they made it sound
            like I was in there. Not that there'd be anything
            wrong—plenty of people have been. Not a big
            deal. Not a big deal. And down there's not a big
            deal. But I was only there for 15, 20 minutes. And
            it was more walking around, looking at things.

BW: I see. And you didn't go again.

TRUMP:	No, I didn't go again. I went one time, very quickly. It was an inspection, and they made it sound like it was—again, Bob, it was during the day.
BW:	Sure, I know. Listen, that's why I'm asking.
TRUMP:	There were very few people during the day. There were almost no protesters.
BW:	And the question is, I mean, people are up in arms, as you know.
TRUMP:	About what?
BW:	About the whole, you know, they want a kind of gee, let the protesters walk around.
TRUMP:	No, that's only if you watch CNN and if you watch MSDNC. Or you read *The New York Times* or your favorite newspaper, *The Washington Post*. Outside of that, the people are very unhappy. These are arsonists, they're thugs, they're anarchists, and they're bad people. They're bad people. Very bad people.
BW:	Even the peaceful protesters? There are a lot of peaceful protesters.
TRUMP:	Uh, there are not many. I'll tell you what. Not many. These are very well-organized things. You'll be seeing that when it comes out. These are very well-organized. Antifa's leading it. These are very well-organized events.

COMMENTARY: Antifa, an abbreviation for "Anti-fascist," is a decentralized movement. It is not an organization and does not have a leader or membership dues.

BW:	Well, we're going into the election.
TRUMP:	Very well-organized.
BW:	Everyone keeps asking, suppose it's a close election, and it's contested. What are you going to do? Everyone says Trump is going to stay in the White House if it's contested. Have you thought—
TRUMP:	Well, I'm not—I—I don't want to even comment on that, Bob. I don't want to comment on that

	at this time. Hey, Bob, I got all these people. I'll talk to you later on tonight. Because I have to go because of the—
BW:	Okay, great. You have a good day, and I thank you for calling, sir.
TRUMP:	Uh, and my guys I know are working hard with you. We'll give it a shot. If I have a fair book, it's going to be a great book. Did you see the book they wrote about Trump and Churchill? Did you see it, it just came out?
BW:	No, I haven't seen that yet.
TRUMP:	It just came out.
BW:	A competition, huh?
TRUMP:	It's doing good. No, it's not competition, but it's a historian who's very respected.

COMMENTARY: Trump is referring to the book *Trump and Churchill: Defenders of Western Civilization*, by Nick Adams, a conservative writer and vocal Trump supporter.

BW:	So you feel—
TRUMP:	And he gave me a rating as one of the greatest presidents ever, because nobody's done what I've done. And it's true. I don't know if you ever got a list of the things that we've done—individual things. But nobody's done what we've done. And now I've got to—and the economy, I'll do it again. It's already started. By September, October, the economy will start heading up. And once it starts heading up, and in big numbers, we're going to have a phenomenal following year. But by September, October—maybe sooner— but by September, October, you'll start to see tremendous jumps in employment and GDP. And by October it'll be really big. And the numbers will be announced, and I'll win the election. Watch. Better than where I was before. Better. Where I was riding high.

BW: Okay. Well this is where we're pointing to. And,
                of course, you bought ownership of the whole
                problem, the racial tensions, by making your
                declaration of law and order.
TRUMP: Law and order, that's right.
BW: You realize that.
TRUMP: I'll take my chances. Thanks, Bob. You're the
                greatest.
BW: Okay, have a good—we'll—I'll call tonight, sir.
                Thank you.
TRUMP: It would be an honor to get a good book from
                you, but that probably won't happen, but that's
                okay, too. Thanks, Bob.
BW: Thank you, sir.

[*Recording ends*]

COMMENTARY: In his Rose Garden address on June 1st, Trump did not talk about racism or the long list of black deaths by law enforcement. Instead, he was quick to label those demonstrating for civil rights as "domestic terrorists" and threatened to "dominate the streets" with "thousands and thousands of heavily armed soldiers."

Trump had met with Defense Secretary Mark Esper and Chairman of the Joint Chiefs General Milley in the Oval Office that morning. He wanted them to bring in the 82nd Airborne. Milley and Esper were both shocked.

Esper explained to Trump the 82nd was trained to take the fight to the enemy with highly lethal combat weapons. They were not trained in crowd control and civil unrest. They were exactly the wrong troops for the job.

Trump asked Esper about the Insurrection Act, an 1807 law that gave the president the authority to use active-duty troops to suppress a domestic insurrection. Esper advised him it was not warranted at all.

Esper brought the 82nd Airborne to Maryland to appease Trump. This would be a very important issue after the election.

In the last two weeks of Trump's presidency, on January 6th, 2021, Trump supporters stormed the Capitol, attempting to prevent the certification of Joe Biden as U.S. President. Trump did not invoke the Insurrection Act, nor did he make any calls for military support.

I had worked as hard as I ever had during May of 2020 since learning about O'Brien and Pottinger's warning to Trump about the coronavirus threat. I completely reconfigured my book to begin with the January 28th warning and set out chronologically Trump's response to the coronavirus. On June 3rd, I sent a 401-page draft of the book to Jonathan Karp, the chief executive officer of Simon & Schuster and my editor for this book.

INTERVIEW 16:
You Really Drank the Kool-Aid

Phone call
June 19, 2020

TRUMP:	You really drank the Kool-Aid, didn't you? Just listen to you. Wow. No, I don't feel that at all.
BW:	You don't?
TRUMP:	I've done more for the Black community than any president in history with the possible exception of Lincoln.

COMMENTARY: Trump called me unexpectedly on Friday, June 19th, the day commemorating the end of slavery in the United States. We had not spoken for over two weeks, as I was working intensely to finish my book *Rage*.

TRUMP:	Hi, Bob.
BW:	How are you?
TRUMP:	How are you doing?
BW:	Well, I'm making progress. Trying to finish a first draft. I was going to try to call you tonight. I appreciate—
TRUMP:	Are my people being good and responsive, I hope?
BW:	Well, I've still run into some roadblocks.
TRUMP:	Where, Bob?
BW:	Well, I'm trying to get those transcripts of those calls, or some part of it—
TRUMP:	With President Xi?

BW:	Yes.
TRUMP:	Okay. Let me work on that. I will work on that. I'll get them and I'll talk to you about them, okay. I'll figure it out.

COMMENTARY: One night, Trump's Chief of Staff in the White House, Mark Meadows, called me at home and said I would never get those transcripts because the transcript of the Zelensky phone call had led to Trump's first impeachment.

BW:	I appreciate it.
TRUMP:	I had very good calls with him, but since they sent us the plague I'm not so thrilled with them, okay?
BW:	Right. I know. You told me that. What do you think's going on? I've talked to all kinds of people. And the Chinese are not only stonewalling still, but there's some evidence that this is quite dark and nefarious. That they're allowing the— allowed the virus to spread. What do you think? I'm turning on my recorder, if I may, sir.
TRUMP:	I'm the one that said that louder and clearer than anybody, if you want to know the truth.
BW:	Yes.
TRUMP:	I'm the leader of that group. Because I think they could have kept it—Now, it is starting up in Beijing, which is interesting. I don't know if you've been seeing that over the last few days.
BW:	Yeah. Of course. Yes.
TRUMP:	So—
BW:	What are they up to? What's their motive?
TRUMP:	Well, I think—I think they could have done a hell of a lot better job stopping it coming out to the rest of the world, including the United States and Europe.
BW:	Do you think they intentionally let it come to the United States and the rest of the world?
TRUMP:	There's a possibility. I don't say they did, but there's certainly a possibility.

BW: Well, you mean that—if they actually did this intentionally, President Trump—

TRUMP: It's definitely a possibility, Bob. You know, the ink wasn't dry on my— You know, I did a great deal on trade. They're buying a lot of stuff. And they're—by the way, they are buying. And that's one of the things I watch every day. They're buying a lot. They're buying tremendous amounts of farm product and stuff. But the ink wasn't dry when the plague came in. And I'm not happy. But with everything being said, Bob, watch what happens, okay. Remember, I told you, the stock market is close to an all-time high and we're not finished with the pandemic yet. I have a rally tomorrow night in Oklahoma—

BW: I noticed.

TRUMP: Over 1.2 million people have signed up. We can only take about 50, 60 thousand. Because, you know, it's a big arena, right? But we can take 22,000 in one arena, 40,000 in another. We're gonna have two arenas loaded. But think of that. Nobody ever had rallies like that.

BW: Okay, I understand that. Now, I really want to spend a moment and dig as deeply—

TRUMP: Okay.

BW: Because this book is designed to understand you deeply—

TRUMP: Good.

BW: Your reaction to the protests. And, you know, I've seen what you've said and so forth.

TRUMP: I think—Yeah, I can give you my reaction. I think that the weak liberal Democrats have handled their cities very badly. And I think the strong people have handled it very well. You'll see what happens in Oklahoma.

BW: Let me ask you this. I mean we share one thing in common. We're white, privileged, who—my father was a lawyer and a judge in Illinois. And we

know what your dad did. And do you have any
sense that that privilege has isolated and put you
in a cave, to a certain extent, as it put me—and I
think lots of white, privileged people—in a cave?
And that we have to work our way out of it to
understand the anger and the pain, particularly,
Black people feel in this country? Do you see—

TRUMP: No. You really drank the Kool-Aid, didn't you?
Just listen to you. Wow. No, I don't feel that
at all.

BW: You don't?

TRUMP: I've done more for the Black community than any
president in history with the possible exception
of Lincoln. And I say possible—you know why
I say possible. Because I'm not sure that Lincoln
started off the way it finished. In other words, you
know, there are those who say he didn't have the
slaves in mind when the Civil War started. You
understand.

BW: Okay. But I don't think it's the Kool-Aid, Mr.
President, I think there is a reality out there that
Black people feel. And part of our job is—I mean,
you and I talked about this some months ago, that
you're governing in an environment where there
are two Americas.

TRUMP: Yep.

BW: Remember that?

TRUMP: And by the way, Bob, it's been that way for a long
time. A lot longer than when I've been here. It's
been that way under Obama, and it's been that
way a long time. There was great division under
Obama.

BW: Sure. But, you know, we talked about this.

TRUMP: The silent—It was a much more silent division,
but there was tremendous hatred and tremendous
division, more than there is now.

BW: You're convinced of that?

TRUMP: Yeah.

BW: And we talked about history's clock, remember that? And I said my analysis was that you came and seized history's clock when you were elected. And that the Democrats and your party, the Republicans, did not know what was going on in America. Remember that? Agree with that?

TRUMP: Sure, I do. I do.

BW: And that—

TRUMP: It's still true. It's still true about, you know, the Democrats and many people in the Republican Party.

BW: Okay, understand—

TRUMP: But I know what's going on. I know what's going on.

BW: Okay. The question is, there's been a shift. And it's substantial. And it's, I think, incumbent on white, privileged people like myself, like you, to say—and I don't think this is Kool-Aid. I think it is understanding points of view that may not come to us naturally.

TRUMP: But I don't have to be there to understand a point of view.

BW: Okay.

TRUMP: I don't have to be Black to understand the Black point of view.

BW: Right. But you—

TRUMP: I don't have to have gone through personal slavery in order to understand the horrible atrocity that—that people have suffered. I don't have to. You know, I don't have to put myself in that position. I can fully understand it without being in that position.

BW: Oh, no, exactly. But do you consider it an atrocity, do you consider—

TRUMP: Oh, absolutely. Slavery? Absolutely.

BW: And what's happened after, up to this day, that we do not have a system of equality and equal opportunity?

TRUMP:	[*exhales*] Well—
BW:	I'm pushing.
TRUMP:	It's been going on for a hundred years, Bob.
BW:	Sure, but—
TRUMP:	It's been going on for a hundred years, plus.
BW:	Okay. You see what I'm asking.
TRUMP:	I fully do. No, it's very fair. It's been going on for a hundred years plus. It's been going on for a long time. And we've made a lot of progress in a lot of different ways. And a lot of progress is being made as we speak. I mean right now. More than you would even think. But this has been going on for many, many years. Many, many years.
BW:	And is not your—we've talked about this—your job is to bring people together?
TRUMP:	I agree. But before I can bring them together, sometimes you have to bring them to a point. You have to bring them to a point. And we're getting close to it. We've made a lot of progress in the last short period of time.
BW:	Let me—
TRUMP:	Don't forget. Until the Chinese plague came in, we had the lowest unemployment in the history of this country for African Americans. We had the lowest unemployment numbers by far, African American. We had the lowest for Asian, Hispanic, too. But we had the best employment numbers in the history of our country. And then we got hit with the plague. Now here's what's happening.

COMMENTARY: Black unemployment had been steadily decreasing for nine years, since 2011. When Trump became president, he also inherited a growing economy from Obama.

| TRUMP: | I'm building up the economy, Bob. And the economy is—Remember, I told you you're gonna have a V-shape? You don't have a V-shape, you might have an I-shape. "I" is almost—Look at |

the job numbers, look at the retail sales numbers. Look at these numbers that are coming in. Wait till you see the third quarter, how good it's gonna be, when your book comes out.

BW: Okay, you've been saying that to me. And the question is—

TRUMP: Well, it's been true. It's been true, Bob. Look at the numbers. We had the highest employment numbers in history two weeks ago. We had the best retail sales numbers increase in history two days ago. In history, Bob.

COMMENTARY: Millions of jobs were added in May and June [of 2020], undoubtedly good news but not historic. More than 22 million jobs had been lost in March and April alone.

BW: Okay, but this—

TRUMP: Wait till you see the numbers come in.

BW: For people out there struggling, for people—

TRUMP: Yeah, but they won't be struggling for long, Bob. They're struggling because we had to turn it off. Because if I didn't turn it off, we would have lost 3 million lives instead of 150,000, or whatever the final number will be. But it will be in that vicinity. We would have lost 3 million lives. And you know what? That's not acceptable, 3 million lives.

COMMENTARY: But two years later, in May 2022, the reported death toll from COVID-19 in the United States was more than one million people.

BW: Let me ask this question, please. Bear with me on this, because I think it's one of the pillars of trying to understand. And if I'm a Black man out there, how am I going to say to myself, ah, President Trump understands my plight, my pain, and he is—the numbers, yes. I understand the work on the economy.

TRUMP:	Wait till you see by the third quarter, by the time your book—well, I don't know when your book is coming out. But by the election, we will have some of the greatest numbers ever released by any country. And it's already happening, Bob. Now, unless some crazy thing happens.
BW:	But do you think that the person out there wants the president to understand how they feel?
TRUMP:	I do, Bob. Let me just tell you, I passed criminal justice reform. Obama couldn't get it done—
BW:	Listen, I understand this.
TRUMP:	I passed opportunity zones. Obama and all these people that came before me, not only Obama, couldn't get it done. Nobody could get done what I got done. I got prison reform done. I got criminal justice reform done. I got—forget all about the good economic numbers, which will be just as good in a very short—because I turned it off and now I turned it back on.
BW:	Okay, I understand. Have you won the hearts of minorities and Black people in this country who feel pain and anguish and are angry? Have you won their hearts? That's my question.
TRUMP:	Okay, you ready? Yes. I did, prior to the plague coming in. But now a lot of those jobs that were, were won—the Black people had the lowest unemployment numbers in history!
BW:	Okay, but they're, if you're—
TRUMP:	They had the best jobs! They were making more money than they ever made!
BW:	Okay, but half the people—
TRUMP:	Have you—
BW:	Half the Black people—
TRUMP:	Yes, but you saw some of my polls with Black— with Black people.
BW:	Okay, but let me ask this, sir. Because I want to understand. Half the Black people now, right on this day in June 2020, are unemployed. And you

	look at the polls, you look at the protests, and you talk to people—
TRUMP:	They'll be employed very soon, Bob.
BW:	And they're—
TRUMP:	It's all coming back. They're going to be employed. Okay—
BW:	Okay, but you—
TRUMP:	Before the plague, they had the best numbers ever. Everybody was doing great. They were getting tremendous increases. They were making more money and people were happy. When the plague came in from China, then a lot of people lost jobs. Those jobs are all coming back. Black people will all be employed very soon, just like they were before. And the numbers will even be better.
BW:	Okay. But as you know and as you've said, the murder of George Floyd triggered something in people. Not just Black people, minorities, but in white people—who are saying, you know, like I'm trying to say, I think I've been a privileged white person. I know you have been, right? [*Three-second pause*] No?
TRUMP:	I don't—I don't get into that argument. I've done a good job for Black people. I've done the best job of any president since Lincoln.
BW:	Okay.
TRUMP:	Other than Lincoln.
BW:	Now, here's the other question.
TRUMP:	I don't get into that. You know, there's no point to getting into it. All I can do is what I'm doing. I have done the best job of any president of the United States history, other than Abraham Lincoln, for Black people. I got criminal justice reform; I got Black colleges and universities.
BW:	Okay. Have you won their hearts? Because this is a business of the heart. I think—
TRUMP:	I'll let you know that at the end of my term when they get their jobs back. Okay? And it's gonna

be before—it'll be before, by the end of the year
you're gonna see numbers like nobody's ever seen
before. And it's already happened, Bob. Two days
ago, you had the greatest retail sales numbers in
history, Bob.

COMMENTARY: He seemed not to understand racial inequality
went way beyond job numbers.

BW:	Okay, listen, I understand this. But some of this, part of this—
TRUMP:	And that will all make a "V." Remember I told you a "V" and you disputed it? You were disputing it. And 90 percent of the people were disputing it, right? Now, now, they're all saying Trump was right. It's beyond a "V." In fact, the market's up today almost 200 points. We're ready to set a record on the stock market, and the pandemic is ending, it's weaving its way out—and by the way, we're going to have a vaccine soon and we're going to have therapeutics soon. Hey, Bob, could I call you later so I can get to these generals to make sure everything's good?
BW:	Okay, that's great. That's—I really want to push, and I need to talk—
TRUMP:	I don't mind.
BW:	I need to talk—
TRUMP:	I don't mind. You're a good man, I hope you're truthful. If you're truthful, you're going to write a great book. And if you're not truthful, you're gonna hit me.
BW:	I—
TRUMP:	Bye, my man, I'll talk to you later.
BW:	Okay, thank you, sir.
TRUMP:	Very good. Absolutely.
BW:	Bye.
TRUMP:	Thanks, Bob. Say hello to your wife. Bye.

[*Recording ends*]

COMMENTARY: I called him again that night. He did not call back. I wondered if that might be the last conversation we'd have. He had said, "The pandemic is ending; it's weaving its way out." That day, COVID-19 cases were rising in 23 states with 10 seeing their highest single day increase.

Senator Lindsey Graham had told Trump, "Right now if the election was held, you would lose."

INTERVIEW 17:
Nobody's Done What I've Done

Phone call

June 22, 2020

TRUMP: Bob, I'm somebody that likes to get things done
                  rather than talk.

COMMENTARY: Trump held his rally in Oklahoma's 19,000-seat
BOK Center on Saturday, June 20th. This was his first public campaign
event since March. City officials had worried about a "super-spreader
event," and urged Trump to cancel it.
     In our previous interview, Trump had told me:

TRUMP: I have a rally tomorrow night in Oklahoma—
BW: I noticed.
TRUMP: Over 1.2 million people have signed up.

Less than half of the arena was filled, and Trump had to stare into
rows of empty blue seats. This was the focus of most media coverage.
     Trump called me on June 22nd, at 8:15 p.m. Protesters were trying
to tear down the Andrew Jackson statue in Lafayette Square. As we
spoke, police began to push protesters away from the still-standing
statue. They were using tear gas and batons.

TRUMP: I just got to the White House, and I'm watching a—
                  an event go down where they're trying to rip down
                  a statue in Washington DC and we're stopping
                  them with great force, I think. I'll let you know. But
                  it's terrible what's going on. Terrible.

350

BW:	What do you think of all that?
TRUMP:	I think it's a disgrace. I think it's disgraceful. You know, it's been going on for a long time, indirectly. But it's gotten more direct. And I've stopped them. On the federal basis I've stopped them strongly. But some of these states are, in some cases, foolish. In some cases, weak. But it's a terrible thing that's going on in that sense. Yeah.
BW:	Well, how—I appreciate you calling. And I'm trying to wrap up the book.
TRUMP:	Okay.
BW:	Have you been able to look through all that stuff Matt Pottinger gave you?
TRUMP:	I have looked through it. And what I could do is I can see if—Bob, I can show it to you, but it would be a big violation to actually give it to you. You know, it's about a conversation. So I could show it to you, you could sit, read it, do whatever you want with it.
BW:	Okay.
TRUMP:	But I think it would be a big violation to go beyond that. You know what I mean.
BW:	Okay. Understand that.

COMMENTARY: Investigations later conclusively established that Trump had a very casual, even reckless attitude toward classified documents and classified information.

TRUMP:	Did you watch the speech on Saturday night?
BW:	Oh, of course. Every word. Every single—
TRUMP:	So it's very interesting. It just came out, that the headline, quote, Trump rally gives Fox News the largest Saturday night audience in its history. I'd say that's not bad, even by your standard, right? Largest Saturday night audience in the history of Fox.
BW:	That's quite something. It was—
TRUMP:	It just came out 10 minutes ago. I thought you might be interested in it.

BW: It was quite a speech. How do you feel? Because
               everyone, or lots of people, are writing about the
               blue empty seats.

TRUMP: Ah, I know, it's disgraceful. First of all, let me tell
               you. For two weeks, these people did nothing but
               talk about, if you go there it's gonna be a death
               chamber. You'll die, essentially. You know, I'm
               exaggerating.

BW: Yes.

TRUMP: But they basically said horrible, horrible things
               about, don't go there, don't go. Don't go. The
               networks. You know, the fake news. Then we had
               protesters there who were quite violent. About
               300 of them, from various groups. Then we had
               curfews imposed on people that got there five
               days early. And, let's see, there was one other
               thing. Whatever.

BW: Yeah.

TRUMP: And we still had a nice crowd. But, Bob, I don't
               know if you noticed, but they like to show the
               upper ring. The upper ring was a little—by the
               way, the first empty seats I've ever had. But I've
               never done one in COVID. You know, I mean—

BW: Yeah.

TRUMP: Now what does make up for that—

BW: Did you—

TRUMP: You know, we had a nice crowd. We probably had
               12,000 people there. That's still a lot of people.
               But it was very hard to get in. You had a lot of
               pro—you know, not a lot, but you had some
               pretty violent protesters.

COMMENTARY: The Tulsa Fire Department said 6,200 people were
in attendance in the arena that can hold 19,000. There were some
heated conversations between Black Lives Matter and Trump supporters, but no violence was reported. Trump opened his rally speech by
immediately blaming protesters and the media for scaring away his
supporters.

Trump refers to his supporters as the "Silent Majority":

TRUMP TULSA RALLY (AUDIO): I stand before you to declare. The silent majority is stronger than ever before.

This phrase was made famous by Nixon in 1969 as he rallied support for the Vietnam War amidst growing vocal public opposition to the war.

The term "silent majority" was his reference to conservative voters who sat on the sidelines and avoided public debate.

A Gallup poll taken after Nixon's nationally televised speech showed that 77 percent of people supported Nixon's policy in Vietnam at that time.

TRUMP:	And I'll tell you what. The speech itself got unbelievable reviews from everybody. I don't know. I hope you enjoyed it.
BW:	How long did you work on it? And you're using the teleprompter on that, you have to?
TRUMP:	No. I would say maybe 25 or 30 percent teleprompter. The rest was ad-lib. How long have I worked on it? Very interesting question. I guess my whole life I've worked on it, right? No, when you think of it. No, I didn't work on it. I just I tend to be able to tell stories when I get up to a microphone. And it did get great reviews from everybody, even the haters. So.

COMMENTARY: His speech received the opposite of great reviews. He did not address the death of George Floyd. He referred to the coronavirus as "Kung flu" and failed to talk about the nation-wide struggle for racial justice.

In a follow up to his speech at West Point a week earlier, Trump demonstrated that he could drink a glass of water with one hand and could walk down a ramp.

TRUMP:	But it was, it was good. And we had a really wonderful—I mean, we had a wonderful

audience. But, again, Bob, if you turned on any newscast—NBC, C— they talk about, how could he do this? How could he bring people in? Why should—why should people go? It's a pretty tough environment to crack. And yet we had a good crowd.

BW: Yeah. And so, yeah. About, well about two-thirds or a half—

TRUMP: I would say it was about two-thirds. Maybe 70 percent, 65, 70 percent was full.

COMMENTARY: I was still trying to get the transcripts of Trump's phone calls with President Xi.

BW: Okay. Here's where I am, and the reason I want to look at those transcripts. Because I understand, from people who I've talked to about it, that you're being the diplomat. You're trying to talk to Xi and say, hey, look, let us come in and let's look at this—

TRUMP: I did.

BW: And he's, he's, you know—resisting you. And saying—

TRUMP: Yeah. I did. I wanted to go in.

BW: And then on March 26th—

TRUMP: I wanted at a minimum, the World Health Organization to go in, which at that time, you know, I'm saving $500 million a year now. I terminated the relationship.

BW: And on March 26th, which is the second call I've asked for, as I understand, President Xi suggested a cause-and-effect relationship between the tone of what U.S. officials were saying about this and the degree to which he would, China would, cooperate with you. Other words, he's kind of threatening you, almost blackmailing you, saying, tone it down or we won't cooperate. Is that right?

TRUMP: No, I would say that he was very respectful. He

	asked me if it would be possible not to call it the China virus.
BW:	Yeah.
TRUMP:	Or the Chinese virus. And the problem is after that, they tried to blame it on Europe, and they tried to blame it on soldiers, American soldiers in Europe. So, you know, you become a free agent.
BW:	But you're trying to work it out with him. You're not angry or threatening. I mean, I understand, and I think this is people who've gone through this—he was kind of threatening you. Look, hey, if you don't, kind of, tone it down, we will not cooperate with you. And, of course, you've got to get cooperation to find out, as you say, what is this plague? Is that fair or not?
TRUMP:	So I'd have to read it. It depends on your definition of who was, who was tougher with who. I don't know. I'd have to really read that. But it was an interesting conversation. And as time has gone by—I think you've probably seen my attitude—
BW:	It's toughened. It's toughened.
TRUMP:	I mean, and it's changing more and more.
BW:	Has he asked to talk to you?
TRUMP:	You have to understand, I made a great deal, and the ink wasn't even dry when the plague floated in, okay?
BW:	Yes, I know you've made that point. Okay. Now—
TRUMP:	You understand that. The ink, literally, the ink wasn't dry. And they could have stopped it. I believe they could have stopped it.
BW:	Okay. Now, the other thing is, I need to talk to Attorney General Barr. Only about the Mueller Report. As you remember, as I remember, two years of your administration was Mueller. And Barr is the one who looked at that and, if I may quote him, said, what the fuck is this? The Mueller Report. Because, as you know, they

	ducked all the hard questions, they didn't say anything.
TRUMP:	They found nothing. At the end of two years, they ruled no collusion. And they just put out some very unimportant things. And it was—and the Attorney General and the staff ruled no obstruction. And there was no obstruction. And also, when there's no collusion, that means there's no case.

COMMENTARY: The Mueller report cited 10 instances of possible obstruction of justice but did not reach a conclusion because of a Justice Department policy that a sitting president could not be charged with a crime.

BW:	But do you see why that's important to my story, because that was two years, and it went on—
TRUMP:	Two wasted years.
BW:	And will you be willing to—
TRUMP:	Two wasted years and billions of dollars, because what it did to the country was so bad. You know, I mean, the focus of that stupidity. And then you saw Mueller testify—
BW:	Yes, certainly.
TRUMP:	And it was like a lead balloon dropped on top of it.
BW:	Okay. Is Barr still working for you? Can you ask? I mean, I know him—going way back decades—to talk to me? I cannot get through. Because I know he's had lots—
TRUMP:	Well, you know he's a different kind. He's a very private guy. He really doesn't like doing interviews. He likes to do the—
BW:	Well, he does it all the time, though, Mr. President.
TRUMP:	Though one thing I will tell you, also—
BW:	Yes.
TRUMP:	You're going to have some very interesting things happening, in my opinion, with respect to Strzok and Page and Comey and all of these people. I think it's gonna be very interesting.

BW:	Well, we'll see this. I mean, this will be chapter two.
TRUMP:	Yeah. You're coming into a very interesting time.
BW:	Will you ask him to talk to me?
TRUMP:	I will, but, um—
BW:	Look—
TRUMP:	It's not his thing. In other words—You know, he's doing a very good job. Really a great job. And we're really breaking up the Deep State, Bob. This was horrible. They spied on my campaign, and they got caught.
BW:	Well, we're gonna find out about that. And it's gonna be very interesting.
TRUMP:	Well, look, they did. When you see Strzok and Page talking about an insurance policy.
BW:	I understand that. But they spent two years, and I mean, here's—here's the little dirty secret of all of this. I know this from going back to Nixon and Watergate and looking at Clinton's case, Reagan's case, Iran-Contra, remember that? You have to have an insider who's gonna come forward and say, this was my corruption. This was somebody else's corruption. But they never had an insider. And so when you look at this, you have nothing. Not after two years, but after a month. Because a good prosecutor, like a good reporter, will say: What have you got? They have—
TRUMP:	They should have ended it after the first four days. Because after that they found out that the dossier was a fake. They found out that Christopher Steele was a fake. They found out— all of these things they knew. And not only that, they canceled, text messaged back and forth—you know, they had text messages—
BW:	Sure, listen, I've looked at the whole thing—
TRUMP:	Bob, hey Bob, thousands of text messages. But you've seen everything. You've seen what the evidence is. Hey look, before you even get to Durham, did you take—I assume you took the

	really tough report that was written on Comey, right? You've seen that?
BW:	Yes, of course. And look, who knows what the ending is.
TRUMP:	They never had anything.
BW:	And if anyone had—
TRUMP:	What a shame. And how unfair that was to me, Bob. Yeah, they never had a damn thing.
BW:	And I need to get Barr's perspective on it. That's all. If you'd ask him.
TRUMP:	I mean the one thing, Bob. He is very busy.
BW:	I know. Listen—
TRUMP:	He's got—he's loaded down with that, you know, that whole thing is moving big. He's loaded down with all of this stuff. And he's not somebody that will easily pick up the phone and say, gee let's talk, or let's sit down. You know, he's a—he's not a PR guy like a lot of these guys. Like Comey.
BW:	I understand. I'll show up at his doorstep. I know where he lives. I'll do that. Anyway—
TRUMP:	I will talk to him. But I just want him to feel comfortable. I think he's doing a really good job. By the way, honey, I'm talking to Bob Woodward. Our great first lady—the great Bob Woodward, honey.
BW:	Melania, how are you?
TRUMP:	The first lady just walked in the room.
MELANIA:	I'm very well, thank you. How are you? [BW and Melania greet each other at the same time.]
BW:	Can I say hello to her? How are you?
MELANIA:	I'm good, thank you, how are you?
BW:	Good. Well, so they did that book on you and they're giving all kinds of credit to you for knowing how to live with this man.
MELANIA:	[laughs]
TRUMP:	I didn't know this. What book is this? I want to read this one.

COMMENTARY: The book was *The Art of Her Deal* by Mary Jordan.

MELANIA:	Bob, it's a book of some correct stuff and some not correct stuff. So—
TRUMP:	You know, she's very popular, Bob. I go out and make speeches, they all held up signs: We Love Our First Lady. She's actually very popular. She's done a good job.
MELANIA:	Mm-hm.
TRUMP:	Honey, you know this man is one of the great legends of all time? He's doing a book on me. It'll probably be atrocious, but that's okay.
MELANIA:	When [is] it coming out?
BW:	It's coming out in September.
MELANIA:	Okay.
TRUMP:	Nobody has done more than Donald Trump in the first three and a half years of a presidency. That I can tell you, Bob.
BW:	Well, see, what—
TRUMP:	And I can tell you that with surety. In fact, we have to send you an update.
BW:	Now, last time we talked, I thought you were upset with me because you said I was drinking the Kool-Aid about—
TRUMP:	With regard to what?
BW:	With regard to the protest movement and so forth.
TRUMP:	Yeah, a little bit, I think so. I think you probably think they're wonderful people and they're not.
BW:	Okay, and let me just follow up and ask this question.
TRUMP:	Go ahead.
BW:	Because it's the great British novelist Graham Greene who says, don't despise your enemies or people who are on the other side. They have a case. And I was arguing with you. And I was arguing, I was pushing. You have to understand— just like I, as a reporter, have to understand—

how people reach conclusions, what their
emotions are—

TRUMP: Okay. I'm okay with that.

BW: You have to step out of your own shoes.

TRUMP: Yeah.

BW: Don't you?

TRUMP: Uh, yeah, you do. But you can see things even
from your shoes.

BW: [*laughs*] Okay.

TRUMP: I think. I don't think you necessarily have to be
there. You know, I see that more and more people
are saying what you—

BW: Okay this is—

TRUMP: —just said. But I think you can do it both ways.

BW: Okay. But this is a big—

TRUMP: I just think that when you have the kind of
violence, the kind of thuggery—and, by the way,
you have legitimate protesters and then you have
people that are agitators.

BW: Sure, you do. But most of it—I mean, I've looked
at it, Mr. President, and I've had one of my
assistants really look in detail at it, and most of
the protests are peaceful. Not all of them, you're
exactly right.

TRUMP: What would you say, though, about, let's say,
Minneapolis, where you have had tremendous
violence. And stores and city blocks burned
down? Or, you know, when you look at, frankly,
I think what's going on right now is a terrible
thing in New York. But in Seattle when you look
at what's happening there where they've literally
taken over a large chunk of a city.

COMMENTARY: Once again, while there was violence, Trump is
exaggerating its scale.

BW: Right. But my question to you—and this is the
Kool-Aid question:

TRUMP:	Go ahead.
BW:	Do you understand people who feel passionately—I mean, the Black Lives Matter movement is real.
TRUMP:	Well, Black Lives, the first time I heard about that, you know the threat was to cops and really to the police. Vicious, vicious statements on police.
BW:	Okay. But—
TRUMP:	You know what the statement was. Do you remember?
BW:	I don't remember, sir.
TRUMP:	Pigs in a blanket.

COMMENTARY: Trump was referring to an incident back in 2015 where a group in St. Paul, Minnesota, chanted, "pigs in a blanket, fry 'em like bacon." The group was not affiliated with the national Black Lives Matter organization. Fox News hosts Sean Hannity and Tucker Carlson, however, had been playing an old video of the 2015 chant.

TRUMP:	You know, it was a whole big thing. It was a very, very nasty—
BW:	But there are a lot of people who are angry and feel pain. I mean, you were saying, hey look, I can't be those people. That's quite true. But I think it's really important to step out of your shoes, and—
TRUMP:	That's okay. I get it. I'm okay with that.
BW:	I think they want—
TRUMP:	No, I'm okay with it.
BW:	And my question to you is—
TRUMP:	I think you can view it both ways.
BW:	Sure.
TRUMP:	Sometimes the view may be different, depending on where you're coming from.
BW:	But, but the question is, and I've got—as I always do, I have my tape recorder on. And I want to—
TRUMP:	That's okay. I don't mind.
BW:	And I want to hear—

TRUMP: You can have it on. I'm a straight shooter.

BW: The president talking to Black people in this country about what you understand they've gone through. And, you know, we can get to what your remedy is and what you're gonna fix. But do you understand, and we talked about this—I mentioned this, you didn't like it. You're a person of white privilege just like I am. And the question is, can somebody like you—because of your position—step out and say, you know, I've got some breaks, I've had advantages. There are people out there who have not, and I understand their anger and their fierce, fierce resentment of people like you and people like me.

TRUMP: Bob, I feel I do understand it. But if I didn't understand it, I would not have done criminal justice reform that nobody was able to do but me. I would not have done opportunity zones which have had a tremendously positive impact on areas that were absolutely dying. I would not have funded long-term historically Black colleges and universities where you know that whole story. Where they would have to come back every year.

BW: Sure, I understand what you've done. The question is—

TRUMP: No, no. But I wouldn't have done it if I didn't understand it.

COMMENTARY: Trump had signed a bill continuing $255 million in annual funding to historically Black colleges and universities and other schools serving primarily minority students.

TRUMP: In other words, if I was not extremely sympathetic to the cause and the plight of what they've gone through, of what, you know, African Americans and the Black community has gone through, I would not have done, you know, a vast amount of money for historically Black colleges and universities. I would not have done, of all of them, criminal justice reform.

BW: Okay, now—let's say, let's say I have—

TRUMP: Bob, that was a very hard thing to get done. Opportunity zones, too.

BW: Okay, I understand that—

TRUMP: That was a very hard thing to get done.

BW: What you've done. The question is, what's in your heart? Because what people want—I don't think people want you to get up and say, hey, look, you know, I'm gonna give all my money to Black Lives Matter. I think people want to understand that you understand. What's the essence of your responsibility as president? We've talked about this.

TRUMP: I think the essence of my responsibility is to do a good job for all communities. All communities. The essence of my responsibility is to help people. And I think that I've helped the Black community more than any president outside—

BW: I know, you've said that.

TRUMP: Outside of Abraham Lincoln. And I mean that fully. Because nobody else has done what I've done. Whether it's criminal justice reform, whether it's opportunity zones, whether it's historically Black colleges and universities, nobody has done what I—

BW: Let's say I had—

TRUMP: Except for the late, great Abraham Lincoln.

BW: Okay. Suppose I had ten Black Lives Matter people here as a focus group.

TRUMP: Okay.

BW: And I said, here's President Trump. And this is what President Trump wants to say to you about how he can step out of his shoes.

TRUMP: Right.

BW: To understand what life is like in your shoes. And what are you going to say?

TRUMP:	Bob, I'm somebody that likes to get things done rather than talk.
BW:	Okay.
TRUMP:	And what I would do is I would not say—I would not think of it the way I believe you would like me to think of it—
BW:	No, I'm not—I don't like you one way or another. Don't get me wrong. [*crosstalk*]
TRUMP:	Rather, I would tell them what I've done.
BW:	I'm trying to understand. I mean, you've been very indulgent with me. I mean, think about it.
TRUMP:	Well, I'm giving it a shot, Bob. I'm giving it a shot. I mean, Bush was indulgent, and you killed the guy. You know, but, you know, I get that. I get that.
BW:	I mean, listen, all I do—
TRUMP:	Hey, I fully get that. We shouldn't be in the war in Iraq, okay? I fully get that. I mean, we shouldn't be in the Middle East. So, you know, I get it.
BW:	And—he had his say.
TRUMP:	Nobody's done what I've done, Bob. Nobody.
BW:	Okay. But sometimes when you get in these things, you have to lay it on yourself. And there's no bigger yourself in this country than you, as president. And I'm not trying to get you to say something you don't feel. I'm asking whether you can understand the plight, struggle, pain of people—I mean it's real. It's been an awakening for me, if I may say that, at my age. I'm older than you—77.
TRUMP:	Wow.
BW:	To see that these people are saying, it's been a raw deal, and I've not liked it, and it's a form of oppression. It's a new form of slavery that has occurred in this country that you're president of. And I want to make sure I understand what you want to say to them. You understand that?
TRUMP:	Yeah, I do, Bob. I think this. I think that I have

	some wonderful—what I can do best is get things done. And I have some wonderful things that I'm gonna be doing for the Black community in the United States. And I did a lot of it until the Chinese virus hit us.
BW:	Well, we'll see. If a member of my focus group said to you, President Trump, do you understand me, what would you say?
TRUMP:	I would say that I really believe I do. And that's why I've done so much for the Black community.
BW:	Okay.
TRUMP:	I've done more than anybody else—and I said it to you—other than the late, great Abraham Lincoln. It's true. It's true, Bob.

COMMENTARY: It's not true. President Johnson had signed civil rights legislation that was one of the hallmarks of his presidency.

TRUMP:	I got it. [crosstalk]
BW:	Do you think there is systematic or institutional racism in this country?
TRUMP:	Well, I think there is everywhere. I think probably less here than most places. Or less here than many places.
BW:	Okay. But is it here in a way that it has an impact on people's lives?
TRUMP:	I think it is. And it's unfortunate. But I think it is.
BW:	You're going to work on the economics and the jobs and so forth. But there's a spiritual dimension to this—
TRUMP:	Yeah.
BW:	—where I think people want somebody to get up and say, hey, I get it. I really am moving toward getting my feet in your shoes. And this is, not just the economic plan. But the idea of what we—I know you wouldn't like this. But remember, Hillary Clinton went on a listening tour?
TRUMP:	Yeah.

BW: Do you need to go on a listening tour and listen
              to people?

TRUMP: I think I listen to people—I think I listen to
              people all the time. I like to listen to people.

BW: Okay.

TRUMP: I hear what people are saying.

BW: Okay.

TRUMP: I think I have a strength, economically, that a lot
              of people don't have. Most people don't have.
              So I'm able to get things done economically. And
              that's a very big part of a problem. I'll tell you
              what, had we been allowed to carry on that great
              economy that got built under my administration,
              me and my administration, I think had we not
              gotten hit by this artificial situation—

BW: No, no, you said that, you made the point—

TRUMP: I think that you would see a very different place
              right now. You know, when you see the wages
              were rising so fast. The unemployment was so
              low. Never been this low for African Americans.
              For almost anybody.

BW: Sure, I understand.

TRUMP: No, but I think you would have seen a very
              different place. And then we got hit. And we
              went into an operation. It was an operation like a
              patient gets operated on. And now we're starting
              all over again. Well, yeah, pretty much. Had I
              not built a strong foundation for the country, you
              wouldn't be able to have the kind of numbers
              that were announced last week on jobs, et cetera,
              et cetera. So, uh, yes. I do hear what people are
              saying. I do understand what they're saying. And
              I'm doing things about it. Including, including
              economic things.

BW: No, I mean—I mean that's the centerpiece of
              it all.

TRUMP: Yeah. It could heal a lot of—a lot of hearts.

BW: Yeah. But—

TRUMP:	There are other things, by the way. Don't get me wrong. But a good economy can take care of a lot of problems.
BW:	Yes, but not all of them. And particularly at this—
TRUMP:	No, no. Nothing gets rid of all of them, Bob. Nothing.
BW:	This is—
TRUMP:	But you add various things together, and problems can disappear. And that's what I'd like to do.
BW:	Do you remember when Bob Costa and I came and talked to you before you got the nomination in 2016?
TRUMP:	I do. At the building. You mean which one? At the building, right?
BW:	Yeah. They were doing renovation on your hotel. And this is—
TRUMP:	We were—we were sort of almost finished. Yep.
BW:	—this is when you said to us, and you said, I bring out rage in people. I bring rage out. I always have. I don't know if it's an asset or a liability. But whatever it is, I do. Is that true?
TRUMP:	I bring out—yes, sometimes, because I do things. I do more things than other people are able to get done. And that, sometimes, can make my opponents unhappy.
BW:	Yeah.
TRUMP:	They view me differently than they view other presidents. A lot of other presidents that you've covered didn't get a lot done, Bob. When you look at what I've done with the military, with the vets, with regulations, cutting more regulations, by far, than any president in the history of our country. With taxes, with the big cuts, with the environment in terms of—many things having to do with the environment, with ANWR.
BW:	Yeah.
TRUMP:	Just ANWR is just one thing of many—

COMMENTARY: He's talking about his administration's plan to open up parts of the Arctic National Wildlife Refuge to development by fossil fuel companies. It was a classic battle between big oil and the climate change advocates.

BW: What do you think, if I can ask this—

TRUMP: —every president wanted to, but they were unable to do it.

BW: What do you think of your Justice Gorsuch, who kind of led the charge against you on LGBTQ issues?

COMMENTARY: Neil Gorsuch had just authored a 6-to-3 opinion ruling that the Civil Rights Act protects gay and transgender people from workplace discrimination.

TRUMP: Well, it's the way he felt, it's the way he felt.

BW: And that's okay with you?

TRUMP: When you say against me, against?

BW: Well, it was against your administration's position.

TRUMP: Yeah, but this is the way he felt. And, you know, I want people to go the way they feel. I mean, he felt he was doing the right thing. I do think it opens the spigots for a lot of litigation.

BW: All that decision said was the freedom of the Civil Rights Act applies to everyone.

TRUMP: Right.

BW: And I thought, suppose Donald Trump was on the Supreme Court, how would he vote on this?

TRUMP: You know, a lot of people thought I wasn't exactly unhappy with that decision.

BW: Is that true?

TRUMP: I don't want to comment. Anyway. Were you surprised by that decision?

BW: I was surprised by it. But I did, 40 years ago, a book on the Supreme Court. And you know what happens when they take a vote, the senior justice in the majority—and in that case it was

Chief Justice Roberts, gets to assign the opinion. He could have assigned himself. He could have assigned one of the liberals. But he assigned Gorsuch. Because I know how this works. You put Gorsuch in a position of, he embraces his vote because he has to write the opinion.

TRUMP: Right. Right.

BW: And it was very smart of Roberts from his point of view.

TRUMP: Are you surprised at Roberts?

BW: I think he's doing exactly the balancing act that a chief justice—I mean I've talked to Lindsey Graham about this a lot. And, as you know, Lindsey Graham doesn't think it's a good thing that you make the courts part of politics. You really want to get people in there who are good lawyers and can think. And if you politicize the courts, particularly the Supreme Court, that's a bad thing for America. Do you agree?

TRUMP: Right. Well, is Roberts doing it?

BW: Well, I think he's been very careful. And I think he finds issues like this issue, you know, I'm pressing. But I think if you were on the Supreme Court, you would have voted for more freedom.

TRUMP: That's very interesting. Okay. Well, I'll never get that vote.

BW: Well, maybe you can appoint yourself.

TRUMP: I am what's good for people. All people. So, you know, that's where I am.

BW: Okay. So how do you feel about the campaign, now? Because, you know, these polls are out there. That can't bring a smile to your face.

TRUMP: You see different polls than I do. I think we're doing fine.

COMMENTARY: Polls showed Biden ahead by a comfortable nine percent. *The New York Times* reported the Trump campaign private polling also showed Trump well behind Biden.

TRUMP:	The campaign hasn't really started. It's starting, you know, over the next few weeks. Let me ask you. So when you see that it just came out that the rally the other day, which had, you know, still a nice crowd by any other standard. But the only time I've ever had a vacant seat. But we have a—I never spoke with the Chinese virus in the room. So, you know, I mean I had a lot of people say, hey, I'll watch it on television. And they did, because it was a very big night. And a tremendous night, even bigger on online. You know that. It was like a—
BW:	Yeah. Well, I'll tell you. My wife, Elsa, and I laughed at your story about going down the ramp.
TRUMP:	Really?
BW:	I thought that was—[laughing]
TRUMP:	That's funny. You know, it was sad, though. Because the news—I made a very good speech and they refused to cover it. They covered that and they were saying, maybe he has Parkinson's.
BW:	I know, I know.
TRUMP:	No, but you know, and they knew that wasn't true. I think it really discredited them. And people knew even before I told the story. And, you know, I had to go inch by inch. And literally, you know, you've done that, where you have a steep surface—
BW:	Sure, sure.
TRUMP:	And I had very slippery shoes. Believe it or not. If you have leather shoes, they're very slippery on the bottom.
BW:	Never wear 'em again.
TRUMP:	And I didn't want to pull a Gerald Ford, which you—I know you remember well, when he fell leaving the plane, right?
BW:	I sure do. Stamped on memories of him forever.
TRUMP:	Well, I don't want those memories. I wouldn't want that memory of me. Can you imagine that story, right? And it's sad. But, you know,

I'm covered very, very unfairly. Including polls. They come out with polls where they totally overexaggerate the Democrats versus the Republicans. Look, I had the same time last year, Bob. I had a poll, the *Washington Post*–ABC poll, two and a half weeks out, I was 14 points behind. And I knew it wasn't true. I knew it wasn't true. In fact, I think that they were going to change it, if you want to know the truth. We complained about it. And you remember, they came out with a poll, two weeks, and I said, there's no way. And we had a poll in Michigan that I was gonna lose by five points. And I won. And we had a poll that I was going to lose Wisconsin. And I won.

BW: I understand. I understand what happened. Listen, I was going on television—

TRUMP: How do you rate that election, Bob, the 2016? Was that one of the great of all time, or was it? People consider that to be a moment in history like no other. What's your feeling on that, because you're really a—you are truly a great historian—

BW: No, I'm not. I'm not.

TRUMP: Even though you don't call yourself a historian, I guess.

BW: I'm just a reporter. My feeling—I was on television saying you could win. And it was on a Fox News show, and people jumped all over me. What do you mean, he can win? I said, I'm telling you, he can win.

TRUMP: I think I'm in much better position than I was then, because I've done a lot. I also think I have a much weaker opponent.

BW: Well, that's quite possible.

TRUMP: Look, she was—whether you like her or not, she's a horrible human being, but whether you like her or not, she was smart. Very smart. And very devious, very tricky, very smart. And you said

	you're 77, 78. That means you're the same age as Joe. But it hasn't hit you. It may someday.
BW:	I hope not. I hope not.
TRUMP:	No, but it has hit Joe. And you know that. I mean look, you see. You see what's going on. It's a weird deal. He couldn't do it in prime time. I used— remember, I used to call him one-percent Joe.

COMMENTARY: This was Trump's way of mocking Biden's losses in previous Democratic primaries. For example, in 2008 Biden received one percent of the vote in the Iowa caucuses before dropping out of the race.

BW:	Well, now they say he's going to debate you three times.
TRUMP:	I mean, that's fine. If he does it. I mean that's fine. Look, can I be honest, he did fine—hold on, let me see something. I'm just seeing something coming across the—oh, that's funny. So, anyway, go ahead, what were you going to say?
BW:	So what's the debate going to be like?
TRUMP:	I thought, by the way, I thought he did okay. I think he did at least even against Bernie. You know. I was surprised that he was able to get through that debate. And he didn't win it, but he didn't lose it. You know, it was a pretty even debate. And you know, I was surprised. So you never know what happens.
BW:	Yeah.
TRUMP:	You never know what happens.
BW:	Yeah.
TRUMP:	But I've had some very good debates. I wouldn't be talking to you if I didn't have good debates. You know that.
BW:	You know, that's true. That's true.
TRUMP:	My best debate was probably the second debate with crooked Hillary. I mean that was probably— that was a great debate.

BW: And this is—we've talked about this, and we talked about this a couple of weeks ago, about history's clock. And the whole business of what happened in 2016. And you came along, and the Democrats and your own party had no idea what was going on in America.

TRUMP: Yep. Got 'em by surprise, Bob. Caught 'em by surprise.

BW: And you did. There's no question about that. And the question now is where's—

TRUMP: I'll get 'em by surprise again, Bob. You watch.

BW: Where's history's clock?

TRUMP: Well, we're going to find out. I've done a lot. China set me back. Hey, Bob. I was sailing.

BW: Are you going to talk to President Xi again?

TRUMP: Uh, yeah. I imagine at some point.

BW: Are you going to call him, or is he going to—what is it? Who?

TRUMP: I don't know, Bob. Look, you know, I told you, I feel so differently toward the whole thing with China. It's just—

BW: I know. Well, listen, I've talked to some of the experts—

TRUMP: This is such a terrible ordeal for the world. Not only just us, for the whole world, what—

BW: Yes. And there is some evidence, as I suspect the experts have told you, that this virus was engineered. That someone told me who knows said, if you were gonna imagine a virus that would attack with such efficiency and be so lethal on somebody's lungs, you could not have designed a better one. And there's some people who think that they manipulated this, as you know.

TRUMP: Oh, sure I've heard that. I've heard many theories. I've also heard that it was incompetence. I have heard that it was a mistake. I've heard mistake, I've heard incompetence, and I've heard, you know—

BW:	Manipulation?
TRUMP:	I've heard every theory there is, Bob.
BW:	And what's the reality? Because that's important.
TRUMP:	Well, I think we may find the reality at some point. But right now, nobody knows for sure.
BW:	If they engineered this and intentionally let it out into the world.
TRUMP:	Well, how come they got hit so hard? Their numbers are substantial. Very, very substantial. You know, when I talk about testing, Bob, so I've done, we have done, an incredible job on ventilators, on testing, on everything.
BW:	Yeah.
TRUMP:	I've made a lot of governors look good because they were dead. They had no chance of ventilators and I got—we make thousands of ventilators a week. And we're helping the rest of the world with ventilators.
BW:	Yeah, I know. I know. I've talked to Jared about that—
TRUMP:	Oh, good. We've done a good job. But testing is interesting. Because, because we do—we did 25 million tests as of today. 25 million. If we did four million or three million, like Germany or somebody else, we would have very few cases. So testing is interesting because it's a double-edged sword. You know I had 155 all-time stock market highs during the, you know, three and a half year—all of these things.
BW:	And you don't—
TRUMP:	And we're going along and flying high—
BW:	Is it true you don't own any stock?
TRUMP:	I'm not allowed to.
BW:	Really?
TRUMP:	I have owned stock over the—I haven't been a big person for stock. You know, I've just—I've liked—I've always liked real estate. But, but, yeah, I've dabbled in stock. But I've never been a big stock

person. But look at what I've done for 401(K)s. But two things. Number one, look at where it is now. It's almost at the same level it was when the plague hit. Okay? I mean, take a look. But I was riding so high, the market was riding so high. But I said, wow. Can we take this all the way to that very special date of November third?

BW: You know, this is going to be a tough road. This is not going to be as easy as it was the three previous years. Of course, you realize that?

TRUMP: I do. But I think that if I get the market going up nicely I think that we're going to be very tough to beat.

BW: Thank you. And I'm glad—

TRUMP: You take care. Say hello to your wife. I'll see you soon, Bob.

BW: Okay, thank you, sir. Bye.

TRUMP: Bye.

[*Recording ends*]

INTERVIEW 18:
I'm Not Feeling Any Love

Phone call
July 8, 2020

TRUMP:	I have done a tremendous amount for the Black community. And, honestly, I'm not feeling any love.

COMMENTARY: Trump called me unexpectedly on Wednesday, July 8th, before his day of meetings with Mexican President Obrador. My goal was now exclusively to finish with small edits and additions to the book in order to get it published before the presidential election on November 3rd.

TRUMP:	I'm so busy, Bob, I don't have time to breathe. What's up, Bob?
BW:	Okay. I wanted to kind of get an overview of everything that, you know, has been going on—
TRUMP:	Okay. I just got some very good poll numbers, I will say that.
BW:	People have—and I'm turning my recorder on for our history, here.
TRUMP:	Okay.
BW:	This will be our 17th conversation—
TRUMP:	Wow.
BW:	For this book.
TRUMP:	Wow.
BW:	And that's a lot. I've taken a lot of your time.

TRUMP:	Yeah, well. All I ask for is fairness. And, you know, I'm sure I won't get it, but that's okay.
BW:	Well, you'll, you'll—
TRUMP:	I'm used to that. But I do ask for fairness because nobody's done what I've done. Nobody.
BW:	Well—
TRUMP:	Did you get the new list of new things that were added on?
BW:	Yeah. I've seen all of this. You know, here's what I think the big issue in the campaign is going to be. And that is, what are you trying to do? I look at those two speeches—the Mount Rushmore speech.
TRUMP:	Right.
BW:	The speech on the South Lawn, there. The White House, over, right after the Fourth of July or on the Fourth of July.

Excerpts from President Trump's speech at Mount Rushmore on July 4th, 2020:

TRUMP:	*Our nation is witnessing a merciless campaign to wipe out our history, defame our heroes, erase our values, and indoctrinate . . .*
TRUMP:	*There is a new far-left fascism that demands absolute allegiance. . . .*
TRUMP:	*We are now in the process of defeating the radical left, the Marxists, the anarchists, the agitators, the looters, and people who in many instances have absolutely no clue what they are doing.*

Both speeches painted divisive portraits of some citizens threatening the country—a kind of reemergence in tone of "American carnage" from Trump's inaugural address.

BW:	What are you trying to say to people with these speeches? Because—

TRUMP:	Well, what I'm trying to do—and they were very well reviewed, as you probably have heard. What I'm trying to do is two things. I'm trying to show where we're going and where we were. Where we were as a country, how we were formed. How we developed as a country. Because I think the past is a very important element as to the future. I really believe strongly in history.
BW:	Sure.
TRUMP:	And in culture. And I believe that the past—you have your tape on, Bob, I hope, yes? You have your tape on, tape recorder?
BW:	Yes, I've got the tape recorder on.
TRUMP:	Good.
BW:	And, but the question is I think the Mount Rushmore—
TRUMP:	No, but I think the past is a very important. I think it's very important that we not forget our past. And that was a lot of the speech. And what I'm doing is we're building an economy that's going very rapidly, Bob. You're going to be surprised.
BW:	Okay, I'm waiting, as is the world. And in the Mount Rushmore speech you talk about a new far-left fascism.
TRUMP:	Yes.
BW:	And, you know, I've done a lot of reporting, President Trump, on this. And there's some people who represent that kind of anger, the radical left. But it's not much. It's not—
TRUMP:	I call them anarchists.
BW:	Yes, I know. And Marxists. You know, if you talk to the experts, there are no Marxists left.
TRUMP	Well, no that's wrong, Bob. Black Lives Matter, what they do is they literally have it in their website that they're Marxists. I mean, they put it down. If you look at their original statements. And they haven't changed.

COMMENTARY: As noted, the original founder of the grassroots Black Lives Matter group described herself and another founder as Marxists back in 2015. Since then, the group has become a national movement and their website as of this recording does not contain any mention of Marxism. *The New York Times* reported in July of 2020 that 15 to 26 million people in the United States participated in George Floyd protests.

BW:	But, you know, look the—
TRUMP:	No, but they literally called them Marxists, you know, Bob.
BW:	Okay. I'm trying to get a 30,000-foot perspective on this.
TRUMP:	Okay.
BW:	That, what are you saying to people? For instance, in the second speech you said, "our movement," referring to your movement and your base. And, you know, we never forget, we are one family and one nation.
TRUMP:	Right.
BW:	Okay. People—Black Lives Matter people—look at all of this and they say they're not being invited in. That you've put up a wall around your base, and they're looking at this—and I think somebody objectively, as I'm trying to do, can look at it and say, now, wait a minute. We're not opening the gate to everyone. And that's my reading of it. And the question is, what's your intent?
TRUMP:	Let me just say—Look, I have done more for the Black community than any other president other than Abraham Lincoln.
BW:	And Lyndon Johnson.
TRUMP:	I say more than Lyndon Johnson.
BW:	Well—
TRUMP:	Okay. I got criminal justice reform.
BW:	Right.
TRUMP:	I did prison reform. I did historically Black colleges and universities, okay, which nobody—I

got full funding for a 10-year period. Nobody was able to do that. Nobody.

BW: Okay. But as you and I have talked about over the months—

TRUMP: No, no. These are big things, Bob. These are things—

BW: Yes. No, but it's about the heart.

TRUMP: Nobody. Obama—Obama never even tried.

COMMENTARY: Trump is overstating what he had accomplished. President Johnson had extensive voting rights legislation and a historic war on poverty. The Obama administration had many criminal justice reforms.

TRUMP: Criminal justice reform, Bob, nobody could believe it. I mean this guy, Van Jones, came into my office. He was crying. He was crying. He couldn't believe it happened.

BW: Okay, but that's—

TRUMP: A week later he goes and bad-mouths me.

COMMENTARY: Van Jones is an American lawyer, CNN political commentator, and progressive activist.

BW: We've talked about this.

TRUMP: Okay.

BW: And it's a question—

TRUMP: No, but Bob, you can't forget that, because when you talk about—

BW: Of course not. But it doesn't define—

TRUMP: I have done, I have done a tremendous amount for the Black community. And, honestly, I'm not feeling any love. Because I was doing very well in the polls. As soon as the China virus came in— as soon as the plague, China virus, came in—as soon as it came in—those poll numbers all of a sudden started inching back to where I started, which is eight or nine or ten percent. And I don't understand that. I don't. Because nobody blames me for the virus.

BW: Okay, because it's a question—we've talked about this, sir. I'm sorry to press, but I want to ask these questions. It's a matter of the heart and the spirit. Are you saying to people who are, you know, Black Lives Matter, who are minorities in this country, you are welcome here? You and I have talked about—we've had some serious conversations about what the job of the president is. And I said to you after doing this for almost 50 years, my definition, the job of the president is to figure out what the next stage of good is for a majority of people in the country. A real majority, not a party. Not interest groups. Not a base. Figure out what that is. And then execute a plan to do—And you agreed. You said, I agree, that's exactly right.

TRUMP: Sure.

BW: And the question is, are people—do they feel you're opening up and saying, come on into my leadership, my values, what I care about? And, as you know, people vote their own interests.

TRUMP: Yeah.

BW: What are my interests in being for Trump? And too much feeling out there that the door's not wide open. And that's the question.

COMMENTARY: His speech about "far-left fascism" and "the Marxists, the anarchists, the agitators, the looters" was probably the most divisive July Fourth speech ever given by a U.S. president.

BW: [crosstalk] Is it really—

TRUMP: Okay. I got it. The door is very wide open. I want to include all people. I want to include all Americans. The door is absolutely open. And that's why I did criminal justice reform and prison reform. That's why I did opportunity zones.

	That's why I did all of this. It would have been a lot easier not to do anything. It would have been much easier for me, Bob. Really.
BW:	Okay, yes. But—
TRUMP:	Very tough getting it done. Obama couldn't get it done. Bush couldn't get it done. Nobody could get it done.
BW:	Okay. You keep—
TRUMP:	I'm the only one who could get it done. And I got it done.
BW:	You keep talking about that. And the question is—
TRUMP:	They are the biggest achievements made for the Black community since—in 100 years.

COMMENTARY: The pandemic had disproportionately impacted Black communities where there were higher rates of death, hospitalization, and job loss from the coronavirus.

TRUMP:	Criminal justice reform was an impossibility to get done and I got it done. Nobody else but me.
BW:	Okay. So, what's your goal here?
TRUMP:	My goal is to do a great job as president, to keep our country strong, to have a great economy so that everybody can have a great job—as I was doing until the plague hit us. And now we're doing it again. Hey, Bob. We just had the greatest job number in the history of our country. New jobs.
BW:	I know, I understand that.
TRUMP:	Five million. That's a big thing.
BW:	And let's hope it comes back. I think—
TRUMP:	It will, it will.
BW:	That would be—
TRUMP:	You'll do a third book in the next year.
BW:	Well—
TRUMP:	Next year's gonna be a fantastic year. Watch.
BW:	As you know, the virus is on fire. Absolutely on fire.

TRUMP:	Bob, it's only on fire because of our testing. Because we're testing 40 million people. The deaths are at a tenfold—
BW:	Well, as you know—
TRUMP:	Did you see the death rate?
BW:	Yes, I know. And it—
TRUMP:	No, but Bob, the death rate, which is the important word, is down tenfold. Ten. Fold.
BW:	Yes, and you heard what Fauci said about this. Said that's a false narrative.

COMMENTARY: Dr. Fauci and other medical experts said this was not true and certainly was not grounds for optimism since coronavirus infections were surging.

TRUMP:	I closed the borders to China. I put a ban on China in January.
BW:	No, I know that. I know that.
TRUMP:	Fauci also said you don't have to wear a mask.
BW:	The question is, where are we now?
TRUMP:	We're in great shape. Most of the country is headed absolutely away from the virus. We're totally set with our hospitals. We're tenfold lower. And I use that because I got it from, I think, *The Wall Street Journal* or one of them. They used the word tenfold, and that's what the number is. We have a tenfold reduction of death. The reason we have so many cases is because we're testing 40 million people.
BW:	Well, as you know, that's under dispute.
TRUMP:	If we tested half the number of people, we would have half the number of cases. No other country tests all these people.
BW:	Okay, but it's on fire, sir. Look at the numbers. Look at what the governors of the states in Texas and Florida—
TRUMP:	No, it's all fine—And you're building immunity at the same time, Bob. And very few people are dying.

BW: But also, it's in young people who can be
           asymptomatic, as you know.
TRUMP: I know, but they say when it's in young people
           and they're asymptomatic, which it is, they don't
           transfer it. It's not transferrable.

COMMENTARY: That's not true. People of any age who are asymptomatic, that is infected but not showing symptoms, can still carry and infect others with COVID-19.

BW: Let me take you to this. Because I think it's
           important to understanding the moment. You say
           we're in great shape. I think, looking at it, I'm not
           wearing any hat in this, President Trump.
TRUMP: I understand.
BW: I am not.
TRUMP: I understand.
BW: You know, the death rate is part of it. But the
           number of cases is, what, 57,000? That's almost
           double—
TRUMP: Bob. Bob, are you ready?
BW: I'm ready.
TRUMP: Germany doesn't test unless somebody is sick.
           Because we did 40 million people, anybody that
           has the sniffles—any kid that has a little bit of a
           cold, they test positive. And it's gonna go away in
           two days. It's frankly, it's ridiculous.

COMMENTARY: The virus was not going away. On July 8th there were 64,775 new coronavirus cases in the United States, and the daily death toll was 1,089.

BW: Okay where's that inform—where are you get—
           what medical—
TRUMP: It's all over the place.
BW: Okay. Let's move beyond testing.
TRUMP: We're the only one that does it.
BW: If you called Tony Fauci in and sat him down in
           the Oval Office—

TRUMP:	He couldn't win that argument with me.
BW:	Pardon?
TRUMP:	He cannot win that argument.
BW:	Well, but, you know he's only done it for about 40 years.
TRUMP:	He was wrong on the China ban. I was right.
BW:	Yeah, well, we know there's a—
TRUMP:	And I was the only one that said we have to ban them.
BW:	Look, there's a—I've talked to—
TRUMP:	We'd have hundreds of thousands of more people dead right now. And let me tell you, Bob, if I went the herd, like they're doing in Brazil and like they did in Sweden, which didn't work, and other places, we would have had three million dead instead of 130,000 as of today. And that will go up somewhat. But we are getting toward the end.
BW:	Okay.
TRUMP:	But we would have had three million people. From two to three million people.
BW:	There's a lot of disputed facts. Like on the China restrictions, I've talked to six people who were at that meeting, and Fauci was for it. For the restrictions.
TRUMP:	No, no.
BW:	And you and I have talked about—
TRUMP:	No, he was against it. And it's been written very well he was against it.
BW:	No, sir.
TRUMP:	He was against it for a month, and then after that he said, you made the right decision.
BW:	Yeah, well, he said at that meeting and, as you know—
TRUMP:	You know why? Because he believed in the World Health Organization that I terminated because they're just a puppet of China and saved $500 million a year.
BW:	Okay, but as you know it was Matt Pottinger who was the—had the expertise, who'd been in China,

who realized what liars they were about things like this. Who, as I understand it, said you've got to restrict travel—people coming from China. And you did that. There's no question about you did it.

TRUMP: What, you mean Pottinger built up—he, Pottinger must have told you that himself, right? Yeah.

BW: Well, no, somebody else involved in—is that true?

TRUMP: No, not that I remember. I just felt I was given a set of facts, and I was the only one in the room that agreed, that felt that we should close the border.

BW: Okay.

TRUMP: I was the only one, Bob.

COMMENTARY: President Trump keeps repeating this, though I knew from firsthand participants in meeting notes that this was untrue.

TRUMP: Now—

BW: Okay.

TRUMP: Maybe Pottinger told me something—I don't know. But I certainly don't remember. It's nice that he tells you he did, but I don't remember it. But maybe he did, who knows. It didn't matter. I made the decision.

BW: You did. I agree.

TRUMP: I think all people, including Fauci, were against it. I made the decision. By making that decision, I saved hundreds of thousands of lives. Hundreds of thousands of lives.

BW: And the Europe decision and the 15—

TRUMP: And the Europe decision came shortly thereafter. And that was because I saw what was happening in Italy, especially.

BW: Yeah, I know.

TRUMP: I said, we have to close Europe. And I saved hundreds of thousands of lives by doing that.

BW: And, you know, a lot of people—

TRUMP:	Most of our country now is in good shape, Bob. Not in bad shape. Like, you're hearing about Florida, which flared up, and other—
BW:	See, what we're—
TRUMP:	But the flare-up is much different than it was three months ago.
BW:	Yeah. Yeah. I—Look, as a citizen, somebody who lives here, I'm worried as I can be about this whole thing.
TRUMP:	Don't worry about it, Bob. Okay? Don't worry about it.
BW:	Now I want to—but, let me—
TRUMP:	If we get to do another book together, you'll find out I was right. Bob, I have the President of Mexico, Obrador. He's literally waiting for me outside. I got to go.
BW:	Okay, good.
TRUMP:	I got to go. I consider you to be very important. But he is literally standing at the door saying please, sir.
BW:	Okay, can we talk later tonight then?
TRUMP:	Yeah, maybe later tonight. If I can, I will.
BW:	Okay, thanks, sir.
TRUMP:	Actually I enjoy talking to you. Thanks, Bob.
BW:	Bye.
TRUMP:	Bye.

[*Recording ends*]

COMMENTARY: Five days later, July 13th, I interviewed Jared Kushner, the president's son-in-law. His voice sounded hoarse.

"What I've learned in the world of Trump is news cycles don't last very long. Sentiment changes."

In relation to the virus, Kushner said:

"He's had a string of kind of bad luck."

Biden continued to lead Trump in the polls by double digits.

"Biden's had about as good a couple months as he could get, you know, being hidden."

Due to COVID, Biden had not traveled much to campaign and had not held public events that would put people at risk.

Kushner said Biden's reliance on Bernie Sanders and Elizabeth Warren's liberal ideas amounted to "a long political suicide note."

On Trump, Kushner said:

"The goal is to get his head from governing to campaigning."

I was incredulous. In the midst of the largest public health crisis in a century, Kushner thought it was time to turn to campaigning?

"So the goal is to get him back to offense."

The offense soon appeared. Trump and the White House launched a public attack to discredit Dr. Fauci and to discredit Joe Biden.

Trump then fired his campaign manager Brad Parscale, who he blamed for the poor turnout at the rally in Tulsa.

INTERVIEW 19:
Failure to Warn. Failure to Act

Phone Call
July 21, 2020

TRUMP: You don't understand me. But that's okay. You'll understand me after the election. But you don't understand me now.

COMMENTARY: Trump called me unexpectedly the morning of Tuesday, July 21st. The manuscript for my book *Rage* was due to my publisher that day. It was done and would be published in about seven weeks. New daily cases of COVID were at about 60,000 with deaths at 1,000 a day.

TRUMP: Hi, Bob. I'm just running out. I called you before to say hello. How are you doing?
BW: Good. Well, I'm sorting it out. Things are getting bad, aren't they?
TRUMP: Bad in what way?
BW: Well, the virus. I mean, it's—
TRUMP: Well, it's flaring up. It's flaring up all over the world, Bob. By the way, all over the world. That was one thing I noticed last week. You know they talk about this country. All over the world, it's flaring up. But we have it under control.

COMMENTARY: I want listeners to hear that again.

TRUMP: We have it under control.

We have it under control. The virus had been out of control in the United States for months. Trump was editing his own narrative. It immediately reminded me of President Nixon in 1973 releasing more than 200,000 words of edited transcripts of his secret White House tapes. They had extensive deletions.

When Nixon personally edited the conversations, he directed his lawyers to insert the following "Materials unrelated to presidential actions deleted," or when there was profanity "expletive deleted."

It was Nixon's way of saying I'm going to tell the parts of the story I want told. Nothing more. This is exactly what Trump tries to do with me. There was no legal or rational reason for Nixon to delete such actions or foul language. But he declared that that's what he was going to do, and his lawyers had to go along. In 1974 the Supreme Court ruled that Nixon had to turn over the raw tapes themselves, free from cuts, deletions, or paraphrasing. These tapes then sunk the Nixon presidency and he resigned.

TRUMP: We had areas that—like Texas and Florida—that we thought maybe were gone, and they hadn't gotten hit yet. So, but we have it under control. We have it absolutely. I believe it's—but it's a tough, no question.

BW: Boy, it is. But as you look back on it, because I'm trying to round up and make a final assessment on this book, what grade would you give yourself on the handling of the coronavirus?

TRUMP: Well, I think I'd give myself a very good grade, Bob, because what we've done is, you know, we were totally—when I took over, there was nothing, there were no provisions, no anything for this.

COMMENTARY: Obama's National Security Council had left behind a 69-page document entitled "Playbook for Early Response to High-Consequence Emerging Infectious Disease Threats and Biological Incidents." The document included precise instructions for dealing with novel influenza viruses.

TRUMP:	And, by the way, there was, if you look, you know I use the expression the cupboards were bare. And they were bare. We didn't have ventilators, nor did governors have ventilators or any of the equipment that you'd need. The governors of the states with almost few exceptions were prepared for something like this. And within a very short period of time, we are now building thousands of ventilators a month and—
BW:	No, I understand that. But—
TRUMP:	Well, I think it's a big thing. And additionally we're making swabs, we're making tests. We will have 50 million tests by the weekend. 50 million.
BW:	I understand, sir. But, you know, this is a genuine crisis. And the question I have for this book is what have you learned about yourself?
TRUMP:	Well, I'm fighting on many fronts. I'm fighting this, I was fighting the fake Russia, Russia, Russia thing, which that turned out to be a total fake. You'll see that—
BW:	I understand.
TRUMP:	—in a very short period of time. We caught 'em spying on my campaign.

COMMENTARY: He was right about the deeply flawed FBI wiretaps on Carter Page. Page was an obscure foreign aid during the campaign, and he had no role in the Trump presidency. According to all the investigations, news coverage, and books, there is no evidence that the FBI spied directly on Trump.

TRUMP:	But you have to understand, Bob, I've been fighting this for two and a half years unfairly.
BW:	When we started talking in December, if I said to you we're gonna have a virus that comes and kills 140,000 people in this country, you would think I was smoking something.
TRUMP:	Well, you know all my life I've heard the word

BW: pandemic. But somehow you never think of that as a modern-day thing that could happen.

BW: I know, but it's happened.

TRUMP: Because not since 1917 have we had anything like this.

BW: And, you know, one of the things Lindsey Graham says as the campaign is obviously heating up with Biden, that Biden is not really your opponent. The virus is your opponent. Do you agree?

TRUMP: Well, I think that's largely true. I do think that's— Well, it's the virus and it's a radical left group of people, and it's the media. The media is my opponent, regardless of anything. No matter how well we do, they will say we didn't do well.

COMMENTARY: He singles out the same bad actors, the media, the democrats, the RINOs (Republicans In Name Only). His contempt for them blinded him to the real opponent in front of him, namely his own actions and lack of strategy and planning.

BW: Okay, but—

TRUMP: No matter how well this is ultimately handled, and if you look at death rates. If you look at a lot of other things, and you compare us to the rest of the world—

BW: I know. But 140,000 people have died. And—

TRUMP: But we have a much bigger country. If you look at China, they have many more people that died. They just don't report it. If you look at Russia, if you look at India—

BW: I think that's right. You're—

TRUMP: If you look at other countries, they don't report. You know, when you have to report, there's a big difference.

BW: Now last week, sir, Jared said you are getting back on offense. And we saw that last week, your press conference where you mentioned Biden 30 times. You replaced your campaign manager. The White

	House attacked Fauci. I mean, is this the strategy? Back on offense?
TRUMP:	I have a very flexible strategy, Bob. I've had it for a long time. My whole life has been flexible strategy and I've done very well. And I had it in the last campaign, too. I was very flexible. I changed campaign managers three times.
BW:	Is it offense now? Or is it governing—
TRUMP:	I view it as starting. Now look—
BW:	You understand why I'm asking—
TRUMP:	I won the last campaign in the last four weeks. But I would really say I won it in the last week. I did rallies, I did many, many things in the last week. And I don't know if you've been seeing what's going on, but I've done these teleconference calls, you know the town halls, and I'm having numbers on them that are record numbers. I'm hooking them into Facebook, and we're getting tremendous—I did North Carolina, I did Michigan. I did a lot of—because with COVID, you really can't do rallies—probably airport rallies—but you can't do stadium rallies, you can't do the indoor arena rallies.
BW:	Okay, but is it offense, or is it governing? Jared says—
TRUMP:	It's both.
BW:	—you're moving from a situation of governing to offense. And—
TRUMP:	I think it's really both. I mean, I'm governing. I govern, and that's what I do. I have to govern. I just spoke to four countries. I spoke with three countries yesterday. I mean, it's a combination of governing and a political campaign. We have 105 days. Now, to me 105 days is a very long time. To me it's an eternity.
BW:	And the question—
TRUMP:	For somebody else, 105 days doesn't sound

	like much. For me, 105 days is all—I won the
	campaign in the last week.
BW:	I understand that.
TRUMP:	Four years ago.
BW:	But there's no reason you're going to remember
	this, but when you and I had a long talk back in
	April, I went over the 12 to 14 things that there
	needed to be a plan on. That was based on my
	reporting.
TRUMP:	Right.
BW:	Do you remember that?
TRUMP:	I do.
BW:	And it laid out, you've got to do this. You've got
	to do that. Now, I'm looking at this as a neutral
	observer. And I'm asking, in July, it's not clear
	what the plan is. And I talk to people who are
	your supporters. I talk to people who are your
	detractors.
TRUMP:	Bob, you'll see the plan over the next four weeks.

COMMENTARY: I could not help but think that Trump's plan, if one existed, would be coming far too late—like the old saying "rearranging deck chairs on the *Titanic*."

TRUMP:	Because what's happening is, even today I'm
	doing a rollout on something.
BW:	I see that.
TRUMP:	We're doing immigration, we're doing health
	care. Because based on the DACA decision, I'm
	going to do things that nobody thought would
	be possible to do. The DACA decision gave the
	president powers that a lot of people didn't know
	the president had. And you will see things in the
	next four weeks—two weeks, but four weeks—
	that will be very impressive for you.
BW:	Okay. About the plan for the coronavirus. Other
	words, what's the—testing, what's the—you
	know, we went through this list in April, and you
	were kind of, I think, not struck by it. And then

at the end you said, whoa, did you write that list down? And I go back and revisit that list, and it was a strategy and a matrix and a road map for— you had to lead. You had to say, this is what I'm going to do.

TRUMP: Well, I am leading, Bob. But, you know, you have a lot of great leaders around the world and their countries are stymied. We're not stymied. But you have a lot of great leaders around the world, and this has affected them very, very powerfully.

BW: Right. But you're running for—

TRUMP: It's not something that oh, through great leadership, everything's going to disappear. This takes a period of time. This is not something that just goes, whoop, and it's gone. You know, you don't just wave the magic wand. We saved millions of lives by doing the initial closing. I saved hundreds of thousands of lives by closing the border to China, by closing it by banning China—

BW: And you told Chris Wallace you had a talk with Fauci. Did you guys smoke the peace pipe?

TRUMP: No, I've never been at war with him. I have people—there are people in the Republican party who do not like him. He's a Democrat.

BW: Well, he's not, actually. He's an independent. I had my assistant—

TRUMP: Well, I would say he's a Democrat. And that's okay. I don't mind. No, I've had a good relationship with him always. I disagreed with him on some of the things. I disagreed with him on the ban. He didn't want to ban China. I didn't. He told me I was right two months later.

BW: He actually did want to ban China and restrict it. And, you know, I have the notes of those meetings. And, but you're right—

TRUMP: Fauci, Fauci was against it at that time. So, you know—

BW: Okay. So why'd you replace Brad as the campaign

manager? Brad is a great digital guy. That's what
he was. And that's where he did a good job for me.

COMMENTARY: After Trump's low turnout at his rally in Tulsa,
Oklahoma, he erupted at his campaign manager Brad Parscale and
fired him.

TRUMP:	But Brad was a great digital guy, and I put him back into the digital world, which is really his strength. And I have somebody that I think is very good. All of these guys, I'm familiar with. You know, they were all with the last campaign. Bill Stepien was in the last campaign, too. You know, they were all in the last campaign. We basically have, with few exceptions, a similar group that I did in the last campaign.
BW:	I've got to finish this book and I have to be very aggressive and tough in my assessment and realistic.
TRUMP:	No, you don't, you have to be fair, I think. I don't think you have to be tough.
BW:	That includes being fair, but there is—
TRUMP:	Nobody's done what I've done, Bob, in three and a half years. The virus came along. That's not my fault. That's China's fault.
BW:	But the virus—Lindsey Graham is right. You are running against the virus. Not Joe Biden.
TRUMP:	Well, I'm running against both. Look, I'm running against a guy that can't put two sentences together, Bob. Okay? So I'm running against Biden, but I'm running against—I'm running against many things. We had the greatest economy in history. I have to get the economy up a second time. And I'm doing it.
BW:	If I polled 100 leaders—political leaders, business leaders—and I don't have time to go around talk to 100 people, and I said, what is missing? They would say, a plan. An organized, this is what—

TRUMP: You will see the plan, Bob. I've got 106 days.
                  That's a long time.

COMMENTARY: I did not know what to say.

TRUMP: You know, if I put out a plan now, people won't
                  even remember it in a hundred—I won the last
                  election in the final week.
BW: No, no. But it's not just put out the plan, it's
                  execute it, isn't it?
TRUMP: No, no. I am executing it. You'll see it starting.
                  I've already started. But you will see things being
                  signed, documents being signed, not just—this
                  isn't just a plan, this is getting it done. I will have
                  immigration done. I will have health care done.
                  I did a thing called transparency in health care.
                  People don't even know what it is. It's more
                  important than health care. Transparency for
                  medical bills. It's bigger than health care. I did
                  it. Nobody else would have done it, nobody else
                  could have done it. It's done. I don't know if you
                  know that. I've signed it. It's done. Transparency.
                  It's a big thing.
BW: Okay, that's going to be the—
TRUMP: These are the things I've done. I've given you
                  the list. Over the last three and a half years, [?]
                  from now.
BW: When you and I talk—
TRUMP: I rebuilt the military, Bob.
BW: —after November. When you and I talk after the
                  November election, it's going to be, what happens
                  with the virus. And whether there is—
TRUMP: Maybe, by that time, Bob, the virus problem
                  will be solved. Because I think we're going to
                  have vaccines come out very soon. Vaccines and
                  therapeutics. With therapeutics right now being
                  more important. Because you'd fix people. You'd
                  get people, you know, better. That's even better.

BW:	Well—
TRUMP:	So no, I think—Bob, I think we're going to have vaccines soon. I think we already have them. But they're in tests. I think we have things that work. But they're in tests.
BW:	Well, we will see. I mean, that's part of the plan. And I know billions of dollars.
TRUMP:	Would you view that as a game changer?
BW:	Well, if it happens.

COMMENTARY: I felt as if I was talking to a drowning man. I then mentioned a mother I knew who had two children, ages six and nine.

BW:	She cannot figure out whether to let them go back to school or whether to buy a cabin in the forest in Pennsylvania and live there. And she is totally perplexed and, if I may say, traumatized about what to do. Should she send her kids back?
TRUMP:	Right.
BW:	And, you know, there are tens of millions of people who are struggling with it.
TRUMP:	Okay. But I think she should send her kids back. I think you're going to have therapeutics. I think you're going to have vaccines very soon. And you're going to see them being announced over the next month.
BW:	Okay. What about the polls? Jared says he has his own polls that show you are either ahead or within the margin of error in all the states you won. Is that correct?
TRUMP:	That's right—yeah. No, I think we're winning. I just got a good poll that we're four up in Michigan. Okay? I think we're winning. Look, these are phony polls. Bob, take a look at the numbers, where they do 39 percent Democrat and 22 percent Republican.
BW:	But it's also—
TRUMP:	They go off a list of registered voters and

they're—some are dead. Why aren't they doing likely voters, not registered? This is a fixed deal. These are suppression polls. They did the same. Look, your famous *Washington Post*–ABC, gave a poll four years ago, a week and a half before the election, that I was 14 points down.

BW: Listen, we've gone over that. That's correct. And it was a surprise.

TRUMP: I'm doing much better this time.

BW: But, as you know, it wasn't a surprise to me because I said you could win. And people on Fox News just about threw me off. Because—

TRUMP: But I think I have a much better shot this time. But you haven't seen the end of the campaign.

BW: Okay. So what grade do you give yourself on the virus for the last seven months?

TRUMP: Other than the public relations, which is impossible because it's a fake media. Fake. They're fake. I know you disagree—

BW: Yeah I do. But I—

TRUMP: Well I think you do agree, but you're not going to say it. Other than the fact that I have been unable to [?] the media for treating us fairly—

BW: So what's the grade, sir?

TRUMP: —for treating us fairly, I give ourselves an A. But the grade is incomplete, and I'll tell you why. If we come up with the vaccines and therapeutics, then I give myself an A-plus. Because we are—you know how many years ahead of schedule? You know a vaccine wouldn't be thought about for another two years if you went by the schedule.

BW: Okay, okay. We're gonna see in November. Now I've talked to—

TRUMP: But, Bob, remember this—

BW: I've talked to lots of your predecessors. I never talked to Nixon, but I talked to many, many of them. And they get philosophical when I ask the question, what have you learned about yourself?

	And that's the question on you. What have you learned about yourself?
TRUMP:	[*Sighs audibly*]
BW:	You have to have learned!
TRUMP:	That I can handle more than other people can handle. Because and I'll tell you what, whether I learned about it myself—more people come up to me and say, and I mean very strong people, people that are successful, even. A lot of people. They say, I swear to you, I don't know how it's possible for you to handle what you've handled. How you've done this with the kind of opposition, the kind of shenanigans, the kind of illegal witch hunts—they're illegal, by the way. I don't know how you do that. A lot of people have said, I have no idea how you were able to handle it.
BW:	It's a tough job and it's been—I mean as Jared says—
TRUMP:	Tougher for me than just about anybody, I would think.
BW:	Jared says you've had a string of bad luck. And he thinks you'll get a couple of breaks in the next couple of months. And of course—
TRUMP:	Well, the virus was bad luck.
BW:	Yeah.
TRUMP:	Now, look. If we didn't have the virus, I was 10, 12 points up. I was cruising to election.
BW:	Yeah. Well, people are worried about the virus.
TRUMP:	I know that, Bob. But the virus has nothing to do with me. it's not my fault.
BW:	No, it does. Because—
TRUMP:	I'm not the one who let the damn virus out. It was China. It's not me.
BW:	Okay. I know. But you have the problem. And I know you've talked to Lindsey and lots of people about this. And the question is, what's the plan? How are you going to lead? And that's the question as I look at this. And I think, from my

sampling of people which I think is pretty good—
people who, you know, you see that interview
that Chris Wallace did. And people were saying,
oh, you were nervous, you were unhappy. You
talk to other people that say—

TRUMP: I don't think I was nervous. I got good marks
on that interview. The only one that said I was
nervous were people that don't like Trump, okay?
Hey, the enemy will say whatever it is. You know,
you do an interview—oh, he was terrible, terrible.
I got great marks on that interview. From the
neutral players.

COMMENTARY: Trump was widely criticized for a combative interview he had done with Fox News host Chris Wallace. Trump downplayed the coronavirus and blamed testing, Fauci, and China.

TRUMP: My base loved that interview, but from the neutral
players, I got great marks on that interview.

BW: Okay. So—

TRUMP: It was 103 degrees out when we did that crazy
interview.

BW: Yeah. So when we talk in November. Hopefully
we'll be talking. We're going to look back and
we're gonna say, end of July, August, September,
October, what happened with the virus? People
want their president to succeed. Now, you're
right. There's some people who don't.

TRUMP: No, no, no. I think you're wrong. No, people
don't want me to succeed.

BW: No, but if you succeed, they succeed.

TRUMP: Even the RINOs, even the RINOs don't want me
to succeed. They'll end up with a Supreme Court
and lots of things that they're not gonna be too
happy with. I have opposition like nobody has.
And that's okay. I've had that all my life. I've
always had it. And this has been—my whole life
has been like this. In the meantime, right now, I'm

looking at the White House. Okay. I'm staring right at the walls of the White House.

BW: Where are you?

TRUMP: I've had opposition all my life, Bob. More than most. And let's see how it all turns out. We've got 105 days. Let's see how it all turns out. I think it's gonna turn out—

BW: Okay. Today, at five o'clock—

TRUMP: I was unlucky with the virus, because it came in and—

BW: Sure.

TRUMP: —whether it was me or anybody else—

BW: But you got it. You got it. The country's got it. And the world's got it. But you're in charge of this country. And, you know—

TRUMP: We've done better than any other country. Just about, than any other country, in handling it. And it's a bigger, more diverse, more difficult country. And we've done better than any—other than with the press. Other than with the press, I've done a great job. But with the press, I can't do a good job because it's fake. It's fake news. It's a fake group of people and you know it, and you won't write it.

BW: Okay, are you going—

TRUMP: It's one of those things, Bob.

BW: Are you going to acknowledge that in the last six, seven months, you made some mistakes in judgment on the virus?

TRUMP: I'll see how it all turns out. Let's see how it all turns out. I took a big chance on vaccines. I upped the program. You wouldn't be looking at vaccines for three years. We're looking at them next week.

BW: No, I understand. I understand.

TRUMP: No, no. But you don't understand.

BW: I do.

TRUMP: What I was able to do with the FDA and scheduling. A vaccine takes years before it ever even gets tested. We're testing vaccines for three weeks already.

BW: Okay. You're in charge of the national interest, and the national interest—

TRUMP: Will I get credit for it? Probably not. But I'll take the credit.

BW: No, no. You are in charge of the na—You know, look. I've learned one thing in 50 years in writing about nine presidents—nine, including you, going back to Nixon. Ford, Reagan, Obama, you name it. And that is, presidents have power—extraordinary power—and people are leaning on you. And I'm saying from my reporting—

TRUMP: —They do have extraordinary power. But in my case, they never accepted it. And they never accepted this president, because they're a bunch of dishonest people. And they spied on my campaign, and we caught them. They spied before and after I won. And we caught them. And we caught them cold. Let's see what happens.

BW: Yeah. We're indeed going to see. Is there any lesson you take? Because I think this is so important, because I'm in the business of trying to understand other people. I keep learning about, how do you really understand people? How do I understand you? I mean you and I—

TRUMP: You don't understand me. You don't understand me. But that's okay. You'll understand me after the election. But you don't understand me now.

BW: You don't think so?

TRUMP: No, I don't think so.

BW: What—

TRUMP: I don't think you get it. And that's okay.

BW: What are the questions I have not asked, that have not been answered?

TRUMP: I think you've asked me a lot of very good questions. A lot of personal questions. I think you've asked me a lot of good stuff. A lot of

	things are happening, Bob. Just remember, it was seven days and I got a *Washington Post* poll that Hillary Clinton was going to cream me.
BW:	No, listen, I know that. I know that.
TRUMP:	And in that seven days, I gave five, six rallies a day. Nobody else could physically or mentally do it.
BW:	Yeah. Okay.
TRUMP:	And I wasn't like Biden, where every time he has a rally he names the wrong location. I mean, Iowa. No, you're in Idaho. You know. I wasn't—I gave six, five, seven speeches a day in front of big crowds. And I won in the last week. That's where I won. And the *Washington Post*—14 points down!
BW:	You understood history's clock. People did not. But, you know, the seed of this as I'm trying to understand it, is that Steele Dossier. And the four—
TRUMP:	Well the seed of it is the Steele Dossier has now been proven to be a total phony.
BW:	And you know what? Everyone should have ignored it. Including you, including the FBI.
TRUMP:	I couldn't have ignored it. Nope, they were going after my life.
BW:	Yeah.
TRUMP:	They went after me. If I ignored it, I wouldn't be president right now. They were vicious. They were terrible. Jeff Sessions was a terrible pick by me. He didn't know what he was doing. It wasn't that he was vicious, he just didn't have a clue. No, it was terrible.
BW:	History's going to have such a big time with all of this.
TRUMP:	It was an attempted coup.
BW:	Well.
TRUMP:	And I had to go through that. And it was all bullshit. And yet I had to be careful. When you say I should have just—I had to be very careful with it. I had to be very careful with it.

BW:	Listen. You know, we've gone through all of this.
TRUMP:	No, but I had to do that in addition to running a country. And nobody's done the things that I've done. When you look at what I've done. The list, you have the list.
BW:	I have the list. But, you know what, number one is the virus. Number two's the virus. Number three is the virus.
TRUMP:	No, no. I agree with that.
BW:	Yes, sir.
TRUMP:	That was thrown upon me when we were riding high. The election was over. I was going to win easily. And all of a sudden we get hit by the China virus. And now I'm working my ass off. So long, Bob. Good luck.
BW:	Okay, sir. Have a good day.
TRUMP:	Thanks, Bob.
BW:	Thanks for calling.
TRUMP:	Thank you. Great guy. Bye.
BW:	Bye.

[*Recording ends*]

COMMENTARY: Seven hours later, Trump gave a long statement at his first Coronavirus Task Force press conference in three months. He spoke alone at the White House. No Pence, no Fauci, no Dr. Birx. He also shifted tone. Everything was not rosy with the outlook for the virus.

> TRUMP: *It will probably, unfortunately, get worse before it gets better. Something I don't like saying about things, but that's the way it is.*

Prior to this, Trump had adamantly refused to wear a mask. Now he was gonna even pivot on that.

> TRUMP: *Wear a mask. Get a mask. Whether you like the mask or not, they have an impact. They'll have an effect and we need everything we can get.*

My wife, Elsa Walsh, who had worked for years as a reporter for *The Washington Post* and then as a staff writer for *The New Yorker*, spent endless hours with me sifting through the story of the Trump presidency. We talked intensely over the whole last year. What was the remedy, the course that could have been taken? Was there a way to do better?

Elsa suggested looking at a previous president who had his own crisis and spoke directly to the American people. The model was Franklin Delano Roosevelt. Over his 12 years as president, FDR gave 30 fireside chats. His aides and the public often clamored for more. But FDR said no. It was important to limit his talks to the major events and to make them exceptional. He also said they were really hard work for him personally, requiring often days of his time.

The evening radio addresses concerned the toughest issues facing the country, particularly after the 1941 attack on Pearl Harbor.

> **FDR:** *We must share together the bad news and the good news; the defeats and the victories—the changing fortunes of war. So far, the news has been all bad. We have suffered a serious setback in Hawaii.*

In a calm and reassuring voice, he explained what the problem was, what the government was doing about it, and what he expected of the people.

> **FDR:** *Your government has unmistakable confidence in your ability to hear the worst without flinching or losing heart.*

Often the message was grim, but FDR invited the American people in.

> **FDR:** *It will not only be a long war, it will be a hard war . . . We are now fighting to maintain our right to live among our world neighbors in freedom in common decency . . . We are all in it—all the way. Every single man, woman,*

and child is a partner in the most tremendous
undertaking of our American history.

For more than 50 years, I have written about 10 presidents from Nixon to Biden. A president must be willing to share the worst with the people, the bad news with the good.

FDR: *On the road ahead, there lies hard work,*
                            grueling work. Day and night, every hour and
                            every minute.

All presidents have a large obligation to inform, warn, protect, to define goals and the true national interest. It should be a truth-telling response to the world, especially in crisis. Trump has, instead, enshrined personal grievance and division as a governing principle of his presidency. On the coronavirus, he denied, concealed and covered up. In my view, it was one of the worst crimes of any president.

INTERVIEW 20:
The Next One I Need Is You

Phone call
August 14, 2020

TRUMP: Gonna be interesting. We have a lot of support.
I don't know if you see it. And we have a lot of
invisible support. More than anyone's—I think,
I'll let you know—

COMMENTARY: On August 14th, Elsa and I were sitting in our den at home. The book was done. It would be on bookshelves in four weeks. There was a sense of relief that almost permeated the room. Ah, it's over, I thought. At least this moment with Trump is over. The phone rang and Elsa picked up. It was Trump. I put my hands over my head in consternation. "You have to talk to him," Elsa whispered insistently, holding out the phone. I took the receiver, and she switched on a tape recorder.

TRUMP: Hey, Bob.
BW: How are you, President Trump?
TRUMP: How are you? How are you doing, okay?
BW: Good.
TRUMP: Good. Hey, Bob, so the deal, I wanted to tell you
a little bit about it. But it was very—we kept it
pretty confidential believe it or not.
BW: Yes, that's a big deal.

COMMENTARY: He wanted to talk about the Abraham Accords, an agreement made the day before among Israel, the United Arab

Emirates, and the Unites States to normalize relations among the countries.

TRUMP:	So here's what will happen, now. Saudi Arabia wants to be in. They all want to be in. Every single country wants to be in. And the Palestinians are all controlled by them. You know, because they all get lots of money from them—that's where they get their money. From the various, you know, very wealthy countries that we're dealing with. And they all want to be in. So I just want to tell you the chips will fall into place very quickly. Very nicely. And you may very well have peace in the Middle East. Real peace, not a peace with, you know, one nation agrees to something. It's a peace where everybody agrees. And I was hoping you'd like it.
BW:	Okay, good. Well—
TRUMP:	We've even been getting coverage from *The New York Times* today, which is shocking.
BW:	Yeah, isn't that something. Well, it's a big deal. And it goes back to Carter's Camp David, when the Israelis and Sadat made peace. So . . .
TRUMP:	It never happened. It never really, you know, it never went anywhere. I mean, the problem—
BW:	Yes, but at least they didn't go to war.
TRUMP:	Yeah, well, yeah, in a way. That's right. You know, what happens here is you'll have all the countries agreeing. And it's gonna happen very quickly because they all like it.
BW:	Yeah.
TRUMP:	You had to break the ice—
BW:	Good.
TRUMP:	—with a highly respected country. And a highly respected leader. I just wanted you to know. Maybe you put your book to bed already?
BW:	No, the book is all done. It's called *Rage*—
TRUMP:	Okay.

BW: —which is something we talked about. It's you know, it's the condition of the world. And I quote you a lot.

TRUMP: No, I like it.

BW: It's a tough book, sir. And you have your say and there's going to be a lot of controversy about it, I expect. Like on North Korea I think they put out that I have those letters and so forth. A lot of people are going to read that and say, you know, Trump made sure there was no war. And other people are going to say, oh, well, that was a risky diplomatic strategy. But anyway, that's laid out. The whole business with the COVID and dealing with that is laid out. And so it's close to the bone and you helped me get there, and I appreciate that.

TRUMP: Alright. Well, we've done better than most countries with COVID. You're starting to see that. Because now all of those shining examples are now blowing up, right? You see that. Germany and many of them are blowing up.

BW: And it's gonna be a tough month in September as the flu comes in and—

TRUMP: You have the flu on top of it, yep.

BW: I mean, one of the doctors told me it's just going to be a hailstorm. So we're in for a tough season. As soon as I get a copy of the book I will send it over to you. And I emphasize it's tough. I had to make my independent judgments on things as you—

TRUMP: So do you think I did the right thing on North Korea?

BW: Um, you know, I think—look, you keep saying it. And I quote you in the book—

TRUMP: Zero. No people have been killed.

BW: No war, no war. And, you know, you make the point repeatedly. Not just about North Korea, but about the Middle East and everywhere.

TRUMP:	This is a big step that, unfortunately, isn't in your book. You know.
BW:	Yeah. Yeah. Well, this—
TRUMP:	That's why I called you. I wish—
BW:	Okay, well I appreciate that. And I'll get the book to you.
TRUMP:	This sort of tells you that I'm right, okay. It'll all fall into place over the next short period of time.
BW:	Okay. Okay, well, we'll talk. I mean, there are parts of the book you're not gonna like. And—
TRUMP:	What won't I like, Bob?
BW:	Well, it's tough times. The virus, as you repeatedly told me, and as you've said publicly, it's derailed things. And it's a big reality in people's lives, as you know.
TRUMP:	You know the market's coming back very strong, you do know that.
BW:	Yes, of course.

COMMENTARY: This was his incessant refrain. He couldn't stop talking about the stock market.

BW:	And—
TRUMP:	Did you cover that in the book?
BW:	Yeah, oh sure. Listen, probably 20 percent of the book are quotes from you about, you know, the interviews we did and the discussions and the phone calls. So you have your say. And the people who offer criticisms and my judgments are in there as you always told me they were going to be. And so, it's going to be one hell of an interesting election.
TRUMP:	Yep. Going to be interesting. We have a lot of support. I don't know if you see it. And we have a lot of invisible support. More than anyone's—I think, I'll let you know—
BW:	Yeah.
TRUMP:	But I think more than anyone's ever had. When

	you look at the polls, when you look at people that don't want to talk to pollsters. And then you look, and I guess I'm getting pretty close anyway. You know, we have polls that I'm up. I'm up in many of the swing states now.
BW:	It's gonna be a contest between you and Biden. It's going to be a contest between both of you and the virus. Because it's in real people's lives. You know, all those tens of millions of people who don't have jobs, who don't have that income.
TRUMP:	I know.
BW:	Listen, I mean, you and I—
TRUMP:	Nothing more could have been done. Nothing more could have been done.
BW:	Well—
TRUMP:	I acted early. I acted early. So we'll see.
BW:	This will be the history that we start the first draft of.
TRUMP:	So you think the virus totally supersedes the economy?
BW:	Oh, sure. But they're related, as you know.
TRUMP:	A little bit, yeah.
BW:	Oh, a little bit? I mean—
TRUMP:	I mean more than a little bit. But the economy is doing—look, we're close to a new stock market record.
BW:	Yeah. But you have tens of millions of people in this country who are your citizens who don't have jobs and don't have that money coming in that came in for a number of months. And I always worry, as you and I've discussed, that in my position of privilege that I don't realize that enough. And, you know, that's—that's gonna be part of the election.
TRUMP:	I agree.
BW:	It's gonna be maybe—
TRUMP:	Oh, it's a big part. You know, the stock market's almost at a new record high. Very close to it.

BW:	Yeah, but as you know—
TRUMP:	That's a surprise.
BW:	It's a surprise. But you talk to the experts about it, and they say there's no place for the money to go. Because you can't make any money by buying bonds or putting it in a bank account. And so—
TRUMP:	For whatever reason, it's where the stocks are. And 401(K)s are doing phenomenally well. You know, they're up—they're up 57 percent since March, Bob.

COMMENTARY: According to *Fidelity*, the average 401(K) balance increased 14 percent in the second quarter of 2020.

BW:	So if there's peace in the Middle East then, you know, that's going to be a big, big deal. And I see Tom Friedman is giving you credit for it today.
TRUMP:	Oh, is he? Tom Friedman? That's nice.
BW:	Isn't that something. So I think—
TRUMP:	It's come a long way. The next one I need is you. But it looks like I don't have it on this book, but we'll get you sometime later, I guess.
BW:	It's tough, sir. Thank you very much.
TRUMP:	Alright. Thanks. Bye.
BW:	Bye, have a good day.

[*Recording ends*]

EPILOGUE

When I relistened to these tapes earlier this year, I realized the real Trump was pounding in my ears in a way that the printed page does not capture.

At one point in June 2020, I asked him if he had assistance with a law-and-order speech he had given. Trump said:

TRUMP: I get people. They come up with ideas. But the ideas are mine, Bob. The ideas are mine . . . Want to know something? Everything is mine.

"Everything is mine." That is Trump's view of the presidency that comes across over and over again in our interviews. The presidency is mine. It is *still* mine. The only view that matters is mine.

Trump does not believe in democracy. That is my central conclusion. The U.S. Constitution is built and structured on divided powers among three branches. No one owns the federal government or its citizens.

There is no King.

As you listened to these tapes you heard Trump's deception, performance, and grievance. You saw what drives Trump.

TRUMP: There's nobody that's tougher than me. Nobody's tougher than me. You asked me about impeachment. I'm under impeachment, and you said you just act like you won the fucking race. Nixon was in a corner with his thumb in his mouth. Bill Clinton took it very, very hard. I don't—I just do things, okay? I do what I want—[*crosstalk*]

He stokes political and racial divisions. If he regains the presidency, he will settle scores.

Trump treated the presidency like his own property. "Everything is mine" and "I do what I want."

The first news stories on my book *Rage* ran on September 9th, 2020, two months before the presidential election. *The Washington Post* ran an excerpt emphasizing the January 28th Oval Office briefing when Trump's national security adviser Robert O'Brien warned him about the virus.

CNN followed with saturation coverage on *Rage* and Trump's efforts to conceal the true threat of the coronavirus.

Peter Baker, the chief White House correspondent for *The New York Times*, wrote: "With an election 53 days away, perhaps no other president . . . did as much to undermine himself."

Dan Pfeiffer, a senior adviser to former President Obama, said, "Trump treated a reporter famous for bringing down a president like his personal sounding board. It is truly one of the most stupid, self-destructive communications decisions made by a politician in memory."

Trump commented on *Rage* on September 16th:

"I said a lot of really good things. I mean, for the most part, people like to turn it around, but I said really good things in that book."

On October 15th, less than three weeks before the presidential election, Trump appeared at a nationally televised prime-time NBC Town Hall. The host, Savannah Guthrie, asked Trump about his response to the virus:

GUTHRIE:	*Can I ask you, did your national security adviser on January 28th in the Oval Office warn you that this would be the greatest national security risk of your administration?*
TRUMP:	*I read that but no, he didn't.*
GUTHRIE:	*He didn't say it or you don't remember?*
TRUMP:	*I read it . . . I read it someplace. Maybe Woodward said it or something. But he did not say that.*

What Trump said is not true. Guthrie could have played an interview from a month earlier when Fox News anchor Brett Baier had asked O'Brien about my book.

BAIER:	*There's a quote in this book about the COVID threat, January 28th in the Oval Office. You're quoted to say to the president, "This will be the biggest national security threat you face in your presidency, this is going to be the roughest thing you face." Is that true?*
O'BRIEN:	*It is true. It was during one of our Oval intelligence briefs and it was something we were concerned about.*

In the end, Biden won the presidential election by seven million votes. However, a switch of 44,000 votes in the states of Arizona, Wisconsin, and Georgia would have given Trump and Biden a tie in the Electoral College. This tie would have kicked the election to the House of Representatives, where states would vote. Since there were more Republican dominated states, Trump would have won.

President Trump strode to the lectern in the East room of the White House at around 2:30 a.m. on November 4th and refused to concede. His tone was dismissive, indignant.

TRUMP:	*This is an embarrassment to our country. We were getting ready to win this election. Frankly, we did win this election. [Applause]*

This launched his claim that the election was stolen from him, as he still insists to this day.

Everything that followed Trump's loss of the presidency to Joe Biden reflects this absolute self-focus and his relentless and dangerous efforts to undermine the Constitution and our laws. He exerted extraordinary pressure on his then–Vice President Mike Pence to block the Constitutional certification of Biden as president on January 6th.

That day, driven by Trump's rhetoric and his obvious approval, a mob descended on the Capitol and, in a stunning, unprecedented act of collective violence, broke through doors and windows, and ransacked the House chamber, where the electoral votes were to be counted. The mob then went in search of Pence—to hang him and to prevent the certification of Joe Biden's victory. Trump did nothing to restrain them.

Criminal and civil investigations into his conduct continue in Atlanta and New York. There are also ongoing investigations into his

conduct related to January 6th and his hoarding of the most sensitive top secret documents at his Mar-a-Lago estate in Palm Beach.
Among the documents retrieved from Mar-a-Lago were the letters
between Trump and North Korean leader Kim Jong Un.

"Oh, those are so top secret," Trump said to me two years earlier on
January 20th, 2020, about those letters. He let me read them. I dictated
them into my tape recorder and quoted the letters in my book *Rage*.

It is still somewhat of a puzzle to me why he talked to me and at
such length. I think he honestly believed he could talk me into telling
the story of his presidency as he would like it to be seen and remembered in history. He saw me as part of the Washington establishment,
which had almost universally withheld approval of him.

TRUMP: My natural inclination is to win. And after I
                    win, I will be so presidential that you won't even
                    recognize me . . . You'll be falling asleep, you'll be
                    so bored.

Few fell asleep and few were bored.

Senator Lindsey Graham had assured Trump that I would not put
words in his mouth. That opened the door initially for these interviews. Trump also seemed to see me as a worthy adversary. Someone
he could win over.

For more than 50 years, I have written books about 10 presidents
from Nixon to Biden. I had interviewed Presidents Carter, Clinton,
George W. Bush, and Obama. That seemed to further legitimize me
to Trump.

TRUMP: You're probably going to screw me. You know,
                    because that's the way it goes. Look, Bush sat
                    with you for hours and you screwed him. But the
                    difference was, I ain't no Bush.

In these Trump interviews, I tried to take him as seriously as he took
himself. I also tried to do my homework. I asked questions directly
and did not adopt a hostile posture. While I pushed him and did not
necessarily agree with his categorical declarations or self-praise, I let
him have his say.

I also believe the tapes show that Trump's greatest failure was his handling of the coronavirus. He ignored the explicit, dire January 28th warning from his national security adviser Robert O'Brien that "this will be the biggest national security threat you face in your presidency." Instead, Trump deceived and covered up.

TRUMP:	I wanted to always play it down. I still like playing it down because I don't want to create a panic.
BW:	Was there a moment in all of this, last two months, where you said to yourself, ah, this is the leadership test of a lifetime?
TRUMP:	No.

I ended my book *Rage* in 2020 with the following sentence: "When his performance as president is taken in its entirety, I can only reach one conclusion: Trump is the wrong man for the job."

Now, two years later in 2022, I realize that I didn't go far enough. Trump is an unparalleled danger. The record now shows that Trump has led—and continues to lead—a seditious conspiracy to overturn the 2020 election, which in effect is an effort to destroy democracy.

Trump is telling his inner circle that he does plan to run again in 2024. "I'm going to do it," he says. One argument made to Trump is that if he runs and wins it will be the biggest political comeback in American, and perhaps, world history. That win will be his legacy. A triumphant Second Act. On November 15, Trump announced he would run again.

If he doesn't run and win, the argument is that his political obituary will be the January 6th insurrection at the Capitol, two impeachment trials, the more than one million deaths from the coronavirus, and hardening political and racial divisions.

In late 2022 as I write this, Trump has the biggest group of followers, loyalists, and fundraisers of any politician in the country. He has a political machine unequaled, exceeding that of even President Joe Biden.

Trump exploits the notoriety of the ongoing scandals, investigations, and political warfare so he can dominate and keep his grip on American politics.

He relishes the combat and defiance. The presidency is his narcotic, fueling heroic energy.

In 2021, I did another book on Trump, *Peril,* with Robert Costa. The book showed how Trump continues to hold campaign-style rallies across the country. Trump's message: "We didn't lose. We didn't lose. We didn't lose." Trump declined to be interviewed for *Peril.* So my last interview with him was August 14th, 2020.

Costa and I asked these questions at the end of our book: "Could Trump work his will again? Were there any limits to what he and his supporters might do to put him back in power?" We concluded: "Peril remains."

These are still the questions in 2022.

The Trump Tapes show Trump in his own words, his shortcomings and his unfitness to lead the United States. Instead of understanding his responsibilities as president to address the crises affecting the country, Trump is consumed by the past and unable to let go of his grievances.

TRUMP: They got caught. This was a treasonous act. This
                     was a terrible act. And if this were Obama sitting
                     in the seat where I am right now instead of me,
                     these people would've been in jail. For 50 years
                     they would've gone to jail. They would've spent
                     50 years in jail, meaning they would've died in jail.

                                    *

BW: I say this to you directly: what happened in the
                     past, it's getting in the way, I think, of you doing
                     the job—I mean, ask Melania. Is the past—
TRUMP: Why do you think that, Bob? I think people tried
                     to—this was a coup. This was an attempted and
                     failed coup.

Trump aspired to be a colossus like FDR. He lives his own self-inflicted melodrama. Everything is mine. I do what I want.

CLOSE

BIO

Bob Woodward has authored 21 books. Fifteen were #1 bestsellers, including three on Trump: *Fear, Rage,* and *Peril.* He has been a *Washington Post* reporter for 50 years and shared in two Pulitzer Prizes.

You've been reading *The Trump Tapes: Bob Woodward's Twenty Interviews with President Donald Trump,* also available as a Simon & Schuster audiobook original.

AUDIOBOOK CREDITS

All interviews were recorded by Bob Woodward.

Studio recording by Terry Hogan and Andre Bellido at Simon & Schuster in New York, and Harry Evans and Mike Goehler at Clean Cuts at Three Seas in Washington DC.

Post-production by Hudson Sound

Fact-checking by Evelyn Duffy and Ben Gambuzza at Open Boat Editing

The associate producer was Claire Tadokoro.

The executive producers were Chris Lynch, Elisa Shokoff, and Elsa Walsh.

The Trump Tapes was produced and directed by Karen Pearlman and Claire McMullen.

Also available from Simon & Schuster:
Fear by Bob Woodward, *Rage* by Bob Woodward, and *Peril* by Bob Woodward and Robert Costa.

APPENDIX:
Kim Jong Un–Trump Letters

These are the twenty-seven letters between North Korean Leader Kim Jong Un and President Donald J. Trump in chronological order. Bob Woodward dictated from Trump's original letters and the English translation of Kim's letters.

———————

[*on White House stationery*]

1 April 2018

Dear Chairman Kim,
Thank you for extending an invitation for us to meet. I would be glad to meet with you to discuss a way forward for our two countries.

I would like to convey my thanks as well for hosting Director Pompeo in Pyongyang. He has my total confidence as my representative in preparing for our meeting.

I look forward to working with you toward greater improvement in our relations and to mutually creating a better and safer future for North Korea and the world.

Chairman Kim
1 April 2018
Chairman State Affairs Commission
Democratic People's Republic of Korea

Dear Excellency:
I am thankful for the personal letter you sent that explicitly laid out your great intentions. In addition, I would like to express my gratitude for sending Director Pompeo as your entrusted delegate to Pyongyang.

Through your personal letter and detailed explanation from Director Pompeo, I fully acknowledge your plans and determination, and I am very encouraged by them. In addition to your great plan, I intend to take big steps to resolve existing issues between our two countries and end negative bilateral relations.

I'm prepared to cooperate with you in sincerity and dedication to accomplish a great feat that no one in the past has been able to achieve and that is unexpected by the whole world. And I am confident that our first meeting will lead to proactive pursuit in this achievement. I eagerly await your momentous decision.

With respect,
Chairman State Affairs Commission,
Democratic People's Republic of Korea
Kim Jong Un
1 April 2018, Pyongyang

[on *White House stationery, undated; 4/3/18 is handwritten in the* corner]

His Excellency Kim Jong Un
Chairman of the State Affairs Commission of the Democratic
People's Republic of Korea
Pyongyang

Dear Mr. Chairman,
I greatly appreciate your letter, which was passed to me by
Central Intelligence Agency Director Pompeo. I agree with
everything you said and have very little doubt that our meeting
will be a momentous one for both our countries and for the rest
of the world. I look forward to meeting you in coming weeks.

Sincerely,
[signed Donald J. Trump]

[on *White House stationery*]

May 24, 2018
His Excellency Kim Jong Un
Chairman of the State Affairs Commission of the Democratic
People's Republic of Korea
Pyongyang

Dear Mr. Chairman,
We greatly appreciate your time, patience, and effort with respect
to our recent negotiations and discussions relative to a summit
long sought by both parties which was scheduled to take place on
June 12 in Singapore. We were informed that this meeting was
requested by North Korea, but that to us is totally irrelevant.

I was very much looking forward to being there with you. Sadly,
based on the tremendous anger and open hostility displayed in your
most recent statement, I feel it is inappropriate, at this time, to have
this long-planned meeting. Therefore please let this letter serve to
represent that the Singapore summit for the good of both parties
but to the detriment of the world will not take place.

You talk about your nuclear capabilities, but ours are so massive
and powerful that I pray to God they will never have to be used. I
felt a wonderful dialogue was building up between you and me and
ultimately it is only the dialogue that matters. Someday I look very
much forward to meeting you.

In the meantime, I want to thank you for the release of the
hostages who are now home with their families. That was a
beautiful gesture and was very much appreciated.

If you change your mind having to do with this most
important summit, please do not hesitate to call me or write.
The world, and North Korea in particular, has lost a great
opportunity for lasting peace and great prosperity and wealth.
This missed opportunity is a truly sad moment in history.

Yours truly.
[signed Donald J. Trump]

HE Donald J. Trump, President
United States of America, Washington

Esteemed Your Excellency,
Allow me to take this opportunity to highly appreciate the
efforts Your Excellency President is extending with a view to
making our upcoming meeting a historic moment.

It is with great expectations that I myself await the DPRK-US
summit, an event the entire world is focusing on. I have no doubt
that our scheduled meeting, the first ever between us, will be a
milestone in the efforts aimed at improving relations between the
DPRK and the United States as well as ensuring peace and security
in the region.

At the same time, I sincerely hope that our first meeting, about
to happen at no small pains, will lead to more wonderful and
meaningful meetings.

I look forward to having a significant meeting with Your
Excellency on June 12.

Kim Jong Un
Pyongyang
May 29, 2018

[*on White House stationery*]

June 15, 2018
His Excellency Kim Jong Un
Chairman of the State Affairs Commission of the Democratic
People's Republic of Korea
Pyongyang

Dear Mr. Chairman,
I just have arrived back in America, and the media for North
Korea and you have been fantastic. They have great respect for
you and your country. I also reported how well we got along
and that we like each other very much—true. See you soon.

Sincerely,
[signed Donald J. Trump]
[*Note: "true" above is underlined in Trump's black magic marker.*]

[*on White House stationery*]

July 3, 2018
His Excellency Kim Jong Un
Chairman of the State Affairs Commission of the Democratic
People's Republic of Korea
Pyongyang

Dear Mr. Chairman,
Our summit in Singapore was a truly historic event. You and I
accomplished a great deal. Our joint statement demonstrated
the determination we both share to bring our nations'
relationship—and the security of the world—into a new era.

To ensure the Singapore summit is remembered as a turning
point in history, we must make fast progress on the commitments
we made in the summit joint statement. It would be a beautiful
thing if we could announce as soon as possible that our two
countries are taking steps to implement those commitments—
steps we have never taken before.

To make this happen, I have sent Secretary of State Mike
Pompeo to Pyongyang with directions to achieve substantial
progress. First, Secretary Pompeo hopes to reach agreement on the
return of an initial set of POW/MIA remains as soon as possible.
Second, the secretary hopes to gain your agreement to permit
a visit by technical experts to the missile engine test site you
pledged in Singapore to shut down. Third and most importantly,
Secretary Pompeo is under my instructions to find agreement with
you on taking the first major steps toward the final, fully verified
denuclearization of the Korean Peninsula and toward a more
peaceful future between us.

I look forward to hearing of progress toward our mutual goals.

Sincerely yours,
Donald J. Trump
President of the United States
[*Note: not personally signed*]

[July 6, 2018]

To President HE Donald J. Trump,
The significant first meeting with Your Excellency and the joint statement that we signed together in Singapore 24 days ago was indeed the start of a meaningful journey.

I deeply appreciate the energetic and extraordinary efforts made by Your Excellency, Mr. President, for the improvement of relations between the two countries and the faithful implementation of the joint statement.

I firmly believe that the strong will, sincere efforts, and unique approach of myself and Your Excellency Mr. President, aimed at opening up a new future between the DPRK and the US will surely come to fruition.

Wishing that the invariable trust and confidence in Your Excellency Mr. President will be further strengthened in the future process of taking practical actions, I extend my conviction with the epochal progress in promoting the DPRK-US relations will bring our next meeting forward.

July 30, 2018

Your Excellency Mr. President,
I express my deep appreciation to Your Excellency for having
a firm faith in the excellent relations established between us
during the first summit and exerting yourself to honor the
promise made in that historic day.

I feel pleased to have formed good ties with such a powerful
and preeminent statesman as Your Excellency, though there is
a sense of regret for the lack of anticipated declaration on the
termination of war. I am convinced that the declaration of the
termination of war would surely see the light of day at an early
date as a world-historic event that encourages the development of
relations between the two countries and promotes global peace and
security.

The first step in improving the DPRK-US relations was taken in
a meaningful way at the Singapore summit, and the next meeting
between us will come to a beautiful fruition bringing even greater
delight and satisfaction to both countries of the DPRK and the US.

I have an unwavering confidence that my next meeting with
Your Excellency would produce a more significant outcome, and
I will make continued efforts and preparations to deliver that
outcome without fail.

I wish Your Excellency good health and bigger success in the
fulfillment of your official duties. I also extend my heartfelt and
warmest greetings to the First Lady and the family members of
Your Excellency.

Kim Jong Un
July 30, 2018

_____

[*on White House stationery*]

August 2, 2018
His Excellency Kim Jong Un
Chairman of the State Affairs Commission of the Democratic
People's Republic of Korea
Pyongyang

Dear Mr. Chairman,
Thank you for your letter, which I received through
Ambassador Harry Harris, my excellent representative to the
Republic of Korea. I've been briefed on Ambassador Harris'
meeting with Vice Chairman Kim Yong Chol and understand
they had a candid and constructive conversation.

It has been almost two months since our historic summit in
Singapore. The deal you and I made was an excellent one, and I
am pleased that there has been progress implementing the joint
statement we signed.

Thank you for fulfilling your commitment to begin the process
of returning the remains of our soldiers and planning for future
joint recovery operations. This was an important step, and it meant
so much to the American people.

It is now time to make progress on the other commitments
we made, including complete denuclearization. To advance this
goal, I would like to send Secretary of State Mike Pompeo back to
Pyongyang to meet with you to plan next steps. I agree you and I
should meet again at a mutually convenient time. Secretary Pompeo's
visit to Pyongyang would be an opportunity to ensure we make the
progress necessary for our next meeting to be another great success.

I look forward to hearing your response soon. I will convey
your warm greetings to Melania. Please give my best to your
family as well.

Sincerely,
Donald J. Trump
President of the United States
[*Written in black magic marker:*] I look forward to seeing you soon—

August 12, 2018

Your Excellency Mr. President,
I received your great letter that contained your will and
intent. Per my previous letter, I am happy to have established
a relationship with a strong political leader (like yourself) who
has great leadership, political sense and decisiveness. (Further) I
have fostered this goodwill toward you in the past two months.

I fully agree with your proposal for Secretary of State Mike
Pompeo to visit Pyongyang. I am prepared to seriously discuss
future plans with the Secretary of State, whom you have appointed.
The work we are currently planning will even be more meaningful
and will lead to a great negotiation resulting in a great outcome.

If our historic meeting two months ago signaled a new
beginning to the DPRK-US relationship, my next meeting with
you will be an opportunity to plan for a safe and solid future.
I'm sure that the effort you and I are putting forth will continue
to bring about satisfactory results.

Your Excellency Mr. President, wishing you good health,
Kim Jong Un
August 12, 2018

September 6, 2018

Your Excellency Mr. President,
I would first like to seek your understanding for having
hurt your feelings even for a moment under unfortunate
circumstances in which Secretary of State Pompeo's visit to
Pyongyang that Your Excellency had planned was cancelled. It
is my thought that instead of having a war of words on issues
that divide our two sides with Secretary Pompeo, who it is
difficult for me to think can fully represent Your Excellency's
mind, it would be more constructive to meet in person with
Your Excellency who are endowed with an outstanding political
sense and have an in-depth exchange of views on important
issues including the denuclearization.

I would like to affirm that I remain unchanged in my resolve
to faithfully implement the historic joint statement signed at the
Singapore summit and that in addition to the steps that we have taken
up front, we are willing to take further meaningful steps one at a time
in a phased manner, such as the complete shutdown of the Nuclear
Weapons Institute or the Satellite Launch District and the irreversible
closure of the nuclear materials production facility. However, in order
for us to sustain the momentum for continuing to take these steps, we
need to feel some changes in our surroundings, even a little, to prove
that the effort we make are by no means in vain.

I still vividly remember the conversation I had with Your
Excellency Mr. President 80-odd days ago on the Sentosa Island
in which we talked about the need to terminate the history
of unfortunate past of our two countries to resolve the issue
of denuclearization on the principle of phased, synchronized
actions and to work together to open a bright future for the two
countries—something no one has done before. If our goodwill
and sincere efforts are properly appreciated and the United States
to take more substantive steps and actions in a phased manner,
significant progress will be made in the issue of denuclearization
that is the focus of the world. And this indeed will be recorded in
history as Your Excellency's great achievement.

I fully support the idea of a second DPRK-US summit that Your Excellency have already mentioned in public and will be glad to meet with Your Excellency Mr. President at any time of your convenience. I am rather curious to know how Your Excellency would think about this, and I really am looking forward to a positive reply.

I am always pleased about and cherish the excellent relationship that I have formed with such a powerful and preeminent President of the United States of America as Your Excellency. This confidence that I have in Your Excellency will never change. I am deeply convinced that the many miraculous changes that we have brought about this year beyond the imagination of everyone will lead to many more in the future on the basis of the excellent relationship that exists between Your Excellency and myself.

I wish Your Excellency Mr. President even greater success in all your important work as well as your good health. I extend my warm greetings to the First Lady and other members of your family.

Please accept the assurances of my highest consideration.
Kim Jong Un
September 6, 2018

September 21, 2018

Your Excellency Mr. President,
I acknowledge that our meeting again in the near future will
be very useful for removing distrust and building confidence
between our two countries and making big progress in the issue
of denuclearization of the Korean Peninsula. I am not sure how
Your Excellency would think about this, but I am confident that
when we meet again we can confirm our respective positions and
certainly reach an agreement that will come to fruition. I have a
feeling that very good results may come about in my next meeting
with Your Excellency and I will work hard to make that happen.

I hope to discuss the issue of denuclearization of the Korean
Peninsula directly with Your Excellency, not with President Moon
Jae-in of South Korea, in future and I think the excessive interest
President Moon is showing as now in our matter is unnecessary.
If Your Excellency agrees with me, please do send Pompeo to
Pyongyang again at an early date. I will meet with the person with
the authority delegated by Your Excellency and discuss and plan
the steps forward, including the time and venue of our meeting.

As I wrote in my previous letter, my confidence and respect
for Your Excellency will never change, though many people are
skeptical about the current status and the prospects of the relations
between our countries about our ideas of resolving the issue of
denuclearization in the future. I, together with Your Excellency,
will definitely prove them wrong. The excellent relations between
us will serve as the basis for the wonderful achievements we will
make in the future and such a belief will be the driving force for all
our successful work.

I sincerely wish Your Excellency Mr. President great success
in your important work. I extend my warm greetings to the First
Lady.

Please accept, Your Excellency, the assurances of my highest
consideration.
Kim Jong Un
September 21, 2018

[*on White House stationery*]

December 24, 2018
His Excellency Kim Jong Un
Chairman of the State Affairs Commission of the Democratic
People's Republic of Korea
Pyongyang

Dear Chairman Kim,
We had a great 2018. I wanted to wish you a wonderful 2019. I
look forward to our next summit and to making real progress
on denuclearization and a really bright future for your people
under your leadership in the year ahead.
    Please give my warmest regards to your beautiful family
and the people of the Democratic People's Republic of Korea.
Looking forward to seeing you soon.
[*signed Donald Trump in black magic marker*]

25 December 2018

Your Excellency,
It has been 200 days since the historic DPRK-US summit
in Singapore this past June, and the year is now almost
coming to an end. Even now I cannot forget that moment
of history when I firmly held Your Excellency's hand at the
beautiful and sacred location as the whole world watched
with great interest and hope to relive the honor of that day.
As I mentioned at that time, I feel very honored to have
established an excellent relationship with a person such as
Your Excellency.

As the new year 2019 approaches, critical issues that require
endless effort toward even higher ideals and goals still await us.
Just as Your Excellency frankly noted, as we enter the new year
the whole world will certainly once again come to see, not so far
in the future, another historic meeting between myself and Your
Excellency reminiscent of a scene from a fantasy film.

I have already instructed my closest and most trusted colleagues
and the relevant organs to speed up the preparations for holding
a second DPRK-US summit and am prepared to achieved good
results with Your Excellency during the next meeting.

Nevertheless, what worries me is that it may not reflect
positively on us should both sides appear to stubbornly insist on
our respective positions regarding the location of the summit. It
could also result in wasting a lot of time. Therefore, my position
is to urgently hold senior-level contact between the DPRK and the
US to internally [translator's note: privately] discuss and coordinate
issues regarding the location.

I hope that Your Excellency will once again demonstrate great
decisiveness and excellent leadership to accomplish results in the
second DPRK summit. I wholeheartedly hope that the things that
Your Excellency seeks to achieve will come to great fruition.

I wish the honorable First Lady, your family and those close
to you good health, happiness, and great success.

Sincerely, with unchanging respect for Your Excellency the
President,
Chairman State Affairs Commission
Democratic People's Republic of Korea
Kim Jong Un
25 December 2018

_____

[on *White House stationery*]

December 28, 2018
His Excellency Kim Jong Un
Chairman of the State Affairs Commission of the Democratic
People's Republic of Korea
Pyongyang

Dear Chairman Kim,
I just received your letter and very much appreciate your warm
feelings and thoughts. Like you, I have no doubt that a great
result will be accomplished between our two countries, and
that the only two leaders who can do it are you and me.
    The location of our next summit, to which I am very much
looking forward, will not be a problem for me. Also I do not
mind meeting closer to your country than mine, [in?] that travel is
probably far easier for me than for you. I have heard that numerous
locations have been rejected but that Bangkok, Thailand or Hanoi,
Vietnam would be acceptable.
    I wish you a prosperous and joyful start to a happy new year
and look forward to meeting you very soon.
    Best wishes to your family and friends.

Sincerely,
Donald Trump
[*"Best wishes" above is underlined in black magic marker.*]
[on *White House stationery*]

January 8, 2019
His Excellency Kim Jong Un
Chairman of the State Affairs Commission of the Democratic
People's Republic of Korea
Pyongyang

Dear Chairman Kim,
I heard it was your birthday and I wanted to wish you a happy
day. You will have many great years of celebration and success.
Your country will soon be on a historic and prosperous path.

Sincerely,
Donald Trump

January 17, 2019

Your Excellency Mr. President,
I express my sincere appreciation to Your Excellency Mr. President for inviting my special envoy and high-level delegation to Washington out of your special and strong aspiration for better relations between the DPRK and the US despite your busy schedule in the beginning of the year. It is indeed a pleasure and relief for me to start the new year 2019 with the expectation that the great relationship between us would continue, and it is my sincere hope that in the new year all the work we do together, hand in hand, will become momentous events that will shake the world.

I would like to believe that while last year was a meaningful one in which we put an end to the longstanding hostile relations between the DPRK and the US and made a commitment to a new future, this will be a more significant year that will see our bilateral relations develop into a new higher stage.

In this respect, a second DPRK-US summit will be a very crucial and weighty historic event equal to the Singapore meeting. I am doing everything possible in my power for the successful opening of a second summit, and I have authorized my special envoy Kim Yong-chol and the high-level delegation to convey my thoughts on the venue, time and agenda for the meeting to Your Excellency Mr. President and your side and have full discussions.

I have no doubt that I would receive a report that this DPRK-US high-level talks in Washington went smoothly and reached a good agreement thanks to the attention of Your Excellency.

I look forward to seeing you again soon, Your Excellency Mr. President, in good health and full of energy in our most meaningful meeting.

Sincerely,
Kim Jong Un

———————

[written by hand in black magic marker, with a slant, covering a whole piece of White House stationery:]

1/18/2019

Mr Chairman,
A great meeting and message. We are together doing something very historic. I will see you soon.

Your friend,
Donald J. Trump

[written by hand in black magic marker on White House stationery:]

February 19, 2019

Chairman,
I look forward to seeing you next week. It will be great!

Best wishes,
Donald J. Trump

[There is page of four pictures of the two of them meeting, possibly from a North Korean newspaper. A note in black magic marker reads: Chairman, so great. Good pictures. Best wishes.]

[*on White House stationery*]

March 22, 2019
His Excellency Kim Jong Un
Chairman of the State Affairs Commission of the Democratic
People's Republic of Korea
Pyongyang

Dear Chairman Kim,
I am writing today to send you warm greetings for the
upcoming anniversary of the birth of President Kim Il
Sung, the founder of your great country. You have carried
forward his vision for your people and you now have an
historic opportunity to fulfill his dying wish—to achieve
denuclearization. I am certain, that under your leadership,
the Democratic People's Republic of Korea will achieve its
enormous potential.

   Thank you again for making this long journey to Hanoi. As I
said to you when we parted ways, you are my friend and always
will be. Contrary to some media reports about our meeting, you
and I have made tremendous progress. Although there is still a lot
of work to do, I have great hope and expectation about what you
and I can accomplish together in the months and years to come if
we remain committed to our shared goals.

   Give my warm regards to your beautiful family.

Sincerely,
Donald J. Trump
[*Note: "warm regards to your" above is underlined in black magic
marker*]

June 10, 2019

Your Excellency Mr. President,
I am writing this letter to you as we are nearing the first
anniversary of our meeting in Singapore on June 12—the
historic moment of great significance that captured the
attention of the world and left an imprint still indelible in my
memory—as well as to congratulate you on your birthday,
which is just days away. I take it as a great honor to be able to
send such a letter to Your Excellency.

I extend my sincere and warm regards to Your Excellency
on the occasion of your birthday. My regards also to the First
Lady and the rest of your family and all your people, and I wish
everyone good health and happiness and hope that everyone's
dream will become a beautiful reality.

Like the brief time we had together a year ago in Singapore,
every minute we shared 103 days ago in Hanoi was also a moment
of glory that remains a precious memory. Such a precious memory
that I have in my unwavering respect for you will provide an
impetus for me to take my steps when we walk toward each other
again someday in the future.

I also believe that the deep and special friendship between
us will work as a magical force that leads the progress of the
DPRK-US relations, clearing all the hurdles we face in the process
of bringing about the developments we seek to achieve.

Your Excellency Mr. President, I still respect and lay my hopes
on the will and determination that you showed in our first meeting
to resolve the issue of our unique style that nobody had ever tried,
and to write a new history. Today's reality is that without a new
approach and the courage it takes, the prospects for resolution of
the issue will only be bleak.

I believe the one day will come sooner or later when we sit
down together to make great things happen, with the will to
give another chance to our mutual trust. Such a day should come
again. It may well be recorded as yet another fantastic moment in
history.

I assure Your Excellency that my respect for you will never change.

Happy birthday once again, Your Excellency. I hope Your Excellency will always be in good health and achieve success in your work. I extend my best wishes on behalf of my family to the First Lady and the rest of your family.

Sincerely yours,
Kim Jong Un
June 10, 2019

————————

[on *White House stationery*]

June 12, 2019
His Excellency Kim Jong Un
Chairman of the State Affairs Commission of the Democratic
People's Republic of Korea
Pyongyang

Dear Mr. Chairman,
It is great to hear from you. Thank you for your letter and warm
birthday wishes. I hope you and your family are doing well.

It is hard to believe that a full year has passed since our historic
first meeting in Singapore. It was on that day, one year ago, that
you and I made a number of extraordinary commitments to
one another—you committed to completely denuclearize, and I
committed to provide security guarantees. We both committed to
establish new relations for our two countries and to build a lasting
and stable peace regime on the Korean peninsula.

I completely agree with you. You and I have a unique style and
a special friendship. Only you and I, working together, can resolve
the issues between our two countries and end nearly 70 years of
hostility, bringing an era of prosperity to the Korean peninsula that
will exceed all our greatest expectations—and you will be the one
to lead. It will be historic!

I agree with you and think it would be a great thing for us to
meet again. There's some work to be done to prepare for that day.
As you said, success requires courage. So in that spirit, let us direct
our teams to meet again in the coming weeks to take a fresh look
at ways to fulfil the commitments you and I made one year ago
today. I look forward to hearing from you.

As always, I wish you good health and great success. Please
give my warm regards to your beautiful family.

Sincerely,
Donald Trump
[*Note: "good health and great success" above are underlined in black
magic marker*]

[*on White House stationery*]

June 29, 2019
His Excellency Kim Jong Un
Chairman of the State Affairs Commission of the Democratic
People's Republic of Korea
Pyongyang

Dear Chairman Kim,
As you may have seen, I am traveling today from Osaka, Japan,
to the Republic of Korea, and since I will be so close to you,
I would like to invite you to meet me at the border tomorrow
afternoon. I will be near the DMZ in the afternoon and
propose a meeting at 3:30 at the Peace House on the southern
side of the military demarcation line. I have no specific agenda
for our meeting, but think it would be great to see you again
since we will be so close to each other. Hope to see you
tomorrow!

Sincerely,
Donald Trump

[*on White House stationery*]

June 30, 2019
His Excellency Kim Jong Un
Chairman of the State Affairs Commission of the Democratic
People's Republic of Korea
Pyongyang

Dear Chairman Kim,
Being with you today was truly amazing. Even the media,
which always likes to say that everything is bad, is giving
you accolades for inviting me into your country. They said
you demonstrated great foresight and courage in accepting
a meeting on such short notice and very public notice. Most
importantly I thought our meeting went very well. The
potential of your country is truly limitless, and I am confident
that incredible prosperity awaits you and your people in the
future as we continue to work together.
    [*handwritten in black magic marker:*] Great being with you!

Sincerely,
Donald Trump
[*"Great" above is underlined with black magic marker*]
[Bob Woodard dictation note: *There is a photocopy of the whole
NYT front page from Monday, July 1, 2019. There is a picture of
Trump and Kim. The headline of the story is "After Twitter overture,
Trump and Kim meet on North Korean soil." The words are hard to
make out. In magic marker, Trump writes:* Chairman, great picture
of you, big time.]

[*on White House stationery*]

July 2, 2019
His Excellency Kim Jong Un
Chairman of the State Affairs Commission of the Democratic
People's Republic of Korea
Pyongyang

Dear Mr. Chairman,
Enclosed are photographs taken at our momentous summits in
Singapore and Hanoi and at our historic meeting on June 30,
2019 at the joint security area. It was an honor to cross into
your country and to resume our important discussion.

I have tremendous confidence in our ability to strike a big deal
that leads to immense prosperity for you and your people, shed you
of your nuclear burden, and inspires generations to come.

These images are great memories for me and capture the
unique friendship that you and I have developed.
[*Copies of 22 photos were included in what was sent to Chairman Kim.*]

August 5, 2019

Your Excellency,
More than 30 days have passed since we have had a meaningful
reunion on June 30 at the North-South Military Demarcation
line, a symbol of hostility and confrontation. Truly even as I
recall it again I'm struck at what a great moment it was.

I'm delighted to receive each and every single picture you
specifically chose from that day, which holds special meaning and
will remain an internal memory from that momentous and historic
day. Those photographs now hang in my office. I express my
appreciation to you, and I will remember that moment forever.

Your Excellency has left an extraordinary historical legacy, and
going forward will continue to lead a great change in history.

Your Excellency, I remember clearly the promise I made 30 days
ago to have experts from our two countries sit down face-to-face
in a few weeks' time to discuss the work that Your Excellency and
I need to do in the future. However, the current environment is
different from that day.

My belief was that the provocative combined military exercises
would either be cancelled or postponed ahead of our two
countries' working-level negotiations where we would continue to
discuss important matters. Against whom is the combined military
exercises taking place in the southern part of the Korean Peninsula,
who are they trying to block, and who are they intended to defeat
and attack?

It can't be that the South Korean forces are discussing the issue
of wartime operational control in order to fight a tribe on the
other side of the earth or to fight against the Iranian army 70,000
kilometers away. Conceptually and hypothetically, the main target
of the war preparatory exercises is our own military. This is not
our misunderstanding.

As if to support our view, a few days ago the person who they
call the minister of national defense of South Korea said that the
modernization of our conventional commercial weapons was
deemed a "provocation" and a "threat" and that if we continue
to "provoke" and "threaten" they will classify my administration

and military as an "enemy." Now and in the future, South Korean military cannot be my enemy. As you mentioned at some point, we have a strong military without the need of special means, and the truth is that South Korean military is no match against my military.

Putting aside the disparity in military strength, I have no intention of either attacking South Korea or of starting a war. I truly do not have those thoughts. The problem is, why do they engage in this noisy commotion with these exercises, saying that they are preparing themselves with the assumption that there will be a bloody fratricidal war that nobody wants to think about it? Instead it would be wiser for them to think of ways to reduce military tensions by improving relations with us.

The thing I like even less is that the US military is engaged in these paranoid and hypersensitive actions with the South Korean people. I do not understand the purpose of having these "wargames" that we consider as threatening at the time when we are looking ahead of this very important meeting. At present, it is very difficult for me and my people to understand your side's and the South Korean authority's decisions and actions. The most important cause of what your side considers the headache of "missile threats" and nuclear problem is the military actions of your side and the South Korean military that threatens our safety. And until these elements are eliminated, no changed outcome can be anticipated.

I am clearly offended and I do not want to hide this feeling from you. I am really, very offended. At every opportunity after we met, you said there are no more artificial earthquakes and no objects flying in the sky. You also said that the detainees have been released and returned and the remains have been returned.

In this vein, I have done more than I can at this present stage, very responsively and practically in order to keep the trust we have. However, what has Your Excellency done and what am I to explain to my people about what has changed since we met? Have actions been relaxed or any my country's external environments been improved? Have military exercises been stopped? It would be a big mistake if US self-assesses this as an accomplishment of US policy toward DPRK through use of pressure and dialogue.

I do not wish to do anything to disappoint you any time soon, nor do I plan to do so. If you do not think of our relationship as a stepping stone that only benefits you, then you would not make me look like an idiot that will only give without getting anything in return.

My letter has gone long, but to state my main point, regrettably now is not the time to engage in working-level talks. It is not the right atmosphere in my country, and if we were to move forward with working-level talks now, our leadership would be viewed as strange by the outside world and by us as well. We will not have to reconsider the working-level talks when the "wargames" of the US and South Korea that I so strongly asked to be stopped becomes a thing of the past weekend. What kind of working level talks could we possibly have? It obviously would not be about the sanctions relief, which I very much wanted, nor will it be about the location of our fourth summit talks.

To put it another way, we are not in a hurry. If this were like Hanoi, just a few months ago, when I held onto the dream of hastening the start of a better life, it would be different. But we are in a different situation, and we are not in a hurry.

And there are now about five months left until the end of the year, which I commented on at one point. In coming up with a good agreement, these months can be seen as long or as short depending on what we do. Please reach out to me again when the "military game" and "wargame" with South Korea has ended. At that time, we will discuss the time and location of the working-level talks.

Your Excellency, I am immensely proud and honored that we have a relationship where I can send and receive such candid thoughts with you. You are a statesman with great might. I consider it an honor to have this special relationship with you. I will put in even greater effort, Mr. President, to protect my faith in you.

As you also commented while we were improvement testing very small missiles, which all nations do, we slightly surprised the fools in the south and it was quite amusing.

I hope that you always enjoy good health, Mr. President, and my wish is for you to realize even greater accomplishments.

To your respected First Lady and your loving family, I send my warm wishes and greetings.

Sincerely,
Kim Jong Un
August 5, 2019